TVA and the Dispossessed

and the
Dispossessed

*The Resettlement of Population
in the Norris Dam Area*

Michael J. McDonald
John Muldowny

THE UNIVERSITY OF TENNESSEE PRESS / KNOXVILLE

Library of Congress Cataloging in Publication Data
McDonald, Michael J., 1934–
    TVA and the resettlement of population in
the Norris Dam area.

    Bibliography: p.
    Includes index.
    1. Land settlement—Tennessee—Norris Lake region.
2. Water resources development—Social aspects—Tennessee—
Norris Lake region. 3. Tennessee Valley Authority.
I. Muldowny, John, 1931– . II. Title.
III. Title: T.V.A. and the resettlement of population in the
Norris Dam area.
HD211.T2M35   307'.2   81-16333
ISBN 0-87049-345-0 (cl.: alk. paper)
ISBN 1-57233-164-X (pbk. alk. paper)

Contents

Illustrations

Acknowledgments

Because so much of this book is based on unpublished sources contained in the various archives and libraries of the Tennessee Valley Authority, our first acknowledgments must go to all those who helped guide us through the labyrnthine files of such a large federal agency. To Jesse Mills, director of the Technical Library of TVA, we owe special thanks. His encouragement, advice, support, and, above all, friendship helped see the project through to its completion. Bill Whitehead and his able staff at the library earned our everlasting thanks for the hours they spent aiding us. The late Stella Lieb of TVA Archives and her successor, Ron Brewer, were most helpful as was Joe Parrott of Land Acquisitions. Sandra Edmunds, now of TVA's Forestry Division, was instrumental in helping set up the initial data tapes and analyses. Paul Evans, former head of the Information Office, made it possible for us to have access to materials, office space, and computer time and was in every respect helpful in the early stages of the project. We do not have space enough to thank everyone in TVA who was helpful to us; and although we have felt at liberty to be critical of TVA in a scholarly sense, we also acknowledge and respect the cooperation we received from all members of the agency.

The late Arthur E. Morgan, former chairman of the TVA Board of Directors, was generous with his time and advice as was Charles Hoffman, former secretary of the board during the 1930s. Nina D. Myatt, head of Special Collections at Antioch's Olive Kettering Library, William R. Emerson of the Franklin D. Roosevelt Library at Hyde Park, New York, and Jim Hall, formerly of the Federal

Records Center at East Point, Georgia, were also extremely helpful. Special thanks are also owed to Alice Beauschene of the University of Tennessee Computer Center for help and advice. During the early stages of our research, we were immeasurably aided by two faculty research and travel grants from the Graduate School of the University of Tennessee, Knoxville. Those grants provided two summers free from any teaching obligations as well as making possible visits to the aforementioned individuals and archival sources.

Our colleagues form the support mechanism without which this book would not have been written. Portions of the manuscript were read by Pete Daniel, Charles Johnson, and Susan Becker of the History Department, and Donald W. Hastings of the Sociology Department. Their criticisms and suggestions were extremely helpful. Bruce Wheeler read the entire manuscript, lent a sympathetic ear, and provided incisive comments as well as strong moral support. Our colleague and chairman, LeRoy P. Graf, was always supportive and tried whenever possible to lighten our teaching responsibilities.

We also owe debts of gratitude for the past work of many of our graduate students. To Ken Landgren and Gabrielle Merrill who spent the better portion of two summers helping code and research TVA questionnaires; to Richard Westbrook, James Shields, Douglas Blair, and the late Cleo Martin Lucas who helped collect the oral interviews; to Brenda Joyner Moore who transcribed most of them; and to all other students whose contributions cannot be easily singled out we are also extremely grateful.

Finally, there was the thankless mechanical task of proofreading and typing the manuscript. To Jeanne McDonald and Evelyn Muldowny who devoted many hours to correcting much of the original and final manuscript; to Debbie Pierce, Janet Hickman, and especially Melinda Murtaugh and Cindy Nichols, who typed various stages of the final draft, we are most appreciative.

Many people whom we have not named have helped and advised us. They and we know who they are and will excuse, we hope, the lack of specific mention. In this book we have tried to convey to our readers something of the quality of life of residents in the Norris Dam region. Throughout the traumatic days of their removal, the families displaced by TVA proved to be an inspiring example demonstrating that the new heroes of history are apt to be more acted upon by forces over which they have little control than to be actors in dramas they compose. No loss of dignity accrues to them because of that—rather the opposite. To them this book is dedicated.

Abbreviations

AAA	Agricultural Adjustment Administration
AFL	American Federation of Labor
CCC	Civilian Conservation Corps
CWA	Civil Works Administration
FCA	Farm Credit Administration
FERA	Federal Emergency Relief Administration
FSA	Farm Security Administration
NRA	National Recovery Administration
NYB	National Youth Board
PWA	Public Works Administration
RA	Resettlement Administration
RFC	Reconstruction Finance Corporation
SCS	Soil Conservation Service
TERA	Tennessee Emergency Relief Agency
TSPC	Tennessee State Planning Commission
TVA	Tennessee Valley Authority
TVAC	Tennessee Valley Authority Cooperatives
USDA	U.S. Department of Agriculture
WPA	Works Progress Administration

TVA and the Dispossessed

1 Introduction

IN THE SUMMER of 1933, amid the agony of a national depression, the Tennessee Valley Authority began to acquire land in the rocky, sloping meadows of upper East Tennessee. Its purpose was to create a storage reservoir and hydroelectric facility at the confluence of the Clinch and Powell rivers, the northeastern tributaries of the Tennessee. Thus the federal agency began a course of action which transformed thousands of human lives and effected multitudinous environmental and economic changes, the repercussions of which are still being felt today.

TVA had been created in the crucible of senatorial and congressional debate in the post–World War I era over the future disposition of the federal facilities located on the Tennessee River at Muscle Shoals, Alabama.[1] These facilities had been constructed in 1918 in a mood of economic self-sufficiency aimed at cutting national dependence upon Chilean nitrates for war production. After the war a debate arose over the peacetime use of the facilities and their nitrate-producing capacities. Once private sale of the properties had been decided against, the discussion expanded during the 1920s into what became the basis of Senator George Norris's federal action program designed to harness the power of the whole river for flood control, power production, cheap nitrate fertilizer production, and navigation.

By the early 1930s, Franklin D. Roosevelt, first as governor, then as president, had added to Norris's program the ideas of land-use planning and regional development. These ideas, together with the concept of multipurpose stream development, brought about the upstream impoundment of tributaries for stor-

3

age and hydroelectric power generation. Thus what had begun at Muscle Shoals among the plantation economies of northern Alabama and lower Tennessee led inexorably to the mountainous highlands of the river's source and to the "hog and corn" subsistence farms of the independent (and poor) white smallholders in the fastness of the upper Tennessee and its tributaries. An experiment had escalated into one of the most exciting and innovative regional development programs in the nation's history.

As noted above, the site chosen to begin the first impoundment was near the confluence of the Church and Powell rivers below the Cumberland Plateau in upper East Tennessee. The two rivers became the Clinch, which with the Holston and French Broad rivers makes up the major tributaries of the Tennessee from the northeast. The location of the first faltering steps in TVA's experiment was not a novel one. Both the Corps of Engineers and the Tennessee Electric and Power Company had shown interest in the site, known to them as Coal Creek. To contemporaries it is better known for the "Father of TVA," George Norris. The Norris Dam and Reservoir, in what will subsequently be referred to as the Norris Basin, provided TVA's first laboratory in regional planning and one of the most important.

The taming of the Tennessee entailed the purchase, under eminent domain, of enormous amounts of land and the consequent displacement of thousands of families from farms where many had lived for generations, the oldest dating back to the immediate postrevolutionary period. The purchase of land and the relocation of families occurred whenever and wherever TVA built a dam and reservoir. But Norris Dam, TVA's first major project, was to displace a greater number of families than any other dam the Authority constructed. TVA purchased 153,000 acres of land, the bulk of it from subsistence farmers and their tenants, some from railroads and the Tennessee Electric and Power Company, to build the dam and form the reservoir. When the project had been completed, the waters formed Norris Lake, which extends nearly seventy miles up the arms of the Clinch and Powell rivers. The land purchase displaced over 3,000 rural families from the Norris Basin.

The process of displacement, and the various ways in which TVA coped with it, form the general subject of this book. Although

4

much has been written about the TVA in terms of its political and economic development, there has thus far been little analysis of the agency at the grass roots. This study examines TVA's intensive confrontation with the people and constructs a view of TVA from the ground up. No better opportunity is afforded for this than a review of TVA's activities in the initial phase of its operations—land purchase, family removal, relocation, and related grass-roots programs.

Specific programs of TVA have naturally been the objects of scholarly attention, and consequently a number of fine studies of scholarly value have emerged. These include Thomas McCraw's analysis of TVA's power program, Wilmon Droze's study of the navigation programs, Joseph Ransmeier's work on water-control planning, and Harry Case's examination of TVA's personnel policy. Victor Hobday has written on municipal power distribution, C. Herman Pritchett on administration development, and Norman Wengert on agriculture.

In addition to analyses of specific programs, many researchers have examined the broader implications of TVA. Herman Finer's examination of TVA's international applications and Clarence Hodge's study of TVA and regional administration are superior examples of this sort of work. Attempts have been made both to analyze TVA's economic impact (John Moore) and to indicate how elusive economic impact analysis is in econometric terms (Lance Davis).

There is a wealth of general studies of TVA's development as seen from within. Three former directors have told the TVA "story" from their points of view (Gordon Clapp, David Lilienthal, and A. E. Morgan), and one former administrator (Marguerite Owen) examined TVA from the vantage point of the Washington scene. TVA has been examined by high-level staff executives (Roscoe Martin), and TVA's published engineering reports alone (on each of the dams) constitute models of their kind throughout the world today and contain much more than engineering specifications. One should also mention Charles Crawford's oral history program at Memphis State University, which allows many former TVA executives and managerial staff to tell of TVA's history from their respective positions within the Authority.

TVA has been the subject of a multitude of newspaper and magazine articles and two extensive journalistic and popular accounts (R. L. Duffus and Willson Whitman). Its architecture has been examined (J. H. Kyle), and its progress and personnel portrayed in popular cinema (Elia Kazan's *Wild River*), in photographs (Lewis Hine), and in film documentaries (*The Valley* and *People of the Cumberland*). TVA's birth has been described in detail (Preston Hubbard); its parentage discussed at length (Richard Lowitt); its progress praised (Lilienthal and Clapp); and its quarrels and personalities laid bare (Lilienthal, Morgan, McCraw, Roy Talbert).[2] All of this literature, however, has provided a view of TVA from above and rarely from the grass roots, which is lamentable if for no other reason than the fact that historically TVA has been acutely conscious of its role as a "grass-roots" institution and has worked to project an image of itself as sensitive to the needs of the Valley people.

One notable exception to the dearth of literature on TVA at the grass roots is provided by the work of Phillip Selznick.[3] He did not examine the actual operation of TVA at that level in any detail, however, but rather subjected to careful scrutiny TVA's conceptualization of itself as a grass-roots institution. Selznick's conclusion was that TVA's vision of the grass roots was obscured by the domination of "agriculturalists" within the agency, whose philosophy of approaching the people and whose definition of the people were highly colored by the attitudes of the Farm Bureau Federation and the agricultural extension program. Selznick feels, in sum, that such a coloration in fact kept TVA from the "true" grass roots. His analysis of the process of "cooptation," whereby the agriculturalists within TVA imposed their philosophy upon important segments of the institution, has been criticized for its lack of evidence, but it is nonetheless a stimulating and elegantly argued position. More important, from the viewpoint of the authors, Selznick, in attempting to interpret the problem involved in TVA's approaches to the grass roots, opened new avenues of inquiry for historians of TVA by creating a theoretical bridge from the agency to the people of the Valley.

The people of the Norris Basin bore the tensions of the immediate confrontation with TVA. They were, in a real sense, the raw material of TVA's planning experiments as much as were the elements of water and land, farms and forest. As Herman Pritchett comments: "Nowhere did the Authority's program have more direct and disturbing effects than upon the hundreds of families who had to abandon their homes and farms to the waters of a TVA reservoir."[4] Part of Pritchett's observation is, of course, understatement—families were removed in the thousands rather than hundreds.

The inhabitants of the Norris Basin, the first host population of TVA, were for the most part isolated and economically disadvantaged, owing largely to geographical location and to the pressure of population on marginally productive land. For the most part they lived in tightly knit and very small rural communities which had poor transportation and health and sanitary facilities. Three of every ten household heads were tenants, while the rest were generally small landowners. Since most were subsistence farmers, only small amounts of cash were generated in the communities. Although life in the Norris Basin did have distinct advantages for some, the communities formed an isolated and static society which generally offered little opportunity for improvement save that which could be gained by moving out of the Valley.

Were it not for the mobility afforded through this out-migration (a mobility which in modern societies has meant the ability to escape the relentless pressure of population on marginal resources), there would be a justification for calling the Norris Basin a premodern society. As it existed in 1933, it was in fact a society in transition to modernity. Certainly a population for which migration is the only answer to a constantly depleted standard of living cannot be classed as consisting of successful participants in modern American economic growth and development. But Norris Basin inhabitants had not been successful participants in that life for most of the twentieth century, and when the Great Depression caused the collapse of the industrial areas to which many had migrated in their need, they returned home and increased the pressure on limited resources, underlining the static nature of the society they had fled. It was into this situation that TVA came, and in 1933 the newly created agency certainly possessed the capacity to alleviate the harsh and unremitting problems of too many people caught in a largely inhospitable agricultural environment.

This capacity historians have called modernization; yet modernization is a word to be construed not simply in vacuo, but rather as representative of, or signifying, a historical process. As such it can be described contextually. To say that TVA was an agent of modernization means basically that TVA possessed the instrumentality and the intent, through programs like regional planning and power productivity, to transform wholly or in part a population removed from the mainstream of American life.

If the Norris Basin were essentially premodern, the task of conceptual definition would be made easier. It is, however, more accurate to describe it as transitional. This quality of being transitional between premodern and modern we have taken to mean as characterized by a number of features: first among these is the dependence upon environmental factors of a limiting nature and the general lack of technological components to overcome or break this dependence. The self-sufficient farm that was characteristic of the Norris Basin relied heavily upon manpower rather than machine technology to feed itself and obtain surpluses for trade and sale. This limitation was imposed partly by topography, partly by lack of capital. The technology was there, but in the main the communities could not avail themselves of it. Second, the relative isolation of the region, coupled with its high human fertility, its reliance upon subsistence farming, row-cropping on poor soil, and the lack of industrial enterprise in the immediate region meant that out-migration was one of the predominant ways in which Norris Basin inhabitants obtained some social and economic mobility. In the period of the Great Depression, out-migration to neighboring or distant industrial centers was no longer a viable solution to the problems of poor soil, isolation, and lack of technology. Third, this combination of environmental, technological, and economic restraints had combined to shape a relatively static society removed not only from the opportunities of modern life but from its amenities as well. Lack of electrical power and machine technology, manpower demands, isolation, loss of mobility and limited educational opportunity, and a high degree of endogamous mar-

riages combined to prevent all but the most favorably endowed
from fully participating in the economic life of the twentieth century.

The nearly premodern configuration of rural communities
whose complete self-sufficiency was broken only by its limited
dependence on a few regional urban markets fairly well describes
the predicament of the inhabitants of the Norris Basin. All of this
was further underlined in the depression years by the closing of the
escape valve of migration. These conditions, then, describe rather
than define what is meant by the "transitional" phase between
premodern and modern.

The instruments of change which TVA possessed—bountiful and
cheap power, regional planning apparatuses, legal strength, and
federal backing were the means by which the regional inhabitants,
and indeed the inhabitants of the entire Tennessee Valley, could
escape the limitations imposed upon them. In addition, it provided
TVA with the means by which it could construct an environment
more open to opportunity and mobility and less dependent upon
manpower and nature. In this sense, TVA can be regarded as an
agent of modernization in the Tennessee Valley generally and in
the Norris region specifically.

Did TVA possess a warrant for planning which would allow historians to construe it as an agent of modernization? Its early history
would certainly seem to indicate so. But that warrant for modernization was ambivalent at its core, for TVA emanated conceptually
from two different sources: George Norris's "action program" for
Muscle Shoals, which stressed flood control, fertilizer production,
power production, and navigation, and Franklin Roosevelt's regional planning ideas. The ambiguity was a matter of emphasis.
While the action program stressed the practical elements of hydraulic management, the planning function moved in the direction
of determining the shape, or the quality, of life that would emerge
in the hydraulic society of the Tennessee Valley. The one was
practical and empirical, the other, more ideological in nature.

Roosevelt had long been interested in the progressive conservation movement of Theodore Roosevelt and Giffort Pinchot, particularly the concept of land planning for the public good. Franklin
Roosevelt's gubernatorial predecessor, Alfred E. Smith, had

utilized the planning efforts of Benton McKaye of the United States Forest Service and Clarence Stein, architect and progressive city planner. As governor of New York, Roosevelt developed in 1930 a regional planning program which specifically called for the withdrawal from private use of submarginal land yielding no profit in crops and favored disposition of this land for reforestation and recreational purposes. Roosevelt stressed that this program would aid in determining the ability of a rural area to support road construction or improvement of school facilities and electric power and telephone lines.[5] Soon after, Roosevelt suggested that some of the same type of work which had been accomplished in New York might be applicable to other regions of the country as well. He particularly had the South in mind, perhaps from observations that he had made while visiting his "other home," as he called it, in Georgia.[6]

In 1931 Roosevelt was the keynote speaker at a conference on regionalism held at the University of Virginia. Tracy Augur, a planner who would join TVA soon after its inception, was attending the conference and, in a 1942 memorandum on the planning sections of the TVA Act, stressed the conference's significance in the development of TVA.[7]

Roosevelt's keynote address was on New York State planning, and Augur noted that the conference

was sponsored by the group of men who had been the progressive element in the planning movement, many of whom had been associated with the New York State plan. Roosevelt, in his speech, referred to the similarity between Southern problems and those tackled in New York, and indicated that the same type of approach might be helpful. Roosevelt stayed on the platform for "nearly an hour" answering questions. . . . I do not recall that the Tennessee Valley region was even mentioned by name, but Mr. Odum [Howard Odum of Chapel Hill] and other southern regionalists were present and it is probable that the relationship of New York State planning techniques to the problems of southern Appalachia were mentioned.

Augur recalled that the Virginia conference influenced TVA in another respect, since the two men who authored the planning sections (22 and 23) of the TVA Act, John Nolen, Jr., and Frederick Gutheim, were also at the Charlottesville conference for an entire week of meetings. "They were in contact," he noted, "with such men as Louis Brownlow, Stuart Chase, Professor Odum, and other leaders of thought on the regional planning subject." McKaye, Chase, and Odum associated themselves in various capacities with TVA in its early years. Augur concluded a section of his memorandum by stating, "There does seem to be a clear relationship between the president's appearance at Virginia and the final introduction of sections 22 and 23."[8]

Whether from past political experience, from personal observations, or from exposure to planning ideas while he was attending regional development meetings, Roosevelt seemed committed to some type of planning for the Tennessee Valley. In particular, he singled out Muscle Shoals for special attention, possibly because it had been the center of controversy as to government's planning role in its operation ever since its inception during World War I. In this endeavor Roosevelt had a cause in common with Senator George Norris, the Nebraska progressive who had been actively promoting government operation of the dam and hydroelectric facility there. As Roosevelt stated in *On Our Way:*

> Before I came to Washington, I had decided that for many reasons the Tennessee Valley—in other words, all of the watershed of the Tennessee River and its tributaries—would provide an ideal land use experiment on a regional scale embracing many states. . . . This Plan fitted in well with the splendid fight which Senator Norris had been making for the development of power and the manufacture of fertilizer at the Wilson Dam Properties. . . . In enlarging the original objective so as to make it cover the whole Tennessee Valley, Senator Norris and I undertook to include a multitude of human activities and physical developments.[9]

Roosevelt's election to the presidency was crucial to the implementation of the Muscle Shoals project: Senator Norris was provided with the favorable circumstances and forceful political leadership needed to carry plans for the federal development of Muscle Shoals to fruition, and Roosevelt gained from Norris's project a concrete base from which he could expand regional planning concepts and by which he could translate long-matured ideas into reality at a time when the nation desperately needed them. The result of their collaboration was a large-scale regional planning experiment—the Tennessee Valley Authority. Norris had supplied concepts of unified river development and power and fertilizer programs through his involvement with legislation on Muscle Shoals, while Roosevelt's initiative supplied regional planning, land use, and development schemes. The two currents seemed to flow together into the TVA Act.

FDR succinctly expressed his broad planning message in a speech made at Montgomery, Alabama, January 21, 1933, after a trip to Muscle Shoals. Roosevelt was, he said, committed to "put Muscle Shoals to work" and then to make of it "an even greater development." He continued: "We have an opportunity of setting an example of planning not just for ourselves but for the generations to come, tying in industry and agriculture and forestry and flood prevention, tying them all into a unified whole . . . so that we can afford better opportunities and better places for living for millions of yet unborn, in the days to come." This language was to reappear not only in the president's message before Congress in defense of the TVA Act but also in section 23 of the act, where marginal land utilization and reforestation were mentioned specifically, as well as in a section in which a phrase concerning agricultural conditions was broadened and changed to encompass "the economic and social well-being of the people living in said river basin."[10]

At first glance the different currents which flowed into the making of the TVA Act appear to be so conjoined in the name of government resource development for public use that their separation appears artificial; yet one must concur with Augur's judgment: "Although President Roosevelt has been a strong advocate of public power while Governor of New York, and hence saw eye to eye with Senator Norris on the power features of the TVA Act, it is interesting that the President's first interest in the Tennessee Valley always appeared to be in the broader aspects of the project."[11]

TVA thus bore the imprint of the dual influences which created it. Tracy Augur noted in 1942 that the planning sections of the TVA Act (22 and 23) deal with "the making of plans as a future basis for legislation" and give the president authority. The remainder of the TVA Act, however, "deals with the execution of plans which had been formulated in greater or lesser degree throughout a long period of discussion about Muscle Shoals" and the TVA board with authority.[12]

Duality carried with it some ambiguity of purpose. Public benefit, in a broad sense, was the aim of both Roosevelt's regional planning ideas and Norris's desire to develop Muscle Shoals. But as Augur indicates, the president's message to Congress was open and nonspecific. TVA was "charged with the broadest duty of planning for the proper use, conservation, and development of the Tennessee River drainage basin and its adjoining territory for the general social and economic welfare of the nation."[13]

Herman Pritchett has indicated that the TVA Act was developed along the lines of previous Muscle Shoals projects and that by the terms of the act, TVA was "directed to take over the Muscle Shoals properties, utilize the nitrate plants in a commercial or experimental program and to dispose of the surplus power generated at Wilson dam over the corporation's own transmission lines." To this was added the "expanded role" desired by the president. One phase authorized TVA to build dams and powerhouses and undertake navigation projects on the Tennessee River and its tributaries. This could be construed as the Muscle Shoals action program, conceived by Norris in extenso. The second role expansion came in the two sections for regional planning and development (22 and 23). Pritchett has argued that the second role expansion was little understood. "It was clear that Congress was still planning for a power and fertilizer corporation, and had attempted no serious and thoroughgoing adaptation of the Muscle Shoals plans previously developed to the needs of the unique type of organization which was now contemplated." Pritchett concludes: "From the statutory point of view, the Tennessee Valley Authority was merely the Muscle Shoals Corporation of previous years, with some additional ill-defined powers and functions."[14]

Although the preamble to the TVA Act and the planning segments of the act itself affirmed a broadly stated public land policy, Phillip Selznick has noted:

> The provisions of the Act which followed the enacting clause neither established machinery nor delegated authority which would give effect to those ambitions. The Authority was assigned power to acquire real estate for the construction of dams, reservoirs, transmission lines, power houses, and other structures, and navigation projects at any point along the Tennessee River, or any of its tributaries.[15]

Selznick, like Pritchett, feels that what he calls the "general welfare" provisions of the TVA Act "are regarded as among its weakest parts." The results of this weakness have led to the implementation of general welfare responsibilities through programs "which did have a sound legal foundation with certain ideals of public policy." Pritchett's view that the planning sections (or Selznick's "general welfare" aspects) of the TVA Act were ill-defined from a statutory point of view, or Selznick's evaluation of them as weak, does not destroy their very real existence as an ideological base within TVA, and certainly Arthur Morgan, the first chairman of the TVA board, embraced the general welfare sections of the TVA Act as the most significant and first in order of priority over the action programs.[16] This fact in itself was to lead to some difficulties, for divergent points of origin and emphasis potentially nurtured the seeds for two TVAs rather than one, a situation underlined by differences in attitude among the general directors.

The spectre of more than one TVA loomed even larger when the appointment of the first directors was announced. Each represented diverse interests and points of view; each was renowned in his field; each would bring the stamp of his own personality to the agency. In addition, the fact that Arthur Morgan was appointed by Franklin Roosevelt to head the agency before the actual act was drawn up makes his appointment crucial, for it was Morgan who as chairman designate was instrumental in influencing the selection of the men who would make up the first board of directors of the TVA.

At the time of his appointment, Morgan, aged fifty-three had already carved out an illustrious career as both an engineer and educator. Born in 1880, Morgan had grown up in Minnesota and had worked first as a surveyor assistant to his father, gradually moving into the field of water-control engineering, where he soon became an expert. By 1910 he had organized his own engineering firm, the Morgan Engineering Company of Memphis, Tennessee.

For the next twenty years he supervised many flood control and drainage projects, but his major achievement was his work in the Miami River Valley of Ohio. There he supervised, in what became known as the Miami Conservancy District, some previously untried flood control measures which gave him national attention during the 1920s.

During that same decade Morgan was also known as an innovative educator. First as a member of the board of trustees, then as president, Morgan made Antioch College, a small liberal arts school in Yellow Springs, Ohio, into a model institution of higher education in America. As a devout believer in cooperation and community spirit, Morgan introduced such innovations as work-study programs and campus workshops where students could put their book learning into practice. What this president envisioned for Antioch was not only a college but a community where education and work could be combined for the benefit of all.

Just precisely how Franklin Roosevelt came to select Morgan as the first TVA director is not entirely clear; some evidence suggests that James Cox, Roosevelt's running mate in 1920, who was familiar with Morgan's accomplishments in his native Ohio, may have mentioned his name to the president; possibly Eleanor Roosevelt, who had helped raise money for Antioch and had read Morgan's ideas in his publication, *Antioch Notes*, might have called him to her husband's attention. In any event, Roosevelt, stressing more the idea of comprehensive regional planning for the Tennessee Valley than cheaper public power or better farm technology, selected Morgan to carry out the administration's goal. And Morgan leapt to the challenge, confessing, "The TVA is the kind of thing I have been wanting to do all my life."

In naming Morgan to the board of TVA, Roosevelt also entrusted him with the task of aiding in the selection of the other two board members. Within limits the president gave Morgan a free hand, suggesting only that he believed it would be sensible to select one individual who was familiar with electric power and one who understood southern agriculture. The Ohioan diligently went about this task, screening candidates, conducting interviews, traveling countless miles before recommending two men, Harcourt A. Morgan and David Lilienthal.

In 1933 Harcourt Morgan, no relation to Arthur, was president of the University of Tennessee. He had come to the university in 1905 to head its agricultural experiment station after teaching and

President and Mrs. Franklin D. Roosevelt with Arthur Morgan, first chairman of the TVA Board at Norris Dam.

becoming an expert in agricultural entomology at Louisiana State University. He got on well with students, faculty, and local farmers, lectured throughout the states on farm problems, and recruited students for the school of agriculture. By 1913 he had been named the college's dean, and six years later he became president of the university.

Harcourt Morgan firmly believed in the future of southern agriculture and saw the TVA as an educational force for its progress and growth. But in Morgan's eyes agricultural change had to be gradual, not immediate nor radical, and thus as a reformer he was much more conservative in outlook than his namesake on the TVA board. Yet for representative of southern agriculture within the TVA, there could seemingly not have been a more logical choice. A friend of the farmer, he became the major policy maker for the agricultural interests within the TVA region.

Morgan's second recommendation was David Lilienthal. Lilienthal's appointment was to satisfy Roosevelt's stipulation that someone familiar with the public utility issue be named to the board. Though the question of public power was to become a critical factor in TVA's development during the next decade, Arthur Morgan viewed it as only one aspect of the Authority's larger mission to effect change in the Valley. Nevertheless, the power issue was important if for no other reason than the fact that during the preceding decade Norris himself had made it an integral part of the Muscle Shoals proposals. No one overly friendly or sympathetic to the power companies would be tolerated by Norris and his congressional supporters; furthermore, Norris in particular seemed to be concerned about both of the Morgans' inexperience with the utility companies, that they in short might not be strong enough to withstand the pressure. All the more reason, then, that someone tough on the power issue should be appointed. Lilienthal filled the bill perfectly.

A member of the Wisconsin Public Service Commission in 1933, Lilienthal at age thirty-three might well have been considered a wonder. He had spent his youth in northern Indiana, attending first DePauw University and then Harvard Law School. His interest in labor law led him to become friendly with Professor Felix Frankfurter as well as with prominent labor leaders such as Wil-

17

liam Green of the American Federation of Labor (AFL) and public figures such as Frank Walsh, whom Roosevelt as governor appointed to the New York State Power Commission.

During the 1920s Lilienthal associated himself with Donald Richberg and Robert M. LaFollette, Jr., men whose ties link them to the old Progressive circle of Bull Moose days. For a time he worked in Richberg's Chicago law firm, later branching out on his own and taking up public utility law. His reputation in that field prompted Governor Philip LaFollette to appoint him in 1931 to the Wisconsin Railroad Commission. Instructed by LaFollette to broaden the power of the commission, Lilienthal was instrumental in drafting such legislation and in the process renaming the regulatory body the Public Service Commission. Pressing hard against all private utilities in the state, Lilienthal soon won their enmity. In fact, so unpopular had he become with the private utility companies that in all likelihood he would have been ousted had he not been appointed to the TVA. But Morgan's recommendation along with Norris's wholehearted endorsement sent Lilienthal to Washington as the third member of the TVA board of directors.

Clearly Arthur Morgan's voice was important in the ultimate composition of the TVA board, but his early appointment also made him a crucial participant in decisions as to how the board might function, particularly because of his attendance at sessions of the conference committee of the House and Senate considering the TVA act itself.

During one of the sessions Arthur Morgan was asked if he preferred to serve the committee as an individual or upon a board composed of several persons. Morgan recounts that he was surprised by the question and hesitated to answer. "In his talk with me," stated the chairman designate, "President Roosevelt had assumed that there would be two other directors and I had accepted that assumption without further thought." The question, however, prompted Arthur Morgan to rethink the problem: "I had quite clear ideas as to what should be the policies of the Authority but on the other hand I thought that three good men serving as equals could greatly strengthen one another. I wondered whether administration under a single individual would have public acceptance. . . ."[17] Morgan explained that after rethinking the question he responded, on the spur of the moment, that a completely equal three-member board would be preferable.[18] Later Arthur Morgan may have ruefully contemplated his quick decision, since dissension among the "completely equal" board members was to appear at the very first meeting, held in Washington on June 16, 1933, which among other things formally incorporated the agency and authorized a seal for the authority. Harcourt Morgan later recounted his disappointment at the meeting's progress, complaining that Arthur Morgan immediately attended to such details as approval of the preliminary surveys of Cove Creek Dam (later Norris) rather than devoting the time to a broad discussion of the TVA Act, its meaning, and its interpretation. Arthur Morgan's version of that meeting and of Harcourt Morgan's reaction to it was: "Harcourt Morgan protested that he had expected the directors to spend considerable time discussing objectives, policies, plans and working arrangement. He felt that I was precipitate."[19]

One excellent analysis of the administrative portents of this meeting points out that the directors possessed three administrative alternatives: "To leave administration in the hands of a delegated general manager, to have one of the directors assume all administrative duties, or to have them shared out among all the directors." The board chose the second option. Chairman Arthur Morgan was designated general manager of the corporation, his duties "to include the coordination and general administration of its various activities, subject to the continuing authority of the Board of Directors acting as a board." This choice was not a good one, for such a system was likely to succeed only "if the administrative member is a very strong personality and the other directors are weak or have only part-time positions. If the statute definitely prescribes the powers and duties of the administrator, there is also a possibility of success. In the case of TVA, none of these conditions was met."[20] If Arthur Morgan possessed a strong personality, so did his associates; in addition they were both ambitious and active.

Arthur Morgan was essentially ill-suited to work that demanded a team effort. He had many of the attributes and failings of an autocrat, combined with a narrow, puritanical concept of personal behavior and the confident righteousness of a self-made and self-taught man. Roy Talbert's interesting and sympathetic biography brings out the tremendous spectrum of ideas that Morgan's mind embraced. They included scientism, eugenics, late-nineteenth-century race theory, Anglo-Saxonism, food faddism, and progressive education. A man whose favorite reading was Max Nordau's *Degeneration* and who authored a biography of Edward Bellamy is impossible to stereotype, but indications are that while Morgan had an immense amount of self-discipline, he lacked intellectual rigor. In an applied science like engineering he was enormously inventive and imaginative. Administratively, however, his inventiveness, broad range of interests, and lack of intellectual discipline combined with a tendency to enmesh himself in details that all too often should have been delegated to others. Morgan lacked the ability to balance broad policy goals and the delegation of routine to subordinates.[21] Some of these failings became clear in an early board meeting of July 30, 1933, when Arthur Morgan presented to his colleagues a series of rather general and vague projects for their approval. Harcourt Morgan immediately branded these as "impracticable and highly visionary."[22]

Among the projects which Harcourt Morgan disliked were "a study of the proper function of the real estate man in organized society," a comprehensive forestry program, total integration of all power sites in the valley, the development of cooperatives, and a general socioeconomic plan for the valley.[23] H. Morgan stated that the projects were "clearly outside the scope of our responsibility under the law" and determined that in order for him to continue as a director, there must be some discussion of the authority "whereby each member of the board would be limited in individual action to those with which each was intimately familiar."[24] Harcourt Morgan related to a reporter from *Liberty Magazine* that "he [Harcourt Morgan] was much perturbed at the way things were going; that he was working to bring the project down to earth; that he was going into a board meeting that following Monday with some trepidation and with that objective."[25]

Harcourt Morgan was clearly concerned with a division of

power in the Authority along relatively narrow lines and in conformity with each director's special abilities. Arthur Morgan's vision of the TVA was, despite the profusion of detailed projects, much more magisterial and in many respects radically different from that of his colleagues on the board. Arthur Morgan did not think the TVA's main purpose was the production of power or fertilizer. He relates of his initial conversations with Roosevelt: "When he spent most of our time talking together not about dams or electric power or fertilizer but about the quality of life of the people of the Tennessee Valley I was quite certain of it [that he wanted the job]."

Arthur Morgan recounts on another occasion that the president spoke to him for an hour and a half, talking not about power development and fertilizer but about the general improvement of the area.[26] Beyond doubt, Roosevelt knew his man.

While it is not the intention of the authors to trace the conflicts which ensued within the board of directors of TVA, it should be pointed out that the first of these discussions ended in a reallocation of duties and responsibilities which in large degree destroyed the uniformity envisaged in the three-man directorate and allowed each of the three to go his separate route. This step took place less than three months after the first board meeting with the submittal, by Harcourt Morgan and David Lilienthal, of a memorandum on organization dated August 3, 1933. The crux of this memorandum was a criticism of Arthur Morgan's administrative position: "There has not thus far been a satisfactory or workable program or procedure of administration developed by this board." The memorandum spoke of inadequate administrative measures as well as confusion in the administration.[27]

Arthur Morgan responded in his defense with a memorandum presented in an August 5, 1933, board meeting. He stated that he had been guided by three principles to date: "First to keep going, to guide, and to bring into control, the activities suddenly thrust into the hands of the Board; second, to set up the inevitable administrative organization which is largely independent of the programs adopted, and third, to secure the assistance of key men who can advise the board in the formulation of policies." It was Arthur Morgan's contention that the adequate development of wide-range administrative programs must wait upon the advice of these properly qualified "key men."[28]

Harcourt Morgan and David Lilienthal outvoted A. E. Morgan, and as a result there was a general division of powers. Administratively it called for a split in the primary responsibility for each phase of the TVA program among the three directors. In each of these areas the director was the "responsible administrative chief." This responsibility included preparation of tentative recommendations on policy, personnel, and budget in each area; the submission of these recommendations to the whole board; and the execution of the program authorized. As one author has commented, this gave each director a dual role; he both formulated policy and administered his special area. The director as administrator was to be responsible to the board as a whole, was to receive his instructions from it, and was to make his reports to it.[29] This arrangement allowed for considerable ease in getting projects under way, but it was essentially "an expedient which could be made to operate only with the conscious effort and good will of the participants." It also made for a confusion of roles.[30]

Arthur Morgan did not feel that the allocations had been carried out so that each man was delegated authority as administrator in the area of his expertise and training. For example, he opposed the placement of the land acquisition function under David Lilienthal's Legal Division; he regarded land acquisition as his own field of specialization.[31] Morgan would later testify to a congressional committee in 1938:

> For instance there was the purchase of millions of dollars worth of real estate. It happened that in handling 50 or more public projects requiring the acquisition of land . . . I had been immediately responsible for, or I had guided the appraisal of over 100,000 tracts of land. . . . I suppose that my experience in that field as 50 times that of the other two members of the board combined.[32]

Under the reorganization Arthur Morgan was to oversee the general engineering as well as the nonagricultural education and training programs. In addition, he was to supervise all land and regional planning, including forestry, the Civilian Conservation Corps (CCC), and subsistence homesteads and to coordinate all social and economic planning. On the other hand, Harcourt Morgan was to control all agricultural matters, which included planning for rural life, chemical engineering, and public relations. David Lilienthal was in charge of all questions relating to electric power, land acquisitions, and legal operations. Since this legislative division clearly earmarked each director's specific role and responsibility, it is not difficult to delineate the differences which soon erupted among them and thus within TVA. Different aspects of the Authority's operation where it affected the grass roots are not so easily discernible or separable, however, for decisions about how to remove and relocate rural people, how to buy their land, or how to plan their future cut abruptly and sharply across the three areas of the directors' practical operations. Given the studies already made on the disagreements between Arthur Morgan and Lilienthal, one knows that the directors were not inclined to work together easily. But did this mean that TVA did not work effectively? Did it mean that TVA did not meet the needs of its grass-roots constituents? Did the internal bickering of the directors harm the objectives of TVA?

The confusion, ambiguity, and hostility engendered by the 1933 reorganization would plague the agency until 1937, when Arthur Morgan and the other directors became so openly embroiled in bitter dispute that Roosevelt was forced to call for Morgan's resignation, a story brillantly told by Thomas McCraw in *Morgan versus Lilienthal*. Still, the history of TVA's effectiveness in the Norris Basin cannot be written solely in terms of its directors any more than the New Deal can as a history of Franklin D. Roosevelt and his heads of agencies and departments. Rather it must be written from the perspective of the way the agents of TVA carried the agency's objectives to the people, to the grass roots. Given the problems involved in just these specific tasks alone, the fact that there existed divisions in responsibilities of power which cut across the necessarily unified problems only made TVA's efforts harder to fathom. In effect, then, dissension and misunderstanding at the top of the agency caused uncertainty to filter down through the administrative and departmental divisions and to deter operations of practical programs to meet grass-roots needs. Theoretical differences among the directors added to the specific division of responsibilities and coupled with the administrative structure of the agency itself all contributed to increasing the confusion of operations at the grass roots.

From the beginning TVA confronted the transitional society of the Norris Basin ambivalently. Rather than a coherent, holistic, and well-formulated grass-roots philosophy, there existed divergence between its action program and its general welfare program; and rather than beginning its work with an administrative structure which would enhance programmatic specificity and unity, it began with an administrative structure lacking a general manager and so constructed as to diminish unity and favor directorial divergence. In addition TVA's posture toward the grass roots was not, unfortunately, the sort of thing which could be allowed to mature in long and well-reasoned debate. The very actions of TVA which most affected the people of the Norris Basin had to begin immediately, and their effect was immediate—land had to be purchased, and people had to be removed. The immediacy of TVA's impact at Norris, then, is one of the factors influencing the length and scope of this study.

The authors have chosen to examine TVA's impact on the Norris Basin in terms of a short to intermediate time period, by which we mean chronologically the years between TVA's inception in 1933 and 1940, the year in which TVA made the final assessment of its work in the Norris Basin and therefore an appropriate terminal date for this study. The floodgates of Norris Dam were closed in 1936, population removal was essentially completed at Norris by 1937, and the period comprising TVA's follow-up studies of its work at Norris ran roughly from 1936 to 1940. To follow the vicissitudes of the removed population, or even to assess TVA's impact beyond 1939–40, would be intensely complex, if not fruitless. A European war had by then begun to transform the American economy and was fast bringing to a close the depression era in which TVA's first experiment had been conducted. The parameters within which that initial experiment took place were radically altered in the war years. It is difficult to separate TVA's wartime and postwar impact on the region from the national economic impact of which it was a part. The coming of war, then, provides a fitting conclusion to an innovative phase in federal planning that was, to a very great extent, depression-induced. Thereafter TVA itself and the populations it affected were subject to an ever-widening set of influences.

The years between 1937 and 1939 can be used in another way to mark a turning point in TVA's history, for they mark an administrative convulsion within the agency which ends with a major congressional investigation. TVA emerged from this investigation with a clean bill of health, but those familiar with the Authority and its history know that the TVA of the wartime and postwar era is not the TVA of the thirties. Indeed the TVA of the late seventies bears more resemblence in many respects to the TVA of the thirties than to that of its "mature" period in between.

Short-term to intermediate-term impact analysis, while defensible, does pose certain complex problems, most of which center less on events themselves than on the ways in which these events are perceived. The concepts of modernization and of transitional modes were accompanied by a variety of images and perceptions. One of the most striking symbols of TVA, as the Authority perceives itself and is perceived by many others, is that of the power transmission line. The power line has been seen as the link between modernization and the rural, isolated community—a link which breaks down the separatism of rural communities and brings them into the mass of American society; a link that brings mass entertainment, mass consumerism, broader educational opportunities, social mobility, labor-saving energy, and increased participation in the national community. The power line, the transformer, and the dynamo were the means of attacking the social and cultural deprivation that characterized much of Appalachia in the thirties, and as such they were the images of progressive modernization. But in exploring TVA's impact on a transitional society, one has to acknowledge that the people of the Norris Basin had an imagery of their own, one deeply rooted in the traditional.

The first groups of people to feel the full weight of modernization, be they communities or nations, are more apt to bear the disruptive effects and tensions of that process than are the generations that follow. So it was in considerable degree in the Norris Basin, where rural communities bore the cost of disruption and dislocation in the short term so that deferred benefits could be gained. If the transmission line and the dynamo are the perceived images of these deferred or promised benefits, the rural community, a repository of traditional values and cohesiveness, may well dramatize the immediate confrontation of the transitional with the modern. For we must remind ourselves that if life in Southern Appalachia was too often characterized by harshness and deprivation, those very characteristics bred values of self-reliance and communal cohesiveness and a sense of self which transcended the poverty of the region. Thus in the historical analysis of TVA's short-term impact on the Norris Basin and its people, one sees the confrontation, conflict, and coexistence of the values and images of modernity and a virtually premodern rurality.

TVA and the people it confronted in the Norris Basin conceived of the present and the future in different and varied ways; nor were their views mutually opposed. TVA and the people were both ambivalent about the experiment in which they were participants. David Lilienthal's paean to the Authority, *TVA: Democracy on the March,* was written with hindsight, the knowledge of the institutional maturity of TVA. The holistic unity so self-consciously adumbrated by the title belies the very real tentativeness and confusion which existed for nearly a decade within TVA. The inhabitants of the Norris Basin were divided: they desired the benefits of the world TVA was in the process of creating as well as those of the world which TVA had doomed. TVA was itself a divided agency with regard to its ideology, its administrative structure, and its directors' concepts—uncertain of the degree to which it could or should shape the society upon which it had intruded and never completely confident or united in its legal limits, purpose, and experimental scope. TVA and the people worked out in their particular ways the conflicts inherent in the confrontation of a modernizing agent and a transitional society, and by focusing on this case the authors hope to further the historical understanding of both the Tennessee Valley Authority and the people it affected. At the same time, in a larger and less particular sense, it is hoped that this work will illuminate our general understanding of the ways in which modernization of transitional societies creates conflict and human doubt which bring unintended consequences.

TVA

PART ONE

The Norris Basin:
Setting for an Experiment

The environment that had shaped the society of the Norris Basin had changed little, in many respects, from the days when the first settlers had pushed toward the Cumberland gap. J. B. Killibrew had visited the region after the Civil War when he was compiling THE RESOURCES OF TENNESSEE *and had praised the strong sense of community and the self-sufficient farming practices which he found. When* TVA *came in 1933, the same characteristics prevailed, though the society was beginning to feel the impact of those great social catalysts the automobile and the radio. But demographic and landholding patterns over the years conspired to make the environment increasingly harsh as population pressed upon land often worked to its limits. From a broader perspective it was obvious that the land and its people stood in need of restoration and some beneficent change that would break the stasis imposed by environmental conditions.*

TVA possessed the power and ideas to do just that. The promise to set in motion programs of flood control, water control on the land, production of cheap electrical power, navigational improvements, conservation, and regional planning was bound to break traditional patterns of life imposed by the interaction of generations stultified in limited physical surroundings. No assessment of the impact of TVA *can be made without attempting historically to reconstruct life as it was before* TVA, *for the very quality and enduring characteristics of that life make it simultaneously an object for change and resistance to change—for transformation and preservation.*

2 Life in the Norris Basin Recalled

NO BETTER INSTRUMENTS for the expression of the totality and resonance of an existence have been devised than the human memory and its voice. Oral history is one of the tools available to the historian in recreating the tapestry of life and expressing it in such a way as to capture its wholeness and richness. Recall over an extensive period is not, of course, error-free, but it allows the historian to provide a reflection of past lives as they have been seen, thought about, and lived. The oral record reveals the conscious and unconscious sources of ambivalence in the face of modernization.

All the people interviewed for this book were residents in the Norris area either just before TVA came or at the time of its coming.[1] Many belonged to families who were displaced, and all were old enough to have historically competent memories of the rural life and times of the 1930s.[2]

An oral interview, whatever its historical warrant, constitutes an intrusion of sorts. It is a tribute to the persons interviewed that they bore this intrusion cooperatively and with consistent good humor. Whatever changes have been wrought in the lives of these people since the coming of TVA, one persistent trait has endured. One can only echo J. B. Killibrew's words in 1873: "Hospitality is a cardinal virtue through the South and East Tennessee is no exception. The well-behaved stranger, whether he comes as a mere passer-by or an immigrant, is sure of a hearty welcome and kind treatment."[3]

THE SELF-SUFFICIENT FARM *Curtis Stiner[4] is still actively farming in the Norris Basin on an attractive farm close to the Clinch River*

arm of the Norris reservoir. He farmed about 300 acres with his
father before TVA came and had also worked running a sawmill
and cutting timber for railroad crossties. When TVA came, he
took a construction job with the agency and worked on Norris,
Douglas, and Cherokee dams. His wife, Vera, also reared in the
Norris Basin, began her career as a schoolteacher in Union
County, where she taught until her recent retirement.

Stiner, a vigorous and imposing man in his sixties, had just come
in from the fields, where he had put in a full day working tobacco.
Reticent at first, he soon began to reminisce enthusiastically about
the early days, speaking warmly about the self-sufficient farming
life he remembered from boyhood. We were speaking of the various connotations of the term "hillbilly" when Mr. Stiner observed
about some people in the nearby Smoky Mountains: "They know
good seed beans from bad 'uns. They still carry on the old way of
living, and I like it pretty well." He and his wife disagreed about
the benefits of modernization, she stating that the old way of life
may have been all right "if you don't have to carry water from the
spring and fill up the oil lamps." Stiner complained about the
dependence upon modern power sources

> with all this pushbutton stuff. Well, it becomes a part of you. You
> can't cook a meal without it; you can't take a bath without it; you
> can't get a drink of water without it, and you can't do nothing
> without it. . . . There you are, you're hooked. If you had the old
> wood stove there in the kitchen, and a pitcher lift pump there on
> the porch run into the cistern . . . , and if the power goes you can
> still get a meal and get your water, and you had an Aladdin lamp you
> could light it and have a good light and go right on about your
> business, see, but you're hooked when the power goes off.

In the twenties Stiner ran a farm of about 300 acres with his
father. He began to grow tobacco first in 1925 ("just a shirttail full"),
then turned to raising beans, potatoes, vegetables of all kinds,
eggs, chickens, turkeys, and fattened hogs ("dress 'em here, haul
'em to town in a wagon") for the Knoxville market. Of farming
during the depression and even before it, Mr. Stiner commented:
"You had food to eat, you just didn't have any money to spend. I've
lived in a depression all my life; that's all I ever knowed. I can't tell
any difference; not between the twenties and the thirties."

To help with the crops, Stiner and his father kept tenants and hired labor whom they paid $0.75 to $1.25 a day. Stiner wanted his father to turn the land the tenants worked to pasture and raise cattle, but "he just fooled with them tenants." The trouble, he said, was that there were too many of them. "They all had to have a corn crop n they all had to have a corn bread 'n meat living, and . . . corn to fatten them hogs."

When Stiner was approached by a TVA agent to become a test demonstration farmer, he revealed a strong sense of independence: "I was cutting wheat up here on this land. I said, 'I don't want nothin' you've got to offer me no way you can preach it or talk it.'" He stated that becoming a test demonstration farmer, which entailed, among other things, accepting free fertilizer, would have obligated him to TVA. "I'd have been obligated. I'd of had to done what they said, the way they said, and when they said. That don't suit me. This is mine. I bought it and paid for it. I sweated it out. If I want to plow straight up and down the hill, I will, but a man's got any sense wouldn't do that."

> Andy Henegar[5] *is now retired from farming and lives in Maynardville, the county seat of Union County. He has been a farmer all his life. When TVA came to Union County, he was operating a farm of 101 acres, which he sold to TVA for about fifteen dollars an acre.*

"It was ridge land. . . . there was some bluffs on it, but it was all farmable land. We didn't have tractors and things to farm with back there, jus' two mules probably." He began to raise tobacco "a few years before they bought us out." He also grew food for the market in Knoxville: "We raised beans and tomatoes, potatoes, Irish and sweet, and put them on the market. We didn't get rich." Before the dam was built, the distance from his house to Knoxville was thirty-two miles.

> After the dam I had to come around this way [through Maynardville], and it kind of doubled the distance. Well, we didn't have a truck of our own for a right smart bit, but we had it [produce] hauled. A man that lived in there had a little pickup truck, and he'd haul our stuff for us, whatever he had to haul.

Henegar spoke of raising sorghum cane for the syrup.

> People would eat 'em [the canes], feed 'em to the cattle, make vinegar out of 'em, sweeten stuff, put it on the table [every] differ-

ent way you could use molasses, 'cause we didn't have the sugar back then like we have it now. . . . They used it more to make moonshine than they used it on the table.

Mrs. Dottie Ousley,[6] *who was present at Andy Henegar's interview, presently heads Union County's federal program for the aged. Her father, one of the five or six doctors in Union County, also practiced in parts of Claiborne and Campbell counties. He had graduated from medical school in 1895 and was still practicing when TVA came. Mrs. Ousley was raised on her father's land, a seventy- or eighty-acre farm worked by tenants and day laborers who sometimes paid for their medical bills through farm work. She later married a doctor from the Loyston area whose own father was also a local physician.*

They used to come in from Kentucky and haul moonshine out by the carloads. There where my daddy was, where he lived, you'd see those Kentucky cars go in, you'd know that so-and-so would be out before too long to pay the doctor's bills, and that night you'd hear those old cars come out of there, rrrrrrrr, rrrrrrrr, they's just loaded down. And then people would come and pay my daddy, because that was the only way they had of making a living, to tell the truth, because they all had big families, because . . . a lot of them lived back on ridge places and they wanted to send their children to school as much as they could, but their farms were run down, a lot of them, weren't they, Mr. Henegar?

"Oh yeah, they farmed 'em to death," he replied. Henegar felt that while some people raised cattle in the years after the coming of TVA, there were very few who kept more than they could use personally. A "good" river farm (about 100 acres), he said, would have brought a good price before TVA came, especially if it had included the much-prized bottom land: "You take the level land— it was higher than ridge land. You take the valley land—it didn't hardly go as high as ridge land because they was too many valley rocks on it. . . . River farms tended to be good because of bottom land, but some river farms didn't have bottom land, just bluffs that ran down to the river."

H. Clay Stiner,[7] *an amiable man of advancing years, operates a small country store not far from the Norris impoundment at a bend in the Clinch River called Leadmine Bend, an area settled by the Stiners for generations. His father was one of the wealthiest men in the region and a large landowner. The land his father*

32

sold to TVA had been in the family since 1820. The store he operates today is just as it was in 1933 when TVA came and in fact was placed on rollers and moved up the road to a new location to avoid the rising waters of Norris Reservoir.

Stiner commented on the scarcity of good bottom land: not many people had it. The average farm, he believed, was about 75 to 100 acres at the time when TVA came. "Most people made just barely to live. They was an honorable people. They'd tell you the truth. I dealt with them, and I'd carry them in the store from one year to the other. Their main cash crop was tobacco. When they sold it they'd come and pay the store account." Much of Stiner's business involved trading his store goods for goods raised by the area farmers:

They'd bring eggs, chickens, butter, ginseng, 'possum hides, chestnuts, everything like that, you know, everything that would sell, and we'd load it on the wagons and take it to Knoxville and sell it . . . , and it'd take us three days to make that trip over there. Come from here daylight in the morning, we'd go to Copper Ridge—John Warren run that livery stable there—stay all night there, get up the next morning before daylight, head for Knoxville, sell our load of produce, buy a load of merchandise, come back to Copper Ridge, spend the night, and come in the next day. We'd have to meet them with an extra pair of mules at the Clinch River, it took four mules to bring them over, it was so rough. In 1925 we got a T-model truck, and it had solid tires. The roads were so damn rough we *had* to have them, and then we didn't do much better than with a pair of mules and a wagon.

Not many people, said Stiner, went to Knoxville frequently to trade. "Now and then some of them would go in with their wagon . . . , but the majority of farmers, they traded here at the store. Back then practically all were people who raised their stuff or canned it. They'd slaughter their hogs to have their meat and lard. Kill a little beef and have it, and all they needed at the store was sugar, salt, coffee, pepper, and stuff like that."

Clay Stiner's father had five tenants on his farm in the thirties, one of whom had been there for thirty-five years. There were also sharecroppers and some day laborers who were paid at a going rate of about seventy-five cents a day. They managed "pretty good. My father gave them a garden, and they'd have a hog, take care of a hog

. . . back then. . . . Everybody had to get it on their own, they knew it, and they'd go after it, 'cause they knowed they had to shine." Stiner stated that it was a more common practice for the younger sons of farmers to try to work on their father's farms and raise part of a crop of their own or some cattle, or do some day labor for pay, than to become a tenant for another farmer. Most of the tenants were not related to the people who employed them.

> Monroe Stooksbury[8] *was thirty-two, married, and living on his own farm when TVA came to the Norris Basin, but he moved to Knoxville to go into the grocery business before the Norris Dam was built. His parents, Sam and Nola Stooksbury, also operated their own farm, which TVA purchased, and an older brother operated a farm which he sold to TVA. While Monoe owned a farm, he was not a full-time farmer, as both he and his wife were elementary schoolteachers in Loyston, where she taught the third, fourth, and fifth grades, and he taught the seventh and eighth.*

Before he became a teacher, Monroe Stooksbury worked on his father's place. He remembered that they grew "a little of everything. We grew corn, potatoes, and just about everything we ate. We fattened our own hogs, we had a milk cow that we had our milk from. . . . Well, we did sell some milk and butter in Knoxville, and we'd send buttermilk in, and butter about twice a week. My mother made it, churned it in the old-fashioned churn. Well, we finally got one of those churns that you turn with a crank, you know."

> Myers Hill[9] *was twenty-six years old when he left Union County with TVA's arrival. He was married and living with his parents on a farm between the Clinch and Powell rivers in lower Union County. His uncle, Sherman Hill, operated a local store which Hill later operated for a while with his cousin, following his uncle's death. Myers Hill's father, Newton Hill, was a farmer and justice of the peace and a member of the county court.*

Myers Hill said that a good many people talk about the life of the "old days," but he is not sure they really mean it "cause you take, we didn't have any convenience of electricity or anything like that. The newspaper we got was day-old when we got it, and all we had was radios and those, of course, were battery-powered radios. There wasn't the convenience that we got after we moved out of up

34

there, and got to where we had electricity and many other conveniences which was available." Large portions of Union County did not receive electricity until the early forties.

Hill's uncle, who ran a grocery store in Union County, committed suicide when TVA came. "Till the dam ran us out," Myers and his cousin operated the store, which was conveniently located across from one of the dozen or so CCC camps, "and had a nice business for a country store at that time." Hill described the store as a general merchandise store: "You know, they carried everything from plow points to dry goods, shoestrings and shoes, and everything that you can imagine can be used in the country. The farmers brought their chickens, sold their chickens, we took the chickens, eggs, butter, anything like that. We'd make our trip to Knoxville once a week in a wagon."

He remembers his father's farm very well and still goes there occasionally to look at the steps of the old home at the edge of the lake, now the only remnant of another life.

> We go back up there once in a while, and of course it's grown up till you have to work your way in there, but they do have a road that goes down in the community, there where I used to live. All the lowland, it was a valley—a "holler," we called it—and the bottomland of the creek along there was very fertile land; and outside of that, the other land was hilly and very steep—some of it very steep, hilly land.

Myers Hill's father's farm was about one-third cultivated and pasture, and the rest was in timber. He recalled that his father raised hay and corn and later tobacco. "Of course, after tobacco came, that was some extra money. Nearly all farmers raised and thatched tobacco to give some extra money. But outside of that it was just corn and other things we raised for our own consumption." Hill mentioned one feature about his uncle's store that he felt was unique.

> People would raise chickens, eggs and . . . butter, and anything they had an excess of, they could tke it to the general store and trade it for sugar and other staples that you wasn't able to raise or didn't have, and if you had something coming to you he'd give you scrip that was different denominations. I think from five cents, twenty-five, fifty and a dollar scrip. . . . that was the only place it could be traded.

Boyd Rogers and Claud Longmire[10] *were interviewed together. The former, a TVA engineer, was raised in the Lost Creek Community in the Central Peninsula between the Clinch and Powell Rivers. The latter was seventeen when TVA came and was living with his parents. They moved after TVA's purchase of Longmire's father's place at the foot of Bear Ridge in Big Springs Hollow. His father, Charles Longmire, worked as a foreman for the Forest Service Division of the CCC camps. Both are Union Countians.*

Boyd Rogers began

Most of the people raised their own back then. They fattened their own hogs, butchered their own hogs, raised their own corn, and they took their own corn to the community water mill. A mill is where they take tolls—take your corn in to grind it, and they take out so many pounds of corn for grinding it for you. You didn't pay money. . . . it's corn by the toll. A bushel of corn weighed fifty-six pounds. I believe that a toll was one-eighth, which would be seven pounds.

Claude Longmire added: "They took out seven pounds for grinding it for you. This fellow told me he went into Rufie Rice's mill one day, and he said he kind of fussed about it, and he said, 'I hear people don't get their just dues here at this mill,' and he said Uncle Rufie told him, 'Well, a lot of them don't get it till they die.'"

Boyd Rogers said that the farmers "in our section over there raised principally everything they ate. Very few reached up and bought things." Longmire added, "So you might have bought salt and what they called coal oil, kerosene, and sugar." Rogers: "And coffee . . . , took the eggs to the store and swapped them for sugar or . . ." Claude Longmire interrupted, "Anything and buy some calico, what they called gingham and calico, and the women'd make clothes out of them—two or three yards of this and two or three yards of that."

The Community

In nearly all of the interviews, some questions were asked concerning the rural communities where individuals had lived prior to the coming of TVA. References to the community's size, cohesion, social stratification, boundaries, composition, and character emerged from these interviews in various forms, but one point which seemed to persist in nearly every direction was the sense of community togetherness and the high value which inhabitants placed upon it.

In H. Clay Stiner's opinion, "Every community lived to support itself," and each took pride in "not having to go to them [other communities] for anything." When asked if Loyston, a community not far away, would be considered a community separate from Leadmine Bend, where he was reared, Stiner replied: "Yes, well, at the last they got to marrying some of our folks. All those Loyston boys would come up here and try to get some of our girls. And then we'd have to visit." The general rule, said Stiner, was that you married within your own community.

Dottie Ousley said that the boys in one community became jealous when young men from another community visited the girls. Curtis Stiner's wife, Vera, said of this particular practice: "They would do what we called 'rocking' them. . . . When the boys take the girl home, and he went back to his community, her friends that didn't want him to come in would be along the road to throw rocks at him . . . , and sometimes they'd get hurt, too."

The process of "neighboring" would appear to have been a matter of course in the communities of the Norris Basin. H. Clay Stiner explained:

> Everybody lived alike. If some of the neighbors got sick and had a crop out, the other neighbors would go in and work his crops or whatever else was needed. They was just a bunch of people that was very close together. [If] one had the sickness, if one didn't have food, they'd take the food into the home. If one died, they'd take care of the body. The neighbors would bring in the rough casket, and I had the handles, and they'd trim the casket right here in the store. It's not like that nowadays, not by a whole lot, and all of these people were honorable and they was honest. If they told you they'd come to work for you tomorrow, they'd be here settin' on the steps when you got up. Was a lot of those people gettin' hard luck and they'd come to my father and want a job of work and he'd have them clean up the farm, fence rows and stuff like that, and pay for what they wanted at the store. . . . the first day's work I'd done I got thirty-five cents a day—the men got seventy-five cents. But that was custom, you don't expect any more because it's custom in the neighborhood—that was the rule. . . . People still travel back here to trade. They seem to enjoy seeing the country. And when they

was leaving here it was just like a funeral here at the store every day. The store set right at the bridge down there [across the Powell River], and those people lived up in the hollows, they'd have to haul heavy stuff out on wagons, couldn't get a truck up in there. They'd haul it here and I'd store it till they could get a truck to move it. And all the neighbors would come in to see those people off. It was just like a funeral—they didn't know whether they'd see them any more in their life.

Stiner felt that religious differences meant no more in the community structure than monetary ones. "No, no, religion didn't never cut no figures. People held to that rule that you had a right to worship according to the dictates of your own conscience, and we were free people and we used that privilege." Asked whether money or land was a divisive social point in the community, Stiner replied, "We were all people, and some people were fortunate to accumulate more than others. But still, at the same time if a man gets a few dollars ahead, he's still a man."

Myers Hill recalls that his father owned some veterinary books which he often studied. "He doctored horses and cows and animals, you know, and studied the veterinarian books and learned something about the different animal diseases and things and how to treat them." His father performed these services for nothing, for

back in those days people didn't think of charging their neighbors for any service. . . . Anytime there was a tragedy in any family, the whole community would come in. Say the head of the house, the farmer, got sick—they would come in and work his crops and take care of him. If he had a house burn down—all the neighbors would get together and help them rebuild a home and supply them with the furnishings and things like that.

Myers Hill echoed H. Clay Stiner's comments on social differentiation.

Not because of being poor or anything like that they wasn't looked down on in the community I lived in, because there wasn't any what you say well-to-do people in the community where I lived. And poorer people, everybody respected them just as much as they did everybody else, just as long as their character was good. The only people who was maybe looked down on was the people who had poor characters. . . . All the rural communities, I think, was pretty much like that back then, to help one another. Seems like they was

Above: Loyston, largest rural community inundated by the waters of Norris Dam, as TVA began clearing the reservoir area. Below: Leaving the Land. Henry Ray and his family, dressed up and ready to move from their land on the Central Peninsula, 1935.

more close to one another, and [there was] more love for one another than there is today. I don't know, that's what some friends of mine and others have talked about, which we wish things could be like they used to be in that one respect, that people showed more love and respect for their neighbor and fellow man than they do today. 'Course they may love them as much today, but they're concerned with so many other activities till they don't get to show it enough, maybe don't have the time.

Myers Hill also spoke of the funeral practices of the times.

There wasn't no undertakers, neighbors came in to take care of them, burial and preparing them for burial and all that. There wasn't no such things as embalmers, only the neighbors did it . . . , and the churches I was telling you about—when somebody in the community died, they'd ring what they called the death bell. And since there wasn't no communication, people'd hear that bell, oh, for miles around. The way they rang the death bell was different from any other. They'd pull the cord—the rope—down and hold it for a few seconds and then let it go back instead of letting it ring the natural ring. Everybody'd recognize the death bell, and they knew there was somebody in the community who was dead. Of course the whole community would come in and prepare food and help and do anything that was needed to be done for the family.

Bill and Lou Emma Taylor[11] *were renting on property purchased by TVA and had to leave and temporarily set up housekeeping in a tenant house on her grandfather's property because rental property was so hard to find after TVA came. Her parents relocated in Knox County, Tennessee, and his in Georgia. Bill Taylor was a rural mail carrier in Union County at the time TVA came, delivering mail in the Central Peninsula on a route of about thirty-five miles which served 200 people.*

"They [the community] worked together. If someone got sick and couldn't work his property, why, people would go in and work it for them and take care of it a lot more than they would now—they wouldn't do it now nowhere, but they did then at that time." Lou Emma Taylor added: "Now if somebody got sick like he says, they didn't let his crop ruin. They went over and worked it out and got in his tobacco, anything like that. It was put in the barn ready for them, and then at night they'd help nurse and set up for them and they just acted like church folks should."

Boyd Rogers spoke of another form of aid for those persons in the community struck by adversity.

I've known them, maybe two or three individuals, to take a wagon and team and travel over the country to make up for them what they called—"making up" for someone—anybody who wanted to give something donated it. If you wanted to donate money, all right. If you wanted to donate clothing, if they had some clothing to fit the family, they'd do that, or something in the way of cookware for the wife. I've seen them do that . . . , or I've seen them have what they called the box supper or the pie supper.

The box supper and pie supper were, said Rogers and Claude Longmire, always benefits which had the added attraction of mixing charitable efforts with recreation. As Longmire pointed out, "The cause and the benefit it was going for was what people looked at mostly . . . had fun out of it, too." Boyd Rogers said, "People are usually pretty level on a thing like that and had a lot of fun as well." Part of the fun of the charitable pie or box supper benefit was the auction, which provided general amusement as well as an innocent courtship ritual. As Claude Longmire tells it, "If a man they knew . . . he was dating some young lady, why if she'd made a pie and it'd go over there and they'd auction it off—they'd try to run it up on her boyfriend, make him pay more for it, because whoever got the pie got to eat it with the girl."

Nearly all the persons interviewed perceived that the rural communities where they lived were generally peaceful. Myers Hill in recalling the occasions when he and some friends went to different revival services as boys, agreed:

> We'd walk four and five miles to go to these other churches. Get in somebody's turnip patches every night coming back, in the fall, you know, and eat them turnips. As to occasional pilfered watermelon, [boys] did that just for meanness, I think—they didn't consider it stealing.
>
> They just wasn't any crime a-going in that area. People'd go to bed and leave their doors open, maybe close the screens to keep the dogs out and think nothing about it . . . , people didn't lock their doors a bit more than nothing. . . . Biggest thing they ever heard of was people getting drunk and getting arrested or something like that.

> Ruble Palmer[12] *was thirty years old and living on a farm in the Big Valley section of Union County when TVA came. Upon relocation he purchased fifty acres of land near Maynardville, the county seat, where he still lives.*

41

While there was nearly universal agreement that people left houses and barns open and that the community engendered a spirit of mutual trust, a note of healthy skepticism on the subject was introduced by Ruble Palmer, who asserted that "a lot of people never did [lock doors], but you could lose things. It wasn't no utopia, but you find rascals everywhere you go, you know."

Perceptions relative to community size varied considerably, but most agreed that a community was quite small. Andy Henegar felt that "every community had one church, maybe two churches in it," and that a major determinant of space was the difficulty in transportation. "People had a poor way of gettin' around, they could not travel too far." Mrs. Dottie Ousley agreed that the rural community was very small, but in terms of social relationships some people had a considerable number of friends outside the community if they were not stay-at-home types. Myers Hill felt a community had at least one church and estimated that the average community might contain 100 to 150 persons altogether.

Mrs. Vera Stiner illustrated community size when she noted that Big Valley, an area that runs for several miles along the north bank of the Clinch River, was made up of many small communities. She spoke of her childhood acquaintance with Dottie Ousley, who lived in Sharp's Chapel, while she (Mrs. Stiner) was reared in Big Sinks: "Well, that's the Big Sinks. And where it got its name, we used to call it Sink Hole, a big hole where the water from all directions comes into that . . . , and it was about four or five miles [from Sharp's Chapel]. Well, we didn't associate in the same group very much." Mrs. Stiner felt the community could be measured not in terms of numbers of families but by area. "I don't know whether you'd count it by families or not, but it was a small area."

For many residents the location of churches was a means of community identification. Myers Hill recalled that his community, Big Springs, had one church.

The one that I showed you was the only one in the community. You go on out to the Bridges community [about five miles]—they had a church, and you go on up the other road there to about five or six miles, [there] was another community, and that's where the Methodist Church was, there. I guess then we had Walnut Grove community. I think it was down near the fork of the river, where

Powell and Clinch rivers come together down there. And it was a Methodist. Had a Methodist and Baptist church both in that community. Back when I was young . . . youngsters used to walk and go to these different churches when they was having revival services, you know. We'd walk four and five miles to go to these other churches.

(Oaks Chapel, Oak Grove, Big Springs, and Blue Springs were within this radius from Hill's community.)

The church's location in terms of the community was interestingly described by Vera Stiner, who stated that people generally went to the one nearest to them. "I know in doing my research on when our church was established, my father's cousin gave the property, because they traveled by horseback, wagon, or buggy at that time, and he said he wasn't going to take any more of his dead relatives in a chokewagon for about ten miles, so he gave the land, and the church was established." Mrs. Stiner and Dottie Ousley, living three miles apart, went to different churches, and Vera Stiner noted that "there was a church every three or four miles."

The church, a provider of communal cohesiveness, played a highly diversified role in the day-to-day life of the community. It was an institutional link to the demographic reality of the community: the newborn and the reborn entered the community through the church, and church cemeteries bore mute evidence of the links of past generations to present ones. The church served as a place of worship, sociability, recreation, and education. The pronounced tendencies in the Norris Basin communities were toward Missionary and Primitive Baptist and Methodist Churches, with Baptists numerically preponderant.

Although sectarianism and religious splintering appear in the proliferation of Baptist and Methodist churches, most of the divisiveness appears to have been occasioned by doctrinal disputes of the previous century and by the splintering caused by the rift between the Confederacy and the Union. As Myers Hill said:

And back there, there were two types of Methodists—the southern and the northern Methodists. The southern was started back during the Civil War—the ones that didn't believe in slavery, you know, that was the only difference. . . . The feeling was that hard from the Civil War . . . that they wouldn't go to the same churches here. The feeling took two or three generations for it to die out. I reckon it finally died out.

Doctrinal differences were revealed in one interview when H. E. Anderson said, "The Primitives [Baptists] have changed. They didn't believe in any missionaries at all; they didn't believe in paying the preacher; they didn't believe in having Sunday school, anything like that, and now they have all that." Vera Stiner, speaking of the Baptists, said that for both Missionaries and Primitives, membership entailed rebirth. "You have to have a rebirth, become a Christian before you could join the church, and when you joined the church, you were a member of the church. The Primitive Baptists wouldn't accept members from a Missionary Baptist church by letter—they had to be rebaptized."

Most persons interviewed recalled that by the time TVA appeared on the scene in the Norris Basin area, there was a relatively open exchange among the different religions. Andy Henegar recalled:

> Every community had a church, maybe two churches in it. We had the Primitive Baptists and the Missionary Baptists and we had the Methodists, that was about it, and the Holiness came in. But back there if it was a Missionary Baptist church, it was goin' to help the Methodists; the Methodists was goin' to help the Missionaries; the Primitive Baptists would help both ways. Denomination did not amount to much because they all worked through each other.

To Clay Stiner, whether or not a church was close to home appeared to affect the size of its congregation, regardless of their denominational preferences. "If it was close, they'd attend."

Myers Hill also discussed the notion of religious discrimination "The Methodists and Baptists would join together in the revival services and meetings. Wasn't nothing thought about the denominations getting together and worshiping together and church services."

H. E. Anderson, eighty-two[13] *left the Norris area in 1937. His home adjoined the TVA purchase. Since most of the area where he taught school was purchased by TVA, he moved to Fountain City, a suburb of Knoxville and started teaching in eastern Union County for forty dollars a month. Anderson went overseas in the First World War, and upon his discharge he taught at Oak Grove*

*School and Hills Academy in Union County. He furthered his
education at normal schools in Eastern Tennessee and Kentucky
and eventually taught at one of the Union County junior high
schools at Leadmine Bend. After the depression he went into the
building supply and construction business. His wife was also a
schoolteacher. He gives a different picture of church services,
with no joint revival meetings.*

"Just one church at a time. There were three denominations
there, the Primitive Baptists, the Missionary Baptists, and the
Methodists. They didn't take together. Later on there were some
of the Holiness churches. And the rivalry between the churches
was in truth pretty keen. The minister of one denomination
wouldn't preach in another one." The variance in preference for
church attendance was often due to the infrequency of services.
Anderson remembered that his minister "had to ride fifteen or
sixteen miles on horseback. Sometimes he'd come into the community on Saturday and we'd have church on Saturday, then he'd
stay in the community there and then have church on Sunday, and
then we had—some of the churches had—Sunday school. Very few
did. The revival was the biggest activity of churches, schools, or
anything else."

Myers Hill, who went to a Methodist church, feels the church
"played a pretty important role. Our churches were on circuits,
and we just had preachin' once a month [but] we had Sunday school
every Sunday." The monthly meeting was Saturday, as he remembers, and "one pastor was pastor of maybe three or four churches."
For Hill the revival was a main attraction. Dottie Ousley went to
both Methodist and Baptist churches. "We'd go to both churches
because then you didn't have services every Sunday, you know, so
in order to keep at a church, we'd skip around." Mrs. Ousley
pointed out that the Methodists were more inclined to having
preachers of the circuit-riding type, and that the Baptists often had
a resident preacher. Ruble Palmer concurred. "The Methodists
had three or four churches and a pastor, but the Baptists, a lot of
them, they just had one church and a pastor." Palmer frequently
alternated attendance from one church to another. "Yeah, I went to
all of them, even the Holy Rollers."

The Holiness church was established well after the Baptists and

45

the Methodists had moved into the Basin. Mrs. Ousley's story, revealing a certain enmity among the religions, cast light on a different sort of sociability concerning the church.

> There was a Missionary Baptist church, then there was a Primitive Baptist and a Methodist. And then there was a Holiness church. I never went to that church . . . because we weren't allowed to, because, really . . . , there was a lot of fighting and drinking and acts of this nature. Well, of course, there were at some of the other churches, too. Some of the boys would come in sort of high, maybe have a little riffraff out in the yard, you know. But if our parents ever knew about that, why, they didn't want us to go. . . . I'll say that the Holiness church has come a long ways, and I think you would feel as comfortable going to a Holiness church as any other church now. But when it first originated over in that area, it was pretty wild. I always wanted to go, but [my parents] never would let me.

One point upon which virtually all of those interviewed agreed was that in the church, all distinctions of social status, whether real or imagined, disappeared. Bill Taylor recalled:

> Most people had suits and were decent, but if you did see them at church and a pair of overalls on, they'd be clean, and have a clean shirt which would be all right, but still he might have $1,000 or $2,000 in his pocket. I know once that it did happen. A lady refused to sit down by a man like that in church, but he had over $2,000 in his pocket. Of course she didn't know it, but he could have bought him all kinds of clothes if he wanted. They were sincere.

> Hubert and Schuyler Stooksbury[14] *are brothers who lived about one mile east of Loyston on their father's farm and moved from the Norris Basin in 1935 when TVA purchased their father's land. Hubert Stooksbury explained how people were judged in their community.*

> There wasn't any looking down on anyone. If they were good characters, they wasn't looked down upon. As long as they were of good character, their standing as far as finances were concerned [wasn't considered]. If they wanted to go to the same churches, they went. . . . If they showed bad character, they didn't want to go to church.

The church was the major center of social life. Some of the charitable functions like ice cream and pie suppers were held at the churches. As Monroe Stooksbury recalled: "They were sometimes held at churches for the young people. That was one way of kinda drawing us to the churches." Myers Hill, although not recalling any functions like pie suppers, felt that the attendance at church constituted virtually all the social functions of the community. "About the only thing we had in our community was just our church activities. . . . Yes, nearly everybody went to church. There was more churchgoing then than there is now in our two because there wasn't any other activities to go to like there is today, you know. . . . That was the only gathering that they had to go to, and . . . there was very few people who didn't go to some of the churches." The extended revival was discussed by the Stooksbury brothers. "Oh, yes, they used to have a two-week revival," Hubert began. Schuyler agreed: "Yeah, they'd have a revival every year, usually in the wintertime. People weren't working, felt they all ought to come."

Dottie Ousley vividly remembered the sociability associated with some church functions.

> Oh, yes! And I remember the Baptists, they had their baptizing and footwashing on the first Sunday in May, and that was really a big day. Everybody had to have their house cleaned and all done, you know, to take care of as high as thirty, thirty-five people for lunch on Sunday. Would you believe at that particular time [the thirties], because I was the youngest of eight children, and when all our friends gathered and lots of the ministers would come to my father's for lunch, and it was quite a day.

Mrs. Ousley felt the church meetings enhanced communal ties because that was where friends issued invitations for supper or lunch.

Vera Stiner remembered the church applying summer activities. "I can remember going when I was a child to singing schools. We'd have them a couple of weeks in the summertime, and everybody'd go spend the day and take some lunch. I used to go to different churches, because we just had services once a month, and I was within reach of a Primitive church the other three Sundays, and lots of times I'd go. That's the only place you had to go on Sundays."

Dottie Ousley differed with the view that the church was the only focal point of sociability and recreation in the Basin: "There was activities in the community when there was no church services. We had some real good music of fiddling and things of this sort, going to various neighbors' houses, and square dancing on Saturday night." Bill and Lou Emma Taylor felt the social life was as rich then as now. "Yeah," Bill Taylor began, "the younger folks, they'd get together about once a week for a square dance, and of course we had our churches and Sunday schools for weekends, and then at the high school they had all kinds of programs . . . and picnics and swimming parties." Myers Hill remembered the grocery store as a recreational facility. "Especially on weekends and Saturday afternoons. People would gather and talk and pitch horseshoes. In wintertime they'd sit around the stove in the store and play checkers and gossip about things."

According to H. E. Anderson, "the general store was the meeting place. They had nail cases, people'd come in there and sit on those nail cases and whittle and tell yarns." Dottie Ousley saw this pastime in a slightly different light: "We also had a grocery store, and they would close the store at lunch to come up to the house to eat lunch, especially on rainy days when the loafers were sitting around. Whoever was in the store would say, 'Well, let's go on up to Dad's house and eat lunch,' and they'd all just push back the nail cans, you know, and come up and sit down and eat."

Andy Henegar remembered with particular fondness the events accompanying the harvesting of the cane in the fall and the processing of it in the mule-powered sorghum mills. When the cane was harvested, there would be a "stir-off" of the sorghum molasses. Dottie Ousley commented: "At night when they'd be havin' that stir-off, the youngsters would gather for miles around. We really had a good time." Henegar summed it up well. "Well, it was about all the places they had to go . . . , apple-peeling, corn-shelling, bean-hulling, and go to church on Sunday night or to a revival."

Monroe Stooksbury spent his spare time with other youngsters. "We'd go to the creek occasionally and go in a-swimming, go a-fishing, and we'd play a little baseball on a Saturday afternoon." In his community (Loyston) everyone gravitated to Caney Stooksbury's or George Fox's store in Loyston. "We'd go there on Saturday afternoon. People from all around the community would come in, you know, sort of a meeting place." The older folks, he related, would watch the younger ones play baseball. Myers Hill enjoyed another type of recreation. "The first radio we had was the Grand Ole Opry, wsm, Nashville—that was what most people listened to. First radio that ever came in our community my uncle got it. . . . I remember an old big . . . round speaker sat on top of it. On Saturday nights several neighbors would gather in and listen to the old Saturday night show."

If the men and boys went to the local stores on the weekends, most of those interviewed believed that the women in the community were too busy to do so except to come in and buy staples. Quilting bees and such gatherings, according to Myers Hill, did not involve large groups of women on a social basis. "Maybe a couple or three families would get together and do something like that, but there wasn't no larger gatherings like they do now when they have something like that." He did say that one form of recreation was for "close neighbors" to get together on the weekend or sometimes at night to "talk about things in the community and about your crops, and just whatever was on their minds, maybe talk about the church, or anything that was of common interest among them. They'd talk about some of their families, or some of their neighbors that was sick or some of them that needed help or a lot of times maybe neighborhood gossip that wasn't of any value."

One of the big recreations in Claude Longmire's community was a game of "townball," played every Saturday at Hill's Academy. Equipment was simple and homemade, for they "always made the ball out of twine, make it real tight out of twine, small, about three times the size of a golf ball probably. Take a timber—and I don't know whether it was two by two or rounded off—was [used] for a bat."

Townball could be played by as many as twenty-five or thirty people.

The rules were there, but you could have as many people as you wanted, and you could bat for somebody. The older folks, say sixty-five years old, would swing, and if they'd hit it, they'd have somebody run for them. And the thing about it was if they crossed you out, if they threw the ball in front of you before you got to the base where you were going, or if they caught the ball on the first bounce, or if they caught it on the fly, on the fly or the first bounce—you were out. Or if you hit a ground ball, and they could pick that up and throw it between you and the first base before you

49

got there, you were out. Or if you was starting from first to second, and they picked it up and threw it between first and second base, you were out. That was townball. And if you hit a home run, that gave you what they called an "extra eye." If you had two home runs, you had two eyes. That means they had to get you out twice before you were out. Well, some man that hit real well—like Obie that you was talking about—a big long rawbone, he'd get out of there and maybe have fifteen or twenty home runs. They'd have to get him out fifteen or twenty times, or he could give it to someone else. . . . I give you an eye and you an eye. He could put his whole side back to bat till he got them all out again. They'd play there and the score would be about 120 to 110, and maybe . . . for a whole afternoon the other side didn't get to bat.

Claude Longmire and Boyd Rogers both remember outdoor basketball games. They also recall going to one of the various stores in the community on Saturday to watch a regular baseball game and, as Longmire jokingly added, "to see who was drunk and fought."

Since education was a valued commodity in the Norris Basin, teachers were among the more esteemed community members. The business of a family farm involved the labor of children as well as adults and consequently reduced the length of the school year, which varied as much as from four to eight months. Most of those interviewed had had some experience in the one-room school-house, either as teachers or pupils, but clearly the days of the single-teacher school were numbered at the time TVA came. The one-teacher school itself was more a product of isolation, poor roads, and bad transportation facilities than of personal choice, and many persons interviewed were more inclined to speak of improvements in the system than of the "good old days" of the community one-room school. TVA could certainly claim with justification that it hastened the advent of a more rationalized and efficient school system, since the purchase of numerous one-room schools hastened the process of consolidation. But while those who attended or taught in these single-room schools were well aware of the shortcomings of such a system of instruction, none would deny that they made the best of what they had, and the education won from such adversity, like the fruits wrung from such often inhospitable soil, was all the more pleasurable.

50

It might also be mentioned that some of the publicity attendant upon the coming of TVA stressed the one-room schoolhouse as a symbol of "backwardness" while ignoring larger and better schools in the area. Of one picture of rustic Oakdale School, taken by Lewis Hine, the famous photographer of America's working people, Herbert Stooksbury commented:

> They *wanted* something like Oakdale; they didn't want something that looked good. They wanted to show the worst side. They took pictures. Well, you've seen them. I know why they do it. You see, movies are made about the South. They'll be hillbillies, and the rough people of the South, when you see the movies. And, well, people outside of the South were viewing this community here. If it had all been spic and span and beautiful buildings, well, it wouldn't have been interesting to anybody.

Even allowing for local prejudices, there were some schools like Hill's Academy near Loyston, a subscription school, which contrasted sharply with many of the one-teacher schools. Whether they had attended a small or large school, the persons interviewed felt that the communities placed a high value on education. Bill Taylor commented: "Everybody made their children go to school, and another thing, a lot of people in that area were educated, not in a high school or in a college, but as to general knowledge, maybe they'd go two years in the eighth grade, we'd call it, as high as they went until they got ready for high school. And they had what we call a 'bay horse sense.' Some of the best-educated people in Knoxville come from Union County." Bill's wife Lou Emma agreed. "They all believed in education, sending them just as far as they could send them." Bill Taylor, as he remembered,

> was raised poor. I'm not ashamed of it. I was raised poor. My father and mother had nine children. We're all still alive. All range from seventy years down into their fifties. The Lord's been good to us, I reckon, and our father would have done anything honest to keep us in school. I don't know how they ever kept us in school. And not bragging, but we still got enough education to where we're all making a decent living. We're in good shape.

Vera Stiner began teaching school in 1924 in Union County, in a "one-teacher school just across the ridge." She taught grades one through eight and had about thirty students. Since her own home was ten miles from the school, she had to board out in the community of the school. Even then, getting to the school was difficult. "I had to cross the river in a canoe—one of those old-timey canoes—twice a day. That was quite an experience for me because I was quite a way from the river before Norris Dam was built." It was customary for teachers to board with one family in the community where they taught, a practice which diminished as automobiles became more popular.

Mrs. Stiner's training was not atypical for the times in these communities.

> I taught school before I went to high school. . . . It seems odd, but we had to take a state examination. It was sent out from Nashville. And I taught two years like that, and then I dropped out and finished high school, and at that time they required one year of college to teach. That gave me a permanent right to teach, and I got, I believe, four quarters before I went back to teaching. That was in, I think, '34 when I went back to teaching, and then I kept working on summer school and night extension courses and night classes.

Mrs. Stiner noted, "I was just eighteen when I started [and] had students just a few months younger than I was."

H. E. Anderson, who was a teacher before he left Union County in 1937 and began a new career as a dealer in building supplies, recounted his first career. "I started my first school . . . in 1916, and I had about thirty or forty pupils. I received about forty dollars a month for teaching and paid board out of that. That was in the eastern part of Union County." Anderson was in the service during World War I and returned to teaching upon discharge.

> I taught at Oak Grove, kept going up, and then I went to school in Johnson City and Lincoln Memorial University and then I went one quarter at U.T.—University of Tennessee. In Union County there were four or five schools called junior high schools, and discipline, there'd been paddling in most all the schools. Not boasting or anything, but I was rated for my discipline. . . . When I quit teaching I'd been a principal at one of those junior high schools five years. During the depression they just started cutting salaries and cutting salaries and kept on cutting them . . . , got me down to about eighty-five dollars a month. Well, that's quite a bit of money then, and I quit. I told them I was going to quit and learn something else.

When he taught in a one-teacher school, he taught everything: "All

52

subjects—and my wife taught in the school. She had about 75 or 80 pupils, and it wasn't one grade at all. . . . At one time they had over 100 students in a one-room school ranging in age from about five or six years old to . . . twenty-one. And they didn't have all the subjects like they have now." When he taught in a two-teacher school, "I had students up there eighteen-nineteen years old, and this was a grammar school."

Myers Hill recalled vividly the school he went to as a boy.

The first school was a one-room schoolhouse . . . , and the grades went from beginning—what they called the primer—on up through the eighth grade. One man taught all grades . . . from time school started in the fall till—I don't remember how many months of school we had back in those days. . . , but there were a lot of pupils who had to drop out of school during the harvesting season to help harvest the crops. We carried water in two-gallon buckets, and most of the children, . . . boys especially, would like to get to carry water to get out of the classroom that long. It would take you, say thirty or forty-five minutes to get a bucket of water, and it would sit in the back of the school, and all of the children would have to come and drink water out of this same bucket. They carried little individual drinking cups back then with the lunch box to drink out of.

There were no wells or sanitary facilities, recalled Henegar.

They didn't even have outdoor toilets. The girls went out in the woods up one side of the hill and the boys on the other side. That . . . seems very primitive, but that's the way 'bout all the rural schools were back in those hills. And if you did something wrong, the teacher had to punish you. Most of the time he'd send you out to get a switch to whip you with . . . , and you better not get one that was too easy to break, 'cause he'd send you back and get another one.

Hill recalled that some pupils would become teachers before even completing the eighth grade.

The one-teacher school was eclectic. As Claude Longmire said:

They taught through the board, you know . . . , and in a way it helped the youngsters learn. [For example], he [the teacher] was at the board . . . going over something with the eighth grade, and maybe the seventh or sixth grade could be watching it, too. Of course, you know, they'd pick up some things, because they was all sitting in the same room . . . . just from the exposure they would learn, a little bit. Some did, some didn't. Like anything else, you had slow learners and some that didn't want to learn.

Sometimes the "ones that didn't want to learn" were held back by generational gaps in schooling. As Longmire related: "We had one [man] . . . that said the schoolteachers was kind of messing his kid up over there. Didn't believe in the schoolteaching because, he said, his kid went to school one day and his teacher tells him that two and two is four, he goes back the next day and tells him three and one is four, and [the father] said, 'My kid don't know what to believe.'"

With so many variant ages attending schools, discipline could sometimes be a problem. When H. E. Anderson returned from military service he

> went to one of these schools which had been having discipline problems, and when I went in there I didn't know what I was getting into. Dr. Monroe was a member of the school board [and] told me what happened here—they'd been taking up the teacher's place. Well, the first morning I was there, I was there early at the school building, long before anybody else got there. I went ahead and cleaned it out and cut me a poker, and the poker I had was a hickory stick (you know anything about hickory—you know they [the saplings] often get as large as your wrist there and after you get them you taper them off to a peak). So I got me one of those to use for turning, but I didn't—that wasn't my main idea. What I meant to do was just beat me some of those fellows . . . , but I never had much trouble, and [it was] a wonderful school.

In the process of consolidation of schools and eliminating some of the one-room schools, the quality of instruction was not always an incentive to leave smaller schools for the larger ones, but other attractions could prevail. In Union County there were five junior high schools: Hill's Academy, Leadmine Bend, Loyston, Maynardville, and Luttrell. When Mr. Anderson went to Leadmine Bend,

> it was supposed to be a consolidated school. All the schools around there [were] supposed to come into that one school—all those little one-room schools. Well, you couldn't get them to come in, they wouldn't come, and they'd have to send a teacher over there to those one-room schools. The first year I was there, the first two weeks I just had, I believe, seven students. I said to my wife, "I'm

not going to stay—we're going to quit that school." She said, "Let's stay a little longer." So I decided to do that, and I introduced basketball into that school—they'd had what you call townball and like that, and I instructed the basketball team there, had a good court, and those other schools, those little one-room schools, had fellows coming in—we just robbed all those little schools. Our school was run over, all the rooms were just flooded. . . . And we just never did have any trouble after that about the consolidation.

Monroe Stooksbury felt that if there were some disciplinary problems, most were averted owing to parental pressure, for "most of the time the students were pretty obedient, and they were taught that by their parents. They really sided with the teacher back then."

Vera Stiner stressed the changes more than the continuity and tradition of the small rural school.

I was also in the first school that served hot lunch in Union County. It was supposed to be a one-teacher school, but there were two teachers in the building. We had a curtain drawn through the center. And this lady who lived near the school cooked. Well, we just had soup and occasionally apple pie and cookies. And she cooked all that at home, and she and the larger students carried it all to school and served it there. . . . I believe it was in 1935, and the supervisor came to our school and asked if we would cooperate with them in trying the hot lunch. We had the beginning there, and the next year I was in a two-teacher school and we raised money and cooked in our kitchen and started that. At first we didn't charge anything for lunch, and we got the commodities that were given out. . . . It was the NYB [National Youth Board] that paid the cooks, and that's why we could feed the children free.

Recreation, education, and a sense of accomplishment combined to make spelling one of the most popular subjects. Boyd Rogers particularly liked the book called "the old redback speller." "I went in this old redback speller one year, I believe, and then they changed books. I regret very much that they changed them, personally, because I would have liked to have gone [on] in this old redback speller. It really had some words in there that were hard to spell." Claude Longmire relived the competition. "It was a disgrace to let somebody spell a word that you couldn't. They what you call, spell you down, you know."

THE COMING OF TVA AND POPULATION REMOVAL

The images which the people of the Norris Basin formed of TVA
are reflections of the way they viewed themselves, their communities and their region. There appears to be a persistent dichot-
omy: as the people of the Basin viewed their lives as difficult,
isolated, and outside the mainstream of modernization, they
tended to form an image of TVA as a factor for progressive change;
because their lives were viewed as neighborly, cohesive, familiar,
and enduring through genetic and historical links, TVA was seen as
a disturbing factor.

The Norris Basin residents could not, as TVA planners could, see
the Authority entirely in the long run. They were forced to assess
its coming in the face of the stark reality of removal. They had to sell
or leave their farms and relocate in often unfamiliar surroundings
and to endure the agony of uprooting themselves from communities where they had been settled for generations. It is not
surprising, therefore, that a myriad of views and attitudes concerning TVA was forthcoming.

John Rice Irwin[15] *was five years old when TVA came to the Norris
Basin. His forebears were original settlers in the area ("back
when there were wolves and Indians"), and he has kept alive the
life of those times by operating a museum of Appalachia near
Andersonville, Tennessee, where he has gathered numerous ar-
tifacts of Appalachian culture. Because of his family connections
and continued interest in the area, he has become an informational link between generations concerning life in the Norris
Basin before TVA arrived. His own eloquent views provide an
excellent summation of the reaction to TVA.*

Well, you know how difficult it is to make general statements about
large numbers of people, but if I were pressed to make a general
statement, I think it would be this: They really had a great emotional attachment to that area. Everyone knew everyone else, of
course. Not only that, but almost everyone else was related in
some way or another to everyone else. Most of the people were
descendants of ancestors who came to that area in the 1700s and
early 1800s. And many of them, of course, lived on farms from
one generation to another. So they felt they really had a great
reticence to leave the area, but again they felt (and here I'm
making general statements), they felt that it was something that
would be of benefit to people generally, and they felt they were

56

doing it for their country, sort of. And I recall many, many times hearing them say that they hated to leave more than anything in the world, but they felt it was a worthwhile project, and they held little bitterness for it. Some of them that held those same sentiments, though, felt that the TVA did not reimburse them enough for the land, and for the inconvenience it caused in moving and relocating and buying-replacing a property. . . . I guess they felt that they were doing it for the benefit of their area, and you know, the East Tennessee region and so forth. And they especially felt this later on, I believe, when they saw what TVA had accomplished. I think it was somewhat similar to a person going into the army, in the past, you know. They didn't want to go, they dreaded to go, and it was disruptive, but at the same time they felt some obligations, you know. My grandfather Irwin . . . , of course, was a descendant from the earliest settlers there. My great-great-grandparents settled there when the wolves were still there and the Indians were still around. This was Big Valley, they called it—that was home, you know. . . . It's very difficult to describe the attachments that they had for their land, their emotional involvement, and the fact that they were going to have to leave all that and come somewhere else. It wasn't just that they had spent all their lives there, you know, but as far back as their grandparents could remember.

Irwin, who has kept in touch with former inhabitants over the years, felt that one aspect of hostility toward TVA was the depiction of the Norris Basin inhabitants as backward, either as a direct result of TVA's own attitudes or those of the national news media which avidly followed TVA's regional experiment.

The biggest concern that I can remember that the people had was in regard to some newspaper articles that came out, apparently in newspapers across the country. I'm not sure about that, but I do remember seeing, and have copies somewhere, [of] a full-page pictorial . . . of the people in that area. Well, they showed the Henry Stooksbury family with the old ladies out in front of the big log cabin with their bonnets, washing their clothes. And people up there felt that they were being portrayed as if they were isolated, ignorant mountain people. And I don't know what part TVA played, whether the pictures were from TVA, or whether it happened at the same time; but that was the one big criticism that I recall more than anything else, I think.

Monroe Stooksbury felt that opinion ran generally in favor of TVA. "I felt most people were favorable, although the people over in that section were so deep-rooted that they didn't much want to leave. I think it may have been a bit of a shock to my parents that were older. . . . They liked the idea of building the dam and creating electricity for the area. They had nothing against the TVA." Monroe's older brother, like himself, sold land to TVA. "He was pretty satisfied because he owed for so much of it and it got him out from under [and] that's the way I was for my property. I owed on it and I was pretty glad to sell it and I think that most people that were kindly depressed were pretty glad to get to sell out. But most of them were not like that—they'd owned their land, been passed down from generation to generation, and they owned their land without being in debt." "I don't think there was any resentment about it[TVA]," Myers Hill added. "I think most everybody understood that it was something that was going to help our country through here and make it better and improve our living conditions. If there was any resentment, it was mighty low, mighty small." One of the best ways to evaluate TVA, Claude Longmire felt, was comparative.

> In those days [before TVA] there was no dairy and no . . . factories. It was just there, just no tractors, a horse, a horse-drawn plow. They call those the good old days. They were good in comparing to some things—far as violence is concerned now. But I'd rather live today [than] to live in those days. . . . I've always felt that . . . for TVA to break them up was probably the best thing that ever happened to those people. Because 'most everybody that left there bettered themselves. . . . I don't know of anybody that left there, I can't recall of anybody that what didn't do better when they left there. And they could look back, of course, they have memories of that—childhood memories or memories as a family would have— but there's nobody that I talked to over there that regretted leaving after they'd settled in other places.

Dottie Ousley recalled her father's attitude toward TVA. "Well, of course, he, my father, was a broad-minded person, and he could see the advantages, but he could also see the disadvantages to what it did to him. But he could also look out into the future and see what it was going to mean to the next generation."

To Hubert Stooksbury removal was a necessity for some people of the Norris Basin, for there was a little place between two ridges over there they called the Dark Hollow, and the people over there, I don't know how—well, they *existed*, they didn't *live*. Now, [for] the people like that I guess in the end it was better—turned out that it was better for everybody that they did move. I know of so many of them, and they've done so well since they left there, and we've often discussed it, about what they would have done if they hadn't of moved from there—those that didn't own property or land. If you owned good land up there, why, you were all right, but those that didn't, I don't know. I guess . . . it was a good thing for everybody that was moved up there. But at the time we didn't think so.

Of the tenants who had to move, Stooksbury recalled, "Most of them, I suppose, went out and bought them a little land, whatever they could—the ones that had anything. But all the same, a lot of them didn't have anything up there. They had to move, they did well, they made money. If they'd stayed there they probably would have never had a dime. That was the best thing, of course, that ever happened to them, to move, but at the time they thought it was very cruel." Of one tenant farmer who had done extremely well, Stooksbury related, "Well, he just had a chance. They [TVA's removal] gave him an opportunity.

Isaac Anderson[16] *eighty-two, left the Norris Basin when TVA came. He rented a river farm in Anderson County, where he lived with his wife, Lucille. His attitude upon leaving was perhaps similar to many other renters and tenants who could receive no compensation from TVA because they had no rights in the land they tilled.*

"Well, I didn't feel too awfully bad about it. One way of looking at it, I just thought that when the government took a notion to do anything they just done it, and I just passed it by, is all I can say. . . . I didn't have too much to think about neither way. If the government wanted to put the dam in, they'd put it in regardless of what I thought about it, and all I could do was get out and let them have it." Anderson left his rented place.

Yeah, I moved up across the Clinch River back on top of the ridge and stayed there one year. They said I had to leave there, they was buying that out. . . . I don't think I was really treated right by it, because they said I could stay there another year—they couldn't move me out but said I needed to be moved out. I knowed it was my

time, I had to go. I knowed that, and so I just give, almost give a
good mare and a fine colt away. I went—I sold them for $80, and
then later I paid $175 for a mule to replace them back. Was that
a-making any money? I had to do that so's I could get ready to farm.
I gave a good milk cow away, and then I had to pay the price for one
back. Was I treated right?

Anderson said his father-in-law got "quite a bit" of money for his
farm, "but it's not money—when a man's really homesick, money
ain't it." His father-in-law, he said, "would have as leave as died as
of left that county."

> Silas Snodderly[17] *was twenty-eight when TVA came in. He was
> living with his father on a farm in Big Valley, between Sharp's
> Chapel and Loyston, at Lost Creek. His father relocated in
> Blount County in 1936, and Silas married and moved to Knox-
> ville. Snodderly had helped survey the dam site for the Corps of
> Engineers in the twenties, before TVA was created.*

TVA "was the best thing that ever happened to that country,"
according to Snodderly. "I think so because they was marrying kin,
you know, and stuff like that. Yeah, well, in other words, we didn't
have no resources there much, and we wasn't close to town where
you could get more than country doctors. Well, you know how it
is—unhappy—but we didn't think so then. . . . And there's a lot of
them hated to leave—the old people. The young people, I don't
know if they cared too much or not."

To many of those interviewed, age was a factor in determining
the reactions of families to the coming of TVA. As Myers Hill said,

> I think it was a problem to them. Some of the older people I don't
> think ever was really adjusted to the new localities. They tried to
> make the best of it, of course, but even though they had better
> living conditions, they were still, I don't think, quite as well
> satisfied. A lot of them would rather have stayed on, even though
> their living conditions wasn't as good as they were where they
> moved.

H. E. Anderson agreed.

> Well, I'll tell you what my father-in-law said. He moved out of the
> dam area up there and bought his farm in Meigs County, and he
> said for the first couple or three years, "I felt like I was visiting
> there." It took him that long to adjust. I know some people up there
> that resented moving at all. In fact I know two who committed

suicide. I knew personally both of them. They bought all around [one man], but he wouldn't sell, and he went down to the pond there and put a rope around his neck and hung himself.

Ruble Palmer felt that

younger people could adjust better than the older people, you understand. Get out, mix and mingle, you know, better than the older people. Well . . . , a lot of the old people never did actually adjust to it. Lived there sixty, seventy-five years. You had to force them out. If they had left there on their own accord, it wouldn't have been so bad, but they had to go, see, and they never did actually adjust.

Bill Taylor had a vivid recollection of one of the sad incidents which had become nearly mythologized among those who moved.

I happened to be within a hundred yards of his house when it happened. This is immaterial, but I was hunting, in fact, and one of his neighbors came through the field to where we were, and said Uncle John—they called him Uncle John—said Uncle John hanged himself down there. And I said, "Well, we'll not be shooting here close to his house," so we left the field. . . . In a way, for the younger generation who had to move out of that area, it may have been a blessing for them. But the older people resented it. That was the history of it. My way of looking at it, the older people were harder hit.

Of course, a high proportion of the population removed was older. As Vera Stiner recalled, "My daughter was here yesterday and I talked to her about the old conditions, you know, and she wanted to know why people left the area—young men, most of them, when they grew up—to Indiana, Ohio, Michigan, to work, because we didn't have any industry in the area at that time. And very little in Knoxville at that time. So they went to the industrial North."

Ruby Hill Sampson and Evelyn Hill Longmire,[18] *sisters, lived on Lost Creek in Big Valley on land that had been in their family "back as far as the first land grant began." Their father, Albert Hill, was a teacher and, later, school superintendent in Union County.*

Evelyn Longmire and Ruby Sampson felt that age made no difference in attitude about removal and that as Ruby said, "most people felt about the same." Evelyn agreed. "The thing that hurt so bad was that we just didn't want to be taken away from the place we loved. Even if we went away, we would like to come back and see the place again. Now it's a hundred feet under water. We can never go home again."

John Rice Irwin's grandparents relocated on "a good-sized 300-acre farm" and had a successful readjustment,

> but I think one of the reasons they were able to adjust was that . . . all the children settled right around them. Three sons and one daughter and all the cousins and my grandfather was responsible for rebuilding a church, you know. And it was a little different from instances of where one family moved out and they were scattered. I had an aunt, a great-aunt, for example . . . , who moved down to Sweetwater by herself. Well, she had some children but they were almost grown. I think they married and left, and I remember visiting her when I was a child, and she lived in this big rambling farmhouse by herself, with all the people she called strangers around her. And she was a very lonely old lady, and I remember [she] was crying when I started to leave because all the good times and all the friends back in the valley were gone.

The whole prospect of appraisal and removal was unsettling. Reactions were very mixed. Some sold quickly and were glad to get the price; others, convinced they should get more, had to decide whether to sell eventually or go to condemnation proceedings. A small number (6 families of a total of nearly 3,000) did nothing, and were forcibly evicted when the rising waters behind the dam made their continued presence dangerous. TVA, of course, was anxious to have its appraisal prices met, but sometimes their efforts met with resistance. Lou Emma Taylor, Bill Taylor's wife, recounts one incident.

> My daddy wouldn't take their price. They [her parents] were old, and they'd bought all this and built all these buildings and everything and always lived in the commuity. And we [she and her husband] had to move because we were renting . . . and we had to move. There wasn't anything we could rent, and on my grandfather's place was an old tenant house. We just went and cleaned this one the best we could and put our things in there and set up light housekeeping. So I went over one morning [to her parents'] and was going to have a little wash, do a laundry, and who set on the porch but one of these men who went around, and they'd done been there and offered—wanted them to sell. And who was sitting

Teacher and Pupils, Okolona School, Union, County, 1934-35.

on this porch but [a man] that was working with TVA, and they [her parents] had refused the price that they'd been offered and was taking it to court, and he came back there, and he had them crying—and them old! I might have too much of a temper, but that would raise the temper of anybody, and I wanted to know what was wrong. My daddy couldn't talk; my mother got out and took my things in the house, and she came in the hall and told me what was wrong, that he was out there telling them they just had so long to get out, and that they had to take that price and they had to go . . . , that just flew all over me, that my old daddy and mother was being rooted out of where they had roots. And then somebody coming along there and treating them like they were simpletons that didn't know nothing and tearing [them] apart like that! I went back there and told him, "Now, listen, they have a lawyer handling this, and they don't have to get out until they get a fair price and they don't have to get out at that time anyway! You just get up and leave them alone! I'm not having my mother and daddy, and them old, stirred up like this and torn to pieces." He didn't allow as how he would, and I said, "There's a good shotgun setting inside that door there, and if you don't get off this hill, I'll use it on you." And my daddy said, "Don't do that." And boy, he got up and moved, and I said, "Don't you come back up here anymore and disturb my daddy and mother! That's enough!" And he didn't come back.

The next morning, according to Mrs. Taylor, her husband's boss, who had received similar treatment from the representative, said, "Well, you tell her I'm going to buy her a steak dinner for talking up to him." Mrs. Taylor did say that other people representing the agency had not behaved in a similar fashion, but she still feels strongly about the TVA because her people had to move. In comparing the Norris removal to the current controversy over TVA's Tellico Dam, Mrs. Taylor mentioned the issue of the snail darter. She said: "We were *people*, and those little old fish that isn't worth two cents, they tried to stop that dam over it. They wouldn't let *us* do that."

Claude Longmire felt that some of the hard feeling about land price was owing to the tremendous stability of the area. "But most of the people took what was offered. Some protested, but the majority of the people accepted what was offered. And come to think of it, I don't recall anybody ever selling land to anybody else over there—they wouldn't sell it. People wouldn't sell their land.

. . . A lot of them was like my granddad, thought you just had to go along and take what was offered, you know."

Hubert Stooksbury reflected an attitude present in many of the interviews, and he summed up the whole problem of trying to get at what a "fair price" really was. "I imagine they paid market price for it. But . . . most people . . . didn't want to leave, and they thought they should have been . . . given something for having to move or being driven out of their homes where they'd lived for generations, their forefathers lived there before them, and I think they should have been allowed some consideration for that."

The power of condemnation, the policy of no-price bargaining, and the inherent psychological attachment to the land made it very hard for individuals to agree on what *should* have been paid as a fair price. Certainly TVA emerged from the scrutiny of a congressional investigation with a clean bill of health in the matter of land purchase—an area which was probably more sensitive to allegations of scandal than any other. Of course, "fair market price" is an elusive term—on the one hand relatively simple to establish, on the other something much more complex. As John Rice Irwin said:

> I don't personally remember at that time, or subsequently, a lot of bitterness toward TVA except there was bitterness, there was criticism, in regard to purchasing of property. And it did not appear to me over the years and does not appear to me now that they compensated the people adequately to take care of the trauma of moving and the appreciation of land price. When you go in and take that many families and then move outward, land prices appreciate. They went up because the demand exceeded the supply. I don't think that TVA took that into consideration.

Interviews with former residents of the inundated communities of the Norris area expressed profoundly both the sense of neighborliness and the roots of deep attachment which the rural community had engendered. These feelings were stated in terms of barn raisings and pie suppers or box lunch auctions for neighbors fallen on hard times; in terms of "swapping work" and helping sick friends lay by their crops; in terms of perpetually unlocked doors and mutual trust. One resident's father who was knowledgeable about veterinary medicine treated all the livestock in the community free. His son remarked, "We didn't charge neighbors for such things then." The experience of death itself was a deeply shared one where, in the absence of undertakers, neighbors prepared the deceased for burial. One of the points over which the removed residents were most deeply concerned was the final disposition of the graves that had to be removed when the area was flooded, a concern that was reflected in an almost mystical reverence for their collective forebears who had settled the community. These emotions are rarely expressed in abstract terms, although one interviewee did say: "We worked hard and we didn't have much, but we were happier. Is anybody content today? Back then it seems like we all were." Curiously, this sense of former well-being is often deliberately contrasted with a feeling of being economically "better off now than then."

The limitations of the rural community and the values and attitudes created by it were all reinforced by the fact that farming in this area was predominantly subsistence. There were economic as well as social ties to the small community, and the virtues of independence and self-reliance were in many respects economically induced virtues. The typical farm, in greater or lesser degrees of abundance, produced all the food consumed. Surpluses were traded at local stores for sugar, salt, kerosene, coffee, and ammunition. The typical store carried, as one resident put it, "everything from plow points to shoestrings" and was the community's social center and source of information. The lack of transportation and relative degree of isolation did not mean the absence of a market for goods. If goods were not traded piecemeal, they could be left at a local store, which became a goods entrepôt for a community whose storekeeper could take them to Knoxville or LaFollette once a week. In some instances local storekeepers actually issued scrip in exchange for goods deposited and took the scrip as currency for purchases. Subsistence economy meant, among other things, an abnormally low amount of cash in circulation,. Barter, trade, and swap closed the circle of intimacy in an economic fashion. One way in which this is borne out is the large number of communities named after local stores.

It is almost impossible to recreate today the sense of closeness which prevailed in these communities. Even justice, in minor civil cases, was meted out by a justice of the peace, one to each civil district. One respondent recalls his grandfather, like the medieval king Saint Louis of France, dispensing justice under a tree on a summer's afternoon. The upkeep of roads, too, was intimately connected to the life of the community, since the head of the family or any male twenty-one or over was obliged to three days' labor a year, filling ruts and digging out drainage ditches with his neighbors.

Finally, the sense of intimacy was nurtured in the very genealogical roots of the families. Many went back five and six generations on the same farm, and some could prove claim to ancestors in their communities who had fought at the Battle of King's Mountain in the Revolutionary era. In a more contemporary mode, the mean age of residency in the same community among landowners was 35 years, with a mean 22.6 years on the same farm. Interviewees spoke constantly of farms that had been in the family "for generations." Their attitudes are often conveyed in terms of pride and satisfaction at having endured, at having planted deep roots in the face of economic adversity. The psychological depth of these feelings is perhaps lost upon our open and mobile society.

These shared experiences indicate that even while modernization may create better aggregate standards, better socioeconomic indices, more mobility, more advantages, and more opportunities, there was a very radical trade-off involved for many of these families. And that trade-off was in the loss of a closeness and an identity not easily replaced in most modern societies. Perhaps the radical nature and enforced uprooting of these families by TVA brought closer to the surface the deep feelings and depth of emotional attachment that at times opposes a general desire for economic improvement. These feelings were summed up by one resident, who said that "it was better for everybody that they had to move" and admitted that his own economic prospects had improved immeasurably by his being forced out of such economic stasis. But he also stated in the same interview that the period before TVA came "was the best part of my life."

For the people of the Norris Basin, modernization has meant more chances for betterment, economic, and otherwise. But like a leitmotif within this sense of modernization runs the desire for the retention of old cultural values associated with a poorer, harder way of life. The ultimate juxtaposition of these two realities came in an interview with one respondent who described his dream: a brand new Sears, K-Mart, and Kroger shopping center where there were no clerks and no credit cards, where each person paid for his own purchases and made his own change.

The perceptions expressed in this dream mirror the type of ambivalence which TVA's appearance created and make clearer the tenuousness of the process of dispossession. The removal of families from the Norris Basin created a fragmentation of both physical and mental landscapes. While the oral record calls up vibrantly the images of both, they must be brought into sharper, more quantitative focus before the whole quality of life in the Norris Basin emerges to our consciousness and before we can assess TVA's impact on the people of the region.

3   Life in the Norris Basin Reconstructed

THE IMAGES of daily life drawn from the memories of the people of the Norris Basin have, in a sense, an elusive quality. While evocative and rich, containing material that increases our empathetic understanding of rural Appalachian life in the thirties, they lack a quantitative dimension. In this chapter descriptive statistics, soil analysis, and physiographic descriptions will be used to provide substance—to enhance the images and perceptions from oral history.

Quantitative information is important first because life in the Norris Basin was shaped by factors such as soil quality, topography, geography, and demographic structure. Their measurement and definition are important, although it is only through the qualitative dimension that their influence can be fully comprehended. Second, only the most comprehensive recreation of life before the coming of TVA will provide the background against which removal and relocation can be assessed and analyzed later in the book. In this re-creation a description of the Norris area is the most appropriate place to begin.

THE NORRIS BASIN PURCHASE AREA

The storage reservoir rises to 1,020 feet above mean sea level behind imposing Norris Dam, located below the confluence of the Clinch and Powell rivers, and extends roughly seventy to eighty miles up the two rivers toward their headsprings in southwest Virginia. The reservoir and watershed purchase area includes portions of five upper East Tennessee counties (Anderson, Campbell,

Claiborne, Grainger, and Union), comprising a total purchase area
of 239 square miles (153,008 acres). Most of the land was purchased
by TVA for the reservoir and dam site proper. Only a small portion
of all the land purchased for the reservoir and dam site actually lies
under water in normal conditions.[1] The large remainder of un-
flooded reservoir land was purchased to form a "protective strip"
around the reservoir for the provision of watershed control. Within
the five counties affected, TVA purchased 14 percent of the total
land area then occupied by roughly 3,500 farm families who would
have to be evacuated from the Clinch and Powell river valleys.[2]

PHYSIOGRAPHY

The Norris Basin is part of East Tennessee's dominant physiographic feature—the Great Valley.[3] Located between the Cumberland and Unaka mountain ranges, it slopes downward from
Bristol southwest to Chattanooga, widening perceptibly along its
length. The Norris Basin lies in its northern portion some thirty-
odd miles north of Knoxville, in a trough formed by the Cumberland Mountains on the northeast and the long ridge of Clinch
Mountain on the southeast. The two rivers which make up the
reservoir enter Tennessee east of Cumberland Gap, the Powell
flowing along the edge of the Cumberland and the Clinch running
at the foot of the Clinch Mountain (see map 1).

The Norris Basin lies on the edge of the Cumberland Plateau, a
broken and rugged terrain in contrast to the gently undulating
central floor of the Great Valley. Geological faulting and folding
along the rim of the Cumberlands, combined with the differential
weathering of the underlying strata (limestone, shale, and sand-
stone), produce in the Norris Basin a series of broken ridges and
steep valleys paralleling the Cumberlands. Among the ridge crests
and valleys there are considerable variations in elevation.[4]

With its characteristically steep slopes and broken ridges, the
Norris area is part of the Appalachian land mass, where for generations the constant pressure of rural populations on the natural
environment has eroded the soil and depleted forest resources.
The most arable and productive lands of the Basin are the river and
creek bottoms and banks. In these hilly regions nature has not

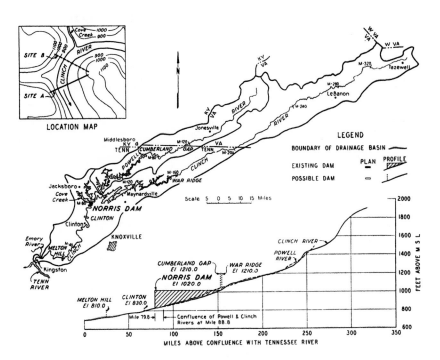

Map and profile of the Clinch and Powell Rivers.

been generous in bestowing lands and rich alluvial deposits; the most arable lands are the scarcest and most highly prized. Once they are in a family's possession, they seldom change ownership.

The advent of TVA and the creation of the Norris Dam and reservoir meant that virtually all of the most productive arable land in the two river valleys would be inundated, leaving a disproportionate amount of the poorer soils. The best land would be the first to go, creating a powerful adverse psychological impact in this closely knit area where bottom lands assumed a symbolic importance far beyond their economic significance, an importance underlined by both their scarcity and their fecundity in a relatively poor region. Obviously, then, to those displaced persons who chose to remain in the Basin, a valuable natural resource would be forever lost, and farm sites would have to be chosen from among the more abundant but less productive soils.

TERRAIN AND SOILS

In the terrain of the Norris Basin, hilly and steep ridge slopes alternate with rolling ridge tops to form the predominant features of the landscape. Although the Basin contains some fine soils of great agricultural range and versatility, especially in the Powell Valley below the Cumberland escarpment, most of the soils are not particularly good. The most abundant soils in the area are classed by the Soil Conservation Service as "fair to poor for crops that require tillage [Class III]; very poor for tillage, better used for pasture [Class IV]; and very poor for tillage, poor for pasture, better used for forest [Class V]".[5] Despite the fact that the Norris Basin in general is characterized by steep, broken terrain and the less productive soils, the area exhibits great range and versatility in categories of farm land, general fertility, and topography.[6]

General categories of farm land adapted by TVA for its appraisals were listed as follows: river bottom, second bottom, and terrace lands; creek and branch bottoms; valley uplands; and hill, ridge, and mountain land. The greater desirability of the bottom, cove, and valley lands brought them under intensive use. In fact, 95 percent of the bottom and terrace lands and 80 percent of the valley uplands were in cultivation or in open pasture when they were bought by TVA.[7] The Authority purchased 136,918 acres for the reservoir and dam site, of which 53 percent (72,388 acres) was cleared. The uncleared land (61,613 acres), the reservoir purchase, was nearly all woodland. The small remainder of the purchase area was uncleared valley upland. A high proportion of the cleared land was in the least arable ridge, hill, and mountain land, the most susceptible to erosion, owing to its rugged topography and shallow humus covering (see table 1).

TABLE 1   *Cleared Farm Land Acreage in the Norris Reservoir Purchase Area by Topographic Type*

Type of Land	Cleared Acres	Amount cleared (%)
1. Riverbottom, second bottom, terrace	5,713	8.0
2. Creek and branch bottom	3,846	5.0
3. Valley upland	6,644	9.0
4. Ridge, hill, and mountain land	56,185	78.0
Total	72,388	100.0

SOURCE: Tennessee Valley Authority, Land Acquisition Division, Appraisal Section, "Real Property Appraisals," table 2.

The struggle of a populous agrarian community to survive economically in a relatively unfavorable environment had led to a continuous utilization of the marginal soils. TVA appraisers found that nearly half of the poor hill, ridge, and mountain land was cleared for agricultural use and of the remainder "only a very small part . . . could have been properly cultivated under the farm practices prevalent if it had been cleared."[8] So much of the poor land had been brought under cultivation that many of the steeper slopes had been abandoned owing to erosion, a sign of land use to the point of marginal return.[9]

At the time of TVA's entry into the Norris Basin, the most arable land of the river and creek buttoms was under intensive cultivation, with the least arable land pressed to its productive limits. Title clearance dossiers compiled by TVA tracing each property purchase back to its original title registry show a pattern of continual and extensive subdivision, generation after generation, of initially large land parcels.[10] As the proportion of arable acreage for farms was reduced over time through the process of subdivision, more and more farms appeared on the less arable land of the slopes and ridges.

In 1907 the U.S. Department of Agriculture compiled an extensive report on the soils of Grainger County, which TVA analysts cited as "fairly representative" of the whole Norris purchase area.[11] The USDA's report indicated that the major agricultural problems of Grainger County were, in addition to the general unproductiveness of the soils, inattention to soil maintenance, lack of improvement in methods of cultivation and tillage, and a serious soil erosion problem.[12] The survey cited continual corn planting without crop rotation as a leading factor in soil abuse and lowered productivity. More acreage, it was noted, was planted in corn than in all other crops combined.[13]

Of the 196,672 acres in Grainger County's land area, there was a scarcity of alluvial bottom and terrace lands with their rich loams, as well as a scarcity of valley and low ridge limestone areas. Roughly 75 percent of Grainger County ranged from "limestones of less productive, less favorable surface conditions to the group of shales, sandstones, and quartzites which were the most easily eroded soils of the East Tennessee watershed"[14] and whose expected average corn yields ranged between five and thirty bushels per acre. These soils were of the same type of ridge, hill, and mountain land that made up 78 percent of TVA's purchase of cleared farm land.[15]

The findings of the USDA's soil report on Grainger County were replicated in a broader study of the Tennessee Valley made in 1933 by Rexford Tugwell, then assistant secretary of agriculture.[16] The Tugwell Report stressed the effects of population pressure in forcing poorer land into cultivation and noted that the fields of the Norris Basin "were approaching the limits of arability." H. H. Bennett of Agriculture's Bureau of Chemistry and Soils, a noted pioneer in soil conservation, stated in the report that land was being cleared on slopes so steep that it would be subject to sheet erosion in three to ten years.[17] Bennett was angered by agricultural conditions which were depleting soil to a point where restoration would become impossible. The farming practices of East Tennessee were, he argued, "little better if any, than that of the early colonial farmers in the tidewater sections of Virginia and Maryland."[18] Farmers of the region paid a high price for these conditions. Declining productivity, poor types of soil, and soil depletion often made life on small self-sufficient farms marginal.

POPULATION: SIZE, DENSITY, AND FERTILITY

A population which depends for its existence on its ability to exploit the natural endowments of a region can be precariously placed if those endowments are relatively poor in quality and have to be worked continuously to provide for an expanding population. It is the implacable growth of population against limited resources that has set in motion waves of Appalachian out-migration, creating a process which, for East Tennessee, has reversed itself only in the present decade. Population pressure, in conjunction with the intensive farming by traditional means, has provided the mechanism which has also led to soil depletion and erosion, two curses of the Appalachian farmer, and is one of the major determinants of life in rural Appalachia.

The factors of the rugged and broken terrain of the Norris Basin and its deficiencies in natural endowments might lead one to expect low population densities. In 1930, however, the Basin counties' population densities were equal to or greater than those of the neighboring counties along the Valley floor.[19] While the term "Appalachian" may denote to many an isolated and sparsely settled hill country, these counties were densely settled,[20] not only in contemporary terms but for some time in the past as well. Figure 1 depicts secular trends in population densities in the five counties. As early as 1870 Campbell and Grainger had densities of about thirty-five and forty-five persons per square mile, and three decades later all five counties approached or exceeded a total of fifty persons per square mile. In the reservoir purchase area of 214 square miles, there was an average density of more than sixty persons per square mile.[21]

Population figures for the five Norris Basin counties bear out Gilbert Beebe's contention that the fertility patterns of the Southern Appalachians are radically different from those of urban and industrial areas.[22] In the decade 1930–40, the counties affected by the Norris purchase showed a high fertility as opposed to a declining fertility for the nation. The crude birth rate for the nation in 1930 was 20.6, while for the Southern Appalachians it was 30.1.[23] All of the counties involved in the Norris land acquisition had higher crude birth rates than the national figure in 1930, and three of the five counties even exceeded the high average figure for the Southern Appalachians. The crude birth rates for the five counties were as follows in 1930: Anderson, 31.0; Campbell, 32.5; Union, 50.2; and Grainger and Claiborne, 25.7.[24] While the crude birth rate fell for the nation between 1930 and 1940 and remained stable for the Southern Appalachians, all the Norris Basin counties save one continued to show increases for that decade.[25]

The general fertility rate was also considerably higher for the Norris Basin counties than for the Southern Appalachian region in 1930 and in 1940.[26] The fertility ratio, however, dropped appreciably in the same decade, a phenomenon which probably reflected out-migration from the area.[27] Three of five counties involved in the TVA's purchase for Norris Dam, even in 1940, showed higher fertility rates than had those of Southern Appalachia a decade earlier.[28] While high fertility patterns can be offset by high death rates and out-migration, the counties of the Norris Basin, which exceeded both national and Southern Appalachian fertility patterns, fell below the average national death rate.[29] The five-county death rate in 1930 was 11.0, as compared with 11.1 for the nation.[30]

Growth in population size and density had occurred most intensively among the Basin counties in the closing decades of the nineteenth century (see table 2). Between 1900 and 1920, however, this intensive growth had either slowed radically or turned to decline. In light of the high fertility rates in these counties, lack of significant population growth must be attributable to out-migration, a phenomenon to be examined in some detail later.

The burgeoning population of the Norris counties at the beginning of the twentieth century pressed against the limited natural resources of the area to create, in the ensuing years before the coming of TVA, a pattern of decreasing mean farm size and an increasing ratio of improved to total farm land. Mean farm size was decreasing in all of East Tennessee during this period. The Norris Basin counties belong to a geographical area containing twenty-eight East Tennessee counties and designated Division 1 by the

TABLE 2 *Population Size and Percent Change for Norris Basin Counties, 1900–30*

County	1900	Gain or loss (%) 1890–1900	1910	Gain or loss (%) 1900–1910	1920	Gain or loss (%) 1910–1920	1930	Gain or loss (%) 1920–1930	Gain or loss (%) 1900–1930
Anderson	17,634	16.6	17,717	0.5	18,298	3.3	19,722	7.8	11.8
Campbell	17,317	28.4	27,387	58.2	28,265	3.2	26,827	-5.1	54.9
Claiborne	20,696	37.0	23,504	13.6	23,286	-.9	24,313	4.4	17.5
Grainger	15,512	17.6	13,888	-10.5	13,369	-3.7	12,737	-4.7	-17.9
Union	12,894	12.5	11,414	-11.5	11,615	1.8	11,371	-2.1	-11.8

SOURCE: Tennessee State Planning Commission, "General Population Stastistics and Trends," table 2, sect. I-D-l.

Tennessee State Planning Commission (TSPC). The commission's 1935 report on population stated that Division 1 contained "the sharpest decrease in farm size among the six divisions of the state."[31] The trend among Norris Basin counties can be seen in the data presented in table 3.

TABLE 3   *Average Farm Acreage for Norris Basin Counties, 1900–30*

County	1900	1910	1920	1930
Anderson	113	88	85	83
Campbell	92	63	63	63
Claiborne	79	72	66	55
Grainger	85	79	77	76
Union	78	74	69	65
Division 1	94	86	83	79

SOURCE: Tennessee State Planning Commission, "General Population Statistics and Trends," table 1, sect. IV–B. (mimeograph)

The greatest decline in mean farm size occurred simultaneously with the period of greatest increase in the ratio of improved farm land to total acreage (see table 4). Both of these trends were associated with the five-county growth in population size and density in the same era. Two decades prior to the arrival of TVA, population density and size of population were reflected in diminishing farm size and a high ratio of improved to total farm land, which underlined the expansion of arable land to marginal limits. These conditions in turn led to a stream of continual out-migration in the 1920s.[32] The Tennessee State Commission on Population gloomily reported in 1930: "It would appear that improved farm land in East

TABLE 4   *Ratio of Improved Farm Land to Total Acreage for Norris Basin Counties, 1860–1930*

County	1860	1870	1880	1890	1900	1910	1920	1930
Anderson	17.8	22.1	29.8	26.6	32.6	34.3	32.4	34.5
Campbell	17.0	19.7	20.2	21.6	23.0	22.7	22.1	26.1
Claiborne	25.6	20.5	27.9	31.7	37.9	42.1	39.4	44.1
Grainger	46.2	46.4	45.4	45.0	52.7	56.8	52.8	53.7
Union	18.6	25.0	42.2	48.7	53.6	56.7	55.0	54.4

SOURCE: Tennessee State Planning Commission, "General Population Statistics and Trends," table 1, sect. IV–C.

Tennessee has reached, if not passed, an economic intensity of use; for its population is dense and the amount of land suited to agriculture is definitely limited."[33] The high fertility of the Basin's inhabitants, together with the limited natural resources of the region, made out-migration the only means to alleviate population pressure, and this in turn resulted in continually diminished returns from the land. The TSPC report of 1935 noted that the problem of rural overpopulation was one of long duration. It had exhibited two responses in the Norris Basin: the need to press into cultivation the less arable land of the slopes or to succumb to the "metropolitan drag" of cities along the Great Valley floor or elsewhere.[34]

While out-migration could allay the worst consequences of population pressure upon limited resources and could ease further erosion of living standards as population pressed upon limited arable land, it was no panacea. By the 1920s the inhabitants of the Norris Basin, isolated as they were, were linked to the economic conditions of a larger society and were subject to forces over which they had no control. One of these factors which even population stability could not evade was the need to expand productivity to offset the continually decreasing price of farm products against the rising prices of manufactured goods. Even self-sufficient farmers had to buy some manufactured commodities, and the rising price of these were eclipsing farm product prices (see table 5).

In the last analysis, out-migration could not effectively reverse the movement from more or less arable land. Continued intensive

TABLE 5 *Index of All Farm Products and Manufactured Products, with Ratio of Prices Received to Prices Paid*

	1910	1914	1917	1918	1919	1920	1925	1928	1930	1931
Index, all farm prices	103	102	175	200	209	205	147	134	117	94
Index, all manufactured goods	98	101	150	178	205	205	159	156	146	137
Price ratio, farm to manufactured products	105	101	118	112	102	99	92	96	80	69

Note: Base figures are for 1910.
SOURCE: Tennessee State Planning Commission, "General Population Statistics and Trends," sect. IV, p. 7.

farming of this land by people caught in a vicious circle of demo-graphic and economic pressures increased the already present hazards of soil depletion, declining fertility and erosion, and the subsequent likelihood of reduced farm income.

TVA planners and analysts, examining aggregate man/land ratios in the Norris Basin for 1930, found the situation unpromising. Rural overpopulation was universally recognized as a major prob-lem of the area and one which by encouraging out-migration de-pleted the productive sector of the Norris Basin's population.[35] One TVA report emphasized the rural population problem by citing Grainger County, which in its estimates "was 43 percent overpopu-lated with regard to land resources and present farm practices."[36]

In the agricultural communities of the Norris Basin there existed a tenuous ecological balance which was essentially a product of population pressing upon marginal resources. By the 1930s it was one which could easily be disturbed to the disadvantage of the area's inhabitants. One factor which disturbed this tenuous equi-librium was the return of out-migrants who had previously left marginal farms hoping for the security of jobs in the cities. Now, due to economic misfortunes, they returned to the soil.

Return-to-the-Farm Movement

Despite their relative isolation, the farmers of the Norris Basin were, by the 1930s, enmeshed in the economic problems of a larger industrial society. In response to rural overpopulation dur-ing the 1920s, many had migrated to industrial and urban areas in the North, the central states, and nearby Knoxville. As the depres-sion deepened, those who had fled the insecurity of a marginal mountain farm were faced with a hard choice: either swell the relief rolls of the metropolises or make their way back to the hard and limited life they had left.

As early as 1930 the movement back to farms from urban centers was noticeable, for both the state and the Norris Basin counties. Census data from 1920–30 for these Basin counties indicate a return-to-the-farm movement nearly equal to that for the state as a whole, and in the case of one county (Union), it is three times higher than state levels (see table 6). The high rate of return,

80

indicative of high out-migration rates in the first instance, appears most visible among the heavily rural farm population of the Norris Basin.[37]

Levron Howard, a TVA analyst, commented in a report on the social and economic characteristics of the Norris Basin in 1933:

> A traveler passing through Union County in 1927 or 1928 would have noticed many apparently deserted farms. These East Tennessee counties, with their poor lands and rocky hills, were not able to compete with the distractions of Detroit and other cities. . . . This movement has now been reversed . . . and if the same traveler returns to Union or the surrounding counties he will find most of the young people back at home with their parents.[38]

Who were these people? Migration can be dealt with either in aggregate terms of net migration or through migration histories of subsets of aggregate populations. The latter is particularly revealing in the case of the Norris Basin. Some profiles are revealed in the data from the questionnaire administered to the population removed by the TVA in 1934. In preparation for the removal of families from the Norris Basin, TVA collected data from family heads which would provide an extensive socioeconomic profile of the removed population and give some insight into their needs in relocating. These data were collected from 2,841 families (1,864 owners and 977 tenants). These did not constitute all of the families

TABLE 6 *Movement of Farm Population in Tennessee and Selected counties of the Norris Basin, 1 April 1929 to 31 March 1930*

Persons who moved	State Total	Campbell	Claiborne	Grainger	Union
To farms from cities, villages, or other incorporated places	21,642	107	148	98	240
Farms reporting	7,046	46	55	43	68
From farms to cities, villages, or other incorporated places	9,970	78	63	48	77
Farms reporting	4,005	41	34	34	29
Net movement *to* farms	11,672	29	85	50	163
Proportion of total population (%)	.45	.11	.35	.39	1.44

Note: These figures are for intrastate movement (i.e., to or from the farm and to or from *a* city, village, or other incorporated place) and omit short-term farm laborers, students, and visitors.
SOURCE: *U.S. Census, 1930: Agriculture*, vol. II, pt. 2, county table 12.

81

finally removed, since changes in purchase policy later increased the total number to around 3,500. Heads of families provided data on the return-to-the-farm movement which were abstracted by TVA for a special report on urban-to-rural migration patterns among the families. [39]

Of the 2,841 families examined, 7 percent of the tenant families and 8 percent of the owner families reported members who had returned home after having previously left to work in some city. Virtually all the tenants who had left were heads of households, as opposed to fewer than half among the owner families, a fact which reflects the much younger average age of tenants than of owners. Ninety percent of the respondents reported that they had left home since 1921, and roughly half of the returnees had come back after 1929. Twenty-six percent of the owner family members and 35 percent of the tenants had gone no further than nearby Knoxville (thirty-five miles away) to seek work in the textile and flour mills of that city, and an almost equal number had established a pattern which came to be well known in the forties and fifties. These individuals sought work among the labor force in the automotive and industrial complexes of cities like Detroit, Akron, and Kokomo. The greater number of those who returned (70 percent) had been away for three years or less, and almost half had been away for one year or less. Work in the cities had been, for many, a stopgap experience and an unpleasant one: 50 percent stated that they would not go back even if given the opportunity. [40]

The families surveyed by TVA were participants in an extensive urban-to-rural migratory flow. This flow increased heavily in the period 1930–35, bringing renewed pressure to bear on the already strained resources of the Norris Basin. Table 6 gives 0.45 percent of the population as the farm return figure for the state in 1929–30. Assuming that year to be "normal" in the context of the back-to-the-farm movement, and using 0.45 percent of population as a multiplier with Tennessee Bureau of Vital Statistics midyear county population estimates as a base for the years 1930–35, one can estimate the number of returnees to the five counties in those years at 2,582 persons. Actual migration data in the interdecennial census of agriculture for 1935 indicate that in the years 1930–35 even greater returnee movements occurred than the estimate using a

1920–30 base would indicate. The census for the five counties reveals that there were 4,817 persons as of January 1, 1935 who had lived on a nonfarm residence five years earlier, a figure nearly double that obtained by the projections from the 1929–30 base (see table 7). The high number of farms reporting three persons indicates that many younger people were coming back to their parents' farms.

The pressure of population on limited resources at the beginning of the century had led to out-migration, whereas the migratory movement out of the region led in turn to a slight but steady decrease of the total amount of land in farms. In the subsequent period of heavy urban-to-rural migration, this pattern was reversed as previously abandoned land was pressed into use to accommodate the influx of farm returnees.[41] By January 1, 1935 the counties of the Norris Basin were registering sharp increases in the numbers of both owner and tenant farms as a result of the return-to-the-farm movement between 1930 and 1935 (see table 8 and figure 2). As the demand for farm land increased through the expansion of owner and tenant farms in the years of peak urban-to-rural migration, mean farm size dropped perceptibly, a significant factor when it is considered that farms in the Basin had already been stabilized at their optimum productive man/land ratio by 1930.[42]

The influx of farm returnees to the Norris Basin counties is also reflected in the data on farm tenancy. Tenancy, decreasing steadily from 1900 to 1925, began to increase noticeably until, in 1935, it

TABLE 7 *Persons on Farms as of 1 January 1935 Who Lived*
on a Nonfarm Residence Five Years Earlier,
For State and Norris Basin Counties

	State	Anderson	Campbell	Claiborne	Grainger	Union
Farms reporting	19,198	305	389	237	220	176
Persons	59,400	1,202	1,660	757	619	579
Farms reporting						
1 person	5,116	51	52	61	66	37
2 persons	4,936	68	84	45	65	43
3 persons	9,146	186	253	131	89	96
Such persons on farms of						
Full owners	29,727	818	877	345	326	334
Tenants	24,780	325	650	345	246	218

SOURCE: *U.S. Census, 1935: Agriculture,* second series, vol. II, pt. 2, county table 4.

had nearly risen to the level of 1900.[43] The increased pressure of population reflected in decreasing farm size and increasing tenancy also resulted in a reduction of the mean amount of cropland harvested. The mean of means for cropland harvested on all farms in the Norris Basin fell from 21.2 acres in 1925 to 15.4 acres in 1935.[44] Out-migration had prevented further erosion of living standards which otherwise would have followed in the wake of natural increases in the population. The reentry of former out-migrants into the economic structure of the Norris area introduced an immediate disequilibrium which is reflected in patterns of decreasing mean farm size and cropland and increasing tenancy. These instant effects of the urban-to-rural population influx were accompanied by another, less immediate one: since the most productive age group

TABLE 8   *Number of Farms, Tenant Farms, and Owner Farms for Norris Basin Counties, 1900–35*

County	1900	1910	1920	1925	1930	1935	1940
			Farms				
Anderson	1,595	1,858	1,677	1,677	1,445	1,975	1,868
Campbell	1,834	2,180	1,892	2,035	1,754	2,299	1,966
Claiborne	2,809	3,238	3,022	3,214	3,298	4,165	2,989
Grainger	2,069	2,379	2,257	2,368	2,140	2,584	2,396
Union	1,952	2,003	2,060	1,986	1,966	2,148	2,060
Total	10,259	11,658	10,908	11,280	10,603	13,171	11,279
			Tenant farms				
Anderson	449	497	296	309	342	555	404
Campbell	652	696	363	334	339	614	478
Claiborne	957	1,010	844	694	874	1,300	394
Grainger	623	731	591	601	598	797	713
Union	580	471	465	361	442	580	322
Total	3,261	3,405	2,559	2,299	2,595	3,846	2,311
			Owner farms				
Anderson	1,142	1,356	1,376	1,362	1,009	1,543	1,559
Campbell	1,181	1,482	1,528	1,699	1,408	1,720	1,549
Claiborne	1,848	2,218	2,176	2,519	2,422	2,879	2,649
Grainger	1,443	1,641	1,662	1,765	1,540	1,818	1,107
Union	1,371	1,531	1,595	1,625	1,524	1,592	1,100
Total	6,985	8,228	8,337	8,970	7,903	9,552	8,564

Note: For census purposes a farm is defined as "all the land directly farmed by one person, either by his labor alone, or with the assistance of members of his household or hired employees." Tracts held of an owner by managers, tenants, or croppers are considered as farms. Farms of three acres or less are excluded unless their agricultural products are valued at $250 or more.

SOURCES: *U.S. Census, 1930, Agriculture,* vol. II, pt. 2, county table 1; *U.S. Census, 1940, Agriculture,* vol. I, first and second series, pt. 4, county table 2.

of the population, both in terms of labor output and of potential fertility, participates in migration, the reentry of the migratory farm returnees added an important element of potential growth.

Of the 2,841 families surveyed by TVA, 76 percent of tenant household heads were forty years old or younger, compared to 24 percent among the owners. The median age of owners was forty-nine, and of tenants, thirty-five. Sixty-four percent of the tenants were twenty to forty (that is, in the productive years), while only 23 percent of the owners were in this age group. The increase of tenancy and the younger tenant age led to rising crude rates of natural increase in the wake of the return-to-the-farm movement (see table 9).

TABLE 9   *Annual Rates of Natural Increase for Norris Basin Counties, 1930–40*

	1930	1931	1932	1933	1934	1935	1936	1937	1938	1939	1940
Anderson	9.9	+12.1	+16.1	−15.2	+18.5	+23.7	−19.0	−17.2	−16.3	+16.6	−11.3
Campbell	15.1	+19.2	+18.3	−15.7	+20.3	+22.5	−16.5	−16.4	+17.4	+18.2	−17.0
Claiborne	10.4	− 9.9	+12.2	−10.6	+11.0	+11.7	−10.0	− 9.9	+15.9	−11.9	+15.4
Grainger	11.2	+13.9	−12.4	−11.3	+13.6	−13.0	−12.0	−11.3	+14.2	+14.9	−12.6
Union	9.9	+17.9	−17.0	−16.1	−14.7	−12.5	− 4.2	+ 6.1	− 5.3	− 4.7	− 4.6

Note: Recorded data only; uncorrected for underregistration rates based on midyear county population estimates.
SOURCE: Computed from State of Tennessee, Department of Public Health, *Annual Bulletins of Vital Statistics* (Nashville, 1930–40).

As urban-to-rural migrants returned to marginal resources already stretched to the breaking point, they found that the urban problems they had attempted to avoid through migration had followed them back to the farms. The Norris Basin counties, in the 1930s, experienced relief rates which were equal to those of neighboring Knox County, which had a large urban, industrialized population in Knoxville—a city from which many who returned to the Norris Basin farms had come (see tables 10 and 11).

The pressure of farm returnees and the increase in tenancy caused many previously vacated dwellings to be pressed into use. While comparable data for earlier periods are not available, the study of rural housing in 1935 by the Tennessee Emergency Relief Agency (TERA) indicated a high proportion of houses unfit for habitation, a situation further reflecting rural pathology in the area (see table 12).

The population which TVA removed from the Norris Basin is

generally representative of the same degree of susceptibility to rural malaise evident in the total population of the five Basin counties. TVA classified the removed population according to how much assistance they would need upon relocation. Group 1 was classed as needing no assistance in relocating; Group 2 was in need of advisory assistance only; and Group 3 was in need of both advisory and financial assistance.[45] Of 2,902 families TVA found that 20 percent (579 families) were in need of some financial aid and were incapable of self-support under existing conditions. Of these families, however, the Authority felt that the majority could become "self-supporting after a period of subsidy" by government loans, homestead projects, and other forms of aid. "These are," the report went on, "in general, relief or borderline cases. Many of them will need only a small loan and some advisory assistance, others will need close supervision in some sort of subsistence homestead for a period of years." At the base of the population, in desperate circumstances, was a group needing the most assistance (about 2.7 percent of the removed population). People in this classification were defined as "incapable of supporting themselves under any circumstances": the unemployables whose ranks were

TABLE 10   *Percentage of Residents on Federal Relief, Norris Basin Counties, Fall 1933 and April–May 1935*

	Percentage on relief	
County	*Fall 1933*	*April–May 1935*
Claiborne	10.1–15.0	15.1–20.0
Grainger	10.1–15.0	15.1–20.0
Union	5.1–10.0	15.1–20.0
Campbell	20.1–25.0	20.1–25.0
Anderson	5.1–10.0	10.1–15.0
Knox[1]	10.1–15.0	15.1–20.0

Note: Figures based on total number of persons on federal relief rather than the number of cases. Based on population figures from 1930 census. Figures include persons on general relief and rural rehabilitation program. For comparative purposes, 11 percent of the U.S. population was on relief in October 1933; 16 percent in May 1935. For Tennessee counties, those located in the Cumberland Tier and Sequachie Valley illustrate the generally higher figures which Campbell County represents. In the 20.1–25.0 and 25.0+ ranges are Campbell, Morgan, Fentress, Cumberland, Van Buren, Sequachie, Grundy, and Marion Counties.

[1]Knox County, predominantly urban owing to the domination of Knoxville, is included for comparative purposes.

SOURCE: Tennessee Valley Authority (Durisch), Social and Economic Division, Research Section, "Map Showing Relief Situation in the Tennessee Valley Area," mimeographed (Knoxville, 1935), 1–3.

rife with individuals suffering from crippling illnesses, severe handicaps, and mental defects.[46]

The 20 percent of the removed population in Group 3 was about equal to the percentage of relief cases in the five-county population. More striking than the total number who fell into Group 3 in TVA's classification was the disproportionate number of tenants in the group, for the lowest of the three classification groups contained 43.1 percent of all the removed tenant families and only 3.3 percent of the owner families.[47]

Even in the early decades of the twentieth century the Norris Basin ecosystem had proven to be relatively fragile. The scarcity of good bottom land and rich soils, when combined with a difficult topography, created initially unfavorable conditions for a population with high fertility rates. Other debilitating factors were continued subdivision of farms under the pressure of population growth, intensive row-cropping, slash-and-burn clearing tech-

TABLE 11 *Tennessee Emergency Relief Rate for Norris Basin Counties, January 1935*

County	Population	Persons on relief	Rate
Anderson	19,722	2,221	112.61
Campbell	26,827	3,829	142.72
Claiborne	24,313	2,867	117.92
Grainger	12,737	1,798	141.16
Union	11,371	2,054	180.63

Note: The state relief rate in January 1935 was 124.21.
SOURCE: Tennessee State Planning Commission, "General Population Statistics and Trends," sect. I–C–1.

TABLE 12 *Substandard Rural Housing in Norris Basin Counties, 1935*

County	All units	Substandard	Percentage
Anderson	3,154	2,063	65.4
Campbell	4,879	2,382	48.8
Claiborne	3,648	2,132	58.4
Grainger	3,100	1,817	58.6
Union	2,124	1,100	51.8

SOURCE: Tennessee Emergency Relief Agency, Rural Housing Survey, 1935, cited in Tennessee State Planning Commission, "General Population Statistics and Trends," table 1, sect. IV–E.

niques, and primitive agricultural practices. The increased cultivation of slopes and an aggravation of erosion problems added to the deterioration of a system which had already been worked to its limits prior to the arrival of TVA, but when the resulting out-migration was turned into return from migration by the economic failures of the depression, between 1930 and the first two years of TVA's presence in the Norris Basin, the extreme fragility of the ecosystem, always latent, was reasserted. Nowhere is this fragility more visible than in the reconstructed aspects of daily life in the Norris Basin.

What was to vanish beneath the reservoir was not so much a way of life as the living social organisms of community, kinfolk, and neighbor—the end products of generations whose visible remnants, the tombstones in family plots, served as mute reminders of the continuity of existence. From data obtained from the displaced families the historian can fortunately not only reconstitute the delicate fabric of families and communities which existed amid the challenge of a harsh environment but also examine the life styles created within this environment on the eve of inundation by the waters. Such a reconstruction would not be possible without the detailed data collected by TVA from the families it displaced, for the Authority's records contain the images of the collective existences which it disrupted.

The most historically significant of these records are the family removal questionnaires. Analysis of aggregate data from questionnaires does not present a detailed picture of the area's residents. Measurements of central tendency are precisely that, and readers are advised to keep in mind the ranges, standard deviations, and frequency distributions in the data which follow, so that the variety in these rural communities will not be obscured. The mean and the median, commonly used, are either too sensitive to extreme values or, conversely, too insensitive to them, and too great a reliance upon them as wholly representative can be misleading. The reader is warned as well that analyses of TVA questionnaire data contain zero values indicating no money spent or received, no goods consumed or owned, and so forth. This makes for very low figures in many cases but accurately reflects the condition of life.

The Family Removal Qestionnaire

TVA's Administrators felt that if a detailed socioeconomic profile were to be obtained from each displaced family, the process of removal and relocation would be easier. Through information elicited from interviews with each family, their individual needs could be ascertained. In the summer of 1934 a detailed eight-page questionnaire was prepared by TVA analysts in the economic research section of the Land Planning and Housing Division. To facilitate the gathering of information from families and to prevent the intrusion of bias against "outsiders," it was decided to have local residents, especially schoolteachers, act as enumerators for TVA.

Since the purpose of the enumeration was to aid in relocation of families in the purchase area of the reservoir, it was decided not to sample the population but to obtain schedules from every head of household in the purchase area who would have to be removed. Data were gathered from nearly 3,000 families.[48] To the historian these data are invaluable for the purposes of description. Virtually every facet of life was examined, including such diverse variables as religious preference, sanitary facilities, books read, newspapers taken, farm income and expenditure, types of personal possessions, and relocation preferences.

The data gathered by TVA comprise nominal, ordinal, and ratio types. The same questionnaire was administered to both tenants and owners and reveals many differences in the life styles and socioeconomic status of these two groups. The method of gathering the data was to have a field worker call upon the family with the questionnaire and enter the responses of the person interviewed. Economic data pertaining to the farm (receipts, expenditures, and so forth) were for the year 1933; other data pertained to present status in 1934. Interviewers asked the family head detailed questions about the amount of food consumed by the family in 1933. These data were given in amounts consumed and were tabulated according to 1933 local market value dollars for conversion into per capita and family living costs. Each field worker was allowed to enter qualitative impressions of the interviews, and by far the greatest number of these indicate that information was freely given in a generally amicable atmosphere. TVA officials checked the arithmetic and tabulated the data from each questionnaire.

The data in the questionnaires were analyzed by TVA and set forth in an in-agency confidential report in 1935.[49] Although this information is currently available, the authors believed that by returning to the original questionnaires and putting the data into machine-readable form, a more detailed analysis would be possible. Unless otherwise indicated, references in this chapter to the questionnaire data will be to our own tabulations rather than to those of TVA.[50]

REMOVED POPULATION: OWNER AND TENANT COMPOSITION

The Norris Basin lies in a region generally noted for a high degree of individual land ownership. In the removed population there were roughly seven owners for every three tenants. The term "tenant," of course, is a very broad classification and covers a number of tenant categories. In general TVA used the same definitions as the U.S. Bureau of the Census. "Tenants" describes those who rent or hire land as opposed to those owning it in fee simple. A cash tenant pays a cash rent, and a share or share-cash tenant pays rent either in shares of agricultural products or in a combination of shares and money. Cash, share, and share-cash tenants furnish stock and tools. A sharecropper pays rent in shares and uses stock and tools furnished by the landlord. In the population removed by TVA there were several squatters, some unspecified tenants, and a number of persons who rented land under unspecified contractual agreements. Classification of the removed population by number and percent is in table 13.

Mean length of residency on the same farm and in the community varied widely between owners and tenants and among various groups of tenants. The owners had long residencies in both categories, as compared with tenants generally, but the residency patterns of tenants who were related to their landlords show considerably longer mean residency than other groups of tenants. The discrepancy between tenant mean year residency on the same farm and in the same community indicates considerable shifting around, a development not surprising in light of frequent renewals of tenant

90

contracts (every year for sharecroppers, roughly every three years for long-term tenants). In tables 14 and 15 is illustrated the variance in residency patterns. Raw frequency distributions of tenant residency, unlike mean residency patterns, reveal the effects of the farm returnee movement and considerable instability of residency for a segment of the population. Of 832 tenants, 32 percent had lived in the same community for three years or less in 1934; a sizable number, 14 percent, had lived in the community one year or less. These figures, contrasted with the high mean years of tenant residency, point to a recently arrived segment of the tenant group.

In addition to variant patterns of residency between tenants who were related to their landlords and those who were not, Levron Howard, a TVA analyst, reported that in four Norris Basin counties there were considerable savings in annual per acre cash rents to tenants who held tenancy contracts from their relatives.[51] But cross-tabulation of quality-of-life variables for tenants, controlling for related and unrelated status as well as various tenant subclassifications, failed to reveal enough significant variance among ten-

TABLE 13 *Distribution of Owners and Tenants*
by Types for Norris Basin
Removed Population, 1933

Type	Percentage
Owner	68.8
Tenant (unspecified)	.8
Renter	6.2
Cash tenant	.9
Share tenant	4.5
Sharecropper	10.9
Squatter	.03
Related tenant (unspecified)	.7
Related renter	1.4
Related cash tenant	.2
Related share tenant	1.4
Related sharecropper	3.8
Related squatter	.07
No response	.3
Total	100.0

Note: $N = 2,699$.

SOURCE: Tennessee Valley Authority, "Family Removal Questionnaire," 1934.

ant types to warrant description of tenants separately by subclassification. Also, in a significant number of cases the number of tenants in a subgroup was too small to generate meaningful data. As a result the material tabulated in this chapter unless otherwise specified refers simply to "owners" or "tenants," the latter inclusive of all types of tenancy.

Tenant residency length indicates elements both of stability (tenant families of long residency on the farm and in the community) and instability (recently returned tenant families). The tenants who had not lived long in the same community were not random urban-to-rural migrants: 90 percent of the heads of all owner and tenant families were entered as residing in 1934 in the county of their births.

Tenant families were less well off than the owners of land gener-

TABLE 14   *Mean Years of Residency in the Same Community by Owner/Tenant Classification for Norris Basin Removed Population, 1933*

Tenure	N	Mean years residency	Standard deviation
Owner	1,846	35.3	19.4
All unrelated tenants	623	15.9	16.0
All related tenants	203	20.8	15.7
Squatters	2	.0	.0
No response	26	—	—
Total	2,699	—	—

SOURCE: Tennessee Valley Authority, "Family Removal Questionnaire," 1934.

TABLE 15   *Mean Years of Residency on the Same Farm by Owner/Tenant Classification for Norris Basin Removed Population, 1933*

Tenure	N	residency M (years)	SD
Owners	1,850	23.0	18.4
All unrelated tenants	628	4.0	6.6
All related tenants	203	11.2	13.9
Squatters	2	0	0
No response	26	—	—
Total	2,699	—	—

SOURCE: Tennessee Valley Authority, "Family Removal Questionnaire," 1934.

ally, but specifically with regard to displacement by TVA, their position was precarious: while owners could expect reimbursement from TVA for the land they sold, tenants could not. They had secured the use of the land by verbal contract of hire or rent, and with no rights of ownership in the land they were not legally entitled to compensation in the event of purchase of the farm they rented. Once removed, the tenants were totally dependent upon their ability to effect new contractual relationships or upon a landowners's willingness to relocate his former tenants upon his new farm. Of 1,857 owners in the removed population, 25 percent rented to tenants: of these, roughly 33 percent stated a willingness to provide land for their tenants upon relocation.

FARM SIZE

The mean farm size for both owners and tenants in the Norris Basin was relatively small. Constant subdivision of farms and the characteristics of the terrain combined to make cropland evenly distributed with wooded land and pasture, with a resulting low mean figure of cropland available for the whole population of 23.7 acres (see table 16). Table 16 gives the median figures for tenant and owner farms according to classes of land. The farms of the Norris Basin were generally more suitable for subsistence farming than the more specialized types of commercial agriculture, although the mean figures must be considered together with the vast range in farm size among the displaced population. While 35 percent of 1,848 owners reported holding 40 acres or less, nearly a quarter of them had farms of 100 acres or more, and there were 41 owners who had farms in excess of 300 acres.

Tenants worked much smaller farms than owners. Of 829 tenants, only 5 percent rented tracts in excess of forty acres, and only seven had farms in excess of eighty acres. The balance between cropland, pasture, and woodland, common on the owner farms, was less typical of the tenant farm. Subsistence demanded that as much as possible of the acreage rented be productive cropland. A number of tenants (18 percent) responded that they rented cropland in parcels of less than one acre. Most of these rented a house with attached garden plot and worked as agricultural day laborers

TABLE 16 *Mean and Median Acreage of Farm Land Owned or Rented, Norris Basin Removed Population: 1933*

Variable	Owners						Tenants					
	N	M	SD	Mdn	Range	NR	N	M	SD	Mdn	Range	NR
Total acreage	1,848	76.2	73.7	60.0	0–975	9	829	26.3	61.8	10.1	0–757	6
Cropland[1]	1,836	29.5	20.3	15.4	0–998	21	829	10.2	12.3	7.0	0–757	6
Woodland	1,837	24.3	27.3	15.4	0–240	20	829	6.4	16.6	.2	0–98	6
Pasture land	1,839	19.6	21.7	14.7	0–340	18	828	5.2	11.7	.2	0–90	7
River bottom	1,838	2.5	8.3	.1	0–98	19	829	1.5	6.6	.1	0–115	9
Creek bottom	1,837	2.3	11.2	.1	0–390	20	829	.7	3.2	.1	0–40	8

Note: No tenants indicated ownership of any land. Though some owners rented land, the figures for owners do not include rented land, only that owned. Figures inclusive of rented cropland used by owners did not alter the mean acreage. NR = not reporting.

[1] Mean average cropland for the whole population was 23.7 acres; standard deviation, 28.0 acres.

SOURCE: Tennessee Valley Authority, "Family Removal Questionnaire," 1934.

or at part-time jobs. Additional cropland was rented by 21 percent of the owners. Although most of these (65 percent) did not rent out any land, some did, but only in small parcels of ten acres or less.

The productive river and creek bottom lands were not widely distributed among the population, as is attested by the extremely low median figures in table 16. River bottoms were rented by 10 percent of the tenants and owned by 18 percent of the landowners. Creek bottoms were being rented by 16 percent of the tenants and were owned by 22 percent of the owners. Level land was also highly desired (if it was well drained), but in this rugged section there was little: 40 percent of the owners had less than 1 acre of level land on their farms (the mean acreage for level land owned was 4.06 acres). Generally the gently rolling to steep land was much more common (owner mean acreage, 35.8 acres). This land was often badly broken by limestone outcroppings, making it difficult to farm the row crops which predominated in the Basin. Much of the rolling land was highly suitable for pasturage, especially the limestone soils, but generally owing to the lack of capital, stock farming was not widely pursued prior to the coming of TVA.

Steeply rolling land was common to the region, and most farms had some (40 percent of the landowners held over fourteen acres of such land). In general this soil was poor, stony, and shaly, of low productivity, but on many of the ridge farms it had been pressed into use. Tenants farmed proportionately poorer classes of land than owners. In level, rolling, and steep land, the mean acreage for tenants was 4.45 acres, 12.0 acres, and 8.3 acres, respectively. Among both owners and tenants the most productive lands were in the smallest proportion to total land.

CROPS

The predominant crop among the Norris Basin farmers was corn. In table 17 are indicated the amounts of land devoted to various crops as well as the yields of corn and tobacco. The concentration upon corn was one of the factors contributing to the erosion which was so serious a problem when TVA came on the scene. Tobacco, while significant, had just recently begun to develop in

TABLE 17 *Mean and Median Acreage and Yields of Cultivated Cropland by Type of Crop, Norris Basin Removed Population, 1933*

Variable	Owners						Tenants					
	N	M	SD	Mdn	Range	NR	N	M	SD	Mdn	Range	NR
Cropland[1]	1,836	29.5	20.3	15.4	—	21	829	10.2	12.3	7.0	—	6
Acreage in corn[2]	1,810	11.5	9.4	10.0	0–90	47	826	6.8	8.7	5.0	0–98	9
Acreage in hay[3]	1,810	5.1	7.9	2.2	0–98	47	826	1.1	5.3	.1	0–80	9
Acreage in small grains[4]	1,812	1.4	3.5	.2	0–42	45	826	.6	2.8	.1	0–50	9
Acreage in tobacco[5]	1,810	8.8	11.6	5.2	0–92	47	826	4.1	6.3	.4	0–40	9
Yield of corn (bu./acre)[6]	1,810	25.4	13.6	25.0	0–90	46	826	16.6	14.2	18.3	0–75	11
Yield of tobacco (lbs./acre)[7]	1,816	606.5	539.1	703.6	0–2,440	56	826	379.9	47.0	4.0	0–2,104	12

Note: NR = not reporting.

[1] Mean cropland for the total population was 23.7 acres.
[2] Population mean, 10.0 acres; standard deviation, 7.4 acres.
[3] Population mean, 3.9 acres; standard deviation, 7.4 acres.
[4] Population mean, 1.2 acres; standard deviation, 3.3 acres.
[5] Population mean, 7.3 acres; standard deviation, 10.5 acres.
[6] Population mean, 22.6 bushels; standard deviation, 14.4 bushels.
SOURCE: Tennessee Valley Authority, "Family Removal Questionnaire," 1934.

the area as a cash crop: 36 percent of the owners and 57 percent of the tenants interviewed had planted no tobacco in 1933.

The variance in acreage and yield between owner and tenant farms points toward a lower quality of life for the latter. The fact that owners held nearly three times as much cropland as tenants indicates a better chance for economic improvement and well-being among owners. Limitations on the amount of cropland for tenants reduced their chances for economic well-being, whatever the variance in the quality and quantity of labor applied to the farm. The smaller amounts of cropland available to the tenant, given the farming practices of the region, made for less flexibility for the tenant farm in crop variation: while owners planted only 39 percent of their cropland in corn, tenants were obliged to utilize nearly 70 percent of their land in the single crop.

For owner and tenant alike, heavy concentration of row-cropping on limited amounts of relatively poor arable land meant a difficult struggle to subsist. There was something of a vicious cycle upon the most marginal of subsistence farms, whether they were owned or rented. Low productivity and little cash inhibited expenditures to raise productivity; farms became poor because they were unproductive and unproductive because they were poor.

FARM EXPENDITURES AND FARM MACHINERY

Census figures show selected farm expenditures in the Norris Basin counties to have lagged behind those of the state.[52] Figures for the displaced population of the Norris Basin are considerably lower than the census figures, but the tabulations for the displaced population include farms reporting zero values, whereas the census figures do not.[53]

Taxes account for the highest mean expense among the owner population but do not directly represent an expenditure related to the improvement of farm productivity. All of the other items of expense do, and among these, livestock and labor expenses were the highest in 1933. The itemized mean labor expense does not directly reflect the amount of labor expended on the farm (outside of family), for in the communities of the Norris Basin, much agricultural labor was traded off among neighbors, and some agricultural labor was paid for in kind. Mean labor expenditure was, however, about equal to the amount spent on livestock. Much livestock, too, was also obtained by trading and swapping; hence cash expenditures are not wholly representative. The total farm expenditures for owners averaged under $100 per household, but few escaped some expenditure for the year. Tenants simply had less cash to spend on the farm, and those who sharecropped, would not cite many expenditures because they were covered under cropping contracts. Not surprsingly, then, a greater number of zero expenditures are reported for tenants, and the median tenant total farm expenditure was $7.66, far below the median owner expenditure of $50.75. Feed expenditures, too, are not entirely representative, since on self-sufficient farms much feed was raised and consumed on the farm. Expenditure statistics thus do not represent the whole picture of the self-sufficient farm unit but rather say more about cash expenditure in proportion to other items making up the income structure of the farm. One feature that characterizes the farm expenditures among the removed population is the large gulf separating owner and tenant.

In addition to spending relatively small amounts of money on the farm, the inhabitants of the Norris basin owned little farm machinery. The terrain imposed limits on the amount of farm machinery which could be utilized, and lack of money prohibited outlays for machinery. Indicated in table 18 are the type and amount of farm equipment owned by the displaced population. Borrowing multiplied the utility of existing farm equipment, and many tenants had access to equipment as specified in sharecropping contracts. Nevertheless, many farms had no farm machinery of value (10 percent of the owners and 39 percent of the tenants). The median value of farm machinery among owners was $70.88, and among tenants, $7.83. A total of 42 percent of the owners and 67 percent of the tenants owned $50 or less in farm machinery (excluding trucks).

In his early study of the Norris Basin, Levron Howard remarked on the lack of farm machinery: "Finding such a paucity of farm machinery in the selected counties of the Norris Basin, one might readily draw the conclusion that most of the labor of the farms is done by work animals and that there would be a large supply of such animals in these East Tennessee counties. This does not seem to be the case, however." Howard's study cited that for the farms in the state in 1930, there were 2.1 horses and mules per farm, much higher than those for the Norris basin counties of Campbell (1.5), Claiborne (1.75), Grainger (1.6), and Union (1.4).[54] The much lower number of farm animals owned by tenants reflects stock supplied in tenant contracts. The inability to finance farm improvements and to increase productivity created, with soil deficiencies and difficult terrain, an aggregate farm income structure that could provide for most necessities of life but few extras.

FARM INCOME STRUCTURE

Before an examination of the numbers that make up aggregate farm income statistics, it must be emphasized that while these figures are low, both comparatively and of themselves, they do not tell the whole story, economically, of the Norris area self-sufficient farms. Many, if not most, of these farms produced the necessities of life. Cash in hand went to pay taxes, rents, and mortgages, as well as many of the necessities which could not be raised or fabricated on the farm. These items, such as kerosene, tools, oil, ammunition, coffee, salt, baking powder, and shoes, could be traded for, if not purchased outright, at local stores. When self-sufficient farms are spoken of in the modern era, however, it is recognized that they are rarely absolutely self-sufficient. Some cash had to be forthcom-

TABLE 18 *Ownership and Use of Selected Farm Implements and Equipment, Norris Basin Removed Population, 1933*

Farm equipment	Owners						Tenants					
	Yes		No		Borrowers		Yes		No		Borrowers	
	N	%	N	%	N	%	N	%	N	%	N	%
Truck	133	7	1,716	93	0	0	33	4	801	96	0	0
Wagon	941	51	763	41	137	7	100	12	526	63	208	25
Limespreader	15	1	1,692	92	135	7	0	0	627	75	207	25
Tractor	21	1	1,686	92	135	7	1	0	625	75	207	25
Baler	27	1	1,680	91	135	7	0	0	627	75	207	25
Thresher	9	0	1,698	92	135	7	0	0	627	75	207	25
Binder	65	4	1,642	89	135	7	0	0	626	75	207	25
Turning plow	1,107	60	601	33	135	7	157	19	470	56	207	25

SOURCE: Tennessee Valley Authority, "Family Removal Questionnaire," 1934.

ing, and in the last analysis, the lower the cash income for a farm unit, the more precarious life could become—the less one could hedge against hard times. Low cash incomes also restricted families in terms of mobility, farm improvement, general quality of life, education, and the ability to take advantage of opportunities if and when they come.

Farm income data obtained by TVA from the removed families of the Norris Basin in 1934 are not truly comparable to census data for the Norris Basin counties compiled for 1929 and 1939. There are no published census data on income for 1935 which can be compared to the TVA material, and in general, falling prices for farm products make any dollar conversions across a ten-year period somewhat precarious. In addition, it is difficult to state precisely what the figures representing farm income and expenditure actually mean in terms of poverty levels, especially when so many of the farm units were subsistence farms. The census information indicates that in 1929 and 1939, the five-county area of the Norris Basin was well behind the state in the value of all farm products sold, traded, or used by the farm unit. In terms of products used but not sold on the farm, the Norris Basin counties were ahead of state averages but lagged behind for crops traded or sold in 1929 and 1939 (see table 19). It would be expected that as a generality the displaced population would share the regional income patterns of similar counties. Carter Goodrich analyzed farms on the nearby Cumberland Plateau as being at the poverty level when the mean per capita gross income fell below $100. This figure was used for the year 1929.[55] Although the Norris Basin mean gross per capita farm incomes were slightly above those in the lowest of the Cumberland coal counties cited by Goodrich in 1929, they were below the $100 per capita line indicative of poverty.[56] Using the reported household size from the TVA data for the removed population (4.9 persons), number of families (2,619), and the total farm income for 1933 ($1,118,538), one obtains a figure of $87.16 per capita gross farm income for the removed population of the Norris Basin in 1933.[57]

In 1934 workers for TVA obtained detailed information on farm income structure from the families who were to be displaced by TVA. Much of this data is presented in tabular form in this chapter,

TABLE 19 *Mean Dollar Value per Farm for Farm Products Sold, Traded, or Used by Farm Households and Farm Products Used by Farm Households: State, Norris Basin Counties (1929, 1939) and Removed Population (1933)*

| | State | | Norris Basin counties | | Norris area removed population | | | | | |
| | | | | | All removed | | Owners | | Tenants | |
Item	Farm M	N	Farm M	N	Farm M	N	Farm M	N	Farm M	N
Dollar value of all farm products sold, traded, or used by the farm household[1]										
1929	$892.53	245,657	$739.86	10,603	$425.34	2,647	$510.33	1,814	$248.80	830
1933	—	—	—	—	—	—	—	—	—	—
1939	631.99	247,617	496.62	10,983	—	—	—	—	—	—
Dollar value of farm products used by farm households										
1929	288.61	245,657	302.94	10,603	275.68	2,647	314.10	1,814	192.89	830
1933	—	—	—	—	—	—	—	—	—	—
1939	195.13	247,617	218.73	10,983	—	—	—	—	—	—

[1]The total value of all farm products sold, traded, or used is the sum value of the following: value of crops harvested (1929, 1930) which were sold, traded, or to be sold; value of forest products; value of farm products used by farm operator's family (including the value of meat, milk, poultry, eggs, honey, vegetables, fruit, and firewood for the use of the operator's family). The sixteenth census used "all farms" and "farms reporting" for 1930 and 1940, respectively. The above table used "all farms" in computing the means so that they would match as closely as possible the figures from the TVA questionnaire which reported zero values. Farms reporting *no* farm products traded, sold, or used are given with percentages in the sixteenth census.

SOURCES: *U.S. Census, 1940, Agriculture,* vol. III, third series, county table, 17; Tennessee Valley Authority, "Family Removal Questionnaire," 1934.

but some generalizations may be useful at this point. The three major income sources are farm income derived from the sale of crops, livestock, poultry and poultry products, dairy products, tobacco, and handcrafts; the dollar value (at 1933 regional market prices) of all food and firewood raised on the farm and consumed there; and finally nonfarm income sources, which are made up of cash on hand, savings deposits, pensions, rents, insurance, labor off the farm, relief, and assistance from children.

Of the various kinds of data involved, there is a striking absence of outside income sources among the population, owner and tenant alike. The number and percentage of those in the population, owner and tenant, who reported no income from outside sources are illustrated in table 20. While in many, if not most, of the other income and expenditure components there is a great difference between owner and tenant figures, in this area there is little variation: both received small amounts of income from outside sources.

More outside income was generated by labor off the farm for owner and tenant alike than from other source. The term "labor off the farm" does not specify nonfarm labor but paid labor not performed on the farm of the respondent. Much of this labor was agricultural day labor, and much of it would appear to have generated only supplemental income, since remuneration was slight: of

TABLE 20 Percentages of Owners and Tenants Reporting
No Income from Outside Sources, Removed
Population of the Norris Basin, 1933

Outside income source	Owners		Tenants	
	N	No income reported (%)	N	No income (%)
Pensions	1,835	95	834	99
Life insurance	1,836	100	834	100
Health and accident insurance	1,836	100	833	100
Savings deposits	1,824	97	834	100
Rents	1,788	89	798	87
Industrial compensation	1,832	100	833	100
Relief	1,816	95	798	79
Labor off farm	1,818	73	817	50
Assistance from children	1,842	95	833	97
Cash on hand	1,777	82	821	91
Other investments	1,823	96	832	98

SOURCE: Tennessee Valley Authority, "Family Removal Questionnaire," 1934.

the 490 owners receiving income from labor off the farm, only 17 percent earned over $400, and 200 of them received $150 or less. Despite the fact that the number of owners in the population far exceeded tenants, a disproportionate number of tenants worked off the farm (403). Half of these made only $100 or less, and only 50 tenants of the 408 made in excess of $275 in 1933.[58]

Crops, poultry and poultry products, livestock, and tobacco sales were the biggest income-producing items on the Norris Basin farms in 1933, with tobacco holding a much lower rank in this regard than it would come to occupy later (see table 21). The most prevalent income producers throughout the population were poultry and dairy products. The traditional "butter and egg" money incidental to farm incomes on highly productive farms was, on these self-sufficient farms, a significant component of farm income. Although a very high proportion of tenants did derive some income

TABLE 21   *Mean and Median Farm Income by Source for Owners and Tenants of the Norris Basin Removed Population: 1933*

			Farm income ($)			
Item	*N*	*No income reported (%)*	*M*	*SD*	*Mdn*	*Range*
Crops						
Owners	1,811	42	61.53	122.18	10.17	
Tenants	831	62	18.66	45.15	.30	0–400
Livestock						
Owners	1,814	46	38.19	100.63		
Tenants	830	70	6.17	70.18	.21	0–280
Poultry and poultry products						
Owners	1,812	19	41.43	56.81	4.15	0–1,000
Tenants						
Dairy products						
Owners	1,814	19	13.26	63.47	24.96	0–766
Tenants	831	89	2.00	12.31	.06	0–300
Tobacco						
Owners	1,813	77	21.50	66.13	.15	0–800
Tenants	831	83	8.72	26.90	.10	0–220
Handcrafts						
Owners	1,815	99	.46	7.99	.0	0–300
Tenants	831	99	1.00	21.20	.01	0–600
Total farm income						
Owners	1,810	8	196.46	349.52	105.06	0–7,875
Tenants	832	29	55.89	78.78	25.47	0–600

SOURCE: Tennessee Valley Authority, "Family Removal Questionnaire," 1934.

from poultry product sales, a large percentage reported no income derived from dairy products. The largest portion of mean income came from crop sales (excluding tobacco). In all the income categories (except handcrafts), tenant farm incomes lagged well behind those of owners. A higher proportion of tenants than of owners reported zero incomes on all items. The family mean farm income of $152.07 represented about $30 per family member for farm-derived income, and the gap in mean income separating owners ($196.46) from tenants ($55.89) was extreme. Given low farm income, the significance of the garden plot on the farm and the possession of a few hogs and milk cows became the fulcrum of quality of life on the subsistence farm.

For the farms of the Norris Basin, the garden plot, which varied from 0.25 to 1.5 acres, was the pivotal component in gross farm income production, the most significant item of which was the food raised on the farm and consumed by the farm family. The resourcefulness, skill, and patience of the family was abundantly tested, for the quantity and quality of the food raised determined whether one fared well or ill.

Twenty-five percent of the tenants and 7 percent of the owners had garden plots of less than 0.25 acre. The tenants generally had smaller gardens—their median size being 0.25 acre to the owners' 0.5 acre, and a larger number of tenants than owners (18 percent against 3 percent) reported zero value in food raised.[59] As in almost all the economic indicators, owners ranked above, and tenants below, the mean figures for the population. The value of food raised on the farm and consumed by the farm family constituted no exception (see table 22). Owner families were larger than tenant families, which accounted for greater gross consumption in total values, but the per capita figures were computed for each household and show lower standards of living for tenants than owners, a fact substantiated by lower tenant ranges and higher percentages reporting zero for amounts of specific food items consumed. Comparison of the Norris Basin figures with those from the censuses indicates that the responses of the removed population were fairly accurate and not out of line with data for the five counties in 1929 and 1939 (see table 19). The farm products raised and consumed by the farm family were the vital element in farm income structures in areas where self-sufficient farms predominate. Among the displaced families of the Norris basin, 68.4 percent of the mean net farm income was made up of farm products raised and consumed on the farm, a higher proportion than the census material shows for 1929 and 1939 in the five counties of the Basin.[60]

Descriptive statistics sometimes fail to bring out the essentially ecological nature of self-sufficient farming communities and the severe limitations which nature imposes upon people. Rugged, often agriculturally unsuitable topography, abundance of the poorer soils, and limited amounts of arable land worked together with population patterns to confine the individual's ability to exploit the soil to advantage. The overall effect was to reduce farm size and agricultural diversity, to lower income, and to depress the quality of life where, in the worst of cases, it was marginal and difficult. The nature of farm life caused these problems to be ramified to a point where they touched the most intimate features

TABLE 22   *Food and Farm Income,*
Norris Basin Removed
Population, 1933

Item	N	No income reported	Value ($)			
			M	SD	Mdn	Range
Total value of food consumed						
Owners	1,803	3	$314.10	$149.43	$302.11	$0–1,100
Tenants	830	—	192.40	144.61	197.90	0–876
Per capita food consumed						
Owners	1,803	3	72.95	42.23	66.12	0–438
Tenants	831	—	42.36	32.80	41.00	0–185
Gross farm income						
Owners	1,787	2	510.33	414.74	437.00	0–8,468
Tenants	830	16	248.81	196.23	239.25	0–1,811
Net farm income[1]						
Owners	1,787	1	369.31	755.69	—	—
Tenants	829	15	116.01	182.12	—	—

Note: Mean and median gross farm income is constructed by computing total income from sales of crops, stock, poultry and poultry products, dairy products, tobacco, and handcrafts together with the value of food raised on the farm and consumed by the farm family. Net farm income is derived by computing total farm expenditures and subtracting them from gross farm income.
[1]Thirty-eight owner families and twelve tenant families showed negative net farm incomes (expenses exceeding income).
SOURCE: Tennessee Valley Authority, "Family Removal Questionnaire," 1934.

of material and psychological existence—the farm home, its facilities, its furnishings and possessions, and its isolation.

Farm Life in the Norris Basin

Lengthy residence patterns, as has been mentioned, were characteristic of the inhabitants of the Basin, especially among landowners. The owners displaced by TVA had lived a mean 35.3 years in the same community and 23.0 years on the same farm. The tenants, who as a group were younger and more mobile, had shorter residency patterns.

Eighty percent of the owner respondents and 94 percent of the tenants came from family units where husband and wife lived together. There were only fourteen divorced and twenty-one separated heads of families in a population of 2,692 persons. The higher number of single family heads in the owner population than in tenant family heads was caused, not by divorce and separation, but by the fact that being considerably older, more owners were widowed than tenants (16 percent as opposed to 5 percent). To enhance the general picture of stability, one should note that 89.5 percent of all the respondents queried by TVA in 1934 were living in the county where they were born. Among the older owner families, the eldest children had left the household, so there was little difference between owners and tenants in the number of children living at home—a median 2.1 for owners and 2.2 for tenants. In table 23 are cited the age and sex breakdown of offspring residing with their parents in 1934, indicating a considerable number in the age groups fifteen to nineteen and twenty to twenty-four. These figures reflect a decline of mobility induced by the depression.

More owner families (30 percent) reported having relatives living with them than tenant families (20 percent), and of these nonnucleic family members, owners had twice as many members classed as "dependents." Few families had more than one "dependent" nonnucleic member; most such people were widowed grandparents or older single relatives.

The mean household size among the removed population was 4.91, with the owner mean at 4.95 and the tenant mean at 4.83.

William Cole, in his study, remarked upon family size as "a fair index to isolation," noting that a median family size of about 4.00 was characteristic of the most isolated segments of East Tennessee: the Cumberlands and the Blue Ridge Mountain section. In fact, five of the ten counties of the state (in 1930) with a median family size of 4.50 to 4.99 were clustered around the Norris Basin in the Cumberlands. In 1934 in the displaced population, the median household size was 4.6 for owners and 4.4 for tenants.[61] The mean household size for the removed population (4.9) compares significantly with the mean number of rooms in the houses of the Norris Basin.

The average dwelling of the Norris Basin was modest—a mean 4.3 (4.1 median) rooms for owner families and a mean 3.0 (median 2.9) rooms for tenants. Between owners and tenants there were variations which averages tend to blur. While 60 percent of the owners were endowed with houses containing four or more rooms, only 12 percent of the tenants lived in dwellings that large. Seventy-two percent of the tenants lived in homes of three rooms or less. Given relatively even mean household size, the more cramped living conditions of the tenants are striking.[62]

What may surprise the historian is the high degree of variation in house size and type. Housing in Appalachian communities is often described in terms of two-, three-, or four-room shacks. In the Norris Basin, however, almost a quarter of the owner families lived in homes of six rooms or more, and there were thirty-seven families

TABLE 23   *Offspring Living at Home in the Norris Reservoir Area, Removed Population, 1934 (in Percent)*

Age intervals	Males	Females
0–4	9.8	9.6
5–9	10.5	10.1
10–14	12.0	10.9
15–19	9.8	8.2
20–24	5.9	4.3
25–29	2.8	1.9
30–34	1.3	.07
30–39	.6	.6
40+	.6	.4

Note: Figures shown are percentages of total population of offspring living at home. $N = 6,828$.
SOURCE: Tennessee Valley Authority, "Family Removal Questionnaire," 1934.

whose homes contained more than nine rooms. The photographs taken by the Land Acquisition Division of the Tennessee Valley Authority attest to the great variation in house size and style, and although the bulk of the population lived modestly in small houses, there was great variation in decoration and general upkeep, and many homes, despite their modest size, were attractive. There were a considerable number of rather poor and substandard houses, but there was also considerable diversity and range, a fact which is obscured by the statistical findings. The tenants were clearly more restricted in their living quarters than the owners, which is perhaps to be expected, but there were not the degree and kind of variance between owner and tenant which one was likely to find in the plantation economies of northern Alabama or western Tennessee. The Norris Basin communities show a range of dwellings from the starkly poor to the nearly opulent—from a one-room log hut with lean-to kitchen and earthen floor to a handsome two-story brick Georgian built for the original owner by his slaves in the decade before the Civil War. The homely prototypes of Kephart and Campbell and the rough-hewn huts of Fetterman's *Stinking Creek* hardly do justice to the variation in dwelling type and degree of comfort which this rural Appalachian community was capable of producing.

The whole population of this segment of rural Appalachia which dwelt in the Norris Basin lived, for the most part, spartanly (see table 24). In 1933 that meant doing without conveniences that would today hardly figure in the construction of most socioeconomic status indexes; indoor toilets and plumbing, telephone, electric lighting, and efficient indoor heating systems. Ninety-four percent of the owners and 98 percent of the tenants were without electricity or phones. Eighteen families of the nearly 2,700 surveyed had Delco or Carbide lighting systems, true rarities for the region. One family owned a kerosene refrigerator, and one cited among its possessions a gas-powered washing machine.

Indoor toilet facilities were about as rare as lighting systems. Surprising to moderns, who judge progress in terms of the possession of flush toilets, in the 1934 Norris Basin this type of measurement was made in terms of who did or did not possess an outdoor privy. Forty-one percent of the tenants and 30 percent of the

TABLE 24 *Selected Living Conditions
and Personal Possessions of the
Norris Basin Removed Population, 1934*

	Owners		Tenants	
Variable	No.	%	No.	%
Living conditions				
Toilet facilities				
None	553	30	346	42
Outside	1,277	69	484	58
Inside	19	1	3	1
Bathing facilities				
None	309	17	136	16
Creek or river	134	7	71	9
Washtub	1,392	76	623	75
Plumbing	8	1	2	1
Water supply source				
None	15	1	5	1
Well	244	13	52	6
Cistern	344	19	114	14
Spring	1,207	65	652	78
Well and spring	13	1	2	1
Cistern and spring	20	1	4	1
Plumbing	8	1	2	1
Electricity and telephone				
Neither	1,737	94	820	98
Electricity	29	2	7	1
Telephone	73	4	2	1
Both	8	1	0	0
Type of heat used				
None	13	1	1	1
Fireplace	1,336	72	545	66
Wood grate	140	8	22	3
Oil stove	1	1	0	0
Coal stove	39	2	22	3
Wood stove	222	12	206	25
Coal grate	62	3	17	2
Other	40	2	17	2
Type of farm				
None	58	3	153	18
General	1,730	94	640	77
Livestock	9	1	3	1
Truck farm	34	2	35	4
Dairy farm	4	1	0	0
Poultry farm	0	0	0	0
Orcharding	2	1	0	0
Mortgage on farm				
Yes	227	12	—	—
No	1,612	88	—	—
Number of tenants				
None	1,385	75	—	—
One	384	19	—	—
Two	77	4	—	—

TABLE 24 *Continued*

Variable	Owners		Tenants	
	No.	%	No.	%
Living conditions (*Continued*)				
Three	22	1	—	—
Four or more	14	1	—	—
Personal possessions				
Car	476	26	132	16
Radio	140	8	25	3
Piano	107	6	14	2
Organ	169	9	18	2
Stove	494	27	232	28
Phonograph	726	39	196	24
Sewing Machine	1,433	78	341	41
Floor coverings	695	38	145	17
Carbide lighting system	10	1	1	1
Delco lighting system	7	1	0	0
Garden plot				
None	121	7	204	25
.25 acre	440	24	255	31
.5 acre	624	34	225	27
.75 acre	128	7	32	4
1 acre	412	23	103	12
1.25 acres	16	1	0	0
1.5 acres	28	2	5	1
1.75 acres	12	1	0	0
2 acres	29	2	5	1

[1]Less than 1 percent.

SOURCE: Tennessee Valley Authority, "Family Removal Questionnaire," 1934.

owners responded that they had no toilet facilities whatsoever. Since much of the population drew its drinking water from springs, streams, and wells, one can only speculate on the dangers from the dysentery-bearing salmonella bacteria and typhoid fever. In all the population, nineteen owners and three tenants had flush toilets. A decade after the coming of TVA, when the Corps of Engineers moved into the Norris Basin in Anderson County to purchase land for the Manhattan Project, they found that many of the wells and springs of the area were so badly polluted that they had to be filled.[63]

Nearly 10 percent of owner and tenant families used adjacent streams and creeks for bathing purposes, but the largest portion of the population had a washtub and brought water from a nearby source. "Nearby" is relative, however, for 65 percent of the owners and 78 percent of the tenants stated that the springs and streams which constituted their water source were a mean 300 yards away, and many families had to fetch water from as far away as a quarter of a mile. Thirty-two percent of the owners and 20 percent of the tenants had wells or cisterns on their property, but differences aside, the bulk of the population was served by the same type of water and sanitary facilities.

The most common form of heat in the home was provided by wood-burning fireplaces, with coal grates and wood and coal stoves following in order of preference. The latter were rare, being owned by a little more than 2 percent of the population, and very a few families owned oil stoves.

The general absence of electricity and the scarcity of lighting systems (only forty-four families had some form of generated power) affected the whole population in terms of luxuries as well as necessities. Radios, a significant factor in reducing rural isolation, were owned by only 8 percent of the owners and 3 percent of the tenants. Most of these were battery-powered. Nine percent of the owners and 2 percent of the tenants had pump organs, with pianos being even scarcer. The phonograph, more easily available on a limited budget and requiring no power source to operate, was more commonly owned—39 percent of the owners and 23 percent of the tenants had one.

The residents of the Norris Basin regarded the sewing machine as a vital implement of farm life and surprisingly, the ownership of them (77 percent owners, 41 percent tenants) was much higher than that of wood-fueled cookstoves, which were owned by only 26 percent of the whole population. The data from the questionnaire, together with photographs of home interiors, indicate a spartan existence for many families. More than half of the owners and three-quarters of the tenants possessed no floor coverings (rugs, linoleum). The mean value of furniture owned by the Norris Basin owner family was estimated by them to be $211.49 (median $200.13), and personal possessions over and above furniture were valued at a mean $107.09 (median $45.32). Tenant figures were generally much less than those of owners (median furniture, $90.11; median personal possessions, $11.80).

While the residents of the Norris Basin lived simply and frugally, many in conditions which today would be regarded as substandard, the population appeared to have been healthy. The death rate, as has been mentioned, was at U.S. standards for the 1930s, and the high average age of the owners attested to extended longevity. Diseases and physical defects were reported by less than one-tenth of the population. The majority of the physical defects were from farm-related accidents: loss of limbs, damaged or crippled limbs, eye injuries, and hernias being the most prevalent. There was little difference between owners and tenants with regard to physical defects and diseases. Age-related infirmities, like eye problems and rheumatism, were higher among the owners, pellagra and tuberculosis among the tenants (especially those on relief). These last, however, occurred for only 2.6 percent of the 630 respondents reporting defects and diseases. Pellagra was no more common in the population than heart defects, and neither occurred in more than 0.1 percent of the population.

The TVA questionnaire asked the number of deaths which had occurred "while living in the present community," a category which blurs significantly any demographic applications, since it is weighted toward owner families. Of the 1,921 deaths reported in the questionnaire, 27 percent were attributable to infant mortality for the population as a whole. Among the relief families infant mortality caused 38.1 percent of the deaths. Generally, tuberculosis and "digestive disorders" accounted for about 7 percent among owners and tenants as causes of death. Premature births and stillbirths as a cause of death were cited by 4 percent of the owners and 4.6 percent of the tenants. Deaths due to pneumonia, heart failure, influenza, paralysis, and strokes were common in the owner population and were virtually unknown among the tenants.

Comparatively speaking, the quality of life of families in the Norris Basin, using selected variables, conforms to the patterns Carter Goodrich found in his analysis of the eighty-four counties of the Appalachian coal plateaus.[64] In many respects it is meaningless to assess these items in dollar amounts. Family heirlooms, cupboards, pie safes, rifles, trunks, pots, utensils, quilts, and numerous other items crafted laboriously and skillfully and handed down from one generation to another are in many respects beyond value, and one feels at second hand a sense of embarrassment in attempting to value the invaluable. But with the constant reminder that the aggregate statistic is nothing more than a fleshless counter, an indicator of sorts, a shadow entity not to be confused with people, we can only conclude that life was plain and difficult for much of the population.

The small communities of rural Appalachia were and are still in many respects products of a high degree of isolation. Separated from one another by accidents of local topography, these self-contained and coherent organisms in the aggregate are also isolated from the wider world of the valley floor in varying degrees, again because of topography plus the relative paucity of automotive transportation, distance, and poor roads. The isolation of these communities from one another and from neighboring urban structures produces dichotomous characteristics. Isolation draws the communities closer together as organic entities and brings out desirable traits of cooperation, closeness, neighboring, and sociability. The same communities, however, viewed from the perspective of distance from a wider world illustrate the population's loss of opportunities to benefit from the alternatives offered by that broader world of urbanism and modernity. In the latter case isolation must be seen in pejorative terms.

One of the keys to an understanding of the lives of rural East Tennessee families in the thirties is to comprehend what their spatial reality was. It is easy enough to speak of the Norris Basin or the counties of the Norris Basin or the Norris area or upper East Tennessee, but these are terms that would have appeared somewhat unreal to the people of whom we are writing. Their spatial reality lay in their communities, and one should really speak of the "communities of the Norris Basin" rather than the counties of the Norris Basin. Counties, in one sense, are most unreal creations, lines on a map, civil districts, broad geographical areas, and administrative enclaves. But communities are living organisms which are permeated by, and which in their turn permeate, the lives of their collective inhabitants. TVA director A. E. Morgan, for example, thought that counties were so archaic that they should be destroyed and supplanted by broader administrative units. What he did not realize was that to the inhabitants of the Norris Basin, the county as an administrative unit was large enough, and as an organic unit of social life, it was much too large.

The residents of the Norris Basin were strongly attached and deeply rooted to the communities, rather than the counties, of which they were a part. These commudities, and their spatial realities, were reflected in their names—the names of geographical details, river crossings, churches, stores, and the intimate experiences of lives that were seldom deeply touched by broader spatial designations and their administrative units. The residents of this part of Tennessee were really residents of Big Springs, Better Chance, Leadmine Bend, Dark Hollow, Poorland Valley, Lost Springs, Lickskillet, and Pinhook. Names like these abound in the rural areas of Appalachia, but one sometimes loses sight of the fact that the names represent communal cells of twenty or thirty families and that the characteristics formed by and within these communities constituted the source of the rural life style of much of Appalachia and the Norris Basin in the 1930s.

The social ties and common interests of the residents of the Norris Basin would appear to have been satisfied by neighboring and churchgoing for the most part. Only 8 percent of the tenants and 17 percent of the owners belonged to fraternal orders and their auxiliaries, although the costs of membership may have rendered such activities more unpopular than would normally have been the case in a more prosperous rural area. Only 1 percent of each group claimed membership in a cooperative—generally conceded as an indicator of progressiveness in a modern farming community.

Families of the removed population in the Norris Basin attended 175 different churches, not all of them precisely within the inundated area. The size of church congregations fluctuated considerably, as did the regularity with which services were held in many congregations. Some churches with regularly attending ministers met weekly, while others, serviced by itinerant preachers and circuit riders, met sporadically. The infrequency with which services were held in many churches helps to explain the numerous crossovers between cited church preferences and the actual church attended by the family. Choice of service would appear to have been predicated less upon denominational preference than upon whatever meeting was frequently available.

Of the whole population, only 109 heads of households claimed no preference in the matter of church denomination. The largest number of families simply stated their preferences as Baptist (1,597 families) or Methodists (448 families). But many others, as expected in an area known as a bastion of Protestant sectarianism, exacerbated not only by past doctrinal differences but by historic disputes over slavery, were more specific in their choices: Northern and Southern Methodists, Northern and Southern Methodist Episcopalians, American Methodists, Missionary and Primitive Baptists, and Baptists who cited themselves as "old school," predestinationist, free will, and Southern. Below the numerous sectarian congregations of Baptists and Methodists, the numbers began to dwindle. The Holiness sect, rising in popularity, claimed thirty-eight families, Church of God four, and Church of Christ two families. There were more Catholic families (three) in the population than Presbyterians (two), and more Mormons (four) than either. The ultimate religious minority in the removed population was the one Quaker family.

The schools of the Norris Basin were not unlike the numerous churches in appearance—small, with one room, and fairly primitive. Schooling in the multigrade classrooms of the rural thirties was sporadic, the school term running regularly for only about six months. Pupils' attendance was often infrequent, owing to the exigencies of farming tasks. During the winter months, some children of the Norris area boarded locally at Hill's Academy as subscription students. The academy, which had a fine reputation locally, offered in its program an advanced curriculum to the older students which included Latin and German. Schoolteachers, mainly young men and women from the area, boarded in the community where they taught and in some cases taught students who were nearly as old as themselves.

There were no radical differences in educational levels between owners and tenants in the area save those attributed to the difference in ages between the two groups. Thirteen percent of the owners and 7 percent of the tenants responded that they had no education. Only 5 percent of the tenant families and 3 percent of the owners were classed as illiterate, however. About one-fourth of the whole population had no schooling beyond the third grade.

The median years of schooling for both owners and tenants was 5.4 years. Twenty-five percent of the owners and 20 percent of the tenants had achieved an eighth-grade education, and 2 percent of the owners and 1 percent of the tenants possessed high school educations. Seven household heads from each group were college graduates. Educational levels of wives were slightly higher than those of their husbands.

The educational levels achieved among the families of the Norris Basin do reflect, if only slightly in some cases, an economic advantage. House size, cropland, gross income, and farm expenditures rose in direct proportion to years of schooling after the sixth-grade level. TVA's analysis of educational level in relation to appraisal value of land purchased in the Norris Basin is given for owner husbands in table 25. TVA also utilized the questionnaire's educational data and some arbitrarily chosen bases to measure retardation of all children of school age in the area. The bases used were that at age seven years "normal" attainment was first-grade level, progressing by grade to age eighteen, where twelfth-grade enrollment was expected. No comparison of Norris Basin schools with other schools was carried out. The results of the TVA survey are shown in table 26. In the population at large there was no radical differentiation in education between owners and tenants, a point which perhaps strengthens the homogeneous character of the population.

Communication with the broader regional entities of East Tennessee took the form of newspaper subscriptions for 50 percent of

TABLE 25 *Educational Attainment by Appraisal*
Value of Land Owned, for Husbands of Owner
Families of the Norris Basin Removed
Population, 1934

				Grade attained (%)				
Group	N	All owner husbands	No schooling	1–3	4–6	7–9	10–12	Above 12
Under $1,000	380	100.0	12.4	17.1	43.4	23.7	3.1	0.3
$1,000–$3,999	896	100.0	6.6	14.8	40.2	31.8	4.8	1.8
$4,000 and over	422	100.0	6.2	6.4	28.9	44.0	9.5	5.0

SOURCE: Tennessee Valley Authority (Durisch and Burchfield), "Families of the Norris Reservoir Area," table 17.

116

the owner families and 25 percent of the tenant families. The most popular paper by far was the Knoxville morning paper, the *Journal*, which contained reports on local market prices for agricultural items. About the same number of newspaper subscribers were taking, in 1934, at least one magazine. The agricultural magazines were the most popular: *Southern Agriculturalist, Home Comfort,* and *Progressive Farmer* were the most widely chosen. Among magazines that were not farm-oriented, *True Stories* was the most widely read, with *McCall's, American,* and *Literary Digest* running close seconds. Tenants who were magazine subscribers exercised the same preferences as owners. Seventy percent of the population regarded the Bible as their reading staple. For those who read books other than the Bible, history was more popular than fiction.

The families of the removed population traded their agricultural surpluses, dairy and poultry products, furs from trapping, nuts, herbs, and other tradable or salable commodities in a number of markets. Forty-one percent of the residents traded at Knoxville, the largest nearby urban center (thirty-six miles distant); LaFollette, the county seat of Campbell County; or in Loyston, a small town located virtually in the center of the area acquired by TVA. If the nearby towns of Jacksboro, Caryville, Coal Creek, Morristown, and Tazewell were to be included, 57 percent of the population would have traded in these centers as well as among the ninety-one small stores scattered throughout the Norris Basin. Given the large

TABLE 26 *Educational Retardation for Male and Female
Children Living at Home for the
Norris Basin Removed Population, 1934*

Parents	N	None	1	2	3	4	5	6+	Total
				Years retarded					
				Male children					
Owners	1,369	37.3	18.4	13.1	11.2	7.4	5.2	7.4	100.0
Tenants	722	31.6	16.7	15.1	12.2	7.9	6.1	10.4	100.0
				Female children					
Owners	1,227	49.4	17.8	11.3	9.2	4.7	3.2	4.4	100.0
Tenants	658	38.0	19.6	15.4	8.5	6.5	4.9	7.1	100.0

SOURCE: Tennessee Valley Authority (Durisch and Burchfield), "Families of the Norris Reservoir Area," tables 22 and 23.

network of small stores, it is hardly surprising that for a relatively isolated area, the median distance from a store for the population was only 5.24 miles.

Knoxville, a significantly large nearby market, was more frequented by owners than by tenants, 41 percent of whom did not go to the city at all. About a quarter of the owners and tenants went to Knoxville once a year, and a small number (9 percent of the owners and 5 percent of the tenants) went more than once a month. The median number of trips per year to Knoxville was 1.4 for owners and 0.9 for tenants. Since cars were owned by 26 percent of the owners and 16 percent of the tenants, and trucks were owned by 7 percent of the owners and 4 percent of the tenants, infrequent trips would be expected. One should not, however, assume that the scarcity of cars and trucks eliminated trading opportunities in Knoxville or other relatively distant markets. Many of the local stores served as entrepôts for goods destined for the outside markets. Store owners would collect these goods and take them to Knoxville, LaFollette, or Morristown at periodic intervals. Sometimes a group of farmers would pool commodities destined for market, and one of their number fortunate enough to own transportation would take them to market, sharing out the cost of transportation from the proceeds of sales. In many cases, farmers simply traded their surpluses at the local stores in return for goods or, sometimes, for scrip which could be saved against future purchases from the stores.

The contracts with a wider world, then, were maintained with varying degrees of frequency through trading and marketing, listening to the radio, and reading newspapers, magazines, and books. Many of the Basin inhabitants whose lives were to be changed by the coming of TVA had already begun to change, and perhaps the more stringent characteristics of isolation mentioned earlier are sharper with reference to the aggregate rather than specific cases. While some families traded in wider circles, read more, were increasingly better educated, and continued for various reasons to participate in a widening circle of connections outside the Basin, the majority of the people did not possess the means of transportation and communication to take advantage of these connections.

The average family continued to live and trade, to worship, and to socialize within a relatively small area. For the rural families displaced by the Tennessee Valley Authority, the mean distance from the home to a store was 1.5 miles; to a doctor, 5.7 miles; to an elementary school, 1.5 miles; to a high school, 8.2 miles; and to a trading center, 4.4 miles. Movement and mobility of these families was complicated by the lack of transportation and the poor conditions of the roads.[65]

The degree to which limits of mobility and restriction of activity affected life is difficult to measure accurately, largely because of the high degree of subjectivity attached to the word "isolation." But some tentative analyses were carried out for the counties of the Tennessee Valley in the 1930s. William E. Cole, an innovative University of Tennessee sociologist who pioneered many sociological studies for TVA, undertook, in 1934, to measure isolation or degrees of isolation on the basis of comparative county percentages dealing with selected variables. These included: location of farms on improved roads, percentage of automobiles owned, possession of telephones, cooperative buying and selling, and population density. Interestingly, the Norris Basin counties were deficient (below state averages) in nearly every respect save population densities. Hence with sizable populations, the counties studied still showed negatively in degrees of isolation.[66] Another measure of relative isolation and smallness can be seen by the dispersal, or diffusion, of the churches and stores which serviced the removed families: nearly 2,700 removed families cited specifically 204 churches where they worshipped, and they specifically named ninety-one stores in the Norris Basin as places where they traded. Other measures of rurality and isolation used by Cole which could shed some light on the population of the Norris Basin counties include sex ratios and libraries.[67]

"Isolation," of course, means different things to different people. To Cole the sociologist, isolation meant that "ignorance is going to be prevalent; schools and churches are going to continue to be inadequate; young people are going to continue to leave the farms; values inherent in farm life are not going to be forthcoming to the extent that they might be under conditions of less isolation."[68] Isolation can, and in some instances should, be expressed in pejorative terms—the distance and lack of ability to overcome it which can be measured in a series of losses: loss of better educational opportunities; loss of cultural opportunities; loss of economic opportunities and alternatives. These losses are real and must carry considerable weight in any assessment of the effects of isolation on communities. But what is perceived as a loss from one point of view may be couched in meliorative terms from another, and the small circle of communality seen as a benefit, not a detriment. The owner population, in particular, with an older mean age, long years in the same community, deep generational roots in their communities, and extended years on the same farm did not see their spatial limitations in a necessarily pejorative sense. These communities were comfortable, consisting of familiar rounds of places easily reached on horseback, by wagon, or by walking. A community consisted of a circle of families with a six- or seven-mile radius within which one could reach the doctor, school, store, and church, or as one respondent put it in an oral interview, a community defined in terms of those who could hear the tolling of the death knell for a departed neighbor or kinsman.

When J. B. Killebrew compiled his classical analyses of East Tennessee farm life in 1873, the South was recovering from the ravages of a bitter Civil War and the effects of the Panic of 1873. More than half a century later, when TVA's sociologists, planners, and economists described the Norris Basin, TVA was attempting to alleviate the ravages of a major depression. Despite the myriad of changes that had occurred in America in the period that separates the publication of Killebrew's *The Resources of Tennessee* and the coming of the Tennessee Valley Authority, the descriptions of the area are nearly identical.[69]

Killebrew was opposed to slavery and romantically extolled the self-sufficiency of the East Tennessee farmer and independent owner who utilized nothing but "his own strong arm" for support. But passing by some of Killebrew's pious hopes and florid prosody in support of the yeoman landowner of the region, one must recognize that the selfsame quality he praised would become, within two generations, a mark of backwardness and derision—the stigma of a population ripe for economic modernization. Killebrew waxed eloquent upon the self-sufficiency and independence of the rural East Tennessean and his ability to live on what he raised:

> The most striking fact in the farming operations of that division [East Tennessee] is that no money crop, so-called, is raised . . . The amount of money realized by the average farmer of East Tennessee is painfully small, yet the people in no portion of the state live so well or have their tables so bountifully furnished. Many a farmer who lives like a lord at his table does not realize $200 in money from his entire farm.[70]

Against the backdrop of economic depression in his own time, Killebrew spoke in glowing terms of a self-sufficiency that enabled one to survive in an intricate network of barter trade carried out in neighborhood stores spaced eight to ten miles apart, where "spun cotton, calico, salt, sugar and coffee are exchanged for feathers, eggs, chickens, dried fruit, etc. These articles after being collected . . . are shipped to Knoxville and other points."[71]

It would, however, be both inaccurate and ungenerous to dismiss Killebrew as a mere Southern romanticizer of yeomanry. What he dreamed of was a regeneration of agricultural practices that would conform to the resources of the East Tennessee region, an agricultural methodology which in his dreams would transform the region: "the development of which will give home markets for their surplus products, and in that happy combination of physical agencies that develop the highest types of noble manhood."[72]

Killebrew's romantic phrase masks a realistic appraisal which unfortunately would be echoed by the USDA and TVA in the thirties. Killebrew may have hoped for the best, but he recognized the frailties of the situation. While praising the independence of the small owner, he conceded that "in the matter of the subdivision of farms, East Tennessee has gone quite as far as seems desirable" (and that at under 100 acres). He argued that there was, in the agricultural system, "scarcely any point at which it does not need improving"; that there was no rotation of crops: "Corn follows corn year after year if the farmer thinks his land will stand it." He argued against the high proportion of row-cropping and a dependence upon corn all out of proportion to other agricultural products. Of the five counties of the Norris Basin, Killebrew wrote extensively on all but Union County. And everywhere he found the same general traits: much land better turned to pasturage (his preference was for sheep) and some very good land poorly worked.[73]

County by county in the Norris Basin, Killebrew relentlessly catalogued the agricultural ills of the Basin in his time: good lands "worn by careless cropping" (Anderson County); "good land small in comparison with unproductive farms" (Anderson County); "want of . . . an orderly and systematic cultivation of farms. The farmers are afraid to spend money for either fertilizer or labor— unwilling to risk the first and having no confidence in the second" [Anderson County]; "farmers have, and for the most part, are still pursuing, an unwise course in the management of the soil" [Campbell County]; "all this wonderful valley [Powell Valley] needs to make it one of the very best in the county, is to produce more grass and less corn" [Campbell County]; "fields are often cultivated until the fertility of the soil is destroyed, and then turned out to grow up in pine forests or alder and persimmon bushes" [Claiborne County].[74]

While Killebrew could well appreciate the social virtues of good husbandry, "simplicity, frugality, and honesty," he deplored "a woeful lack of enterprise" which he found among many farmers of the Norris Basin. In his inimitable prose he vented his scorn upon careless and wasteful practices: "The pernicious habit, and one that argues no rights for prosperity, prevails, to some extent of opening lands, and by ceaseless and careless tillage, exhausting their fertility and thus cheating the soil of its opulent privilege of production."[75]

These appropriate, if colorful, admonitions against some bad practices appear to have gone unheeded. Certainly H. H. Bennett, in the Tugwell Report, found that Killebrew's dream had gone unachieved and his worst fears had been realized. The same life which, seen through Killebrew's optimism, was ringed by the virtues of independence and self-sufficiency had become less attractive with the passage of years, the shrinkage of farms, and the unremitting exhaustion of man and soil alike. The virtues were still there in abundance, but in the face of continuing want and deprivation, the land, to many, had taken on the same characteristics which Killebrew had divined in the faces of hard-working women of these lands: "There is a careworn expression about their countenances, and oftentimes a wasted frame that speaks too plainly of overwork, anxiety, and consequent premature old age."[76]

The situation Killebrew found in the Norris Basin in 1873 had not, in most respects, improved by 1934. It had been tenuous then; time had not brought relief, and the coming of the depression and the return to the farm brought pressures upon communities which, being static, lacked the flexibility to adapt. At this point TVA entered, and its effects must be measured against the backdrop here described.

TVA

PART TWO

The Experiment in Action

The second part of this work introduces TVA in those areas of its administration where it indelibly impressed its image on part of America at the grass roots: land acquisition, population relocation, and grave removal. From the standpoint of the Norris Basin family which was removed, the selling of the land, the relocation of the family, and the removal of the dead were inexorably linked—all constituted a total and wrenching break with a familiar generational consciousness.

For TVA, however, each of the three facets of dispossession was regarded as an administrative task, and each was handled by a different administrative unit. It is unusual, given the divisiveness which existed among the board of directors, that each of the three facets of dispossession was ultimately handled by a different director. David Lilienthal was responsible for land acquisition, Harcourt Morgan for population relocation, and Arthur Morgan for grave removal. This approach to the problem of dispossession justifies separate treatments of each of these major topics.

For the dispossessed farm families of the Norris Basin, the coming of TVA was traumatic. For TVA, the experience of dispossession was also in a sense traumatic, for the agency was convulsed as it attempted, amid tension and conflict, to identify its social role. As each relevant unit within TVA began to cope with its "task" of dispossession, variant and conflicting concepts of TVA's role and scope as a modernizing agent began to appear. The resolution of what was psychologically and emotionally a holistic problem for the dispossessed became for TVA an agonizing and continual appraisal of its role at the grass roots.

125

4 Buying the Land

SINCE CONSTRUCTION was the only immediate panacea to the desperate problem of regional unemployment in the midst of the depression, and since no construction could begin until land was acquired, the development of a workable land acquisition policy constituted one of the earliest and most important phases of TVA's work. More significantly, in purchasing land, the agency would be brought into immediate contact with the people of the Norris Basin. Armed with cash and, ultimately, the right of eminent domain, TVA soon found itself the target of much public scrutiny and adverse criticism which soon made the policy of land acquisition a stormy issue.

The formulation of policy itself was a process fraught with tension, for buying land was the initial step in setting in motion the machinery of removal and relocation which would eventually engulf families, graveyards, churches, schools, and communities. A lack of success in land acquisition or any false moves or missteps which might stir the communities of the Norris Basin to resistance could imperil the success of the whole project. Thus TVA was inordinately cautious in setting up a program of land purchase.

One of the initial difficulties of developing land acquisition procedure was the necessity of establishing a boundary within which TVA would purchase property for the dam site and reservoir at Norris. This boundary, called a taking line, constituted the Norris purchase area. Sequentially, the establishment of a taking line was the first step in land acquisition; but in this early development of TVA, the establishment of a taking line was much more a mere procedural step, for the amount of land to be acquired was soon to be at the very core of the removal process. In a densely inhabited region like the Norris Basin, an extended taking line directly increased the size of the population to be removed, thus intensifying the complexity of the removal process.

In the early years of TVA, decisions about the amount of land to be purchased immediately caused conflict among those who favored minimal purchase policies and those who favored "heavy" purchase or overpurchase policies. The opposing views involved a confrontation of philosophies and interpretations regarding the meaning, direction, and intent of the TVA act and the corporation itself in regard to the question of land policy. What the debate boiled down to was the question of "overpurchase" of land in fee simple in support of conservation, afforestation, and the retirement of marginal land as general welfare goals of TVA, as opposed to the more pragmatic goals of the agency in purchasing flowage easements only to the reservoir's edge.

Land to be actually covered by the reservoir waters at normal pool elevation (expressed as the number of feet above mean sea level attained by the reservoir) was naturally purchased by TVA in fee simple. But the Authority had to be able to establish control over land at the edge of the reservoir which "may be covered intermittently from at least once a year to once every fifty years." Since 1941 this land had been purchased as flowage easements rather than in fee, giving TVA the control it needed without purchasing additional land. As a former TVA official put it:

> Fee simple purchase of this land means more dislocation of families, whereas purchase of flowage easements means that farmers can continue to function as economic units, leaving the owner possession to the water's edge, suject to all the rights TVA needs and has bought.

Described as the policy which "disrupts production and community life the least," such a policy has been in effect in TVA's modern era.[1] But between 1933 and 1941 TVA pursued a policy of heavy purchase of land in fee simple.

For the construction of Norris Dam and its reservoir, 153,008 acres were purchased by TVA. These properties, called "Norris Reservoir area properties," consisted of the following classifications: tracts for the Norris Reservoir and dam site, access right-of-ways and properties for the Norris Freeway to Knoxville, marginal lands, the townsite of Norris, and other miscellaneous sites. By far the largest single class of purchased lands was the Norris Reservoir tracts, which consisted largely of farm land. Of the total of 153,008 acres, 136,867 were Norris Reservoir tracts.[2] The second largest single category of land purchased by the Authority at Norris was the 11,688 acres of marginal land, much of which was not really necessary for the reservoir but which was purchased for the purpose of retiring it from cultivation and to avoid the expense of building bridges to areas isolated by the reservoir.[3] In contrast flowage easements were purchased on only 51 acres at Norris.[4]

At Norris, TVA acquired an enormous amount of land above the normal pool elevation of the reservoir—120,000 acres, or 78.4 percent of all the Norris purchase. The debate over acquisition caused division within the fledgling agency. As one source explained: "This policy was arrived at after vigorous discussion among the TVA staff. On Norris, the foresters, recreationists, engineers and public health people advanced reasons for a large purchase program, and only the agriculturalists were opposed."[5]

One of the obvious points of divergence over purchase policy had its origin in organizational difficulties which, as has been mentioned, were exacerbated by friction among the directors. If, as has so often been alleged, Harcourt Morgan sided with David Lilienthal in the reorganizational structure of August 1933 in order to obtain a free hand with the agricultural program, the debate over purchase policy was to widen the already existing gap between the two Morgans.

The purchase of reservoir land is a main component of the tasks called "water control on the land." In 1937, after the completion of Norris Dam, a department by that name was created and placed under an official called the "chief conservation engineer." But during the building of Norris, water control on the land fell into three separate components: the fertilizer, agricultural, and forestry programs. Fertilizer and agriculture programs fell under Harcourt Morgan's supervision, while forestry remained the responsibility of A. E. Morgan.[6] Given earlier disputes between the two men, further friction was inevitable, especially since Arthur Morgan's ideas about afforestation of marginal land conflicted with those

129

behind Harcourt Morgan's agricultural program. When land acquisition procedure was taken from Arthur Morgan in the August 1933 reorganization, he as chief engineer was still left with the authority to determine what land should be taken. As Charles Hoffman, an early assistant secretary of the TVA board, noted:

> In performing that function, Dr. Morgan and his staff established the boundaries of the reservoir water storage area and then added a belt of land approximately ¼ mile wide around the periphery of the reservoir. . . . It was necessary to stop soil from washing into the water storage reservoir, prevent malaria by destroying the anopheles mosquitoes, control access to the reservoir waters, and to regulate development of recreation facilities along the shore. The purchase of the belt of land along the periphery of the water storage area enabled the TVA to perform all four functions.[7]

The reasons Hoffman cited were significant, since none were in effect separable from the evolution of action programs linked to the normal development of water control on the river and on the land. Fear of excessive siltation from erosion in particular was a convincing argument for heavy purchase of land above the normal pool elevation. The Norris Basin—like much of East Tennessee—was afflicted with the common and persistent problem of erosion, and the purchase of land to prevent reservoir siltation entailed land acquisition in a watershed pattern up the slopes and sides of the valleys to the ridges. Although Hoffman attributes to A. E Morgan reasons for heavy purchase that are all within the purview of the action program of TVA and not its general welfare goals, there was little doubt as to Morgan's feelings in the matter. In his book Morgan recalled the occasion when Roosevelt first broached to him the idea of becoming director: "When he spent most of our time together talking not about dams or electric power or fertilizer but about the quality of life of the people of the Tennessee Valley, I was quite certain of it [that I wanted the job]."[8] Claude Nash, in a study on reservoir land management, asserts that the heavy purchase policy was modified toward flowage easements "as accumulated experience began to show that erosion and siltation were not the immediate problems to the reservoirs that had been feared."[9] Morgan, however, in a personal interview given to the authors, indicated that he never regarded the siltation argument for heavy purchase as decisive as the argument in favor of the retirement and afforestation of marginal land.[10]

The overpurchase policy, then, had two sharply edged arguments. It could be justified by the pursuit of the action program in the protection of the reservoir from siltage, the recreational enhancement of the reservoirs through the provision of limited access, and the prevention of disease through malarial control measures. The purchase of a broad protective belt could be justified by any one of the above arguments. But heavy purchase was also a means by which the general welfare program of TVA could be approached, however obliquely, and Chairman Morgan made no secret of his ardent interest in making conservation through the retirement of marginal land a major aspect of TVA policy. This view was supplemented strongly by the recommendations of the Tugwell Report, which urged the retirement from cultivation of much East Tennessee farm land because of its unproductive character and the abuse it had suffered through row-cropping.[11]

Arthur Morgan was particularly vocal on the issue of erosion and poor use of the soil as one of the principal waste-producing afflictions of the area as well as the nation. He spoke about it in literally dozens of speeches and repeatedly argued that the legislation should be considered to allow the government to dispossess farmers from land which they were incapable of farming properly. He was strongly in favor of the removal of marginal land from cultivation and was particularly interested in the best methods of land use for the area. Charles Hoffman, who attended all board meetings, had left this impression:

> I recall Dr. Arthur E. Morgan advocating at one meeting of the TVA Board that the TVA undertake a survey of land use in the Tennessee Valley. He thought such a survey was mandatory before anything could be done to make use of the valley land. He had in mind pinpointing abused and misused land and spotting areas with high potential which had not been developed for their best use. Various state and federal agencies which he had sounded out were markedly interested in such a survey and had assured him of their cooperation in making good use of the findings.[12]

As an integral part of his land use concepts and of his vision of TVA raising the quality of life in the Tennessee Valley, Arthur Morgan believed that upon the retirement of marginal land and its afforestation, "forest districts of a few thousand to several thousand acres" should be developed. "Many forest areas were large enough to support a small community by forest work with the help of small valley gardens that could be developed along brooks and rivers."[13] To "a creative and energetic young forester," Edward C. M. Richards, Morgan attributed the idea of using for community support systems marginal forest tracts gained through heavy purchase. Recalling the communities that he and Richards had envisioned, Morgan waxed nearly lyrical:

> Mr. Richards marked the boundaries of one or two such forest districts and began to train a group of foresters to manage such tracts. He also planned to employ and train local residents for this purpose. Besides preventing forest fires, they would cut out trees and species unsuitable for lumber and sell that part for firewood or use the best of it for cabinetwork. The several lumber centers would develop varied technical uses for wood products. In some cases, the local timber industry would produce special woods, such as walnut, cherry, white pine, or the rare bird's-eye maple. Some of the tracts would be large enough to support schools for training cabinetmakers, breeders of large fruit trees, and dairy farmers. People could raise their food in the little mountain valleys or become members of bean and tomato cooperatives (like those being developed in another of my projects). Here and there a tract would be especially equipped for training people in forestry or in crafts related to forestry. The people who worked each forest would have the opportunity to build a community center if the tract was not located close to a town or village.
>
> This program would make possible varied industrial development, very different from the vast individual timber holdings that leave the little mountain valleys uncultivated, with few or no woodwork craftsmen and most of the local people working as hired laborers. While extensive tracts owned by large companies might be left intact for purposes such as papermaking, it seemed more socially desirable to have a variety of local industrial centers, each with its population center. The extent to which development of special-wood industries was feasible could not be determined quickly, but one such unit had been organized and was at work; it included small-scale farming and a residence center.[14]

Appointed by A. E. Morgan, Richards was "the most aggressive proponent of extensive acquisition." He was convinced that forest, critical erosion, and marginal land areas within the Tennessee Valley were not being used constructively and in effect were holding down the standard of living:

> In the case of critical erosion and marginal lands, the need for discussion and definite commitment of policy is in one way even more imperative and pressing than in the case of forest lands, for the reason that, for the most part more people are endeavoring to live and earn a livelihood on such areas than on forest lands.[15]

Richards then issued a clarion call for ownership of land in fee by TVA to prevent the destruction of the soil and those who farmed it. Fee-simple purchase could be appreciated as well by planners and recreationists who felt that the natural beauty of the reservoir would be enhanced. It should also be mentioned that at Norris it was policy to avoid breaking up part of a farm by purchase: to avoid severance, the whole farm was bought in fee simple. One former TVA official stated that many of those in favor of the heavy purchase policy had a "gut reaction" against the inequity resulting when individual landowners prospered simply by virtue of the fact that the existence of the reservoir placed them advantageously at the water's edge.[16]

The purchase policy pursued at Norris was a victory for the foresters, recreationists, planners, and engineers. The purchase of a protective strip all around the reservoir an average of one-quarter mile wide was considerable acreage when one considers that the two arms of the reservoir, extending back up the Clinch and Powell river valleys, are seventy to seventy-five riverine miles in length.

The opposition of the agriculturalists was vociferous. Charles Hoffman reported that while neither Lilienthal nor Harcourt Morgan was favorably impressed by A. E. Morgan's notions of land use, Morgan in particular was much opposed: "Dr. H. A. Morgan contended that the owner of the land could do with it as he pleased and that nobody had the right to tell him how he could and could not use the property."[17] The agriculturalists' major argument against such an intensive land acquisition policy was that it "would eliminate large numbers of farms, primarily of the family subsistence type, and would adversely affect the economy of the region."[18]

Had there not been a problem of population pressing so heavily upon the land in the Norris Basin, the overpurchase policy would not have made a great difference in the population removal problem. But this population by pressing arable land into cultivation upon the slopes of the river valleys had created a poor man/land ratio. Heavy purchase would guarantee retirement of marginal land but also removal of a large number of marginal families. The greater the number of economically marginal families on poor land who would have to be moved, the greater the problems of removal and relocation.

Afforestation of marginal land and the heavy purchase policy had much merit. The removal of subsistence farms, with their heavy row-cropping and persistent soil depletion and erosion, was not to be lamented in most cases. Despite Harcourt Morgan's axiom that each man's land is his to do with as he pleases, there seemed little merit in the preservation of an unremunerative way of life for subsistence farmers. There is reason to doubt that Harcourt Morgan was even very well attuned to the needs of the smallholder, for as Charles Hoffman has noted, although he had an admirable "integrated view of the agricultural problems of the Tennessee Valley" and was "acquainted with the Valley's overall needs, [he] was relatively unaware of the problems of the farmer who had a small hillside farm and was growing row crops such as corn and tobacco with the help of a mule."[19] Hoffman pointed out that Morgan's entomological study of the boll weevil in the South had brought him into favor with large landowners, and his career as Tennessee state entomologist, dean of the University of Tennessee Agricultural School, and later president of the university had brought him into contact with the more successful farmers. Hoffman further stated, "He seems to have worked largely with successful farmers who owned large tracts of land rather than with the farmer who was trying to eke out an existence by growing row crops on about 40 acres of marginal hillside land."[20]

Opposing views on land purchase such as those advocated by the two Morgans were, in the long run, irreconcilable. With reorganization in 1937 and the decline of A. E. Morgan's infuence, Neil Bass became chief conservation engineer and, as such, the administrator of both agricultural and forestry programs as they pertained to water control on the land. This brought first the opposi-

tion and later the bitter resignation of E. C. M. Richards, who as
A. E. Morgan's appointee as chief forester shared enthusiastically
the afforestation views of his superior.[21] Soon after this reorganization, the heavy purchase policy succumbed to pressure from Harcourt Morgan and his associates, and a policy of flowage easements
was adopted.

The overpurchase policy, which took excessive amounts of land
out of circulation, would have been judicious if and only if the
Authority had the means to provide for the dispossessed farmer a
better opportunity than that afforded by the marginal subsistence
farm. In short, it was probably advisable to retire unproductive
land from use only where the farmer benefited equally with the
planner, the engineer, the forester, and the recreationist. Such
unfortunately was not the case. As will be discussed later, the small
farmer did not for the most part benefit. Instead, he suffered the
worst of all possible situations—removal without great benefit to
himself. Again there was a striking difference between rhetoric and
reality. Rhetorically, afforestation of marginal land with a high
population density of subsistence farmers could only exist within a
structural framework which afforded great flexibility in the development of a socioeconomic program which would successfully
resettle displaced farmers. Where such a structural frame was
wanting and the policy was pursued nonetheless, it became an
exercise in futility. What was ironic was that the director who had
the vision to provide a corrective to the situation of displaced
families completely lacked the power to do so; while the director
who felt the strongest about the farmer's freedom to do as he
wished became the administrator of the resettlement program
whose implementation was made more difficult by a purchase policy he opposed.

That the heavy purchase policy gave the agency more land than
was really necessary once the forestry program was attenuated can
be borne out by the land review policy followed at Norris Reservoir. Land review practice declares as surplus land those tracts that
have already been purchased but are no longer regarded as necessary, and these tracts are sold at public auction.[22] In the first review
of Norris land purchases, from August 1945 to December 1946,
51,000 acres were considered surplus. In 1952, an additional

15,000 acres were released, and shortly thereafter 4,400 acres were turned over to the state of Tennessee and various local agencies.[23] Using Nash's figures of "heavy purchase" (120,000 acres above normal pool elevation), it is at least conceivable that 58.66 percent of the Norris Basin purchase area was unnecessarily negotiated for. Given an average of 50 acres per farm, one could speculate that nearly 1,500 families were removed unnecessarily. In all fairness, it should be pointed out that the large block purchase of the Central Peninsula, a large portion of land between the confluence of the Clinch and Powell rivers, was made because a large portion of this property was submarginal and because a large part of the population would not have had ready access to trade centers outside the reservoir area without the additional expense to TVA of providing extensive road and bridge connections.

The debate over the theoretical issues of purchase policy within TVA ultimately boiled down to how that policy was applied at the grass roots: in short, the relationship between the ideal and the real. What the TVA agriculturalists, engineers, foresters, planners, and recreationists debated as they strove for agreement on the establishment of a taking line was not known to the inhabitants of the Norris Basin. Yet the decision regarding overpurchase, pursued idealistically within TVA, was to have a very real effect on the lives of thousands. The distance which separated Norris farmers from the debates over heavy purchase was immense; yet that distance between administration and the grass roots was to narrow perceptibly and quickly with the actual purchase of tracts. In the actual acquisition of land, policy was again defined in a statutory and an ideal sense; yet its application at the grass roots illuminated further some of the problems which developed between TVA and its host population.

Considering the grand scope and novel process of the land and of the acquisition undertaking, it was inevitable that errors in judgment, incompetency, and indecision would at times plague agency officials as they sought to go about their respective jobs. Ordinarily federal land purchase was carried out through numerous federal agencies and offices: the Department of Justice, the attorney general's office, and federal district attorneys. TVA, as an autonomous regional agency, kept the process in its own hands, using its own personnel and policy in the contradistinction to processes developed by the comptroller general.[24] TVA also deviated from general procedure by following a policy based heavily upon voluntary purchase as opposed to "blanket condemnation." As noted earlier, section 4(i) of the TVA Act enjoined TVA against blanket condemnation, urging it only in the event of failure to sell at a "fair and reasonable price" as determined by the board of directors.[25] In order to obtain fairer treatment of all sellers of land to the agency, TVA adopted a policy of "no price trading." All appraisal procedures of land (with a few exceptions such as transmission line easements) were the same, and the owner was offered the appraisal price with no changes except when TVA was convinced that an appraisal error had been made. Consequently, large and small landowners received equal treatment.[26]

In preparation for purchasing tracts, TVA appraisal personnel analyzed the factors affecting local land values.[27] Following these analyses, the appraisers made individual tract appraisals, many of which were made independently of one another. The figures were then presented to a committee for review. Ultimately, each tract was inspected by at least one member of the review committee, and owners were notified prior to the initial appraisal date to allow them to accompany TVA's personnel into the field.[28]

Constitutionally TVA was bound to purchase land at a "fair market price," and the TVA policy of purchase has been interpreted as "liberal" in the sense that in seeking a voluntary conveyance of the land, it did not pay the lowest appraisal price but attempted "to leave the landowner in as good a financial position as he occupied before his land was purchased."[29] If TVA's Land Acquisition Division could not obtain voluntary conveyance of lands at its appraisal price, the tract was referred to the Authority's Legal Division, where condemnation proceedings and "title and possession were obtained through the use of the declaration-of-taking procedure."[30]

TVA followed a special condemnation procedure covered under section 25 of the TVA Act.[31] This procedure included the appointment by U.S. District Court of a three-man commission of disinterested local residents who determined the value of the condemned tract. If either party found the word of the commission unsatisfactory, exception was filed so that the case was heard before three federal district judges for a trial de novo. This award could be appealed to the Circuit Court of Appeals, "and the said Circuit Court of Appeals shall on the hearing of said appeal dispose of the same upon the record without regard to the awards of findings theretofore made by the commissioners or the district judges. . . ."[32] The condemnation proceedings for the TVA Act were specifically drafted for protection against "unreasonable jury awards," and one TVA official felt that "much of the success of the TVA land acquisition program is traceable directly to the condemnation procedure prescribed in the TVA Act." Indeed, given the complicated kinship networks of the region and its general reputation for litigiousness, if jury trial procedure under common law had been followed in condemnation proceedings, it is doubtful that TVA could have successfully acquired the necessary land save at an exorbitant cost. Under the system of condemnation used by TVA, the uniformity of condemnation awards brought about "the realization by the landowners that there is little probability that they will obtain through litigation a substantial increase over the amount offered" and that this process "has contributed greatly to TVA's success in acquiring the land needed for its projects by voluntary purchase and sale."[33]

That TVA was successful in its land acquisition policy from the point of view discussed above is certain. In 1949, when TVA's land acquisition program was analyzed, only 3 percent of the tracts acquired was the result of contested condemnation proceedings. On this basis, the initial experience at Norris was below average. Of the acreage acquired, 94.2 percent of the tracts were voluntarily conveyed, with 1.5 percent being condemned for title purposes and 4.4 percent condemned for refusal to sell. The analysis concluded with this statement: "The experience of TVA with these policies establishes that a land acquisition program can be a source of positive benefit to a regional agency instead of a source of conflict with the landowners."[34] Considering the very real problems involved, the report was either somewhat naive or indirect in its assessment.

From the earliest days of TVA, Arthur Morgan was sometimes unable to articulate his legitimate concerns about the operations of

TVA to his fellow directors. He was, for example, deeply worried about possible abuses arising from TVA's purchase of enormous tracts of land; however, in an early board meeting, this concern was presented to the other directors in the form of a project to study the "role of the real estate man in organized society." Harcourt Morgan found such a project alarming and impractical, but Arthur Morgan reflected that earlier speculation in land at Muscle Shoals was intolerable; he was legitimately afraid "that people would get in our reservoirs, and buy up land, or buy up mineral rights, and so forth, and then try to sell them to us as intermediaries. . . . If we could stop that, it would be a good thing."[35] Arthur Morgan had developed principles for the purchase of land which became part of TVA's program. One example was his position on no price trading: "We shall avoid the method of offering less than we intend to pay and then haggling and bickering like oriental traders." He also stressed the need for good appraisals of the land by "disinterested men of good judgment" and urged that the appraiser "should, if possible, visit the man, get his story, and learn of any elements of value or expense that might otherwise be overlooked."[36]

To Arthur Morgan the government agencies involved in land purchasing had paid little or no attention to "human welfare."[37] Since he was primarily concerned with smallholders who had to adjust to difficult conditions, he proclaimed:

> The man, often with a family, who sold his land, had to live while finding a new home. He was hunting for a new tract when numerous persons whose homes had also been bought were also looking for land, so that vacant homes were not abundant. The small amount he had received for his home was soon used up and the family was broke. Having paid the price, the government considered the transaction finished.[38]

It was clear that to Morgan land purchase did not stop with the transaction. In a speech to some students at Norris (ironically enough, exactly a year from the date of his loss of land acquisition power), Morgan discussed what he thought property acquisition should entail:

> To find suitable homes for these people, so they can move into a situation where the roads are well laid out and the land is fertile; where they will have a water supply and decent houses and electric-

ity and some guidance as to farming. . . . Suppose we do buy a tract of land and build houses with water and electricity and good facilities and, possibly, with a central creamery. Will the people accept it or will they want something else? Nobody knows the way. We are exploring, that is one of the characteristics of a job like this.[39]

To him land acquisition and resettlement of the reservoir population were all one process. Unfortunately, neither of these processes was to come under his administrative control. That responsibility was to fall to David Lilienthal.

Lilienthal's first task as the administrative head of land acquisition was the appointment of "General" James Cooper to head the land acquisition effort for the Norris Dam. Cooper, a Tennessean from White County and a law graduate of the University of Tennessee, had served after World War I as a state tax commissioner. Prior to his employment with TVA, Cooper had gone into private practice and had been general counsel of the Mizner development project at Boca Raton during the Florida land boom of the twenties. Between 1927 and 1933 he had been assistant attorney general of Tennessee and in that position had been in charge of land acquisition and title work for the Great Smoky Mountains Park Commission.[40] On the basis of his credentials, he seemed a sound choice.

Since Cooper did not have sufficient maps of the tracts to be acquired in the Norris Basin, his work as land commissioner began slowly, not getting well under way until the winter of 1933–34. Almost immediately he found himself the target of much abuse, the first documented case being a complaint from a woman to Arthur Morgan about unfair treatment in land sales. When queried about the complaint, Cooper claimed that a land appraiser had begun all the trouble "by telling people what his appraisals were, which was about 25 to 50 percent too high," and that "they have all got the idea that they can subdivide their land and sell it off in small lots."[41]

In February two more serious complaints were lodged against General Cooper—both in the form of petitions sent to Senator Kenneth McKellar. The first, from "Democratic and Republican citizens of the county of Union," was mailed February 24, 1934; and the second, from "citizens and landowners of Big Valley Community, Union County," was dated from a February 26 meeting.[42]

The first petition charged Cooper with political favoritism toward Republican state senator W. P. ("Press") Monroe, the leader of one of Union County's two Republican factions and a contender for the office of county judge. It was alleged that Senator Monroe's uncle, though inexperienced, had received employment with TVA as a deed abstractor through Cooper's patronage. The petition complained that both in and out of the inundated area, Cooper had "lauded and praised the said W. P. Monroe." The latter for his part was said to have "openly boasted that he [was] the only person who [could] procure an appointment for anyone with the Tennessee Valley Authority." More significant was the fact that the petitioners very reasonably believed:

> That Senator Monroe, through great favoritism shown him by General Cooper, [could] have a great influence in determining the amount of compensation that they [would] receive for their lands . . . and those politically opposed to the said Senator Monroe [had] a great deal of anxiety as to their plight in the matter when their lands are sole and taken by the TVA.[43]

More serious were the charges laid against Cooper's office by the residents of Big Valley Community in Union County. These people complained of "inequitable treatment at the hands of the Tennessee Valley Authority and its agents and land appraisers" and believed that they were receiving "inadequate compensation" for their lands. The price given by TVA, it was alleged, did not provide for the cost of moving to similar farms at new locations and did not take into consideration "the values of our attachment to this region; or to breaking of ties of friendships; or for attachments to our ancestral homes." It was pointed out that many had refused better offers for their land than those set by TVA appraisers and had complained:

> those employed by the said authority do not possess an adequate knowledge of land values in this locality; and that their untactful utterances, in public and in private, derogatory to our farms, our communities, and to our modes of living have rendered them incompetent to deal with us in the capacity of land appraisers.

Finally it was argued that while they had to bargain for new farms after selling to TVA, the agency would not bargain with them in the sale of land.[44]

141

A TVA Roundup at Loyston School, October 1934. Representatives of TVA met with
local residents to explain how the dam and its flood waters would affect the community.
Residents of Norris basin sometimes protested TVA's land-buying policies at such meetings.

In a confidential note to Arthur Morgan, one of his aides expressed concern about the petition and warned that "the matter brought out by this complaint can develop into a very serious situation. In view of the large number of farmers signing and the careful wording of the document, it is hardly felt that you can entirely ignore the situation." In suggesting that Morgan look into the matter, the aide commented that "the entire subject of land purchasing [should] be considered. The whole machinery seems to have bogged down."[45]

Although Cooper openly denied the charges contained in the petitions, the board of directors nevertheless authorized Neil Bass, assistant to Harcourt Morgan, to make an investigation of the matter. Curiously enough, one of the first things Bass did was to write to Senator McKeller, "Our Board has asked me to make an investigation of the matter, and I would appreciate so much your advising me of any conclusions you may have reached."[46]

In the exchange of letters which followed, it is clear that Cooper regarded McKeller as his political patron. It is likely that McKeller and Cooper were being referred to later when Arthur Morgan testified:

> I might say that I was under intense pressure from a member of Congress to appoint a certain man head of our real estate purchasing here [Norris]. I talked over with that man what his principle would be. He said the thing to do would be to go around and pick up all the land for the people that would sell easy, pick that up at a low price, and when you cannot do that any more pay a big price to the folk that held out.[47]

It is certainly true that Cooper was not appointed land commissioner until land acquisition was taken from Morgan's hands. Indeed Morgan emphatically stated that when land acquisition responsibility was taken from him in the 1933 reorganization, the other two directors "appointed in my place a local man who was completely lacking in the knowledge and competence necessary for the job. I talked with him and told the other directors that he was not qualified."[48] There is also evidence in at least one other case that Cooper was quick to act in terms of political patronage to the extent of overriding, with Lilienthal's consent, the recommendations of the personnel division, which was committed to a nonpatronage position.[49]

When McKellar was queried about the allegations made against Cooper by the Union Countians, he responded that Cooper had "answered the complaints in full."[50] Better than a week after consulting McKellar, Bass made his report to the board of directors, saying that they (Bass and J. C. McAmis, also of Harcourt Morgan's office) had spoken to the superintendent of schools who had mailed the petition. The results of the conversation were not discussed in any detail, nor were any allegations made in the petition discussed. The brief report simply concluded: "I do think that General Cooper has stimulated the prejudices of one of the factions because of his visits with Senator Monroe. . . ." Bass said that for better public relations, Cooper should visit both the factions or neither of them and that the matter should be dropped.[51] Despite the fact that Cooper was given an ostensibly clean bill of health following Bass's inquiries, there was growing dissatisfaction regarding Cooper's work as land commissioner.

Even while the charges against Cooper by the Union Countian were being examined, land acquisition procedure was being carefully studied. While the origins of this study are somewhat obscure, there is probably cause to assume that Cooper's personal behavior had something to do with this reevaluation of land acquisition procedures. The study of land-buying procedure under General Cooper was carried out by John I. Snyder, who would later replace Cooper as head of the land acquisition department.[52] At the time he made the study, Snyder was assistant general solicitor to director Lilienthal, who in addition to being a co-director was general legal counsel for TVA. In his capacity as assistant general solicitor, Snyder had defended Cooper against allegations similar to those produced in the first Union County petition.[53] Although the origins of the evaluation of TVA's land acquisition procedures were vague, charges against Cooper which came to Chairman Morgan's attention were probably instrumental in the reexamination policy. In a lengthy letter drafted to President Roosevelt by Arthur Morgan but never sent, Morgan stated that he had had little to do with land acquisition after the August reallocation of board duties in 1933, information came to me from time to time that this work was being incompetently handled, and that at the prevailing rate of acquisition our entire program of dam construction [both Norris and Wheeler] would be held up. . . . After this program had been under Mr. Lilienthal's direction for about eight months [March 1934] I took the liberty, during his absence, of appointing a committee consisting of the personal assistants of the three directors to investigate the land acquisition program. The conditions proved to be far worse than I supposed. It was a chaos of confusion, inefficiency and political patronage.

This committee, said Morgan, consequently worked out a reorganization; Lilienthal gave up direct supervision and "an entirely new directive staff took charge. The present director [John I. Snyder] has stated that the first year's work was so badly done that his program would have been less difficult if nothing had been done at all by the former administration."[54]

John Snyder, who carried out the examination of Cooper's work as land commissioner, had a slightly different view as to the origins of the reevaluation, which does not fully corroborate A. E. Morgan's version. In the investigation of TVA in 1938–39, Snyder testified that

during the early period of the Authority's organization, we soon became cognizant of the fact that land acquisition was not proceeding as rapidly as necessary to meet the closures of dams, and pressure was exerted from Reservoir Clearance and Construction Departments [under A. E. Morgan's administrative direction] that they weren't getting the services that they needed so as to carry on their work properly.[55]

Under further examination by Francis Biddle, general counsel of the congressional investigating committee, Snyder stated that it was Lilienthal himself who authorized the examination and "complete investigation" of land acquisition procedures, "and on the basis of my report to him, and in a recommendation of how the work should be carried out, which was made, and which he recommended to the Board of Directors the division that was then sent up [Land Acquisition Division]."[56]

Snyder's examination of the work of the land commissioners (Judge Roulhac at Wheeler and General Cooper at Norris) enumerated some problems which plagued land acquisition at both dam sites. It emphasized that land acquisition was proceeding too slowly, that one of the main reasons was the policy of abstracting all the way back to original titles, and that the current land acquisition procedure was slowed by the practice of negotiating individually for each tract. A more systematic and rationalized system of appraisal, the preparation of land books, the clearing of titles, and review of appraisals was suggested—in other words, a complete reorganization of title certification, abstraction, and appraisal.[57] While Cooper had taken part in conferences leading to revision of acquisition procedures, the actual memorandum was not sent to him for any suggestions. Instead, it was sent to coordinating and engineering divisions with the instruction that "if no comments or suggestions are received before Saturday, March 24, it will be assumed that the memo is acceptable to your respective divisions."[58]

Sending these recommendations on land acquisition procedure to the division heads involved was certainly routine, but the exclusion of Cooper from the approval process was puzzling. Certainly Cooper regarded it as the proverbial handwriting on the wall, as far as his position with the agency was concerned, but it was not until April 6, well after Snyder had gained approval from the relevant divisions, that Cooper was able to respond to Snyder's plans for the reorganization of land acquisition activities.[59]

Cooper wrote two lengthy memoranda to Lilienthal in response to Snyder's plans for reorganization. Both bear the date of April 6, 1934, but while the first was a formal response dealing point by point with Snyder's suggestions, the second was intended for Lilienthal's personal file and was an up-to-date report of his activities as land commissioner. Despite later disclaimers that Cooper found Snyder's suggestions impracticable, at the time he told Lilienthal that they were "in the main workable." What led Cooper to take umbrage was the accusation that land buying had proceeded sluggishly under his direction and the implicit suggestion of the Snyder report that he should be replaced as chief land buyer at Norris. To the criticism of tardiness in purchasing land, Cooper replied with some justification that he had not received proper maps until the close of December 1933 and that this problem had naturally retarded the work of land buying. In addition, Cooper clearly rejected the idea of his replacement by Snyder. Partly this seems to have been due to some misunderstanding of the administrative structure of TVA, for as Cooper commented to Lilienthal:

> I think there should be a director at the head of it who is responsible to you only. I thought at the time I was employed that I was to be this director, but in some way which I have never learned, the department was placed under the legal division, why or when I do not know.[60]

Cooper was much opposed to what he regarded as the "mass buying" suggested by Snyder. Finding it preferable to deal with owners individually, he felt that the principle of no bargaining favored by Arthur Morgan was not a good idea, either:

> I have always thought that we should be given some right whereby we could trade with the landowner. Nobody seems to realize that we are dealing with free-born American citizens, most of whom have earned their property by the sweat of their brow, and feel like they have the right to some say as to what they shall be paid for their property. It must be realized that most of these people are anchored and do not want to leave, and at least they should be consulted about the price paid for their land.

This was not an entirely altruistic move to satisfy the desires of the people, however, for it was also Cooper's contention that the land could be purchased more cheaply by the agency in this fashion. While he had agreed initially to the no-bargaining policy, Cooper said that he saw it as experimental only and "I always had some reservation in my mind as to whether it was workable or not."[61] To illustrate his point Cooper stated that he had in his files a resolution of a mass meeting of landowners and passed it on to Lilienthal with the following comment: "I do not agree with the statement that they are not being paid enough for their land, but am passing it on to you to show how they feel."[62]

Cooper, who did not agree with the no-bargaining position, had evidently chosen in some respects to ignore it. Snyder would later testify that Cooper had not organized the work at all, that in many instances the land appraisers in the field simply acted independently of the board of appraisals and review, established by the board of directors, and that often they were simply sloppy and incorrect appraisals. When asked if under Cooper there had been a real attempt to hold to the principle of nonnegotiating, Snyder responded:

> There was a policy that they would have a fixed price which they would not offer above or below. Unfortunately however, that was only policy. They [Cooper's men] would give to one owner a longer surrender of possession date, or they would permit him to take his timber, in other words, other concessions were made, a minor sort of trading went on.

Under such a policy pursued by Cooper, Snyder said that at the time of reorganization (June 1934) there was a whole list of appraisals which had been made too hurriedly and were too low. These properties were placed upon an "agitated list," and their purchase was suspended while the major work of land buying went on.[63] Snyder also said that under Cooper there had been no attempt to organize the work on a "large scale." "In other words," he stated, "they were trying to move a mountain with a wheelbarrow."[64] Arthur Morgan would later say that it was not until Cooper's resignation and the reorganization of land acquisition that his initial principles regarding land purchase were reinstated. In his later book on TVA, however, Morgan, while acknowledging that Snyder was competent, characterized the new purchase policy as "proceeding in the arbitrary and inconsiderate way that at the time characterized land purchase by federal agencies." Morgan evidently was satisfied by neither the old nor the new purchase policy.[65]

Cooper's rather inept defense of himself against the Union County petitioners and the charges of mismanagement brought against him by Snyder put the land acquisition program in jeopardy. But it would be erroneous to accept at face value the vision of near-total incompetence which A. E. Morgan's and Snyder's testimony established in 1938–39. Cooper had some additional points in his defense, and these should be seriously considered. In his personal letter of April 6 to Lilienthal, Cooper acknowledged that there had been multitudinous problems associated with the first period of land acquisition, but he felt that despite this situation a "personal injustice" had been done to him and that he had received "little cooperation" in his work. More pertinently, Cooper felt that his way of doing things had been to get closer to the people themselves, that at the inception of his work he had been given assurances that the TVA "would take care of those people in the pool area whose land was to be encumbered" and that he had fully committed himself in public meetings to the reiteration of this point. As an integral part of this process, Cooper had understood that farmers would be allowed to stay on their land after purchase until TVA had need of that particular land. He claimed rather that the agency had withheld payment until the land was vacated, thereby retarding the work of land acquisition, and said that he had even been issued a specific memorandum on February 28, 1934, to refuse permission to landowners to remain on the land after payment had been made. To the land commissioner, such policy was injurious on two accounts. In the first place, it made allegations of his slowness in buying land unwarrantable, but more importantly it was an affront to the local population and would make them impossible to deal with:

> It is crop time, and all these people want to make a crop, and unless they know they will be able to harvest their crop, they are not going to sign a contract to sell the land. A number of these landowners are in debt. In fact, practically everyone whose land we have purchased owe money and are being heavily pressed therefore, and the delay in closing with them will necessitate the expense of foreclosures and lawsuits.[66]

The general alleged that he could not secure land acquisition contracts owing to a policy of withholding money until possession. This constituted, he said, a change in policy which had been made without his being consulted, "and I have been more or less embarrassed in not being able to carry out promises which I made in compliance of my understanding of what the policies were." Cooper also felt strongly that the TVA had neglected the needs of the people whose land it purchased in that the agency had not constructed a service to provide help in relocating families. Such a service, thought Cooper, should have been developed to work simultaneously with land purchases in the Norris Basin, for its creation would have greatly speeded the work of purchasing land.[67]

There are good reasons to sustain Cooper in his criticisms about the lack of a relocation service and the confusion which surrounded the issue of whether families should stay on the land to make additional crops after the land had been purchased. On the former point, while Arthur Morgan may have differed with Cooper about his methods, he concurred with Cooper on the matter of relocation services. Although this matter will be investigated later, it is pertinent here to note A. E. Morgan's position. In the Congressional investigation of TVA, Morgan was asked by Congressman Wolverton (Rep., New Jersey) of the joint committee what had happened to the removed families: "Did TVA make any effort to place them elsewhere, or what was done to assist them in what might be described as their disaster?" Morgan responded that the question had touched a tender spot and that he had proposed at the beginning that there should be a resettlement program.[68] Such a program was not developed until land purchases had been under way for a year.

Snyder's report, which clearly heralded a change in the development of policies concerning land acquisition, led to the creation of the title of coordinator of land purchases, a position filled by John I. Snyder. Snyder's criticism of previous land purchases and his subsequent elevation to a position above Cooper was regarded by Cooper as a demotion. Consequently, on May 24, Cooper submitted his resignation. He felt that there had been no substantive charges or criticism against either his conduct or the execution of his duties as "commissioner in charge of land acquisition and titles." Despite that, he argued, "Another having been selected and placed in charge of the land acquisition of the Tennessee Valley Authority, I do not feel I can any longer render such services to Tennessee Valley Authority as I should render." Cooper contended that he was close to the people of Norris Basin and had gained their confidence and that the rationalization of land acquisition procedures would be fatal to TVA's development:

> It [TVA] is a great undertaking and should be carried out, but in my humble opinion it can't be a success under the policies now being pursued by the Tennessee Valley Authority and by treating its employees as I have been treated.[69]

Cooper lashed out at TVA in an extensive interview with the *Knoxville Journal* on May 25. Not only did he repeat the comments made in his resignation letter, but he insisted that he had received absolutely no cooperation in his job and that he had been superseded owing to the fact that he was a native Tennessean. Cooper was adamant in his accusation that director Lilienthal had reassured him on three separate occasions that there would be no changes in land acquisition procedure without prior consultation with him (Cooper).[70]

In Washington, two days after his resignation, Cooper hinted at the need for a congressional investigation of TVA. While indicating his accord with the agency's program and aims as set forth by the president, he went on to comment:

> The program can't be properly carried out until it is placed in the hands of people who deal fairly with the public, and who have some comprehensive idea of the difficulties of the people who are being moved out of their homes in the flooded area.[71]

A close friend of Cordell Hull and a protégé of Senator McKellar, Cooper was intensely aware of the fact that aside from Harcourt Morgan's assistant, Neil Bass, he was the only Tennessean high in the TVA organization. "Mr. Lilienthal's interest in Tennessee is evidenced by the fact that there has not been a single Tennessean employed in an important capacity in this organization except Bass and myself."[72] But Cooper seems to have reserved some of his bitterest remarks on the theme that TVA was not acting in the best interests of the people: "I told him [Lilienthal] my idea was to build up that department and establish friendly relations with the people within the area. . . ."[73] Cooper felt that the agency's treatment of him was in a sense symbolic of the agency's move away from life at the grass roots of the Norris Basin.

The fact that Cooper was an important Tennessean and one of the luminaries in the state Democratic establishment meant that there would be bitter reactions from the Tennessee delegation in Congress. The most significant of these came from Senator McKellar, long a proponent of the use of political patronage in the agency's employment structure. McKellar found it particularly galling to hear of Cooper's plight, since "he was one of the very few men from Tennessee that you gentlemen have put on." He found it objectionable that John I. Snyder was from New York and initially came to TVA at considerably less than the salary he would receive as head of land acquisition. Of Snyder, McKellar remarked that while his title was officially and nominally different from that previously accorded Cooper, he was, in reality, superseding Cooper:

> It just does not seem to me that that is fair. I cannot imagine what a New York lawyer would know about the land values and people he has to deal with in the Cove Creek section. . . . To increase the salary fifty percent in six months seems to be a wonderful increase in salary.[74]

The state's attorney general, Roy M. Beeler, and former Governor A. H. Roberts sent letters and telegrams of protest. The latter's telegram to Senator McKellar asking that he do what he could for Cooper concluded: "Think it would be a great mistake to yankeeize TVA."[75]

Lilienthal's own comment on the resignation was that Cooper's job was in no way affected by a move which simply aimed at coordinating land buying with various other activities of the agency. Lilienthal also deplored the fact that TVA's enemies could use Cooper's resignation and criticisms as a means to obstruct and defeat a large TVA appropriations bill then pending in Congress.[76] Benton Stong, editor of the *Knoxville News-Sentinel*, felt that Cooper's resignation would aid the power interests in their fight against TVA as well as work to defeat TVA's congressional appropriation of $48 million.[77] Stong's contention may be borne out by one of the telegrams among the many which Senator McKellar received: "Understand Tennessee Valley Authority has dispensed with services of James W. Cooper as attorney stop we are deeply interested in Mr. Cooper and trust you will use every effort to have him reinstated." This came from the commissioners of the Tennessee Railroad and Public Utilities Commission, which had recently come into conflict with Lilienthal over rate reductions for domestic consumers of the Tennessee Electric Power Company.[78] If James Cooper had truly hoped for vindication at the hands of a congressional investigation, he was to be disappointed. Despite support from the Tennessee congressional delegation, an investigation never materialized, and within a short time the incident was forgotten.

The allegations and counterallegations surrounding James Cooper's resignation, with their aura of Byzantine politics, are difficult to evaluate. Dissension and conflict among the board members would of necessity cause comparable dissension among the component parts of the agency's organization, creating a situation accounting for much conflict in the early years of the Tennessee Valley Authority. Clearly, there is evidence of this in the Cooper controversy. What must also be considered is the simultaneous early tasks of the TVA—buying land, beginning construction, and assembling an administration. Each of these would be formidable in their own right but when TVA had to do all together, confusion was only compounded. The Cooper case graphically illustrates this. In light of the rather uneven development of land acquisition policy, its relative slowness with respect to construction demands, and the public outcry against land purchases expressed in various petitions, it is not surprising that a rationalization of the acquisition process would have to be undertaken. Hence there developed Snyder's investigation and the reorganization under his charge of all land acquisition. But while all this is understandable and rationally explicable, there remains the fact that for nearly a year TVA had carried out a policy which in many respects was inefficient, especially in the absence of a workable resettlement program to aid the dispossessed people of the Norris Basin.

The objections of Senator McKellar and others to Cooper's treatment by TVA may have had some validity. Cooper had had extensive experience in purchasing land for the Great Smoky Mountains National Park, an area in many respects comparable to the Norris Basin, and he knew intuitively the type of people that he was dealing with. His claim that the population from whom the land was purchased expected to be able to negotiate was in many respects correct. "Bargaining" was almost a psychological and social necessity among these rather fiercely independent communities, and the people could be expected to condemn, to a degree, a policy which allowed them no recourse but the courts to adjudicate appraisal prices.[79] In sum, the lengthy Cooper controversy, his subsequent resignation, and the amount of publicity which it produced do illustrate certain shortcomings in land acquisition, not all of which were Cooper's fault. The lack of a resettlement program, the onus placed upon bargaining, and the failure of concerted measures to educate the population of the Norris Basin about the land purchase and removal program all point to the fact that the policy could have been much improved in several areas.[80]

It would seem that Cooper's behavior in office, the complaints he made against the revised mode of land acquisition's mass purchase, and the public charges against him reveal the difficulties of the land acquisition program at the grass roots. Perhaps all this Cooper controversy suggests that while it would be desirable to have participatory grass-roots democracy within federal agencies, it is not always feasible or possible. And TVA's initial experience with General Cooper and land acquisition in the Norris Basin may well bear this out.

But the debates over land acquisition also reveal the linkages between acquisition and relocation, and the fact that there existed no administrative structure for relocation that could operate simultaneously with the purchase of land—a structure that was desperately needed and which should have been constituted even before land purchase began. The degree to which administrative squabbles over purchase procedure masked this lack is obscure. What is certain is that agreement over relocation policies was as difficult to arrive at in the early years as agreement on land acquisition and, for those at the grass roots, more consequential.

5 Planning for the People

IF TVA's acquisition of thousands of acres of land represented a firm commitment to carry out the more specific provisions of the 1933 legislation, the Authority's policy of removal and resettlement of families in the Norris Basin provided something of a microsomic testing ground for one of the Tennessee Valley Authority's larger goals, articulated by Franklin Roosevelt in 1940: "to raise the standards of life by increasing social and economic advantages in a given area."

EARLY RESETTLEMENT CONCEPTS IN TVA

In the chaotic first year of the Authority's existence, no substantial program was developed to meet the needs of the farm families displaced from the Norris Basin despite the fact that obtaining land through purchase and condemnation proceeded at a regular if fairly slow pace throughout much of the year. It was not until nearly a year had elapsed that the Authority established any kind of substantive program to aid the process of relocation and resettlement.[1] The delay in constructing administrative machinery to resolve difficulties among the displaced families appears to have been occasioned by a lack of decisiveness in working out plans and details rather than a lack of concern for the removed families. To be perfectly fair, one must consider the fact that the alternative methods of approaching the problem of resettlement presented themselves in a bewildering variety in this, the first year of the Authority's existence, amid the confusion of building a large and complex organization faced with a number of immediate priorities. Not the least of these was that land had to be purchased before construction could begin, and upon construction hinged the opening of new employment opportunities. The immediate need for the purchase of land and construction of the dam pushed the displacement of families well ahead of the Authority's ability to develop a comprehensive program of resettlement.

A brief look at some of TVA's resettlement concepts in 1933 gives an idea of the complexity involved in solving what appeared, on the face of things, to be a relatively simple problem. Much of the initial effort came from Chairman A. E. Morgan, some of it in the days before the board reorganization of August 1933, when the chairman was trying to cope with a multitude of problems and would, in fact, incur the displeasure of his co-directors for going off in all too many directions and proposing more programs than could be effectively promulgated. It was not the best of times to attempt to initiate a program of population removal and resettlement, even if such a program was sorely needed.

In July 1933 A. E. Morgan anticipated that as much as $2.5 million in federal funds would soon be made available for the building of subsistence homesteads in the TVA region. In a memorandum on the subject, he commented that expenditure for subsistence homesteads would be justified "on the grounds that only in the Tennessee Valley area will this work be part of a general plan for an economic and social program." Anticipating the establishment of homestead colonies by the spring of 1934, Morgan thought feasible the creation of a separate staff and a director to locate large landholdings "in and near" the Tennessee Valley region and to engage tentatively in the purchase of land suitable for subsistence homesteads if the price was sufficiently low. The chairman concluded with a vision of subsistence homesteads—one that was to be reiterated in literally dozens of his speeches and addresses:

> To carry out this policy properly we need a general program which we will not have time to develop fully. It may be that several subsistence units should be parts of a larger community with a single water supply, etc. The location should be suitable for small industries. If a body of virgin timber were part of the holding the communities might revolve around wood product industries.[2]

Following his rather brief memorandum of the subsistence

homestead program, Chairman Morgan made a draft proposal concerning resettlement on August 15, 1933. Making reference to the rural families which were being displaced by the National Land Use Program, Morgan pointed to the need for agencies to aid in the relocation of families displaced by federal projects. "The need for such an agency," he wrote, "is especially acute in the Tennessee Valley, where several thousand rural farm families are at the present time in the process of removal from the impounded areas above the power dam sites." Morgan proposed that such an agency, created under the aegis of TVA, have as its express purpose to assist "these people in the selection of desirable areas, in financing the purchase of more productive land, and in facilitating their readjustment to new conditions on a permanent basis." While Morgan pursued the idea of a TVA subsistence homestead program (the federal subsistence homesteads program was not actually organized under M. L. Wilson until August 23, 1933), he also mentioned four specific agencies which could be utilized by TVA as part of its resettlement program: the Agricultural Extension Service, the Reconstruction Finance Corporation (RFC), the Farm Credit Administration (FCA), and the Federal Emergency Relief Administration (FERA).[3]

Morgan was acutely aware of the problems involved in providing for some program of resettlement, especially for tenants who possessed "little more than household goods" and who would receive no money from the Authority with which to buy lands for resettlement. Even for those who received money from land that they owned, the problem of relieving distress would be present, since relocation was made precarious by the "relative scarcity of productive lands," soil type variation, and real estate speculation.[4] Consequently he felt that any resettlement plans should be "correlated" to regional planning programs within the Tennessee Valley Authority.

Morgan hoped to create within TVA a land corporation with a "revolving fund" to acquire title to lands available for resettlement.[5] The corporation's funds were to provide advances to qualified individuals (those who were "good moral risks") for Farm Credit loans.[6] The RFC, FCA, and the FERA were to be the major participants in the funding of the proposed corporation in the following manner: TVA would advance $100,000, the RFC $900,000, and the FERA would contribute through its Federal Surplus Relief Corporation. The latter would advance "that proportion of $500,000 which it will expend in the purchase of sub-marginal land." It was planned that the money received by owners of submarginal land purchased by the Surplus Relief Corporation would not go to them individually but would be funneled into the proposed TVA land corporation. The sellers of submarginal land would be asked to agree that the money "may be used by the corporation in relocating them." This money would be added to a revolving fund created by TVA and the RFC, the aggregate used "to finance those persons selling out to the Federal Surplus Relief Corporation who are eligible for Farm Credit loans." To that point, landowners would be the major beneficiaries of the proposed corporation. But what of those who owned no land, or what if owners were paid too little for their land? TVA proposed that the revolving fund "should be supplemented to the extent of approximately $1,500 for each person of this class." This sum was intended to enable tenants to qualify for a Farm Credit loan. At the end of a ten-year period, $500 was to be paid back on the basis of a reappraisal and refinancing of the mortgage by the FCA, with the remaining $1,000 considered as a "frozen investment amortized during the next twenty-six years."[7]

As TVA began to purchase land for the dam, other plans for resettlement circulated within the agency. One such idea was provided by General James Cooper, whose role in land acquisition has already been described. Cooper strongly urged the establishment of what he termed a "replacement bureau" and argued that such a bureau could take the money that TVA paid the owner for his land and use it for the purchase of land in large enough parcels to establish "model villages" for ten to twelve families. Cooper felt that such a bureau would establish good will for TVA among the inhabitants of the Norris Basin and would make the purchase of land easier. Since the bureau would funnel purchase money back into a fund to buy land for homesteads, he asserted that the arrangement would "prevent money from being turned over to people who are not accustomed to using it and who will, almost inevitably, in perhaps a majority of cases, dispose of it unwisely, and be left a charge on the community."[8] Although it was possibly a workable alternative, Cooper's proposal died when he resigned.

In the meantime, nothing came of Morgan's proposal for a land corporation in conjunction with the RFC, FCA, and FERA, although something similar to it would be brought up again in 1934. As a purely interim measure, the chairman suggested in September 1933 the creation of a small temporary bureau which would gather, by means of a census, information about the relocation desires of the removed families. After processing the information, the bureau would compile lists of available farms within the area, along with prices and details of sales terms. With this information in hand, Morgan hoped that the owners would be better able to relocate themselves upon removal. The chairman proposed that this small service be kept apart from any land acquisition procedures in TVA and that it be placed in the hands of his co-director, Harcourt Morgan. While the temporary nature of this organization was stressed, suggestions for a more permanent resolution of the resettlement question continued to be formulated.[9] Ironically, this interim proposal was destined to become the nucleus of the only permanent plan for the resettlement of removed families until the establishment of the Family Removal Section on August 1, 1935. Morgan's proposal contained in embryonic form what later became the Relocation Service, formed in 1934 by a contract between the Agricultural Extension Division of the University of Tennessee and the Tennessee Valley Authority (hereafter it is referred to as Extension Relocation Service).

Robert Sessions, a TVA attorney, formulated in February 1934 a plan similar to but not as detailed as A. E. Morgan's suggested loan and mortgage corporation. Though the plan was never adopted, the prefatory remarks in Session's proposal are informative. Linking the whole TVA policy of raising farm standards of living and purchasing power to the issue of population removal at Norris, Sessions argued that some firm arrangement had to be made to get farmers off unproductive land and to assure that they not be resettled on submarginal land. Sessions warned that policies must be formulated early in the TVA's program:

> This problem, moreover, will recur as soon as, and to the extent that, the Authority formulates the policies of the Act with the reference to the construction of other dams, reforestation, the attack on

soil erosion, and regional land planning generally. Moreover, there is an obvious correlation between these phases of the policy of the TVA and the broader policies of the Administration with reference to the retirement of marginal and sub-marginal land. . . .[10]

In the early months of 1934, Morgan again assessed the resettlement issue in a lengthy memorandum which examined the means by which land could be obtained by TVA or some agency under TVA's direction. Morgan, overly solicitous toward the owners who were being displaced by the Authority, revealed his paternalistic attitudes in his remark that whatever arrangements were to be made, it was preferable that there be "no actual transfer of funds [money received by the owners from TVA] into the hands of the landowner." The chairman had an intense dislike of land speculators, whom he literally saw "in the field waiting to grasp the funds of the landowners as soon as they are paid off." He knew of the speculation that had taken place during the development of Muscle Shoals and, believing that speculation inevitably followed large bloc purchases under eminent domain, was determined that the TVA would not contribute, even unwittingly, to such practices.[11]

Morgan's memorandum examined five different modes through which financing land purchases for resettlement purposes could be made: the Subsistence Homesteads Division (of the Department of the Interior); the creation of a mortgage loan corporation under the National Recovery Administration (NRA) which would qualify for Reconstruction Finance Corporation loans; funds channeled from the RFC into the Electric Home and Farm Authority or the Tennessee Valley Authority Cooperatives (TVAC); direct operation under the TVA Act with TVA funds; or a loan from the Public Works Administration to the Tennessee Valley Authority.[12]

A. E. Morgan remained impressed with the subsistence homestead idea and made specific reference to a project in Georgia which, he wrote, "is most interesting for our purposes." He was attracted to the project by virtue of the low interest rates for twenty-year mortgages that enabled farmers to purchase homesteads with little or no down payment.[13] Morgan pointed out that the difficulties involved in the TVA's duplication of the Georgia subsistence homestead project were numerous. While the

Subsistence Homesteads Division had some attractive features for cooperative ventures with the Authority, the most notable being that there was no limitation on the location of their projects, cooperation with it would entail incorporation by the TVA of the "ideas and principles" of the division, and TVA "might not be able to go this far in relocation work." Other disadvantages that were discussed were the allocation of control into the hands of the Subsistence Homesteads Division and the possible lack of funds. The preference set forth in the memorandum was that the Subsistence Homesteads Division lend the money directly to TVA to use as it desired, but it was thought very unlikely that the division would consent to such an operation.[14]

There were special difficulties with the creation of a mortgage loan corporation which qualified for loans from the Reconstruction Finance Corporation. Especially notable was the difficulty in justifying such a corporation under the interpretation of section 1 of the National Industrial Recovery Act. It was suggested, however, that if a sufficient number of landowners would agree to pay the money received from TVA through the sale of their lands into a corporation, that corporation could use those funds as capital against which the RFC could make loans. As a further selling point, it was also argued that the Electric Home and Farm Administration had already gained acceptance from the RFC as a mortgage loan corporation, although it was correctly pointed out that an agency to aid in the purchase of home electrification devices was a far cry from a farm mortgage corporation. But the TVAC was a different matter. Funded by the Federal Emergency Relief Administration to aid in the development of farmers' cooperatives, it could be expanded "into more of an ordinary mortgage loan company" if Harry Hopkins, its director, agreed to it. This was considered a good possibility, since "it would dispense with the additional expense and trouble of forming a new corporation as well as the possible unfavorable criticism against the formation of numerous subsidiary corporations."[15]

The most significant feature of the 1934 memorandum of assessment on relocation pertained to the idea of a resettlement program funded and operated by TVA. Its significance lay in making an implicit correlation between resettlement and the intention of the TVA Act. On a number of grounds it was stated that resettlement as a TVA project was legally justified by the legislation empowering the Authority. Since the TVA Act contained provision for reforestation and the "proper use of marginal lands," the act was seen to justify the removal and resettlement of those who had lived on such lands and were being displaced by TVA. Section 4(h) of the act, which empowered TVA to purchase or acquire real estate to accomplish the purpose of the act, was deemed to provide for resettlement, and the power to convey title might be derived from, and be incidental to TVA's construction of dams:

> While apparently such relocation work has not been taken in connection with any previous purchase and condemnation of lands by the government or any other public body, such work would not seem much less incidental to the building of the dam than is the construction of a town for workers at the dam (Norris).[16]

More tellingly, it was pointed out that the general tone of the act, and Roosevelt's interpretation of it suggest "that the TVA will consider the general welfare of the citizens of the Valley Area in carrying out the physical and engineering projects of the Act."[17] The latter consideration would require the formulation of a concrete relocation plan.

An examination of alternative paths to the resolution of the population removal and resettlement question indicated that while each solution presented obstacles, the Authority could quite probably find ways to overcome them if it was willing to shoulder the added task of resettlement. More importantly, the memorandum suggested that the TVA Act itself contained ample justification for undertaking a permanent resettlement program.

Certainly one major obstacle to the many proposed options was the possibility of conflict between TVA and other government agencies, a problem which could render difficult the implementation of interagency cooperation for resettlement. In and about the TVA region were many operating programs of government agencies. Cumberland Homesteads, a project of the Subsistence Homesteads Division, was in nearby Crossville, Tennessee. The Forestry Service was considering purchase of extensive forest tracts in the TVA region to put them under public management, and the Surplus Relief Corporation of the FERA had made inquiries regarding submarginal land purchases within the Tennessee Valley. TVA was also the recipient of federal funds from FERA to the Tennessee Valley Authority Cooperatives as well as funds from the Civil Works Administration (CWA).[18]

RELOCATION ALTERNATIVES

Earle Draper, the division head of land planning and housing within TVA, was greatly concerned that rehabilitation activities might be undertaken in the Tennessee Valley by other agencies without making coordinating plans with TVA. Draper felt that if agencies were allowed to develop uncoordinated plans, TVA's ability to develop social and economic improvement in the valley would be impaired. He suggested that perhaps TVA could become the coordinator of federal agencies doing rehabilitation work in the valley, becoming the director of such work.[19] Draper's concept of planning would undoubtedly have committed TVA to some extensive resettlement work for the social and economic improvement of displaced persons. Although Draper was enthusiastic about his concepts, others were not, especially the agriculturalists, whose chief spokesman was Harcourt Morgan.

In October of the previous year Morgan had candidly argued for limitations on the planning functions of TVA. He was convinced that the Authority should keep rigorously within the letter of section 22 of the TVA Act and conduct planning only through duly constituted state agencies. He felt that the agency should not undertake such plans independently. "Where no existing Valley Agency is available or can be set up, and only then, the Authority will set up an organization to develop studies, surveys, and plans." Harcourt Morgan's interpretation of TVA as a grass-roots agency was that it cooperate primarily with state and private universities, state colleges of agriculture, their research experimental stations and agricultural extension divisions, state departments of agriculture, and state farm bureau organizations.[20]

CREATION OF A RELOCATION SERVICE

The sort of policy deviation between planners and agriculturalists which was evolving between 1933 and 1934 was to have some repercussions, especially since in those months Harcourt Morgan's influence was rising within the internal administration as A. E. Morgan's declined. This would, however, become more apparent later when open breaks among the directors occurred.[21] Insofar as resettlement of displaced farm families was concerned, however, it was Chairman Morgan's proposal for a small interim "service organization to help landowners" which first bore fruit. Harcourt Morgan had seen and approved the chairman's draft proposal and had offered his help in the implementation of it, his suggestion being to incorporate the plan in conjunction with the Agricultural Extension Service at the University of Tennessee. He instructed his administrative assistant, Neil Bass, to have the director of TVA's Agricultural Division, J. C. McAmis, draw up suggestions for such an incorporation.[22] This directive was given at the time of Chairman Morgan's initial suggestion (September 1933) but was not acted upon until the spring of 1934. McAmis initially responded to his charge in a manner which reflected many of the ideas generated by A. E. Morgan and the planners. But it was precisely these items which would later be deleted from the final proposal. McAmis pointed out that while the least productive tracts were generally small, the most productive lands were held in large tracts and were usually heavily mortgaged. In addition, while owners often resided on the unproductive lands, large productive tracts were often farmed for absentee owners. Helping owners move from least productive to more desirable lands, argued McAmis, could best be accomplished through group purchase of large tracts which could then be farmed individually or cooperatively. "It will be to the advantage of individuals if a large number of them can purchase and develop adjoining tracts into an *organized, planned community*, provided the area can be kept free of land speculation." McAmis supported Chairman Arthur Morgan's earlier notion of a financing agency equipped with revolving funds to "option, purchase, sell, or exchange lands" and to loan money at the same rate[23] of interest as the FCA. McAmis proposed that TVA sponsor such a corporation.

The concrete project request which McAmis eventually drafted, however, did not in any sense incorporate the concept of group purchase, communal farms, or planned communities. On the contrary, such plans were conspicuously absent. Rather, the proposal reflected the conservative position of Harcourt Morgan on planning in TVA. What it did propose for displaced farmers was rather minimal:

> a systematic program of study and instruction to enable them to choose the most favorable locations; to protect them from the dangers of land speculation and unsound investment; to assist farm families to find new locations and adjust their plans of home and farm management to their new conditions.

The modesty of the effort may be inferred from the project's 1934 cost estimate, roughly $8,000. McAmis's proposal for a relocation service fulfilled the administrative intent of Harcourt Morgan, since in its operation it was to be staffed and run by the University of Tennessee Agricultural Extension Division. A contract was to be drawn up between TVA and the Agricultural Extension Division to provide for surveys or censuses of families to be displaced and to help them formulate relocation plans by providing them with lists of available real estate. Extension agents were then to accompany prospective buyers on trips to available sites, with transportation furnished by the Authority. The proposal provided for a "follow-up" of relocated families and the rendering of assistance from the Farm Credit Administration in appraisal and financing for "qualified persons."[24]

Although the project title mentioned owner *and* tenant relocation, it was clear from the procedure that the aim of the plan was to relocate owners who could purchase new lands. Certainly the choices open to poor landowners and tenants in terms of buying new lands and obtaining FCA credit were slight. The minimal activities charged to the relocation service were severely criticized by Earle Draper and others of the Land Planning and Housing Division.

Draper continued in numerous letters to Chairman Morgan to foster the relocation concept as it related to resettlement communities. He specifically cited "as comparable to our situation" (at Norris) the development of homestead colonies for the resettlement of owners and tenants displaced by purchases in Virginia and by the Shenandoah National Park land acquisition, which he praised as a reversal of earlier National Park Service land purchase policy in the Smoky Mountains—a policy of "paying money for land without any attempt to assist those who sold their property." Land purchases at Norris dictated, thought Draper, an urgency to develop policy: "It seems to me that no time should be lost if we are going to work out the basis of subsistence [homesteads]."[25]

The limited aspects of the relocation proposal approved by Harcourt Morgan were also criticized by Tracy Augur in the regional planning section of Draper's Land Planning and Housing Division.[26] Augur felt that the McAmis proposal was "one merely of guidance and protection from unscrupulous land salesmen." It was the static nature of that proposal that Augur most objected to. As he saw it:

> . . . no attempt is made to secure a better population pattern than now exists, or to furnish a more stable economic base than is given by the practice of Agriculture. While the project is undoubtedly a worthwhile one it strikes me as being purely negative in character, that is, it protects the people from exploitation but offers them no improvement in their social or economic status to compensate for leaving their old haunts and habits.[27]

Augur felt that resettlement must be accomplished in planned "community groupings" which would allow services to be rendered to people in ways that would be impossible if they were scattered in isolated tracts. Augur felt that modern standards of life required access to educational and economic services which could not be obtained by populations scattered over the area. He further argued that this was a particularly acute problem in light of the fact that in East Tennessee families must not continue to exist on a "purely agricultural basis" and must be so placed as to take advantage of other forms of employment. "In other words, a population pattern which distributes families over the Valley merely on the basis of available agricultural land does not at all fit into the modern picture, and leaves the people defeated by forces which they cannot influence and control, and which are too involved even to be properly understood."[28]

Augur was particularly struck by the absurdity of collecting enormous amounts of socioeconomic data from families to be relocated in the absence of a well-developed regional plan which would have to serve as a frame for the data, which the project lacked in content and goals. Plans should not, Augur asserted, be made "as an incident to the process of removal." He believed that plans should be made beforehand and presented as a definite offer acceptable to removed families which "also satisfies the purpose of the authority to give them an opportunity which is genuinely better than that which they now enjoy." Augur's conclusion on McAmis's plan for the Relocation Service summed up the difficulties inherent in interpeting the whole function of TVA with regard to planning, resettlement, improvement of the quality of life, obligation, and aim:

> while admitting that this project probably more than fulfills the obligation of TVA to conduct its business relations with fairness, it does not at all fulfill the Authority's opportunity to improve the status of those with whom its work has brought it into direct contact. In fact, it tends to perpetuate a condition which is admittedly bad, and which it is one of the Authority's functions to improve.[29]

The planner's criticisms were brushed aside, however, and McAmis's project was implemented through a contract between TVA and the University of Tennessee Agricultural Extension Division May 1, 1934, thus creating the Extension Relocation Service. This office began work in the late summer and early fall of 1934 by collecting detailed socioeconomic data from the families who were to be removed.

The debate and criticism which surrounded the establishment of the Extension Relocation Service continued. It had served to refine everyone's ideas toward resettlement, but at the same time it had raised issues which continued to divide the agriculturists and planners. It is interesting that the data gathered from removal families in the survey conducted by the Extension Relocation Service provided more hard facts upon which to base resettlement options. In the fall of 1934, the first of many tabulations of the relocation census was released: T. Levron Howard's analysis of the tenant families of the Norris flowage. As a member of the economic section of the Land Planning and Housing Division, Howard's study received immediate attention from the planners, especially as they concentrated their efforts toward the tenantry and toward those owners who were literally mortgaged up to the hilt or who held unproductive land. The situation was summed up rather well by one of the planners who wrote to his chief:

> any attempt to set up a colonization scheme with families that have cash will either force us into a strictly NRA project with attendant high costs, or into a project that will arouse private and union interest because it will compete with them at every turn. Families on relief, on the other hand, constitute no potential market for profit-making goods and should be free to combine in any kind of effort to better their lot. This means that a cooperative enterprise of some sort with attendant reductions in the amount of cash needed to finance the project would be possible. The precedent has been set by rehabilitation projects and some of the subsistence homestead schemes.

The memorandum concluded that the tenants as a class were not accustomed to making decisions and would have to be "carefully directed" in whatever scheme of resettlement was chosen.[30]

RELOCATION RESPONSIBILITIES AND TENANT RESETTLEMENT

Conflicting attitudes toward resettlement continued, with the disagreements becoming more pointed as removal deadlines came nearer. The continued circulation of Levron Howard's study of the Norris tenantry also had its effect. John I. Snyder, now in charge of land acquisition, took the view that TVA's business was the continued purchase of land to meet the deadlines of construction (by March 1, 1935, all families below the 870-foot contour were to be removed), a process that should not be delayed:

> It is the very necessity of their [the tenants] having to go which will make them find their own solution to their difficulties. I believe that the Authority should interest the proper federal agency which has charge of this type of work and ask them to handle the situation. The foregoing may not seem as humane as many of the ideas I have heard expressed in this organization, but I think that in the long run it will be the most helpful thing we can do.[31]

In the ensuing months, as the deadlines for removal approached and the plight of the displaced tenants became clearer, the discussion over resettlement escalated, and the ensuing debate brought

TVA's legal experts fully onto the scene. In January 1935, Tracy Augur, who was the branch chief of regional and town planning in the Division of Land Planning and Housing, issued the opening salvo in the debate. He approached Floyd Reeves, one of A. E. Morgan's men in personnel, with a scheme for tenant resettlement. Reeves, one of the ablest and most foresighted men in the A. E. Morgan entourage, had made the training and employment procedures of the Authority a model for contemporaries. He was a likely person to promote the scheme Augur had in mind.[32]

What Augur proposed to Reeves was the selection of removed families who desired "colonization." These families would then be placed in a training program to fit them for colony membership: "The men might be making furniture and farm implements for their new homes, the women work on other house furnishings, and all receive some instruction on modern farming and housekeeping methods." When instruction got far enough along, Augur proposed that work begin on the homes. He proposed that the "colony" be temporarily housed in a CCC camp, and that the cost of training and housing be borne by TVA, who would "have these people on its hands in any case."[33] It should be kept in mind that the proposal for colonization and training in the CCC camps at TVA expense was intended for tenant families and not for all the removed families who desired it. The planners in TVA were acutely aware of the plight of the tenant, who received no compensation of any kind for removal. Tenants constituted the major part (though certainly not all) of the families classed as "in need of assistance in relocating," as was made manifest in a new supplemental report to Levron Howard's initial study of Extension Relocation Service data.[34]

While it was the planners who were most aware of the agency's organization of the need to extend aid to relocated families and who were the supporters of the most advanced notions of resettlement, they were also consciously aware of relocation as social experimentation. In this light their remarks are revealing. The standards of physical environment of the tenant families in the Norris Basin, wrote planner Carrol Towne, were far below minimum American and English standards: the utilities practically nonexistent, and the springs, which most used for water, would probably be con-

demned by health authorities. "Existing conditions with respect to
toilet facilities are astoundingly poor, and the question therefore
seems to be [whether it] will be possible to condition these people
to anything more elaborate or modern than a privy installation."
The logic of his argument appeared to have been that since they
had been so deprived, the tenants might not be able to get used to
much more than minimal improvement. He therefore opposed the
idea of construction designed to make permanent dwellings (at this
point the town of Norris was still seen as a possible relocation
project) and reduce maintenance costs: "a low first cost coupled
with more careful maintenance would be a better solution."

Towne, like many of TVA's planners, wondered if the characteristic extreme individualism attributed to the local residents was due
mainly to isolation. "This is a condition and not a characteristic, and
in many cases may be forced rather than desired. If this is true, no
one can judge without experiment what the results will be if these
people are forced into a close-knit colony.[35] Draper himself maintained that such a project "might give tenant farmers [more of] a
chance to advance and make something of themselves than they
will have with their own plans for relocation; and on our part a
chance to show what might be done in such a community, as
perhaps a demonstration might be valuable to the country in connection with submarginal land projects and movement of farm
families from poor to better areas."[36]

Despite the guarded optimism of the planners that the project
for the relocation of tenants was feasible, it was about to drift onto
legalistic shoals and be abandoned. The scheme of tenant resettlement had been widely circulated and eventually was taken up in
discussions between TVA's lawyers and Lawrence L. Durisch, Levron Howard, and J. Ed Campbell of the social and economic section of the Land Planning and Housing Division. The lawyers
responded to the planners and economists with a strict interpretation of the TVA Act. It is somewhat fascinating that the Authority's
legal minds, so innovative and energetic in the struggles with the
power companies, were so timid in the face of social reform.

The Legal Division examined the TVA Act under a number of
points to determine whether the Authority could legally use its
funds for a resettlement scheme of the type contemplated. First

the lawyers argued that TVA was obligated under section 26 of the act to pay in condemnation proceedings "the value of the said property sought to be condemned" and no more, thus excluding tenants from receiving remuneration from TVA; and further, if justification were to be sought, it would have to be found elsewhere in the Act.[37]

The logical place to justify the expenditure for tenant resettlement would be in the very broad "planning" apparatus of section 22 of the act, which allowed for surveys, general plans, experiments, and demonstrations such as

> may be useful to Congress and to the several states in guiding and controlling the extent, sequence, and nature of development that may be equitably and economically advanced through the expenditure of public funds, or through the guidance or control of public authority, all for the general purpose of fostering the orderly and proper physical, economic, and social development of said area.

In the letter cited, only the first portion of section 22 was quoted, ending with "expenditure of public funds," and there was no mention at all made of section 23, which directed the president to recommend legislation to Congress, as needed, to carry out the purpose of the preceding section (22), which was specifically to include the "economic and social well-being of the people living in the said river basin."

Lawyers for the Authority argued that "no matter how laudable, from a humanitarian standpoint," there was no justification for the tenant resettlement project as anything but a "temporary expedient," which would certainly differentiate it from any type of planning project which might be "useful to the Congress or to the several state legislatures."

The Extension Relocation Service had been funded two times since its inception under section 3(g) of the act, which conferred upon TVA "such powers as may be necessary or appropriate for the exercise of the powers herein specifically conferred upon the corporation." But to extend these incidental powers for the expenditure for the proposed project would be erroneous, claimed the lawyers, because incidental powers could not "be construed broadly enough to nullify or override the limitation imposed in connection with powers specifically granted." In other words, an examination of planning sections necessitated a legal retreat to the initial limitations of section 26 of the TVA Act. This somewhat tautological exercise was followed by the advice to seek federal and state agency support to resolve the issue of the tenants.

The purely legal arguments were then followed by some stuffy pronouncements which have a Spenserian ring to them. Considering the certainty of future population removal as work on other dams progressed, it was held that TVA should not commit itself to "gratuitous aid" to needy families because it would "create a dangerous precedent," which would "stultify the initiative of other families" who would claim that they, too, must be so aided. Once the Authority committed itself to such aid it would "be exceedingly difficult to persuade them to separate themselves from such bounty." The lawyers, through the process of some rather tortuous logic, were convinced that the Extension Relocation Service to landowners fulfilled "morally and legally" any obligation on the part of TVA to removed populations and that there was little if any justification for the expenditure of Authority funds on such projects as had been proposed by the planners.[38] This view was more strongly stated by the general solicitor of TVA, James Lawrence Fly, who wrote to Levron Howard that in his (Fly's) opinion there was "no authorization for the expenditure of the Authority's funds for or upon such a project."[39]

Arthur Morgan had written a strongly supportive memorandum on the proposed tenant relocation project to the general solicitor of TVA, arguing that it was the obligation of TVA "to provide shelter and care for the destitute, exposed, and homeless people during the emergency period and pending readjustment." Even with this wording of the proposal, responded Fly, the problem was still one for the regular relief agencies, and "it would seem to this extent that the authority is in danger of being turned into a relief and charitable agency, and of course we cannot construe the statute to have such a meaning." Fly thought that for TVA to open itself to such action, the agency would make both people and relief agencies dependent upon it, and that the latter should be served notice that TVA was not going to do their work for them. He concurred in A. E. Morgan's "humane considerations" but adamantly refused

TVA such a proposed role unless the regular organizations outside TVA failed, and then only on an emergency basis.[40]

RESETTLEMENT AND INTERAGENCY COORDINATION

TVA's Coordination Division undertook to follow the advice of the Legal Division in the matter of resettlement, and to this end coordinator C. W. Farrier went to Washington to confer with the assistant FERA administrator and specifically suggest the possibility of purchase of land and resettlement of families under FERA auspices. Farrier was referred to Judge Barton Brown, the TERA director in Nashville, to explore the feasibility of such plans.[41] At the end of March 1935, Judge Brown had conferred with TVA representatives and agreed to consider the subject.

One serious problem in the provision of federal and state relief for families displaced by TVA was that the local and national relief scene kept rapidly shifting. No sooner had Farrier, TVA's liaison with relief agencies, approached FERA-TERA about resettlement than Public Resolution 11 of the Seventy-fourth Congress was passed (April 8, 1935), removing FERA and TERA from the resettlement field and allocating their duties to the Works Progress Administration (WPA). This resolution, known as the Emergency Relief Appropriation Act, authorized funds under the act for making loans to farmers, farm laborers, tenants, and sharecroppers for the purpose of buying land, with the stipulation that the loans were then to be paid back on a long-term basis. Accordingly, Farrier was instructed by A. E. Morgan to request the Legal Division of TVA to draft an executive order for presentation to the president which would authorize TVA to proceed under provision of the Emergency Relief Appropriation Act with funds transferred to TVA's credit.[42]

Farrier pointed out to Fly that surveys made by the TERA before the Norris project was begun had already shown "a very large shortage" of houses and farms and that TVA's population displacement had "greatly increased" this shortage to the point that some subdivision of large farms into smaller units would have to be undertaken to provide 1,500 family units for the displaced families of the Norris Basin alone.[43] In contrast to Fly's attitude that TVA should not engage in resettlement work, Farrier urged that while the executive order should make clear that TVA did not want to collect the monies for the loans, it should "definitely provide" that TVA direct the resettlement work through its staff.[44]

No sooner was this move undertaken by TVA than in April and May a series of executive orders created the Resettlement Administration (RA) an agency which absorbed the functions and funds of the land programs of the FERA (Rural Rehabilitation Division), and the functions and funds of the Division of Subsistence Homesteads, Department of the Interior. Rexford Tugwell was appointed administrator of the Resettlement Administration, and TVA quickly arranged meetings with his acting assistant and appointed C. W. Farrier the formal liaison officer.[45]

Toward the end of June, Tugwell himself visited the TVA area and had discussions with TVA administrators on the problem of reservoir family displacement.

> Dr. Tugwell [wrote Farrier in his notes] gave oral assurance of the cooperation of the Resettlement Administration in the problems on the basis that while many of the people were not now on relief, unless assistance was given them they would go on relief because of being displaced from the Reservoir areas and being unable because of the congested farming conditions in the vicinity to obtain another farming location.[46]

The consolidation into the Resettlement Administration of parts of various federal agencies heretofore charged with resettlement programs made it simple for TVA to perform liaison work with respect to population removal. And Tugwell's assurances doubtless gave heart to critics of the Extension Relocation Service within the Authority who had observed inadequacies in its operations from the beginning. But TVA's major population removal program difficulties stemmed more from limitations imposed by construction deadlines and rising water than from the bureaucratic complications of other federal agencies. The target date for removal of families from the reservoir had been December 1, 1935, but by the end of summer of that year there were still more than 800 families remaining in the reservoir area. Clearly the removal service had reached its limits, and other steps remained to be taken.

FAMILY REMOVAL

During the summer of 1935 various propositions for the creation of a new unit to expedite family removal were discussed, and on September 1, 1935, the Reservoir Family Removal Section of the Coordination Division was organized and funded under the direction of W. G. Carnahan. One of the chief social caseworkers of the section, Marshall Wilson, recalled the steps leading to the establishment of the section:

> By mid-summer, 1935, it appeared that there were a great many families on land purchased or to be purchased, who could not be served by the Relocation Service because of their economic poverty, ill-reputation, mental and physical incompetency, or uncooperative attitude toward the program. A danger was also recognized in that a large number of families were living below the 940 feet contour and, due to the progress of dam erection, they were in danger of flood waters in the event of heavy rains. Consequently, the Family Removal Section . . . was established by the board of directors on September 1, 1935, to cope with these problems.[47]

The newly created section was charged with "removing families . . . by persuading those who have sufficient resources to move and by referring others to existing governmental organizations equipped to assist in the problem of removal." The new creation was budgeted at $40,785 for the year, the bulk of this sum absorbed by the salaries of the sixteen social caseworkers assigned to the section.[48] In the broadest sense of the word, the Reservoir Family Removal Section was a service organization existing to bring resources and individuals together in such a way as to solve the various problems of removal. The most valuable function which the new section would perform was the careful personal attention which it paid problem removal cases. The case files of the section make fascinating reading and attest to the precise and patient attempts made to enlist agencies, charities, church groups, and relatives to help with removal problems. The caseworkers were trained for two weeks and were described as "having previous social work, experience, and training" and being "familiar with rural people such as those in this area."[49]

It must be remembered that the Removal Section was not a

permanent or even temporary resettlement unit. The body was created not as the result of long-range planning but as an expedient afterthought to implement a removal process which had broken down through limitations in removal techniques as practiced by the Extension relocation service. Family removal was to effect immediately the removal from the reservoir of families still living there; to solve immediate, not long-range and intermediate-level, problems in relocation. Even with the work of both the Extension Relocation Service and the Removal Section, TVA still lacked a comprehensive plan to benefit tenants who would receive no money from land sales by their owners or owners who received so little that they could not relocate satisfactorily in something more than a temporary sense.

Social caseworkers of the Removal Section began their work vigorously, interviewing all families still living on land contracted for purchase by TVA. Families were classed according to their removal and relocation needs, and caseworkers attempted to explain fully to each family in detail "the intentions of the Authority in acquiring the land." Workers attempted to isolate the major factor preventing successful removal and relocation and to search for resources which would remove the problem and thus allow the family to leave the reservoir. Diagnosis and application of suitable action followed. In many cases no direct action was required, "the presence in the field of social case workers, and their patient explanation of the situation being itself a stimulation for family action. . . ." The latter point leaves some doubt as to the prior effectiveness of the TVA's public relations at the grass roots.[50]

A wide spectrum of services was rendered by the removal section, ranging from connecting families to federal, state, and local agencies to salvaging building materials from surrendered sites and trucking them to new locations. The caseworkers of the family removal unit provided invaluable aid in helping removed families locate prospective jobs, creating intercounty job transfers, establishing relief cases on new county rolls, and seeing to it that families were properly registered in new school districts.

Within the organizational framework of TVA, the Reservoir Family Removal Section functioned as a relocation services brokerage or clearinghouse, providing hundreds of examples of interdepartmental and intersectional cooperation. The ways in which such exchanges could affect a successful removal are numerous, but a typical case might involve the following TVA units in family relocation: Norris construction units for obtaining scrap lumber; reservoir clearance section for providing personal service contracts for the removal of property; engineering services to survey disputed property lines on new sites; Land Acquisition and Legal divisions to provide statements on the legal status of various tracts of land, land transfers, leasing rights, and so forth; and the Forestry Division for the provision of land for subsistence gardens and temporary leasing arrangements for grazing and croplands.

Beyond this inner circle of involvement, the Reservoir Family Removal Section worked with the Resettlement Administration through TVA's Extension Relocation Service and had direct liaisons with representatives of the Works Progress Administration, the U.S. Post Office, the Tennessee Welfare Commission, local school boards, charities, and church organizations. Throughout the process of removal of families from the Norris Basin, the section operated effectively at a grass-roots level, bringing together removal clients with friends, neighbors, and relatives willing to help. Marshall Wilson wrote later of this network of friends and relatives: "These were the greatest single resource available to needy families. Without their cooperation with removal workers, the accomplishment of this task would have been impossible."[51]

Matching the resources and capabilities of removal families to various kinds of available aid proved to be a difficult task. Marshall Wilson, a chief social caseworker with the Removal Section, drew upon his field experience to create in a memorandum to the section the classification of removal families under five headings which give a good synopsis of the situation. First were the families who had the resources to move and needed only "stimulation" by the section to effect their removal; second, families approved for Resettlement Administration aid under current guidelines; third, families who could move but needed TVA assistance in obtaining building material; fourth, those famiies with inadequate resources for removal; and fifth, those who could move but who refused to move. These last cases were turned over to the Legal Division, and even though in some cases forced evictions resulted, there were only five such cases among all the removed families.

The families of the fourth group, those with inadequate resources, were the most difficult and desperate cases. Wilson's memorandum said the group was made up of "economically marginal families, submarginal families, and a few socially undesirable families." The only way these could be helped was through the Resettlement Administration's purchase of land in the counties where the families then resided. They would receive temporary construction with building materials loaned by TVA either to individual families or to the resettlement agency; submarginal land through TVA's Forestry Division for crops or grazing; and transportation provided by TVA's Family Removal Section. Wilson admitted that such relocation was "but temporary and socially unsatisfactory,"[52] but time was pressing on. At the beginning of January, a month past the target date for removal of families from the reservoir area, 90 landowners and 133 tenant families still remained, many of them badly in need of some aid. The magnitude of the problem was increased when TVA decided to purchase the Central Peninsula, a rugged strip of land lying between the Clinch and Powell rivers composed of predominantly small farms. This land was purchased because it was cheaper for TVA to buy the land than to build access points to it. The purchase meant roughly 300 additional families to be removed from the reservoir area.

After conversations with R. W. Swatts, state representative of the Resettlement Administration, Carnahan wrote to Bruce Poundstone, regional chief of the Resettlement Administration, that of the families displaced by TVA's activity, "at least 800 definitely need resettlement aid," and that of the 538 families remaining in the reservoir as of January 11, 60 needed aid urgently and 300 more "definitely need some."[53]

During January 1936, as construction on the Norris Dam was proceeding at a pace fast enough to force more rapid family removals, the bureaucratic mill ground slowly. In this month alone, while eighty-six families were being removed from the basin, Bruce Poundstone wrote to TVA to thank them for sending the actual numbers of people in need of help: "We are using them in presenting resettlement project proposals to the Adminstrator."[54] On February 28, 1936, the Extension Relocation Service finally drew up a working resettlement project for persons displaced by TVA at Norris and sent it to the Tennessee agent for the Resettlement Administration.[55] By the time this project, "frequently discussed with you," reached R. W. Swatts, the Family Removal Section chief, Carnahan, could write to a colleague: "You might be interested in knowing that we have only 76 persons [families] remaining in the Norris basin area. We have made plans for 70 of these, leaving only 6 for whom no plans have developed."[56] On March 4, 1936, the filling of the Norris Reservoir commenced, and the emergency family removal period ended. At this point only forty families had received aid from the Resettlement Administration.[57]

Julian Brown, the Alabama state director of the Resettlement Administration, told Carnahan that his agency's program in the Tennessee Valley had been hampered by the "scarcity of land and the high rental" as well as the fact that opportunities for part-time employment offered by TVA in land clearance and other temporary jobs caused families to seek that alternative rather than resettlement aid. "Of course, we make no effort to place them on our program where they have this option, and frankly they may be better off if they can retain their contact with the soil and secure this outside income."[58] Brown felt that the Resettlement Administration had done "everything humanly possible to place families in line for rehabilitation," and TVA's Extension Relocation Service concurred that their effort had been commendable at Norris, even though the families had already moved; but the service noted that many relocations were only temporary and had created "maladjustments" among families forced to move.[59] The latter problem, it was certainly true, was more owing to TVA's lack of planning and foresight than to removal efforts of the Resettlement Administration in the Norris area, but Carnahan, who had been in charge of the family removal work at Norris, found fault with the way the agency operated.

John Holt, from the Division of Farm Population and Rural Life of the Bureau of Agricultural Economics, USDA, had queried Carnahan on methods used by the Resettlement Administration in choosing rehabilitation clients.[60] In reply, Carnahan wrote a long and detailed letter laying bare some of the problems which afflicted the whole process of family removal. He argued first that there was a need for some government agency to devote its efforts to the resettlement of groups displaced by federal action. Second, he urged a process of selection "so that all able-bodied families, without sufficient resources for adequate relocation, would be automatically selected to receive benefits through the Resettlement Administration." The emphasis of such a selection process, he insisted, would be on the *readjustment* of displaced population and not on a program designed to give credit to families who met all credit requirements but had low credit ratings.

Carnahan specifically cited the Norris population displacement as an example of the weakness of the Resettlement Administration's policies:

> The Tennessee Valley Authority enlisted the cooperation of the Resettlement Administration in relocating these 3,300 [removed] families, but due to the very high standard required in the selection of families, only 40 families have received aid. . . . We believe that at least 500 families would have been greatly benefited by the assistance of the Resettlement Administration. [61]

The comments made by the chief of the Removal Section at Norris on the involvement of the Resettlement Administration in family removal problems are valuable not just for the light they shed on that agency but for the fashion in which they illuminate the whole family removal and relocation process initiated by TVA.

Of the 500 families cited as needing resettlement aid, "at least 50 percent . . . did not apply for, nor did they particularly desire aid from the Resettlement Administration. They were willing to accept the very poor living conditions that were made available to them by private landowners and private industry." The reason why they did not choose the resettlement aid, according to Carnahan, was that they did not understand the benefits conferred, desired to remain debt-free, were ignorant of resettlement possibilities outside their immediate communities, and maintained a sentimental attachment to their communities. Obviously the removed population would have to be "reeducated" to the benefits of resettlement, or as Carnahan put it, "to benefit this group of non-applicants, it would be necessary to *sell* the Resettlement program rather than to *select* families who had applied for assistance." This reversal of policy would have been necessary to benefit those displaced by government action.[62]

The chief of the Removal Section at Norris pointed out that among the remaining families, there were some who, because of lack of education and "general lack of stimulating environment," would automatically be refused aid by the Resettlement Administration. But they should be helped, he pointed out, not because "submarginal adults" should be aided, but as an "investment in the future generation." Selection for relocation was ipso facto a product of government action, but those families who were considered submarginal should be given some aid, even if they did not meet Resettlement Administration norms.

The question of resettlement aid rested on a hypothetical proposition which Carnahan posed: Did the government have a moral obligation to maintain and/or raise the standard of living of numbers of families displaced by TVA? He responded that an attempt should be made to cushion the adverse effect of dislocation by providing a resettlement program which would prevent a further lowering of living standards and would ensure a minimum standard of living for all families displaced by governmental purchase. Simultaneously, current Resettlement Administration programs could be continued "whereby families who are able to show particular progress would be selected for more ideal and planful economic advancement."[63] Since the Family Removal Section was created to facilitate removal of those families hardest hit by TVA's intrusion into the Norris Basin, Carnahan's closing remarks are highly significant:

> Certainly, both Resettlement Administration officials and Tennessee Valley Authority workers agree that we have lowered the standards of living for numbers of families displaced by the Norris Dam development. We attempt to justify ourselves by hoping that the future progress that will result from the building of the dam will in some way enable these families to raise their standard of living.[64]

RESETTLEMENT AND INTERAGENCY EXPERIMENTS

Conflicting goals and means of the relocation agencies within TVA had been very much in evidence during the process of relocation of families from the Norris Basin. By the summer of 1936, with most of the families removed, more attention was paid to reassessing the past two years' work. In particular, the Reservoir Family Removal Section, in an attempt to reexamine its bases, asked the caseworkers of the programs to comment on the removal process. W. C. Carmichael, who had been a Norris caseworker for the Reservoir Family Removal Section, was critical of the Extension Relocation Service:

> I believe that it is not necessary in part, and probably not fully justified. . . . In my opinion too much effort has been expended in helping that part of the owner group who received above $2,000 [for their land]. . . . I believe it is socially undesirable in that the relocation workers [relocation service] have paid little or no attention to the social aspects of individual families.

The lack of a system, felt Carmichael, ensured that the wealthy would be taken care of first, leaving a "residue of owners and tenants who needed help badly . . . , who needed more time and effort on the part of the service and probably received the least."[65]

While Carmichael's reactions were not unique among the Removal Section caseworkers at Norris, they were well thought out and well formulated. The major faults of the program of family removal, he believed, lay with TVA itself for not developing coordination of efforts and centralization of administration.[66] The "fundamental weaknesses" of population readjustment were described by caseworker Carmichael as:

> First, lack of authority to handle particular Tennessee Valley Authority problems by existing agencies, and lack of real interest on the part of these agencies due to pressing problems of their own; second, lack of coordination of different readjustment activities, caused partly by not having one agency directly responsible . . . ; third, lack of follow-up work by the proper agency. . . .[67]

Caseworker Carmichael felt also that while the Legal Division of TVA could not be "charged with a failure to cooperate, yet there seems to be a lack of understanding as to just what unit is responsible for the performance of certain legal tasks and also the action taken seems very slow even after their responsibility has been admitted." He felt that outside agencies could not be counted on[68] and concluded that "if some existing agency does not admit responsibility for Tennessee Valley Authority population readjustment and show that they have the authority and ability to handle the problem, the only other recourse is to ask for Congressional action."[69]

Despite numerous criticisms of the Relocation Service by workers and directors of the Reservoir Family Removal Section agriculturalists were strongly of the opinion that, as Carnahan put it, "the entire responsibility of family removal and population readjustment should rest with the Relocation Service." Carnahan, who was considering other employment in the fall of 1936, said that his experience as population readjustment adviser in the Reservoir Family Removal Section pointed to the opposite conclusion: that there should be within the departmental level a coordinator who would delegate cooperation with outside agencies while at the same time bringing under a single coordinated effort all factions within TVA which worked in population readjustment.[70]

Carnahan's analysis of his three years' experience in population readjustment was that unless the effort was made cohesive rather than being organizationally fragmented, it would lose its significance. He urged the creation of a separate department of population readjustment for the momentum that it would carry in TVA conferences and for the implications of TVA's whole program:

> The organization of such a department would give new impetus to the development of a practical social and economic effort, usually thought of as a function which TVA was intended to fulfill, but which function has been approached somewhat haphazardly in my opinion and without concrete general objectives consistent with the TVA Act.

Carnahan then placed his finger on one of the issues that had made the population readjustment program within TVA so tension-ridden and conflictual. The disadvantages of such a department within TVA, he said, "would depend largely on considerations as to whether or not the organization of such a department would tend to cause TVA to accept more responsibilty for alleviation of difficult basic problems which it has only discovered, or in some instances aggravated." His own analysis was that the creation of a department of population readjustment would help TVA in its effort to correct these "difficult basic problems" while at the same time showing a commitment by TVA to cooperate with other agencies. Such a commitment, in his eyes, was vital because whatever the means, TVA's population readjustment program should have as its general objectives both the replacement of "as much income base as is displaced in a given area" and the encouragement of changes of vocation from "strictly agricultural to agricultural-industrial vocations . . . to alleviate the conditions which are inevitably brought about when in already over-populated agricultural areas large blocs of land are diverted from cultivation and the people who are using this income base are thrown back on other already over-populated areas." The formulation and pursuit of these objectives was regarded by Carnahan as "a challenging problem which merits the thoughtful attention of those who formulate the policies of the Tennessee Valley Authority."[71]

Theoretically a proponent of cooperation between TVA and outside agencies, Carnahan was an activist as well. Throughout the fall and winter of 1936, he had been supplying the Resettlement Administration with data on removed families at Norris and elsewhere in order to facilitate closer cooperation with that agency. In 1937 these exchanges had borne fruit. Paul Taylor, an agricultural economist with the Rural Resettlement Division of the Resettlement Administration, had been in particularly close touch with Carnahan. At the end of 1936, after visits made to the Norris area, he composed a report which was to influence his agency's attitude toward TVA's population readjustment programs.[72] In his report Taylor stressed particularly that population removal by TVA had worsened an already acute problem of rural overpopulation in the Norris area. Taylor found that as of the end of November 1936, more than 300 families were in need of immediate aid in resettlement. Of these, 165 had resettled "on land unsuitable for permanent tenure," and the rest were still in the area, either unmoved or living in temporary housing. All of these, he believed, needed immediate aid.[73]

Taylor had formed a liaison with C. W. Farrier, the assistant coordinator of TVA, as well as with Carnahan, and had recommended that the latter contact E. R. Henson of the Rural Resettlement Division of the Resettlement Administration. Carnahan had done so, and toward the end of December 1936 he wrote to

Henson: "We realize that the land acquisition activities of the Authority have tended to reduce the number of available farm units in the Tennessee Valley Area. This fact increases the farm population readjustment problem which was already acute before the advent of TVA."[74]

Carnahan and Taylor had evidently been jointly supportive of the concept of a "recreational cooperative" on the Clinch River to be jointly sponsored by TVA and the Resettlement Administration, with land supplied by TVA and the development provided for by the Resettlement Adminstration. Carnahan noted that the TVA board was in general supportive of such cooperation, since the Authority had issued a resolution stating that "serious maladjustment" of families in TVA's area of operation had occurred and that studies of more than twenty years back showed that a number of farm families "cannot make satisfactory adjustments because of existing overcrowding conditions prevailing in the valley unless they receive financial assistance." TVA recommended that such satisfactory adjustments rest with the Resettlement Administration.[75] To this end, Carnahan made contacts with relevant divisions within TVA.[76]

In his report on the difficulties created by TVA's population displacement, Paul Taylor had cited the Clinch River recreational project specifically as an aid to some of the disadvantaged families and had argued for its funding and support by the Resettlement Administration as a "project which might well serve as a type demonstration of a number of similar projects which can be located at carefully selected points along the various reservoirs being formed by the Tennessee Valley Authority."[77] In conjunction with effort through the Clinch River Recreational Cooperative to solve some of the problems of families removed from Norris, Taylor also recommended reviving for TVA's displaced families the Morristown [Tennessee] Tenant Security Project developed by the Resettlement Administration as a part of a Holston Valley Project and abandoned early in 1936, after the optioning of 8,000 acres of land. Taylor asserted that an "infiltration type of settlement" of tenants in the Holston Valley was not the most favorable, but scarcity of farm land made buying contiguous land parcels difficult. He felt that the project should be revived before the options of the land ran out.[78]

Taylor was more enthusiastic about the possibilities of the Recreational Homesteads Project on the Clinch River in the Norris Basin, since unlike the infiltration type of farm settlement, the recreational cooperative would employ farm families in nonfarm occupations:

> It is realized that the greater part of the land in the surrounding counties which is suitable for the production of agricultural crops is already populated to excess. Also, many families are farming lands which are unsuitable for cultivation and incapable of producing sufficient income. . . . The lands suitable for farming near the reservoir site are more congested now than they were prior to the initiation of the Tennessee Valley Authority's program in this area.[79]

The employment of families in a recreational cooperative would ostensibly be an example for taking pressure off the land and channeling productive energies into recreational and handcraft-oriented jobs. Taylor urged the support of his own agency, stating that the Resettlement Administration and the TVA

> have a moral if not a legal obligation to these people. Also, both agencies are receiving a considerable amount of adverse criticism in connection with these particular people. Therefore immediate action on the problem will not only fulfill a moral obligation on the part of the Resettlement Administration, but at the same time it will demonstrate to the Tennessee Valley Authority that this administration is not bluffing with respect to assisting families already displaced, or to be displaced, through the land purchase program of the Authority.[80]

THE CLINCH RIVER BRIDGE RECREATIONAL COOPERATIVE

The evolution, development, and resolution of the Clinch River Recreational Cooperative plan stands as an illustration of the difficulties TVA faced in population readjustment in the Norris area: It involved the hard-core disadvantaged among the displaced population at Norris; it was a test of interagency cooperation in resettlement problems; it was meant as a demonstration of what could be done in the whole field of population readjustment; and finally, and perhaps most importantly, it was to serve as an example of rehabilitation in placing farm families in nonfarm occupations. As Carna-

han put it in a letter, TVA and the Resettlement Administration
concurred in farm infiltration projects as a last resort, "but . . . it is
the consensus of opinion that agriculture alone cannot bear the
entire burden of support of the population in the area if the
minimum American standard of living is to be attained." The recreational cooperative, it was hoped, could become a model of providing increased and stabilized income.[81]

Tennessee Route 33 from Knoxville past Maynardville, the
county seat of Union County, crosses the Norris Reservoir em-
bayment at what was once the Clinch River. The area has always
been an attractive, accessible site affording great recreational potential on the reservoir. As early as October 1935, at the instigation
of C. W. Farrier, assistant coordinator of TVA, the Land Planning
and Housing Division had assessed the site as a recreational possibility to be developed with Civilian Conservation Corps labor. The
project was dropped and then resumed in 1936 as a result of "requests from displaced reservoir families for some type of assistance
from some governmental agency that might assist them in obtaining income for the support of their families."[82] Carnahan, in re-
questing board approval for the recreational project, noted that at a
state planning meeting in Nashville in October with Resettlement
Administration and TVA representatives present, discussion of the
Bankhead farm tenant security bill had led to the conclusion that
nonfarm income was necessary to rehabilitate the Southern Highlands region because of overcrowded conditions on agricultural
land. The question of recreation resources came up, and the Resettlement Administration representatives stated that if recreational
cooperatives could be organized, funds were available for loans to
them.[83]

Before the recreational cooperative was presented to the board
of directors, various representatives met with Brice Mace, a representative of the Resettlement Administration, to discuss the project. The ensuing discussions were illuminating.[84] Carnahan, who
opened the meeting, stressed first of all the problem created by
population removal at Norris:

> three thousand families moved out of the Norris area and divided
> into other economic units, in many instances right around the pro-
> posed location of this cooperative. About 150 families are located on

> 10, 12, 15 acres of land up to considerable acreage, but it does appear that there is a great need for additional income. . . . Memo after memo has come from our field offices about this need.

Mace regretted the fact that the only money available was loan money or loan funds rather than "development" money a certain portion of which could be charged off to relief. Throughout the discussion of the project which followed, L. N. Allen of TVA's Reservoir Property Management Department which would eventually absorb the Reservoir Family Removal Section, was rather cold to the idea that TVA should support such a project. At one point he asked if anyone "had felt the pulse of the Board." Walter Kahoe, an administrative assistant to Arthur Morgan, responded that he believed the board would support the group's decision without delay.[85] When Carnahan urged immediate TVA subsidization to the extent of drawing up plans for the cooperative, saying in effect that TVA had a moral obligation to support this type of planning, L. N. Allen argued: "When you subsidize this particular project you are subsidizing families that have been removed, not only here, but all up and down the valley." As the meeting wore on, it was evident that forestry, planning, and the Family Removal Section were supportive of the project, with Allen conservatively opposed, saying at frequent intervals that all depended upon the opinion of the Legal Division. Brice Mace disappointingly thought the investment would run at about $7,500 per family, an amount considerably above the $6,000 he estimated for resettlement of a family on rural land. Goulden of the Forestry Division rightly pointed out that there was no comparison of benefits in the two cases, because after resettlement on agricultural land, "You are going to get your income from selling agricultural produce, and it seems to be plenty of that already." The Resettlement Administration's representative, who seemed more concerned with the whole concept from an investment point of view, concluded that the best plan would be for TVA to develop the whole project and then rent it to the cooperative, which could borrow money from the Resettlement Administration to run the project and guarantee TVA the rent. This would lessen the risk to the Resettlement Administration but would possibly involve TVA beyond its legal limits. Construction by TVA at its wage base "with its merit and efficiency basis" would, it was feared, "run the costs up and that would not give participants a chance to buy stock while working on construction jobs."[86] The meeting revealed some of the limitations under which TVA operated as well as the inflexibility and caution of the Resettlement Administration, doubtless induced, among other things, by the need to defend congressional appropriations.

Resettlement Administration authorities had, in the interim, examined Paul Taylor's report on the resettlement problem of TVA and had forwarded to Carnahan a proposed general program which included most of Taylor's recommendations. Early in February, Carnahan sent it on to John Blandford, Jr., the general manager of TVA.[87] It was an ambitious program, taking note of the fact that TVA construction at Norris, Wheeler, Pickwick Landing, Guntersville, and Fowler's Bend had already displaced 6,590 families, of whom 2,050 (as conservatively estimated by TVA) needed help in relocation: "most of these families are tenants with little or no cash, and only a small amount of livestock, equipment and household goods. Since these families are being displaced as the result of land purchases by the Tennessee Valley Authority, the government is morally obligated to assist them in relocating on farms equally satisfactory to those operated in the reservoir." For Norris Reservoir families, the Resettlement Administration proposed the infiltration type of settlement near Morristown, Tennessee, in Hamblen County (25 families); the development of the Clinch River Bridge Recreational Cooperative (25 families), and an extension of the Cumberland Mountain Farms Project (225 families). The last project was expected to resettle families from other TVA dam projects (1,100 families at $4,000 per family). Anticipated funding for the Clinch River Bridge Recreational Cooperative was $150,000, and for the Morristown project, $80,000. A meeting between representatives and Resettlement Administration officials was suggested,[88] but an anticipated early conference in February was postponed until later in the month, while the approval of the TVA board of directors was sought for the tentative Clinch-Norris Recreational Cooperative. Aside from planning and providing lands to be leased, the proposal to the board stated that no "direct contribution" to the project would be made by TVA. On February 16, 1937, the board approved the project, and a conference was arranged a few days later.[89] It was not a success. Although L. N. Allen reported to the general manager that lines of communication were to be kept open between TVA and the Resettlement Administration and recommended that Walter Packard and possibly the regional directors of the Resettlement Administration come to Knoxville for a several days' visit (to "become acquainted with the problems here which affect his program"),[90] Allen was more candid in his formal assessment to Director H. A. Morgan:

> We understood that the object of the conferences was to work out closer relations with RA in particular reference to resettlement of problems families disclosed in the regular course of our reservoir family work.
>
> RA, however, seemed to understand that we were creating problems which required, for adjustment, the services of an agency other than ours. We repeatedly called attention to the fact that while we are aware that mal-adjustment was not created by TVA but existed long before TVA came along; that instances of mal-adjustment were discovered in the course of our routine work, that we thought the information thus secured would be valuable to RA in carrying out its routine work.
>
> The conferences were not concluded as scheduled owing to the necessary return of RA officials to Washington at an hour earlier than anticipated. Before leaving, the RA officials asked that TVA address a letter to the Secretary of Agriculture pointing out that resettlement problems exist here and that there is urgent need of immediate action. We understood that this letter was to be used in securing appropriations for the work.
>
> The letter was not written.[91]

Such an attitude was not conducive to good cooperative efforts between the agencies, and when the options ran out on some of the land designated as part of the Clinch River Bridge cooperative, the plan was turned down by the Resettlement Adminstration, in part because TVA, in its proposals, "was lacking in more definite information as to what the Tennessee Valley Authority, which we understand has the responsibility for the development of the proposed site . . . is prepared to do in the way of improving and conditioning the site."[92] This was not, however, the end of the Clinch River recreational project. Although the work of relocation in Norris was virtually complete, the Farm Security Administration (the successor to the Resettlement Administration) remained concerned with TVA's removal problems in its other dams, and Paul Taylor was selected to go to Knoxville as a liaison between TVA and the FSA. The project was revived and discussed and in the spring of 1938 received its death warrant from the same L. N. Allen who had earlier claimed to Harcourt Morgan that the Resettlement Administration was blaming TVA for maladjustments for which it was not responsible. Allen wrote to Paul Taylor that in 1938 TVA could "more fully grasp the problem than was the case when this cooperative was proposed two years ago." Allen argued that reasonable profit could not be expected from a recreational concession unless the operators were experienced and highly trained; that only a small group of people could benefit; that TVA advisers on cooperatives felt that because most of the proposed cooperators would not be employed on the project that the proposed arrangement would not work for "the fullest harmony and combined effort as would be the case if all cooperators were employed"; and that if the recreational service were run by experienced personnel "sympathetic with the conditions that exist," local people would benefit in any case.[93]

In reality, the population removal program for the inhabitants of the Norris Basin and for removed populations in other areas where TVA was then at work was a minimal program with very little vision. It was this very lack of vision which mired the resettlement program in a routine which fell far short of the intentionality of President Roosevelt's idealistic conception of TVA. No one summed up the dilemma better than Tracy Augur, who had been with the agency since its earliest days. In 1935, in response to a request from his chief, Earle S. Draper, for comments on the problem of relocation, Augur wrote a compassionate and human response whose observations were as valid after the Norris project was completed as they had been at the time he wrote them. Augur offers a vision of what TVA's relocation and resettlement program might have been if its ideals had been maintained and pursued.

> I still feel, as I have felt from the beginning, that the problems of relocating families displaced by TVA operations present both a direct responsibility and an opportunity for constructive planning, and that neither is being satisfactorily met. The problem seems to be looked upon as a small and incidental one containing nothing but

191

trouble for the Authority, whereas it is a large and important one which will recur continually as the program progresses. Much more trouble will be caused by an attempt to side-step or soft-pedal the issue than will be caused by tackling it.

Shifts in population are being, and will continue to be, caused increasingly by operations of the authority and of other federal and state agencies in which the authority is interested. If no improvement is made in the character of the population pattern and the social and economic status of the people involved in these shifts, then it seems to me that we must renounce any claim to be able to successfully tackle the larger problems concerning the general composition of the valley population.

There seems to be a too prevalent tendency to look at the limitations and difficulties in the way of such a program, instead of considering its purposes. It is the old story of emphasizing how something cannot be done rather than how it can be done. We are told that the TVA is limited in its activities in terms of the Act, that the FERA is limited in some other way, and so on, through all the housing and financing agencies which have been set up.

The spirit of the president in undertaking the New Deal was just the opposite. He apparently tried to visualize the problems that needed solution, to find out what the best solution was, and then to devise means of achieving it. Certainly there is an opportunity now as never before to follow that course. There are literally dozens of federal agencies set up to help in the readjustment of distressed population groups, and if there is not in the present set-up a means of properly assisting those displaced by TVA operations there is ample opportunity to make up the deficiency through corrective legislation.

Assisting displaced farm families to locate new farms, and protecting them by competent advice on soils and land prices is of course an important and valuable service, and I do not mean to minimize its value when I say that it is only meeting half the problem. Case work among families which are indigent or which are afflicted by physical or mental disability is also important and essential. But this should not close our eyes to the problem of the many families for which a new independent farm does not offer a real future, and which have no permanent disabilities making special cases of them. . . .

We are constantly told that there is no expansion of industry in progress, and that therefore any plans for the resettlement of displaced populations which depend on new industry are futile. I might point out that there is also no expansion in sight for agricultural production except as it is offered by the possible demands of new industry. The family which is made dependent upon new agriculture is therefore no better off than the family which is made dependent upon industry. The only apparent item of difference is that the family with agricultural facilities can at least raise its own food, but under any proper plan of industrial housing the same opportunity is open to the industrial families. In other words we may assume subsistence in any case, whether relocation is founded upon an agricultural or an industrial base. It is possible that a mere subsistence level of living is all that may be counted on for several years for the majority of families with which we are concerned, but I contend that the opportunities for a living derived from expanding industrial employment are as good, if not better, than those dependent upon expanding agricultural employment.

When we turn to other important questions as the social composition of the population and the economy and the efficiency of government, I still feel that there is a stronger case for the creation of new industrial communities, or for well-planned additions to existing ones, than there is for the creation of additional small farms scattered hit-or-miss over the face of the valley. Families can subsist just as well as in an industrial community that is waiting for industry, as they can on scattered farms that are awaiting a profitable market for farm products. During this period the schooling of their children and the rendering of other governmental services can be carried on more economically in the industrial community than on widely scattered farms.

In speaking of an industrial community I am not of course thinking of a single-industry mill town, or of the existing small industrial cities in which congestion has been allowed to destroy the opportunities for pleasant living. I am thinking of new towns created on principles which will insure diversity of employment, garden space for every home, and good community organization. I do not care thru what agency or agencies they are achieved, so long as the attainment is not strangled by monetary limitations. I have very little sympathy, as you know, for the attitude that such things can't be done. If the Tennessee Valley Authority is to make a real contribution to the life of the region it will have to discover or develop the methods by which it can be done. . . .

It has apparently been assumed in the past that the proposals of this division have called for a specific type of community with a certain lot size, a certain total population and a certain method of building and financing houses and acquiring land. This has not been the case. We have merely asked that the principle of resettlement in new communities be accepted as one of the means of assisting in the relocation of displaced families, and that the best type of community and the best means of accomplishing its establishment be worked out. I will never feel content with a program which refuses to investigate the merits and the possibilities of such community development, or which takes the attitude that the problem of displaced families is one which we are best rid of if we can find any other agency to take it, regardless of results. . . .[94]

Despite these sentiments of disappointment over the failure to deal successfully with the problems of removal and resettlement, TVA almost simultaneously had to face an even more sensitive issue, the relocation of thousands of graves in the Norris Basin. Once again the agency would face the challenge of evolving a basic, comprehensive policy. And once again the challenge would be a formidable one.

6 Reburying the Dead

IF THE RELOCATION AND SETTLEMENT of some 3,000 living families had not always been effectively coordinated between various groups and agencies, it was ironical that the reinterment of the dead buried in local communities—over 5,000 graves in scattered burial plots, in numerous churchyards and family burial grounds, many of them unmarked and dating back to the eighteenth century—should be carried out much more efficiently.

TVA's arrival had meant to many of these families a disastrous wrenching away from familiar surroundings and a disruption of a sense of community established through generations. This sense of community was conservative, embracing the dead as well as the living, and it was symbolized by the local church and its burying ground as well as by the numerous kinship ties that bound family to family.

The many small rural communities of the Norris Basin demonstrated a deep sensitivity to and an awareness of their existence as long-established social entities. This sensitivity was enhanced by deeply abiding religious sentiments and was nowhere more apparent than in the concern evidenced by the communities over the final disposition of the graves of their families. To the displaced and uprooted living, these graves were mute evidence of the continuity of their own existence, proof of the permanency of the past, and an irrefrangible link to their collectively shared communal and familial memories.

The reverential attitude toward the dead, expressed so strongly by the concern of these families in the matter of the removal of graves, constituted one of the more delicate matters which the

195

Tennessee Valley Authority had to face. Its resolution of the problem can qualify as a very real test of its ability to function at the popular level in a potentially explosive situation and as a tangible test of sensitivity and restraint in the use of federal power. While the agency was, in time, to develop a structured bureaucracy to handle the problems of grave removal, much of the initial work was delegated to W. R. Woolrich, a mechanical engineer from the University of Tennessee and an assistant to Harcourt Morgan.[1]

There is no available evidence to indicate that public opinion surveys were taken among the populations of the five affected counties as to the disposition of removed graves. A memo from Woolrich to Morgan, however, did refer to a meeting in Union County near Maynardville, Tennessee, as an "independent meeting of residents of the valley" to be held on August 19, 1933. Woolrich's comments to Morgan would indicate that the Authority had somewhat made up its mind as to what type of cemetery would be suitable for the reburied dead: "Will meet with these people. Have asked Draper [Land Planning Housing Division] *to supply information available on design* and will take some pastors to accompany me to keep spiritual leadership in the foreground. Some more thought should be given so that all answers can be made without late reversal."[2]

One of the pastors asked to attend was John D. Freeman, executive secretary and treasurer of the executive board of the Tennessee Baptist Convention in Nashville, Tennessee. Since he could not come, he asked Reverend Wyatt of Knoxville to attend in his place. Freeman wrote to Woolrich, "It is our purpose to try to aid the churches of that area . . . in combining them into larger and more efficient units."[3] At the meeting, attended, not surprisingly, by only Union Countians (Dixie Miller, a prominent resident, was chairman), Woolrich announced that the agency had decided upon a national memorial cemetery, and the group purported to offer its support for the idea. There is no record that the residents of the other four affected counties were consulted. Stranger yet is the fact that at this Union County meeting a resolution was presented and passed "recommending full cooperation, thru churches, with the TVA plans." Woolrich's alleged response was that the TVA "deeply appreciated your assent to these plans. We plan to make all arrangements through your respective churches." Two Knoxville ministers were present—W. B. Morgan of the First Methodist Church and T. C. Wyatt, pastor of McCalla Avenue Baptist Church—who said they would "advise or assist their Union County representatives."[4]

Two days after the meeting with Union Countians, the Tennessee Valley Authority's board of directors voted "that a national cemetery be established, to be maintained by the Authority, to receive the remains of those now buried within the limits of the reservoirs." The Authority agreed to establish full responsibility for disinterment and reinterment to the proposed cemetery and for those not desirous of placing their dead in a national cemetery, space would be provided elsewhere, with compensation equal to the cost of removal to the national cemetery.[5] At this early point in the agency's thinking, it is clear that such a concept loomed large. The agency proposed a TVA National Memorial Council to carry out the establishment of such a cemetery. Following the board of directors meeting a TVA press release floridly stated:

> The Tennessee Valley Authority is arranging to transfer the remains of early patriots from pioneer burying grounds within the area to be flooded by the great Norris dam at Cove Creek, near Knoxville. Some of these old cemeteries date from the days our hardy forefathers first pushed westward across the Alleghenies. Buried here are many soldiers of the Revolution, including some heroes who fought in the notable engagement at King's Mountain, also relatives of Daniel Boone, Davy Crockett, John Sevier, Sam Houston, Andrew Johnson, and others whose names figure on history's pages.[6]

To serve as liaison between the agency and the various religious denominations, three Knoxville clergymen, two of whom had been present at the Union County meeting, urged the formation of a Tennessee Valley Church Advisory Committee and were subsequently asked by the Authority to become the executive committee of a group consisting of fifteen members. According to reports, TVA averred that these men "have taken a leading part in the problem of removing graves." While not wishing to represent the Authority, Dr. Wyatt said, "We will assist it and we will represent the people of the section thru the various denominations." Besides

Wyatt and Morgan from Knoxville, representatives also included Harry Cooke of the First Christian Church, Knoxville (the third executive committee member), and Sam White of the Deadrick Avenue Baptist Church in Knoxville. Two Methodist members were to be moved by Bishop Wallace Brown, and Cooke himself was to appoint two others for the Christian Church.[7]

At this point it should be considered that at best, the decision for a national memorial cemetery had been hurriedly undertaken, and without due consideration of the Norris Basin residents. The advisory committee was largely self-created from the nucleus of Knoxville ministers present at the Union County meeting on August 19 who had actively solicited the Authority's support. The concept of a national memorial cemetery had been officially promulgated by the Authority and had been given nationwide publicity before August 25.

The advisory committee itself, which had gained the approval of TVA, can hardly be called representative of the Norris Basin area. The numerous small rural churches, heavily concentrated in the Primitive and Missionary Baptist sects, could hardly identify with the congregation of urban Knoxville—a city whose shared characteristics were more in line with great Valley towns like Roanoke, Virginia, than with the rural communities below the highland rim.

The Authority, then, with its hurriedly concocted and promoted scheme of a national cemetery and its "official" Church Advisory Committee, which represented Knoxville, not the Norris Basin, had taken at the outset a rather unilateral and high-handed position on grave removal. A prize-winning feature story in the *Chattanooga Sunday Times* (September 13, 1936) would clearly delineate how crucial an unrepresentative position in this case could be:

> Funerals in rural communities are far more solemn and impressive than in the busy rush and bustle of the Metropolis. The stroke of death makes a far wider circle than in the city throng. The fixed and unchanging features of a rural community also perpetuate the memory of a friend or neighbor. . . . His grave is a constant reminder to the survivors. . . . Such was the typical situation in the Norris Reservoir area; each mound held some perpetuating and enduring memory for the individual community circle.[8]

Despite the agency's efforts to promote denominational support for a national cemetery, a religious group much closer to the immediate interests of a large portion of the affected population and one which represented the single largest religious sect in the Norris Basin called a meeting to present their own plans and resolutions to TVA. This group, the Campbell County Missionary Baptist Association, held a strongly divergent attitude from TVA in the matter of a national cemetery.

In the political organization of Baptist churches, ultimate decisionmaking rested in the hands of totally autonomous congregations. The constituency of the Missionary Baptist Association of Campbell County alone was composed of nearly fifty such congregations scattered through four of the five affected counties. Although there were also large congretations of Primitive Baptists, that sect could generally be expected to share similar attitudes toward the buried dead of the area. Instead of letting TVA canvass people on the relocation question, the Campbell County Missionary Baptist Association preferred to conduct its own opinion surveys. Convening on August 25, 1933, for a general business session, the association resolved, in light of the impending construction of Norris Dam, that a survey be made among its constituency "for purpose of presenting to the Tennessee Valley Authority a definite plan for the relocation and organization of the churches to be removed and of other Baptist churches to be organized in the Norris Dam area." To this end three trustees of the association, Dr. G. L. Ridenour, J. P. Meredith, and W. A. Woodward, were instructed to meet with the Baptist congregations in the Norris Basin.

The association was much concerned over the disruption of its churches by the creation of Norris Reservoir and fearful that once the church lands were sold to TVA, the congregations would disband. Thirteen churches within its constituency were scheduled for physical removal, and thirty-four churches altogether would be effectively disorganized by the displacement of part or all of their congregations. The association estimated that in Campbell County alone, 4,000 persons, the majority of whom were Missionary Baptists, would be affected by the Norris project.

Despite the fact that their organization did not lend itself well to a unified social effort, the Missionary Baptist Association was well aware that building Norris Dam would necessitate mission work among the removed population. In expressing this need, the association showed a penetrating social awareness of the area's problems concerning the tenants, the sick and aged, and the general dislocation which would follow in the wake of TVA: "The most grave problem in the area is the demoralization of the churches in the communities to be abandoned. Unrest, discontent, breaking with social ties, the loss of religious responsibility make it imperative that the missionary agencies of the denomination serve the population with workers during this time of emergency." The report also examined the particular problem of the cemeteries to be removed as a result of the anticipated flooding and stressed the character of the rural cemetery, with its "spiritual and sentimental value that does tie the people to their religious institutions."[9]

Specifically appointed to aid the churches in their work of relocation, the three trustees were instructed "to prevent the dissipation of any properties in the communities to be abandoned." The association requested the Tennessee Valley Authority to encourage the consolidation of churches in the new communities where families were to be moved and also urged, apropos of this request, the agency to experiment in community planning with a view to easing the situation of tenants—a problem rendered particularly acute because tenants, without ownership rights in the land, could expect no reimbursement upon resettlement. TVA was encourged to allow the Baptists to own church property and land for cemeteries and other religious purposes in any experimental or model communities. Undoubtedly these comments were precipitated by the wave of publicity which, preceding the arrival of the agency, had often made reference to the possibility of experiments in living to be conducted on federally owned property.

In its closing remarks the association reiterated its stand on the cemetery issue. Any contemplation of a centrally located cemetery for the buried dead of the area which did not provide for the future interments of families that now lived in the Norris area "would deny them the property rights which they now possess—that of free burial." Speaking "as Baptists" the association protested the establishment of a proposed memorial cemetery as "an invasion of our rights as members of a religious organization. The members of our early churches were buried within this section they helped to develop. To deny these [descendants of] pioneers the right of Christian burial near the church or in the communities of their faith is to outrage the sentiment of families in this section and will violate the spiritual background of the people of this county."[10]

Despite these objections, plans for the national cemetery proceeded. On October 11, 1933, TVA released to the press a statement which reaffirmed its intention to "relocate a majority of these graves in a National Memorial Cemetery which will be a fitting and lasting tribute to those resting therein." Citing the work of the Tennessee Valley Church Advisory Committee in Knoxville for aiding in the relocation of churches and graves, the report also pointed out that several sculptors, including Gutzon Borglum, had "volunteered to make appropriate memorial statuary, all without cost."[11]

The work of the advisory committee continued to find substantial support for the memorial cemetery, particularly among Union County residents.[12] Encouraged by these sentiments, the regional planning section of the Division of Land Planning and Housing looked favorably on a site in Knox County near the proposed Norris Freeway (Hall's Crossroads) as a location for the memorial cemetery. While this site would be more convenient to residents on the south side of the Norris Basin (mainly Union Countians), a large number of Campbell County residents would have benefited from a more accessible location near LaFollette. Furthermore, the land planning staff pointed out that no matter what site or sites were chosen, it would take more than a year to develop a national cemetery and would necessitate reinterment of bodies in temporary locations.[13] The Tennessee Valley Authority had already begun, in the fall of 1933, the work of making plane table surveys, photographing, indexing, and mapping grave locations prior to disinterment when vocal opposition appeared from two local groups.

In November 1933, TVA received communications from both the Campbell County Missionary Baptist Association and the executive board of the Tennessee Baptist Convention. The association adamantly opposed the plan of a national memorial cemetery and claimed the right to have their dead taken to church cemeteries of their choice at a cost not to exceed that of removal to a proposed memorial cemetery.[14] The Tennessee Baptist Convention whole-heartedly supported the work of the Reverend George Ridenour, moderator of the Campbell County association, and furthermore requested the Authority "not to provide at federal or state expense any houses of worship in the proposed model villages and not to maintain thereby any form of religion by supporting ministers of worship."[15] In petitioning for the right to organize churches in the model villages and to own in fee simple any land for churches, parsonages, and cemeteries, the executive secretary of the convention expounded to TVA:

> Baptists would not wish to enter into any contract with the government or its agents whereby they would lease ground on which to build their meeting houses. They own property in the area in fee simple. Every church house they have ever owned has been on their own ground or on ground donated for the purpose by some private corporation. Age-long has been their opposition to any kind of contract with a state involving their rights or interests.[16]

The Authority's response to these new pressures was twofold. In the case of Baptist purchase of the fee-simple title in model villages, it replied that it had no legal right to convey federally owned land, that it would be detrimental to other denominations to offer the Baptists a long-term lease on such property, and that it would stimulate religious competition. The agency thought that unless they formed a nondenominational unified church, the only solution for the Baptists would be to build outside federal properties.[17] In response to the Campbell County Missionary Baptist Association's position regarding disinterment and reinterment, the Authority arranged a conference for December 15, 1933, between the Reverend Mr. Ridenour, speaking for the trustees of the Campbell County Baptist Association, and TVA officials involved.

Ridenour declared that the association trustees wanted to appoint their own contact man for the removal and relocation of graves to cemeteries of their own selection. "What we should like to do," stated Ridenour, "would be to have a policy of removal in the County Association, allow the trustees to employ someone who knows the folks and locally to do the removal and relocation also."

Not only did the association desire to move the graves to the relocated sites of removed Baptist churches, but it desired to do the work of identifying and enumerating graves, a process already begun by the Authority. Owing to their sensitivity to local feelings, argued Ridenour, the trustees of the association could carry out the entire process of grave removal better than the agency. It became clear in the course of the conversation that Ridenour had moved so far in this direction as to sign up families on his own initiative for the removal of their buried dead.[18] In point of fact, even before this meeting took place, he had solicited tentative bids for removal from an undertaker in Clarksville.[19]

On January 26, 1934, a second meeting attended by Woolrich, Ridenour, Gen. James Cooper, then chief of land acquisition for TVA, and J. C. Carden, a local undertaker, took place in the Authority's offices in Knoxville. Under discussion was General Cooper's suggestion that Ridenour be employed as liaison for grave removal. Speaking for the cemetery board, Woolrich offered no objection to removal by the trustees of the association of graves under their care but opposed the selection of a denominational contact man for the work. As to Cooper's argument that Ridenour was the popular choice of Norris area Baptists, Woolrich replied, "He is denominational—folks in that area do not want him—and I know from material that I have in my records that he is not acceptable and I have to take that in mind." The major purpose of the meeting, however, was an attempt by Cooper and Ridenour to persuade TVA to develop alternatives to a national cemetery. Both claimed that the agency's plans constituted an undue interference with the local populations, while Cooper went so far as to tell Woolrich, "You are making the people do something that they do not want to do." Woolrich angrily retorted that Cooper and his land purchase policies were to blame for much of the opposition against TVA's plans, and he told Carden and Ridenour that "they had run away with the apple cart" as far as the plans for a national cemetery were concerned. Ridenour and Cooper continued to voice complaints against a planned national cemetery on the grounds of religious and geographical diversity in the region. Ridenour averred that residents of one county in the Norris Basin would not "cross the river" to another county to a centrally located graveyard, and he hinted that TVA had rigged favorable responses for a national cemetery from the area Methodists without consulting the Baptists, who were the dominant group in the Norris Basin.

In response to these allegations, Woolrich claimed that although the Authority had not "definitely" decided upon a national cemetery as a solution to the grave removal problem, it nevertheless felt that Reverend Ridenour had so "stirred up the population" that there would be difficulty in implementing the original plan for such a cemetery, should TVA desire it. Given the objections to a national cemetery, added Woolrich, an alternative course might be for TVA to pay the churches for the land within the taking line and leave to them the responsibility of purchasing land for cemeteries and for assuming the responsibility of burying their own dead, thus removing TVA from any responsibility regarding the establishment of denominational cemeteries. Woolrich's statement coincided perfectly with TVA's announced intention of purchasing no grave sites other than for a national cemetery, and he totally rejected Reverend Ridenour's objective of denominational graveyards underwritten by TVA.

In truth, the Campbell County Missionary Baptist Association's protests had, at the very least, forced TVA into a reassessment of its situation. Submitted to the engineering memorandum which, internal criticism indicates, was written during this time, setting up costs estimates and general procedural outlines regarding the feasibility of a national cemetery. The memorandum stressed the necessity of close cooperation between TVA's agents and the local churches, fraternal orders, social organizations, and ministers, as well as the urgency of finding some person of "mature judgment, persuasive and forceful personality, religious, and dignified bearing" to handle personal relations with the next of kin. After graves had been identified and permission granted to move them, TVA would undertake all costs of reinterment; unidentified graves for which there was no request for removal would be left untouched in their original location. While TVA was willing to compensate those families who preferred private removal, it argued that the work would be done more efficiently by the agency and with less disruption of normal work on the Norris Dam. It was also felt that if individuals and churches undertook

Above: Okolona Missionary Baptist Church, Union County, 1935, with graves being removed from cemetery at rear. Below: Grave Removal. A disinterment in old Baker's Forge Cemetery being inspected by the Campbell County Baptist Association, November 1934.

the work of disinterment and reinterment, there was a stronger chance of the mislocation and improper identification of remains.

In this highly significant report, TVA examined critically the concept of a national cemetery and made an attempt to develop viable alternatives. From the standpoint of aesthetics, regional planning, and easy identification of graves, a national cemetery would be ideal; yet its estimated cost would be very high, future interments of kin would not be allowed, and temporary reinterment would double the outlay. Therefore, the report maintained, "It appears that the easiest and most economical method for the TVA would be to reinter the bodies in the nearest or most convenient existing or new public church or private cemetery or to a higher elevation in the same cemetery."[20] This "easiest and most economical" arrangement would be eminently satisfactory, since "the natives should appreciate this idea, for the bodies will be finally located nearest their original location of interment and available space allowed for future interment of the kin." The remainder of the report, largely devoted to the technical aspects of grave removal and interment, stressed that regardless of who accomplished the actual removal, control and inspection would be handled by the Engineering Services Division of TVA itself. The cost projection of grave removals, including provisions for a national cemetery and temporary reinterment on a basis of cost plus 10 percent estimate, came to $422,000 and $209,000 without temporary reinterment.[21]

Taken as a whole, this memorandum was indicative of TVA's willingness to reexamine its goals and plans critically in the face of local opposition. The national cemetery was no longer to be regarded as an immutable necessity in grave removal operations, though the concept of a national cemetery, once seized upon by TVA, continued to be defended in something of a rear-guard action. TVA, according to a letter from Woolrich in response to inquiries made by Senator Kenneth McKellar, had been somewhat taken aback by the Reverend Ridenour's "repeated objections" to its policy, for Woolrich claimed that a survey made in 1933 under the auspices of both TVA and the Civil Works Administration showed the "majority of the inhabitants . . . in favor of having their dead removed to a national cemetery with permanent care." Ridenour's repeated objections and apparent inability to understand the Authority's nondenominational policy had made it necessary to record and stenotype all the subsequent conversations between Ridenour and representatives of the Tennessee Valley Authority.[22] While Ridenour's proposal for hiring, which had been supported by General Cooper, was opposed by the Authority because of his strong denominational bias, the public opinion against a national cemetery which he had apparently encouraged had to be reckoned with. Accordingly, a new policy on grave removal, based upon Woolrich's suggestions of January 26 and upon the unsigned draft memorandum, was adopted and approved by the board of directors of the Tennessee Valley Authority on February 15, 1934.[23]

Basically the new policy urged TVA's purchase of land presently being used as cemeteries so that the establishment of new burial grounds for those desiring them could be facilitated, with the location and mode of acquisition to be left entirely to the discretion of the churches involved. The only land TVA intended to purchase for specific burial grounds would be that for the Tennessee Valley National Memorial Cemetery. Any other removal would be undertaken under TVA auspices and would be subsidized at twenty dollars per grave, thus relieving the agency of all further legal responsibility for removal. Best estimates were that TVA would be moving some 4,500 graves to the national cemetery, leaving about 1,500 to be moved by others.[24]

Although still committed to the concept of a national cemetery, TVA moved to conform more to the sentiments of the local population by calling meetings and informing relatives of those buried within the reservoir area to identify graves and to sign the necessary removal permits. Relatives were also to be told that removal was not mandatory, and graves would be left undisturbed if so desired. Although TVA insisted upon exercising close supervision and absolute control over every phase of disinterment and reinterment, attempts were made to mollify the public. A close relative or another person designated by the family could witness the disinterment, removal, and reinterment, except in cases of danger from infection from contagious diseases. A promise was also made that only personnel who were deemed sensitive and respectful of the rights of the dead would be chosen for removal work and that "anyone manifesting disrespect for the dead or behaving in such a way as to result in harmful comment by the natives should be discharged for cause."[25]

In early June 1934, the agency finally accomplished with some thoroughness what should have been done a year earlier: public meetings and interviews with concerned citizens were carried out to determine the method of removal and the place of reinterment most in conformance with their desires.[26] The results indicated that there was no desire for a national cemetery and that individuals or church groups should have a choice of burial grounds. These expressed attitudes of the populace resulted in a final and dramatic reversal of the agency's position in 1933. Instead of formulating policy and creating sentiment to support it, TVA was now determined to ascertain and follow public opinion.

TVA saved face by conceding that there was "no rank and file opposition" to their grave removal policy but that there had been agitation against that policy by influential leaders who had accused the agency of "autocracy, disrespect, autocratic activity, and disregard for personal feeding." TVA must show itself to be more humane so that the people of the Norris area would not feel that they needed the protection and intercession of the various groups to protect them; rather, the agency should develop a policy which allowed for the next of kin to establish within the broadest possible limits the place and manner of reburial. If TVA showed itself more humane in this regard, "people would prefer to deal directly with us rather than allow those [to do so] who have already [been] or may be clothed with the authority of a trustee and who may prove to be more contentious than the relatives would be."[27] Through this reorientation TVA could move closer to life at the grass roots and at the same time lessen the local opposition to its policy.

The first concept to fall victim to this reevaluation of popular sentiment in the Norris area was the grand plan for a national memorial cemetery, which had increasingly become the focal point of criticism from local individuals and church groups. Their arguments had centered around the idea that removing the dead to a central location would destroy the unity and identity of the communities within the Norris Basin, that denominational rivalries might well intrude upon the sanctity of the burial ground itself, and that the strong desires of the living to be buried beside their dead relatives might so crowd facilities that restrictions would have to be placed upon burial sites. Thus the grand design shrank to a proposed small, central burial ground within the Norris basin.[28] In view of the fact that so much publicity had been given to a national cemetery, this latest decision represented an attempt to maintain some semblance of commitment to a central burial ground. Why did TVA find itself at the core of contentious debate on the issue of a national cemetery? One reason would appear to be that the agency was guilty of thinking too much in national and regional terms and too little in local terms. While Norris area residents were not unaware of the national "pioneer heritage" of their forebears, their tendency was not to think in terms of vague historical entities but rather in terms of concrete lines of genealogical heritage of families whose least common denominator was the kindship tie and whose broadest was the local church affiliation. The two points of view were in the last analysis antithetical.

Moreover, the debate over the national cemetery had been of a conceptual rather than a pragmatic nature. The agency had been floundering in its attempts to bring policy into conformity with opinion in the absence of hard guidelines in the matter of practical procedure. But on the eve of the commencement of grave removals, it was precisely these pragmatic decisions which were needed. At this point it was TVA's Legal Division which appeared to give concise procedural shape to the whole removal process.

The second victim of TVA's policy shift in the matter of grave removals was, ironically enough, the Missionary Baptist Association—the group which had opposed the national cemetery in the first place. While TVA was reevaluating its cemetery policies, the Baptist association was circulating petitions seeking to add its own trustees to the boards of existing churches and to act as negotiator and recipient of the sale of church property to TVA. Generally speaking, the association spoke in terms of three trustees, but in reality the only active member was the Reverend George Ridenour. From the outset the legal branch of TVA opposed the association's plan, for it appeared to infringe upon each church's right to negotiate the transfer of the fee title of church properties and cemeteries to TVA. TVA argued not only that this would mean dealing with six trustees rather than the usual three but also that negotiations would be made difficult by the presence of Ridenour, who despite his apparent popularity was not universally liked. Opinion surveys of various individual churches had indicated that resolutions made supporting the association were not understood to do more than approve sympathetically the association's aim of seeing that graves were properly removed—an attitude much in line with the political organization of the Baptist churches. Support of the association did not mean that it would be legally empowered to act in the sale of church lands or in the receipt of monies. It was TVA's conjecture that the Reverend Ridenour hoped to gain legal control over the purchase money in negotiations with TVA while making it appear that the agency rather than he was responsible for the purchases.[29] Therefore TVA's Legal Division suggested that the acquisition of fee title be pursued as *regular* purchases under normal land acquisition routines rather than through regular boards of trustees to which Ridenour had been added as a representative of the Missionary Baptist Association.[30]

The association was also involved in the matter of moving graves, a connection which the Legal Division asserted was "entirely independent" of the fee title acquisition of cemetery and church lands. Ridenour's position was that once an individual church had signed a resolution with the association, he was, with the general consent of TVA, free to remove all graves without further permission from any of the families involved. TVA's response was that while fee title to a cemetery was generally held by the boards of trustees of individual churches, the individual descendants of the buried dead were endowed with a burial easement which, according to Tennessee law, could be terminated only by giving notice to the family to remove the remains. It followed from this position that since TVA purchased cemetery lands and thus acquired the fee, the agency alone must give notice to the family of the deceased and allow them an opportunity to remove the grave. Because Ridenour had obtained the permission only of the church congregation at large rather than that of each individual family, cemetery removal would fall completely under the justification of TVA. Still open was the possibility that some kind of agreement could be worked out with the association whereby it would move each family's grave after obtaining permission and would be subject to the same regulations and procedures as TVA. Legally, it was established that TVA did not have to deal with the association. The report concluded, "It is doubtful whether as a matter of policy the TVA will gain anything by permitting the Association to remove these graves."[31]

After more than a year of hearing various proposals and counter-proposals concerning cemetery relocation, TVA by midsummer 1934 had done much to clarify procedures. Various divisions were charged with specific responsibilities—engineering services with photographing, mapping, and recording graves; land acquisition with rechecking appraisals and purchasing property; and industry with maintaining public relations contacts through church and community leadership. Despite progress in all these areas, final removal plans were still stalled and hampered by the lack of permanent sites for grave relocation.[32]

On the eve of actual grave removals, legal precedents and implications were still being examined and formulated by TVA. Precedent for the disinterment and removal of graves was to be found neither in Tennessee statute nor in the decisions of the state supreme court; rather, the laws appeared to "import perpetuity of burial."[33] There was, however, in the statutes of the Code of Tennessee some precedent recognizing "by implication" the natural rights of relatives to remove the bodies of deceased persons.[34]

Legal counsel felt that most decisions rendered on the subject had occurred prior to the establishment of the state health department and that the statutes concerning the health department "are very broad and vast, and vest in said commissioner plenary powers to make rules and regulations for the best interests of the public health."[35] The conclusion reached by the cemetery board's legal counsel was that grave removal at Norris fell under the powers of the commissioner for public health. The Authority sought the cooperation, therefore, of the state commissioner of public health in the matter of approving TVA's grave removal plan and contacting the relevant county health offices for cooperation in letting the disinterment and removal commence. Legal counsel also laid down the fundamentals of grave removal policy that should guide the work of the agency. Essentially, these were that since the agency had invoked the necessity of removal, it must pay the "reasonable cost" of removal according to the "reasonable" wishes of living relatives, and removal must be to the "same general or a similar environment as much as possible." When such was done, the rights and easements of the living relatives shifted automatically from the old location to the new, with care and upkeep in the hands of the living relatives, not TVA. Hence the duties of TVA toward the resting place of the deceased ended with each reinterment.[36]

The approval of TVA's methods by the department of public health, and the establishment of a set of fundamental legal principles finally allowed the tremendous task of disinterment, removal, and reinterment to get underway. The legal fundamentals which ended the Authority's obligation at the point of reinterment led to the countermanding of the order to purchase land for burial purposes, and even the vestigial remnants of the scheme for a national cemetery were dropped forever.[37]

The essential character of the new plan was to persuade each congregation to go ahead and contract for new church grounds and cemeteries so that TVA could remove the buried dead while appraisals were still being made and titles still being acquired to the various church properties to be flooded.[39] Specific guidelines were set forth placing in the hands of the Authority primary responsibility for removing graves below the 1,030 contour. All specific removals, whether done by TVA or private firms, would be duly recorded and supervised by TVA.[39] By September 29, some 848 contracts had been obtained, the great majority of which provided for removal by the agency; only a small minority (thirty-three persons) chose to have private undertakers remove the dead, and an even smaller number (thirteen persons) desired to leave the graves undisturbed. Later records were to show that this ratio was largely maintained throughout the remainder of the program. The relative smoothness with which this program worked pleased all members of the cemetery committee.[40] But the Authority, taking nothing for granted, continued to oversee closely the work of its field personnel, particularly cautioning their contact men to refrain from any "high pressure salesmanship" which would make it appear that private undertakers were being discouraged from participation in grave removals. As a further sign of cooperation, TVA arranged for an inspection tour of its removal work by representatives of the Campbell County Missionary Baptist Association.[41] Underlying all considerations was the fact that the process of grave removal had not been taken for the financial benefit of the government, undertakers, or any specific group of individuals, but for the purpose of discharging a regrettable but necessary public duty.[42]

The Authority was confident, in the last analysis, that its removal procedures were compatible with the desires of the local population. In the face of open and vehement criticisms from local undertakers who regarded TVA as an unfair competitor, the cemetery committee's legal counsel declared that their criticisms would, in the long run, redound to the credit of TVA. The lawyer's contention would appear to have been borne out, for by the fall of 1934, removals by local undertakers represented a minuscule proportion of the total number of graves removed."[43]

From our survey of TVA's grave removal program, it would appear that the agency ultimately formulated a plan which proved workable and successful. Initially lacking guidelines or precedents, TVA tried always to work in close conjunction with local residents and churches. Even TVA's idea of a national cemetery was explored thoroughly and had more than a fair hearing among resident church groups and the local population before being rejected as too impractical, too impersonal, and too fraught with legal complications. Yet throughout hearings, discussions, and meetings on grave removal problems, TVA seemed always painfully aware of the necessity of having grass-roots support for its program.

Considering the magnitude of the grave removal problem—the sheer number of disinterments, the lack of adequate grave markers and proper identification, and particularly the need to avoid alienating the local population in their religious sentiments, TVA performed rather admirably in an area where there was always potential for local antagonism and hostility against the agency. Thaddeus Adams, one of TVA's leading attorneys in setting guidelines to the grave removal procedure, would later write: "The people in the basin among whom we worked, and whose buried dead we were removing, were usually always reasonable, kind, and cooperative."[44] Firm legal guidelines and a willingness to modify policy to conform to local sentiment had much reduced the kind of feeling that had caused a local Baptist preacher to remark to his Sunday school at the beginning of 1934: "It was high time that the Baptist[s] organize to combat the horde of atheists invading the community." That the agency was able to deal with the manifold problems of grave removal successfully in Norris was in this particular case an exercise in the sensitivity and restraint of federal power at a local level, but in the last analysis a restraint which grass-roots agitation had induced. TVA's performance was even more commendable when compared to the confusions and failings of their previous efforts in land acquisition, removal, and resettlement.

ᚂᚃᚐ

PART THREE

The Experiment Assessed

One of the more ironic themes in the history of TVA *is contained in the juxtaposition of the effects of population removal in the Norris area with the planned town of Norris. Both themes are the subject of this final section of the study. The irony is that the town of Norris, near the dam itself, was from the outset to have been a vision of what* TVA *planning could accomplish in a rural setting. It was to have been a showcase of rural electrification, industrial decentralization, greenbelt planning—in short, a community which was to demonstrate how the limiting effects of rural Appalachia could be overcome. The removed families of the Norris Basin were, in many respects, the end results of these rural limitations and should have been, indeed were initially intended to be, the beneficiaries of such planning integration. In this sense the removed families and the town, which should have been a model of* TVA's *social action at the grass roots, never materialized. This failure pointed up once again to* TVA's *inability to formulate a successful policy.*

The dispossessed families of the Norris Basin were allowed, on the one hand, to disperse themselves randomly in the same general areas of rural overpopulation that they had left, with little attention paid to the socioeconomic costs of relocation. The planned town of Norris, on the other hand, never realized the communitarian dreams it was supposed to embody. Planning and the grass roots, instead of complementing one another, evolved in such ways that by 1940 regional planning elements within TVA *were congratulating themselves on having "opened up" the Norris area to the opportunities of a wider world through out-migration, while the model community of Norris existed as a white-collar enclave—a professional suburb of TVA—in the midst of an Appalachian poverty that is still only slowly being eradicated and a drain of youthful population that has been reversed only in the last half decade.*

7   Norris: Suburb in the Wilderness

IN ALL of TVA's preparations for the construction of Norris Dam, some ideas about regional planning underlay the authority's program to remove and relocate both the living and the dead. In addition, President Roosevelt's acknowledged interest as well as the specific provisions of the TVA Act itself prompted some gestures toward planning, conserving, and developing the natural resources of the area.[1] But as has been noted before, the authority never really acted directly on any mandated plan for social change but rather relied upon a series of specific programs which only indirectly increased social and economic advantages. To be sure, from the outset some TVA officials had plans for remodeling the life of the valley and for benefiting its inhabitants through agency programs. Admittedly, some of the ideas for improvement came from various writers, newspapermen, and academics who, after briefly visiting the Tennessee Valley, called TVA "a prevision of Utopia" and made statements suggesting that if there was to be a new civilization in the valley, the customs of the countryside would have to be made over by the inhabitants' adaptation to new realities of life.[2] At the same time there were individuals within the agency who believed that TVA should be something more than a dam-building, power-generating, fertilizer-producing organization. No one individual worked harder for this utopian vision for the Tennessee Valley than Arthur E. Morgan, and no single aspect of TVA's performance reflected this more than the town of Norris.

In speeches and articles delivered and written throughout 1933–35, Morgan outlined his ideas for the future of the Tennessee Valley. Despairing that the region had been out of the mainstream of economic and industrial development for decades, Morgan proposed the creation of small local industries to complement the agriculture of the region. Deploring the fact that the United States had moved more toward mass production and away from small, individual industries, Morgan cited France, with its smaller industries and units of production, as the example to be followed for the Tennessee Valley rather than Germany with its large, heavy industries. He urged that the Tennessee Valley region be made into the "France of Production," not the "Ruhr of Production"; for in his view it would be possible to develop products of individuality and character which would be preferable to mass-produced items.[3]

To implement this concept of small industry in the Tennessee Valley, Morgan proposed the idea of cooperative industry with its own local economy. As Morgan outlined it, this scheme might encompass "a co-operating central purchasing-organization, a central sales' organization, a distributing-organization, and perhaps its own credit in payment for goods—credit which would be good for cooperative products, but not for foreign goods." While people would be compelled to buy from one another, not all business would be conducted in this way, for money would also be necessary. But Morgan hoped that by forcing individuals to buy from each other, economic life in the Tennessee Valley might be improved without resort to the introduction of heavy, mass-production industry.[4] A series of such experiments, he thought, would discourge reliance of the region upon products imported from outside.

By 1934, with TVA's encouragement, a number of cooperative industries were actually begun. There were half a dozen cooperative canneries at work in counties where a large proportion of the population was on relief. Payment for work was made partly in money, partly in assorted cases of canned goods, and some attention was paid to better dietary and nutritonal care for relief families. Other enterprises in operation were two creameries and two poultry-raising cooperatives. Morgan also envisioned cooperative undertakings in such areas as "the production and sale of split-oak shingles, the home production of a variety of wood products, and the production, collection, and sale of handicraft products such as knit goods, rugs, bed quilts, and other textiles, pottery, wood carving and furniture." While estimating that more than 10,000 people were already getting part of their incomes from handcrafts in the region (later data which TVA gathered on farm families would show this to be an overestimate), he also admitted that marketing facilities were poor, standardization of quality was largely lacking, and fine design was much needed.[5]

From the very beginning Morgan had always conceded that cooperation was an attitude toward life which was often difficult to develop, particularly among people who in the past had been very individualistic; but cooperation proved even more difficult to implement than Morgan had anticipated, and as TVA moved further in the direction of electric power, flood control, and better agricultural technology, regional planning was slowly abandoned. Only in the development of the town of Norris did regional planning really survive, and then in a very limited form modified from what Morgan had envisioned.

Apparently the first discussions concerning the town of Norris predated the appointment of the full board of directors, for in a series of meetings with the president, Arthur Morgan and Roosevelt agreed on the need for some kind of model community which would be more than just a construction camp for Norris Dam.[6] The president and Morgan envisioned the town of Norris as a logical extension of their ideas on regional planning, which they believed would aid in bringing solutions to both rural and urban problems. Roosevelt had become interested in regional planning when, as governor of New York, he had encouraged the New York State Commission of Housing and Regional Planning to urge the relocation of industries in rural areas in order to redistribute population better.[7] Sensing the possibility that Norris might well be a small-scale model for future planning on a national scale, Roosevelt pressed Morgan to consider such an alternative. Morgan, who needed no further convincing, suggested at the first meeting of the board of directors that a permanent town be constructed near the dam site. Earl S. Draper, who was then director of TVA's Division of Land Planning and Housing, was asked to prepare a detailed town plan.[8]

During the next six weeks, while Draper and his staff proceeded with the task of selecting potential town sites, Morgan called for continued commitment to social planning by TVA. Hoping to win support and financing from the Division of Subsistence Homesteads, which had been created by Roosevelt within the Interior Department, Morgan in late July laid before the board a proposal which would begin a training program for dam workers.[9] In order to provide permanent homes for these people, one or more towns would have to be built in the vicinity of the dam. As a rule, there should be from one to five acres of tillable land for each house, though not necessarily adjacent to it. Also outlined by Morgan was a town plan which would combine agriculture, handicrafts, and small manufactures and would "supply some of the local needs of the locality and possibly produce goods of such a quality that they would find a quality market outside."[10]

In early August, Draper submitted his recommendation for the location, a site four miles south of the dam, with "considerable good agricultural land which can be used for subsistence gardening . . . and from the standpoint of topography, situation, relation to dam, accessibility to Knoxville, Clinton, and other towns, and all purpose usefulness seems to be the best in the entire section."[11]

On August 5 the board approved the choice and laid out plans for the immediate construction of 250 homes, later to be expanded to 1,000 if necessary.[12] Morgan, who had hoped that part of the financing of the town of Norris might be underwritten by the Division of Subsistence Homesteads, received authorization to seek such funding from the board of directors in September.[13] By late fall, however, when it had become apparent that these funds would not be forthcoming, the planning staff of the Land Planning and Housing Division under Tracy B. Augur began to think in more modest terms. Since it had also been decided that the first 150 homes would be equipped with electric heating, would serve as models for other electrical equipment, and would thus be more expensive to build, the initial projected figure of 1,000 permanent homes had to be scaled down. In the face of the economic realities of escalating cost and the necessity of having rapidly to construct houses for dam workers, the initial figure had to be reduced dramatically, so that it came closer to 300.[14] In addition, while Augur and his staff wanted to copy features that they had seen in other model cities both in the United States and in England, they were able to incorporate only a few of these design innovations, most notably the establishment of a surrounding greenbelt of unoccupied land to preserve the natural beauty and to protect property values from commercial encroachment.[15]

Building of the workers' dormitories began in October 1933, with the first houses under construction by January 1934. Workers began moving into the dorms in early 1934, but houses were not available until the early fall. Because of the need to house workers near the dam site, Norris as a town possessed from its very beginnings a dual purpose, serving as both a temporary and a permanent settlement. The urgency of finding homes for construction workers undermined some of the long-range planning which TVA envisioned for Norris and initially diverted attention away from permanent home construction. Indeed, Augur and his staff did not completely finish the design plan for the town until August 1934, long after the site was already in use.[16]

Once dormitories had been completed, construction on the remainder of the town proceded relatively on schedule. During 1934, TVA had bought additional land so that in its final form the town contained about 4,200 acres, with about 1,000 of these designated for homes and related community structures and facilities. Augur's plan had three focal points: a town center including the community school and shopping area; a construction camp site which might later be converted to offices for community use; a shop area which would contain space for present and future small industries. The greenbelt area south of the town site was to be used for the access to the Norris Freeway connecting Knoxville to the dam, while the northern portion would be used for a town forest and park. From his proposals evolved the final town plan on which TVA completed construction in the spring of 1935.[17]

In view of the proximity of the dam site to town and the rapid appearance of workers' dormitories, Norris seemed always to bear the stigma of a temporary, construction, or even company town. Certainly the first workers' houses were simple in construction and provided little privacy, but they were built on brick foundations, with light construction-grade timber, and were aesthetically compatible with the surrounding landscape.[18] A staff dormitory for engineers and a women's dormitory provided more working and

Model Homes in Norris.

living space than the workers' dormitories but were also not considered permanent. Since dining and recreational facilities had to be provided, too, construction was undertaken on a dining hall and a community building. Because of the various work shifts, construction workers would be eating at irregular hours, so a cafeteria food service building was designed. The basic design of the building included two wings, each with rows of tables surrounded by one central service area. The building had a seating capacity of more than 500 persons, and it was estimated that as many as 900 persons could be served in a single meal. The community building was a multipurpose structure containing a post office, library, meeting rooms, auditorium, offices, and gymnasium. Designed to serve the leisure time of the workers, the building would later be remodeled into the town restaurant, with space for stores and concessions.[19]

Since the construction camp had always been considered temporary, as soon as it was feasible a permanent residential section was built, which consisted of 152 electrified and insulated houses, 130 lower-cost cinder-block houses, 10 duplex houses, and 5 apartment buildings. In addition, some 30 existing farmhouses in the immediate vicinity were remodeled and reconverted to various forms of employee housing during the dam's construction. Included in this complex was a two-story, twenty-room, electrically heated school building, with a capacity of 400 pupils. Partially built with county funds and completed in February 1935, the school was used by children from both Norris and Anderson County.[20]

If the number of permanent houses disappointed the planners who envisioned a more grandiose town site, those same planners were also disappointed in their hopes that Norris would be a haven in which agriculture and small industry would complement each other. Indeed, so high were these hopes that in 1934 construction began on a community building which might fulfill both of those needs. The plan provided for a farmer's market alongside small handicraft and farm supply shops, but this concept soon had to be abandoned when it became clear that neither agriculture nor small home-craft industry could support the town. Remodeled from its original conception, this agriculture building ultimately became the home of the local drugstore, food store, telephone exchange, and post office.[21]

At its completion in the spring of 1935, Norris had cost TVA twice as much as had been originally budgeted. Extolled by many as a model town, a planned community, or the first all-electric town, Norris basked in the sunshine of favorable publicity, for although the cost had been high, the town had fulfilled its primary purpose of providing housing for the men working on Norris Dam. In 1935, about 1,250 men had moved into the construction camp dormitories, while about 1,100 people were living in the houses. Virtually everyone living in Norris at that time was in some way related to the construction of the dam, and thus there was what one observer has called a remarkable "esprit de corps."[22] This common bond among the residents transcended the various regional backgrounds of the residents, for while the majority of the laborers and the craft employees came from the surrounding areas, the professional people came from many states. Interestingly enough, there were few, if any, relocated families living there. In addition, there was present among the townspeople a freshness of approach, a willingness to experiment, and an eagerness of accomplishment which tended to discourage factions and cliques.

In view of the fact that the authority operated practically everything in the town and the workers worked a relatively short thirty-three-hour week, TVA took steps to introduce educational and training programs for its employees. Among the opportunities available were classes in English, history, government, arithmetic, drawing, shorthand, and typing. In conjunction with these courses there was training in the use of wood-working and metal-working machinery, smithing, dairy farming, gardening, handicraft work, electrical wiring, and automobile repair. In the hopes of providing a more stable and comfortable home life, the Authority also proposed programs in home planning and management.[23] The planners hoped that these educational and technical activities might eventually be housed in the Norris school and that both adult and child education might be carried on simultaneously. This concept went along with the cooperative and community spirit which seemed to mark Norris's early years. But both the necessity to scale down the size of the school and the fact that adult education was spread out over so many different fields made it impossible to realize the concept of a total, all-embracing educational program under one administration.

The role of TVA in Norris's development was also evident in the medical services provided the townspeople. Initially employing physicians to give physical examinations to prospective employees and to give emergency aid on the Norris Dam project, the Authority quickly saw the need to provide some form of medical services to the town. Employing a plan used extensively by private industries at the time, TVA furnished various types of medical care for the payment of a certain fee per month. Participation was voluntary, but approximately 250 families and a large number of the men living in the bunkhouses subscribed to the plan, which remained in effect throughout 1936.[24] Other services which TVA, rather than private interests, carried out were the operation of a cafeteria, creamery, filling station, and auto repair shop. There was even a resident landscape architect available to help with local beautification by providing grass seed, fertilizer, and shrubbery to all who asked for them and to stimulate interest in the formation of a local garden club.[25]

Lest it seem that TVA did everything for Norris, it should be pointed out that in some areas the residents themselves did act independently. One such example revolved around communication and the dissemination of information. In the early days of the town the only telephones were construction phones operated by a common battery system and used only for official business. To send messages, a courier system was established in each block, with wives acting as messengers to deliver information. At the same time, the training division within the Authority printed an information sheet which served as a newspaper until May 1935. One of TVA's employees subsequently transformed this sheet into a larger publication which relied on volunteer reporters, printed editorial comment, and in general proved to be one of the more worthwhile private ventures of the community.[26]

Perhaps most enterprising of all the private ventures in Norris in the summer of 1935 was the establishment of several cooperatives. The Norris Cooperative Society planned to rent space from TVA and to operate various service facilities.[27] One of its initial prob-

Houses Overtaken by Norris Dam.

lems was to raise sufficient capital to support the enterprise, for even in 1935 it was evident that many workers and families then residing in the town would be leaving once the dam was completed. Although the cooperative was initially capitalized at $2,400, the TVA board of directors specified that it should increase its operating capital to $3,500. The society reached its goal through additional investments from stockholders as well as through the recruitment of new members but wound up supporting only a food store and a service station, neither of which could be considered an unqualified success.[28] Because its business involved catering to both residents and tourists, however, the service station always turned a profit, often carrying the food store with it.[29] According to TVA estimates, the food store should have been doing close to $12,000 worth of business per month, but in actuality it was doing about one-half that volume.[30] TVA auditors found the bookkeeping sloppy, for the store manager, in seeking to cut costs, did not hire enough clerical help to do the job carefully. While stock was adequate and well displayed, service was efficient, and meat and grocery prices were competitive with those in Clinton and Knoxville stores, some customers did complain about the lack of variety of green vegetables.[31] Because of the lack of produce, some potential customers went elsewhere to buy groceries, thus further decreasing the profits of the store.

During 1936 the grocery's financial situation did not improve very much, and TVA sought to help by waiving payment of the store's rent and by postponing indefinitely its other outstanding financial obligations.[32] None of these gestures helped, and the store struggled on, though its future seemed precarious. The basic problem facing the store and Norris itself was the declining population. With completion of the dam, population of the dormitories declined from a high of 800 to almost 60 at the end of the year, while the number of people living in houses fluctuated between 1,100 and 900. The composition of the town also changed, with a significant rise in the number of professional people, many of whom worked in Knoxville and commuted daily.[33] Clearly the town was changing, and one of the most important transformations occurred in the realm of self-government.

Recognizing that with construction ending, the town would

need some type of government, TVA encouraged the formation of an advisory town council. Composed of representatives from agencies and groups in Norris such as the various cooperatives, the Parent-Teacher's Association, the Garden Club, the Tennessee Valley Workers' Council, it was made up of representatives of unions active in the Norris area and the medical and health councils.[34] Established to act in a bargaining capacity where rents were concerned, the council was also to help formulate policies relating to the residents' living conditions. In addition, such matters as the centralization of social services, the adequacy and quality of the various governmental services, and plans for suitable medical and dental care came under consideration by the council.[35] Nevertheless, although the council operated successfully in those areas, it was felt both by the Authority and by many of the residents that the council as organized was not sufficiently representative. Accordingly, the council studied the development of some method of selection of its members that would assure Norris's citizens of adequate representation. After some deliberation, it submitted a plan calling for an election at large, with proportional representation, and put it into effect by year's end of 1936.[36]

Even though the adoption of self-government represented a positive step in Norris's development, there was no hiding the fact that completion of the dam and the consequent loss of population continued to have adverse effects upon the town. Many of the activities in the field of adult education and training contracted, and what remained was placed under one community educational program. Gone were the trades training programs (though a shop was retained where people could voluntarily do wood working and metal working), the dairy farm, and all other agricultural programs. The community library, which had existed as a separate entity, was combined with the school library, while arts and crafts were also brought under the school's supervision. The medical and dental programs underwent revision as well, as the Authority phased out its responsibilities for those services. Thus it fell to the council members to take up the slack which they did by successfully advertising for private medical and dental practitioners.[37] In short, all of these activities were clear portents of change which seemed to be drawing Norris further away from the model-community concept first envisioned by its planners and moving it closer to a middle-class suburb. Some had recognized this evolvement earlier and had commented upon it, often in very critical terms. One of the most outspoken attacks upon Norris had come from Negroes, who charged that TVA discriminated against blacks in employment, vocational training, and housing opportunities at Norris.

Beginning as early as 1934 and 1935, articles appeared in various black publications citing instances of discrimination within TVA and contrasting the agency's promises of social reform and change with the realities of continued black subordination. While admitting that blacks were being employed at the dam site, the Negroes claimed they were placed generally in the more menial jobs, and the strongest complaints centered around the questions of training and housing opportunities at Norris. What stimulated much of this black reaction to TVA was an article published in *Collier's* magazine in 1934 entitled "There'll Be Shouting in the Valley."[38] Uncritically extolling the promises and achievements of TVA to date, the article also described Norris in almost ecstatic terms:

> You behold three or four hundred houses in which the architects have had a free hand. They are lighted, heated, and air-conditioned by electricity. You cook with electricity, heat water, clean floors, wash clothes and iron them, dispose of garbage, play music. . . . There are sleeping porches, cedar closets, shower baths, and heaven knows what—and all for the gracious rental of from fourteen to forty-five dollars a month, depending upon the size and construction.[39]

This glowing commentary, coupled with such words or phrases as "hard to believe," "astonishing," "worth seeking," "trouble wrenching ourselves away," marked the tenor of the article and precipitated some answers, particularly from the black community. Although not denying some of the potentially idyllic and pastoral qualities of Norris, critics singled out the housing provisions and training programs as being discriminatory. To blacks, Norris was lily-white, for they charged that TVA, by not allowing Negroes to occupy houses in Norris "because Negroes did not fit into the program," excluded them from the "ideal" American community, even though both races lived side by side in many other parts of the Tennessee Valley.[40]

Blacks were also concerned about the inadequacies of TVA's training and vocational programs where, they maintained, no attempt was being made to educate the black nor to diversify his skills. To maintain the black economic status quo was the Authority's goal, even to the point of appointing a white to be chief cook in the Negroes' barracks and of allowing white carpenters to build the cottages for black families. TVA provided training neither in carpentry, metal trades, automobile mechanics, and other skilled work nor in foremanship but rather continued to confine blacks to their customary Valley trades as drillers, powder men, and concrete pourers. In short, black critics railed against the fact that racial discrimination was being fostered by federal funds from a governmental agency.[41]

In attempting to answer these charges, Chairman Morgan chastised black authors about speaking out so sharply on these questions, for he felt that "much more of lasting accomplishment for Negroes could be secured by a policy of 'inching along,' a policy of cautious procedure so as not to raise to its highest pitch the anti-Negro sentiment in the Tennessee Valley."[42] Such criticism, Morgan continued, would jeopardize what steps had been taken to date by TVA in behalf of black employment. With 1,000 to 2,000 Negroes employed throughout the entire Tennessee valley operation, agency officials believed that they were doing as much, if not more, for the blacks than any other federal agency created by the New Deal.[43] Yet these reassuring statements did not muffle criticism from black writers about alleged TVA discrimination at Norris.

Some of the other criticisms of Norris were trivial, exaggerated, and difficult to verify. Most of these centered around complaints about poor service and high prices in Norris. For example, one man complained that he was charged twenty-five cents for a cup of coffee, and a woman lamented that service in the barber shop was so slow it took her two children hours to get a haircut.[44]

Other criticisms which on the surface appeared to be minor blew up storms of controversy. One of the most notable of these was the charge that Norris was a "Godless town." Initially stemming from statements made by a Chicago minister and given nationwide distribution by the *Chicago Tribune*, the controversy centered around the charge that Norris had been left "without provisions for religious worship."[45] While conceding that no churches had been built in Norris, nor had any ground been assigned for churches, TVA noted that it had hoped to avoid competition among religious sects for control of the town, at least until it had more permanent foundations. Periodicals such as the *Christian Century*, one of the leading religious magazines of the day, deplored these attacks, which they interpreted as also being directed against the entire TVA program. Although appreciating the Authority's concern over excessive competition, the magazine cautioned the agency not to act too arbitrarily, that they should not treat religious and business matters as synonymous, that having two churches was not the same as having two competing drugstores in town. Recognizing the difficulty of trying to bring democratic practices to bear upon religious matters, the *Christian Century* acknowledged the Authority's dilemma when it stated:

> The region near Norris happens to be a hotbed of holy rollerism and similar forms of religious obscurantism. Should the permanent population of Norris be drawn from this region, it is conceivable that a majority vote would favor a Holy Roller church. Or if the majority in the community should vote for some other form of church, it is still possible that the Holy Rollers, disdaining comity agreements, might try to storm the place anyway. Is the TVA, its friends might ask, to be expected to acquiesce in either of such developments? Does not its very attempt to build a *model* town lay upon it the responsibility to see that Protestantism is not represented in any such fashion?[46]

In actuality, despite criticism, the evolution of religious life in Norris proceeded in a most orderly and routine fashion. As soon as construction had started on the town, men in the dormitories began holding religious services. Local pastors representing area church denominations also offered their services and frequently appeared at informal Sunday evening services. By April 1934, sufficient interest had been shown to organize Sunday school classes. Because many men left Norris over the weekends, religious services were held on Thursday evenings, attracting an estimated 50 to 300 people, while at the same time the more traditional Sunday morning worship was also instituted, presided over by an ordained minsiter who was also an employee of the Authority.[47]

Recognizing that some more permanent type of religious program had to be implemented, TVA authorized the circulation of a petition to determine the religious preferences of people in the town. Almost unanimously the townspeople who responded voted in favor of a community, nondenominational church. Officially recognized in the last months of 1934, the church was called the Norris Religious Fellowship, and an ordained minister was brought in to work half time for it.[48] Near the end of 1935, the minister left Norris, and the officers carried on without a minister until a full-time clergyman was named in April of 1936. Paid entirely by the religious fellowship, he held Sunday services in the school building. In the next several years, as the population of Norris shifted and declined, the religious fellowship survived and continued unmolested by any more cries of "Godless town" from the outside.[49]

Of all the community services which TVA and Norris provided, none succeeded so well as the Norris school. Designed, built, and staffed by TVA, the school was one of the truly innovative features of the town, as it successfully integrated the school program with the community and was one of Norris's principal attractions as a place to live.

The modern, twenty-room school building was designed to house roughly 400 children in grades from kindergarten through high school. Costing about $170,000, the school initially provided educational opportunities only for Norris children,[50] but when it became evident that the town was not going to grow and expand as planned, educational opportunities were offered to children outside the Norris community. By 1935, a plan had been drawn up whereby approximately 100 high school students from Anderson County were admitted to the Norris school at a tuition of $50 per pupil per school year. Anderson County provided the transportation for its students and in addition paid the salary of an agriculture teacher.[51]

The impact and influence of the Norris school, however, went far beyond Anderson County. Under another contractual agreement, the Norris school served as an experimental and demonstration school for the University of Tennessee. The primary purpose of that program was to show teachers how an educational program can be developed to meet the particular needs of students.[52]

Teachers from the surrounding areas—Anderson, Union, Claiborne, Campbell, and Grainger counties—all visited and observed the methods employed in the Norris school. In addition, the teachers were usually given a tour of the school's physical plant, the library, nursery school, kindergarten, playgrounds, and all departments of instruction. From all reports, county school supervisors indicate that these visitations served to improve both classroom environment and instructional procedure in the respective county schools.[53]

The Norris school also sponsored an adult education program which was primarily for town residents but was available to others who cared to participate. Activities sponsored included workshops for musical and dramatic activities, weaving, pewter pounding, and leather work, and other crafts. Classes in crafts and art were conducted in town or in surrounding schools, and thus a small art center developed out of the federal art project. Also undertaken was a modest health program which combined both public health and physical education. In addition, library facilities were made available to the community, and more than 1,000 books were loaned free to courthouses, schools, and interested private groups throughout the Norris region.[54] Thus Norris's educational record was most impressive and represented the closest approximation to the ideals of its planners. One observer called the community-centered school "the heart and soul of Norris," and perhaps he was not too far from wrong.

Unfortunately for Norris, not everything worked out as well as the community school, and the town never realized the potential that its planners had hoped for. By 1937, the transformation had become painfully obvious. Even though for the first time there were a small number of families who had no connection with TVA, the majority were still employed by the agency, and almost 80 percent were professional people such as engineers in the design departments, regional planning experts, and members of the personnel and legal departments. The craftsmen and laborers who remained were used to operate the dam and powerhouse, to work in forestry projects, and to operate the properties. Of the total population of 1,100, almost one-third now commuted to Knoxville each day, many of whom had no connection with TVA but were Knoxville businessmen who sought out Norris as a suburban retreat.[55]

This large residue of professional people raised average family income to $2,600 per year, and with this rise came growing disinterest in community-sponsored activities. Almost all the consumer cooperative organizations disappeared. The Norris Cooperative Society, after operating the food store at a loss over a considerable period, asked to be released from its rental agreement with TVA. The Authority established a reasonable rent and advertised for applicants who might be interested in the store as a private venture; the Norris council was instructed to make a selection which would be in the best interests of the town. Under private operation, the Norris grocery managed to survive. The barber shop, restaurant, and drugstore, all operated by the Authority, were disposed of in similar fashion, but the filling station remained in the hands of the cooperative society.[56] With the elimination of these TVA services, Norris now bore little resemblance to the image that Arthur Morgan and others had tried to create.

Indeed the tragedy of Norris, if it can be called that, was that despite the best efforts of civic and social planners, the Norris experiment never really took hold. Even with its pleasant country setting and atmosphere, the protective greenbelt against commercial encroachment, and a modern freeway for access to Knoxville, the town was never able to establish for any length of time any true identity of its own. Beginning as essentially a company or construction town, Norris briefly fulfilled its expected potential as the increased work force rushed the dam to completion, only to begin the decline to its ultimate state as a kind of rural retreat or refuge for the Authority's employees—a TVA suburb. Never able to recover after the mass exodus of its construction workers, Norris could not thrive and prosper because it did not offer enough to attract the average family. Despite all the training programs and classes for workers and residents, TVA really failed to develop a program that would significantly help the local, rural population. Arthur Morgan had articulated these kinds of sentiments when the town was being planned, but his ideas were never really followed up, and by the mid-1930s Morgan himself was in no position to implement ideas which did not seem of prime importance to his other two directors on the TVA board. Thus what was made available appealed to the more professional and skilled workers and in effect excluded all who did not share these more intellectual and cultural interests. Faced with operating on its own, the town, even with Arthur Morgan's residence as moral encouragement, could not stem the inevitable tide of population attrition. By the late thirties, the once grand model town, while not a ghost town, was only a shadow of its earlier self.

Over the next ten years, as costs and expenses for the town rose, Congress finally demanded that Norris be put "on a self-sustaining basis . . . or . . . be promptly disposed of." TVA also agreed that Norris could be successful only if it could be "made to integrate properly with a system of local government commonly employed in the Tennessee valley."[57] In short, Norris had to stand on its own without further government support. These steps paved the way for TVA's final disposition of the town which had once been visited by dignitaries like Eleanor Roosevelt, praised by rural and urban planners, and in general trumpeted as the wave of the future.

On June 15, 1948, Norris was sold as a unit at public auction. So was lost to TVA another opportunity to formulate, coordinate, and execute a workable grass-roots policy which would have truly benefited residents of the Norris Basin.

8 The Dispossessed Revisited

I N 1940, four years after the floodgates at Norris were closed, and almost ten years after its inception, the immediate impact of TVA on the Norris region was summed up by a TVA analyst:

> As the circle [of impacts] widens to include adjoining counties, these early tangible results become less and less significant and eventually fade out altogether as discernible quantities. The broader more generally distributed results of the development program come to the fore, such as the calculated benefits of flood control and navigation to the economy of the Tennessee Valley and the extension of rural electrification and low cost power to people and industries within several hundred miles. It is to obtain these widespread objectives that large expenditures of federal funds have been made in the Norris area.[1]

One might well amend the last sentence properly to read: "It is to obtain these widespread objectives that large expenditures of federal funds and unremitting personal sacrifices and hardships on the part of local inhabitants have been made."

This amendment would at least serve to make us aware of the human costs of obtaining long-range planning objectives. Yet to some that reminder seems inappropriate, a small issue to set in the balance against long-term goals and achievements. TVA's history, unlike that of most New Deal creations, continues to be made at this very moment. The "development" program's objectives cited in the quotation above continue to be achieved, for good or ill, as the case may be. Some could argue that to examine the Norris project and its short-term impact alone is to isolate unfairly a segment of TVA's history. Can the disruption of the familiar lives of a rural population nearly half a century ago be balanced against TVA's broader achievements over the past decades? Unless historians adopt the old-fashioned positivistic notion that all material progress justifies any immediate social sacrifices, the answer is yes.

Assessing the most immediate consequences of TVA's regional impact is admittedly to concentrate upon one problem to the exclusion of long-term goals, imagined or achieved, that lie well beyond the time span 1933–40. But it is essentially through the examination of TVA in numerous regional and chronological settings that a different pattern can be constructed than the one which now exists in most New Deal histories—one which tends to cast the TVA in an almost heroic mode. Most histories have qualitatively examined the TVA's long-term development program rather than its immediate effects. TVA, in assessing itself, has often fallen victim to that same myopia.

Attitudes and Expectations of the Removed Population

In 1934, when TVA administered its family removal questionnaire, one of the purposes of gathering information was to determine the needs of relocated families. The interview of family heads included their responses toward the interview itself as well as toward TVA. The interview technique required TVA's field worker to enter responses of the family head. For the questions, "How did the individual respond to the interview?" or "What is his [the respondent's] attitude toward TVA?" the field worker had to check off one of five responses. The responses of the two questions were worded differently. For the interview attitude questions, the responses were: "antagonistic, suspicious, indifferent, interested, and gladly cooperated," while for the TVA-attitude question the choices were "antagonistic, critical, neutral, interested, and active booster." The responses, then, indicate not the respondent's attitudes as evaluated by, or expressed by, himself/herself, but the respondent's attitude as seen by the field worker. This consideration, plus the change in wording of responses from "suspicious" and "indifferent" for the interview response to "critical" and "neutral" for the TVA response, introduces a high degree of subjectivity in the wording of the responses.

The field workers were also allowed comments supporting their judgment in answer to the question: "Do you feel there are any special problems in the moving of the family that need further study?" They were also encouraged to "give gist of the conversation with family." The written answers to these various questions were sometimes lengthy, too much so to be analyzed quantitatively, and so were reduced to key words and phrases and placed in machine-readable form. The types of comments appended to the questionnaire were too varied to yield strong tendencies. Many field workers simply remarked upon the ability of a family to relocate, citing poverty extremes, medical and aging problems, and the like as barriers to successful relocation. The most persistent comments had to do with complaints about TVA's land purchase policies. Altogether, 46.1 percent of the 1,785 family heads interviewed had complaints about field workers appended to the questionnaires. Of these, 15.3 percent complained about land purchase policies, specifically about low prices. Only seventeen of the heads of families interviewed had favorable remarks about land acquisition and prices. Many favorable and unfavorable comments such as "TVA is good for the country" or "TVA is rotten," simply could not be categorized. Those complaining about land prices constituted roughly 7 percent of the total removed population, a figure not much above the percentage of the population who challenged TVA's purchases through the courts.

Respondents were generally positive toward the interview. Of 1,857 owners, only 1 percent were antagonistic, 6 percent suspicious, and 12 percent indifferent. Thirty-six percent of the owners were interested, and 45 percent gladly cooperated in the process. Tenant figures do not show much divergence from this pattern: fewer were regarded as suspicious (2 percent of 835 tenants), a slightly greater percentage were indifferent (13 percent), about the same were interested (34 percent), and more actively cooperated (51 percent). It must be kept in mind that since the interviewers were local people, a favorable response to the interview would be likely.

The expression of the respondents' attitudes toward TVA was different from that expressed toward the interview. By far the largest response from both owners (40 percent) and tenants (57 percent) was "neutral," with an additional 14 percent of the owners and 7 percent of the tenants being "critical." One percent of the tenants and 4 percent of the owners were regarded as antagonistic. Fewer owners (32 percent) and tenants (27 percent) were "interested" than "neutral," and only 8 percent of the tenants and 7 percent of the owners were "active boosters" of TVA. A response of "neutral" might be an expression of anomie by some respondents but, since the answers were tabulated in the late summer and early fall, while land purchase was still going on, might be explained, among owners, by a fear of lessened land prices or some sort of imagined retaliation. At any rate, while responses to the interview moved from "interested" to "gladly cooperated" (85 percent of the tenants and 81 percent of the owners), responses to TVA were grouped at the "neutral" to "antagonistic" end of the spectrum (owners 60 percent, tenants 65 percent).

Expectations upon relocation were very modest. The number of rooms desired in the new location was essentially comparable to the number being lived in at the time of the interview (owner median 4.3 rooms; tenant median 3.6 rooms). Eighty-five percent of the owners and 83 percent of the tenants wanted to relocate on a farm. With regard to possibilities of other development being sought upon relocation, 10 percent of the owners and 4 percent of the tenants had made no decision. Seventy percent of the owners and 58 percent of the tenants hoped to farm exclusively, while a combination of part-time industrial employment and farming was hoped for by 23 percent of the tenants and 12 percent of the owners. Nine percent of the tenants, as opposed to 2 percent of the owners, wanted industrial employment. Small numbers among owners and tenants contemplated the possibility of working in a garage, in stores, or at teaching jobs. Employment and relocation preferences would seem to show greater willingness on the part of tenants to combine industry and farming or select industry for a future job. But tenants were younger, and their population had been increased by the back-to-the-farm movement following the depression, so that proportion is not unexpected. In general, relocation did not work to change the Norris Basin inhabitants' expectations of the future. Life upon relocation was expected to cast itself in much the same mold that it had prior to the coming of TVA.

On relocated farms, 47 percent of the owners and 58 percent of the tenants wanted no electricity, though this response may have been induced as much by the fear of what it would cost as by a desire to maintain a familiar life style. The farms provided for relocation were expected to be modest. Small amounts of cropland were felt to be necessary by both owners (median 19.9 acres) and tenants (median 14.4 acres), though the number of desired acres of cropland for tenants was well above what they had farmed prior to the coming of TVA. Owners hoped for median pasture land of 9.7 acres and 5.2 acres of woodland; tenants, 4.3 and 1.3 acres.

The ideal of a small, self-sufficient farm was one that removed communities expected to retain. The degree to which this reflects desires to continue the same type of life which TVA disrupted is really impossible to determine. Modest expectations could equally be created by pragmatic analyses of just how far (for the owners) TVA's payment for land could stretch. Whether out of a desire to maintain the past, or a very realistic fear of the future, the responses do not point to altered expectations because of TVA's coming. Responses recorded in 1934 during the actual process of uprooting would be bound to reflect insecurity and fearfulness, a desire to cling to the familiar ways. It may have been, as oral respondents would later say, a "good thing" that people were wrenched out of the rural environment of the Norris Basin and forced into a wider and "modernized" world, but only retrospection could provide that. For most, in 1934, the only thing which lay on the horizon was the spectre of an uncertain future. For many, their worst fears would be realized as they pulled up stakes and sought to take up their old lives in new locations.

The years between 1933 and 1936 were traumatic for the residents of the Norris Basin. Thousands of families left behind farm lands and shared lives for new locations as the rising waters of Norris Reservoir closed over the lands that had been an integral part of their environment. To a modern generation in high-industrial, mass-consumption societies, mobility is the accepted pattern. People uproot, leave, and reestablish themselves viewing improvement in life style as a necessity. This change was not so easily accomplished in the traditional, nearly premodern rural society. Uprooting was not the customary pattern. With what trepidations, what visions of the future did people leave friends, neighbors, relatives, and communities to commence life in a new location? While such feelings can be only guessed at, there is concrete evidence about the outcome of the process of relocation. It is to this evidence that one must turn to complete the assessment of TVA's population removal in the Norris Basin.

TVA's Relocation Analyses and Their Sources

In the assessment of TVA's Norris project and its effect upon the removed population which follows, the year 1940 marked the last point at which TVA carried out an analysis of its project in Norris. Immediately thereafter the nation began to remove itself from the doldrums of the depression by virtue of a war-related economic upturn. After 1940, even on a regional basis, it becomes difficult to separate regional benefits or deficiencies conferred or created by TVA from those attributable to a generally invigorated national economy.

It is incumbent upon any scholar working in the field to acknowledge the assiduousness and thoroughness with which TVA continued to assess its own work in population removal and land acquisition in the Norris area. The conclusions reached in some of these reports are, of course, open to questions and criticism, but there can be no doubt as to their intellectual honesty and intent. All of the reports can be designated as impact assessment, or follow-up, analyses of the effects of population removal and land acquisition utilizing two major approaches: assessments of impact on the rural economy and the problem of rural overpopulation and assessments of impact in terms of tax-base loss through the purchase by TVA of exceptionally large amounts of rural real estate and its removal from county tax rolls.

A brief discussion of the various reports aids in the examination of these impact statements. The most valuable and extensive of these was written in 1937 by Harry Satterfield and William Davlin for the Social and Economic Research Division of TVA.[2] Its sig-

A Homestead near Andersonville. This 350-acre property was also submerged beneath the waters of Norris Dam.

nificance lies in the fact that the data came from a three-page follow-up questionnaire given in August and September of 1936 to a sample of the relocated population, precisely two years after the original eight-page questionnaire was given to potential evacuees from the reservoir area in 1934.[3] Regrettably, the raw data for the follow-up study are unavailable, and the Satterfield/Davlin report is the only source which remains.

It is curious that while TVA was conducting its own follow-up investigation, the Agricultural Extension Service of the University of Tennessee, under contract to TVA for phases of population removal, was conducting its own survey between 1936 and 1938, administering a lengthy schedule to a sample of removed families. Pat Kerr, supervisor at the Extension Relocation Service, was in charge of this work and wrote up the conclusions in a report in 1939. Neither the report nor the raw data are now available. At one time housed in the Agricultural Extension Division offices at the University of Tennessee, the reports and the raw data have since been destroyed, and Mr. Kerr has been dead for a number of years. The only available record of the schedules and reports is contained in an M.S. thesis completed for the College of Agriculture by Ralph Leighton Neilsen, who had access to some of the data. Neilsen's study, "Socio-Economic Readjustment of Farm Families Displaced by the TVA Land Purchase in the Norris Area," is based essentially upon Kerr's reports and evaluation. Research strategy dictated the decision not to utilize the Neilsen data because of some defects which would render it unrepresentative.[4]

While the Kerr study and the Satterfield/Davlin report were administered at roughly the same time, neither appears to take notice of the other. There is no record of the Kerr report in TVA's archives, and it is curious that the Social and Economic Division would have been unaware of the Extension Relocation Service's follow-up, since both were working in the same area at the same time. Nielsen does not even cite the Satterfield/Davlin report in his thesis but relies essentially upon Extension Relocation Service materials. The existence of two simultaneous reports reflects the antagonism existing within TVA between the agriculturalists and the planners.

Satterfield and Davlin used 618 relocated families as a sample.

They compiled an alphabetical list of relocated families for each county in Tennessee and for three Kentucky counties contiguous to the Norris Basin: Bell, Laurel, and Whitley. Every third relocated family was chosen from each county's list for the sample. According to the authors of the report, there was neither time nor money to do a more complete survey, but it was felt that the sample constituted "approximately 35 percent of the number of reservoir families who relocated in each county, allowing a 10 percent margin for families who might not be found by the fieldmen who administered the questionnaire."[5] One weakness of their follow-up report was that the results were not weighted in any way to account for the length of time which had occurred between removal and relocation. Not all the answers on the questionnaire were tabulated and analyzed. Although the number of families who removed and relocated out of state was not very large, they were not in the sample, and data on these families would have provided some useful information. Finally, no match-ups were made to the 1934 questionnaires, and the questionnaire of 1936, like those of 1934, suffers from some subjective interpretation.[6] Despite some weaknesses, the Satterfield and Davlin report is the only one produced by TVA which can be said to make an adequate comparative analysis of families after relocation and judges the effectiveness of the relocation services provided by TVA.[7]

A different but not unconnected analysis has to do with the effects of TVA's land acquisition policy. The major impact of land acquisition was the removal of rural real estate from the tax rolls of the counties, which in turn brought about reductions in the tax bases of local governments. Between 1934 and 1940 the Tennessee Valley Authority made three studies of the effect of its land acquisition policy upon local government and finance. The last of these reports, made by the Department of Regional Studies, is the most complete and extensive as well as being the most useful, among other things, for the period of time which separates it from the initial movement of TVA into the region.[8]

Not only does the regional studies report, the last of these analyses, incorporate the materials from the previous two tax studies, but in its own right it constitutes the final comprehensive report on TVA's impact in the Norris region through both land acquisition and population removal. Robert Lowry, its author, was with the Social and Economic Research Division of the Department of Regional Planning Studies, whose director was Earle S. Draper. The report was assembled by the end of 1939, and its tentative conclusions and summaries were submitted to and approved by TVA's regional planning council.[9] The completed regional studies report of 1940 sent to the general manager of TVA, Gordon Clapp, provides an interesting contrast with the Satterfield/Davlin report. The former deals with more aspects of impact, some of them strained, and for the most part balances off the short-term ill effects upon the rural economy through TVA's population removal and land acquisition by projecting the alleged beneficial effects of long-term improvements wrought by the coming of TVA. The Satterfield/Davlin report, by comparison, is more critical, does not include peripheral information, and scrutinizes very carefully the actual effects of relocation and the work of relocation agencies which the Lowry report does not appreciably touch upon. The regional studies report devotes a disproportionate amount of analyses to tax-base reduction and its effects. Of the two reports, both of which constitute final assessments of short-term effects, the Satterfield/Davlin is the more conscientious in adhering to its data and more honest in its criticism. The Lowry report is self-serving in many areas and reduces the weight of critical problems through overly optimistic projections or by making local institutions bear much onus for situations created by TVA's removal and land purchase programs.

POPULATION REMOVAL: ASSESSMENT AND APPRAISAL

One point upon which there was nearly unanimous agreement was that the Norris area suffered primarily from a problem of rural overpopulation which aggravated, and in turn was aggravated by, poor farming practices, crowding of arable land, and intensive farming of marginally productive land. All of these elements contributed to erosion and general soil exhaustion. Fear of siltage in the storage reservoir from lack of water control on the land was one of the contributing factors mentioned earlier in the formulation of a "heavy-purchase" policy which, by increasing the number of displaced persons, brought pressure upon the relocation programs.

The problems and consequences of rural overpopulation were in existence before TVA came to the Norris Basin. Out-migration to industrial opportunities in the North had been a safety valve against the worst aspects of this problems, but that valve had been cut off by the depression. Whatever relief had been supplied through out-migration was terminated, then reversed, as a back-to-the-farm movement accelerated between 1930 and 1935.

As mentioned earlier, the USDA, in a study completed in 1935, found the Norris region at that time to be "one of excess population in relation to economic opportunity," and a TVA study found that Grainger County, one of the counties directly affected by population removal and land acquisition, was in 1936 still 43 percent "overpopulated with respect to land resources and present farm practices."[10] TVA intruded into this dense host population in 1933, displacing over 3,000 families, taking from agricultural use 14 percent of the rural real estate in the five-county area (including some of the best agricultural land in the state in Powell and Big Valley), and removing through purchase and federal tax exemption millions of dollars worth of assessable property from local tax bases.

Intensive farming practices in an overpopulated rural area and the coming of TVA drove land prices up drastically in the Norris area between 1930 and 1935. Increases in the average value of farms were reported in only three counties in Tennessee, and two of these were Campbell and Union, central to the Norris Basin. The Lowry report noted that three of the four counties in the state showing an increase in average value of farm land per acre were in the Norris Basin. Furthermore, such increases were essentially limited to the eighteen civil districts immediately surrounding the reservoir, which showed an aggregate rise in farm value from 1930 to 1935 of $5,000,000, or 42 percent, as opposed to farm values in civil districts contiguous to those surrounding the reservoir area, which rose by only 6 percent. By contrast, farm values throughout the state fell by 25 percent.[11]

The removal of the Norris families was carried out against this backdrop of rising farm values, intensive agriculture upon marginal land, and rural overpopulation. If the movement of the Norris farm evacuees had been beyond the tier of counties surrounding the reservoir, perhaps the pressures created by TVA's intrusion would have been more lightly borne, but either through a sentimental attachment to their homes or the inability to purchase better land outside the basin, much of the removed population doggedly clung to the region where they had been raised. Relocation surveys showed that of the 2,587 families removed as of December 1936, 62 percent remained in the same five-county area. Only 176 families located outside the state at all, and more than half of these went into nearby Bell and Whitley counties in Kentucky. Not only did 62 percent relocate within one of the five Norris basin flowage counties, but an additional 20.4 percent relocated in a county contiguous to one of them. Only 10.8 percent of the removed families crossed an intervening county to establish a new home in Tennessee.[12]

The returns from the follow-up questionnaire revealed that home ownership had "increased slightly" among relocated tenant families (75.1 percent of whom remained in the reservoir area), but examination of the schedules of these thirty-four former tenants, now owners, revealed that thirty remained within the reservoir and were troubled by land shortages. Seven of these were not farming, four families because they could not find cultivatable land to rent. "It appears," said Satterfield and Davlin, "that the former renters who have become owners, purchase of a farm or even a dwelling place was often a necessity because none were available for rental." Only six of the new owner families owned farms of more than twenty-four acres, and from data on twenty-six new owners engaged in farming, it was found that ten had to rent supplemental land.[13] These new owners claimed a median ten acres of cropland as opposed to twelve prior to removal. The land they purchased was not very good: it averaged under twenty-nine dollars an acre, little more than half of what was paid by former owners who relocated (fifty-three dollars). The authors of the report concluded, "The foregoing observations make it difficult to conclude that the change from tenant to owner status among these families has proceeded upon sound economic bases."[14]

There was some further change in status among tenants, as twenty-two former sharecroppers and share tenants who had ostensibly moved upward by becoming cash tenants were actually renters who had discontinued farming "and rented buildings for cash because they were unable to rent land to cultivate."[15] Thus while these elements of apparent upward mobility would be taken as signs of successful relocation, close analysis appears to reveal that these were simply adjustments, not improvements, brought about by the lack of rentable land and houses.[16] This conclusion is significant in that other TVA studies would cite the apparent upward mobility of tenants as an argument in favor of successful relocation practices.

In relocation analysis those points which bear upon farming are the most significant by far, since 83 percent of all the landowners and 79 percent of the tenants examined were engaged in farming upon their removal. In the sample population farming had decreased 7.5 percent upon relocation. Points which cannot be shown to bear upon farming may well enhance other portions of the population but cannot be said generally to affect appreciably the status of the relocated families.

The follow-up study indicated that most removal families kept to the same dominant subsistence farming which they had pursued prior to relocation, hence making a comparison of farm size and values before and after relocation possible. Owner families did not generally spend on their new farms the equivalent of money which they received from TVA.[17] In part this was due to the fact that before the money for the sale was paid over to the former owner by TVA, back taxes, mortgages, and any liens on the land were deducted. It must also be kept in mind that some money had to be kept back by the removed owner to establish himself and his family in a new location. Rising farm values around the reservoir automatically dictated that even with an equivalent amount of money to spend for a new farm, one would be able to purchase less land than one possessed previously and in many cases land of inferior quality.[18] The number of owners holding farms of less than $1,000 in value doubled upon relocation, while those with farms valued at more than $4,000 dropped 10 percent.[19] (see table 27).

Families who managed upon relocating to push outside the immediate tier of counties around the reservoir toward the center of the valley found that the farm prices were (and had always been) considerably higher than with the five-county reservoir area. In

Knox, Hamblen, Jefferson, and Hawkins counties, the average price per acre for farm land in 1936 was sixty-one dollars. The tendency to remain in the county of the old home, already strong in terms of social affinities for the tried and familiar, was reinforced, especially for the poorer families, by the attractiveness of comparably cheaper, if poorer, lands in the reservoir area. Immobility was essentially an economic *and* psychological phenomenon. Unfortunately, many owner families who would probably have benefited most from the acquisition of lands in other counties simply could not afford the opportunity to relocate outside the reservoir area. In fact, 85.4 percent of the families who purchased farms for less than $1,000 relocated in one of the five reservoir counties. Rural overpopulation, then, was made substantially worse by the random process seemingly followed by TVA in relocation. The one area which did not need more people was inundated with them, and with a high proportion of the poorest, creating a problem which merely exacerbated an already precarious economic situation.[20]

As might be expected, the displaced farmers put nearly all their money into their new farms. Only 7 percent of the owners made investments other than in farms, and a substantial number of these were moderate investments.[21] The median size of farms for the sample owners prior to removal had been 60.5 acres; after removal it was 49.3 acres. Tenants in the sample dropped from 12.6 acres prior to removal to 8.2 acres.[22] In addition to smaller farm size, relocation brought about a reduction in cultivatable land, with a higher number of sample families reporting no crops for the year of

TABLE 27   *Distribution of Owners*
by Appraisal Value of Former Farms and
Purchase Price of Present Farms

	Former owners		Present owners	
Value	No.	%	No.	%
All farms	376[1]	100.0	368[2]	100.0
Less than $1,000	43	11.4	89	24.2
$1,000–$3,999	193	51.3	179	48.6
$4,000 and over	140	37.3	100	27.2

[1]Five of the 381 families gave indefinite answers.

[2]The amount paid for present farms was indefinite for twenty-one of the 389 families.

SOURCE: Tennessee Valley Authority, Department of Regional Planning Studies (Satterfield and Davlin), "A Description and Appraisal of the Relocation of Families," table 2.

the survey than prior to relocation (11.5 percent as against 6.1 percent). The owner families in the sample cultivated a median 21.7 acres prior to removal; the median was 16.9 acres thereafter. Sample tenants' cultivated land dropped at about the same ratio.[23] Tabulations of landholding by the sample population before and after relocation are in table 28.

Significant transitions occurred in land cultivation according to the place of relocation. Among relocated owners in reservoir counties, 43.3 percent cultivated fewer than ten acres, a figure which dropped to 20.3 percent among owner families in the first tier of counties beyond the immediate reservoir area and then to 6.0 percent in the third tier of counties and beyond. Those who moved out of the reservoir relocated more successfully than those who remained.[24]

Considering land scarcity and rising land costs in the reservoir area, as well as comparably higher costs outside it, relocated families possessed only a minimal capacity for expansion and improvement on new farms. In the sample, 80 percent of the relocated families showed no change in the ownership of farm machinery, and 75 percent showed no change in the ownership of live-

TABLE 28 Relocated Owners and Tenants
Owners and Tenants of the Norris Flowage,
by Number of Acres Cultivated (in Percent)

| | Relocated families | | | | All families prior to removal | |
| | Owners | | Tenants | | | |
Number of acres cultivated	Present farm	Former farm	Present farm	Former farm	Owners	Tenants
All families	100.0	100.0	100.0	100.0	100.0	100.0
None	6.9	4.4	19.2	9.2	3.6	22.5
0.1–9	25.2	16.2	40.7	34.5	21.7	37.8
10–19	26.0	25.9	27.5	33.2	26.0	25.0
20–29	14.7	21.6	7.4	13.5	19.6	8.5
30–39	9.3	11.1	2.6	8.1	11.9	3.5
40–49	6.2	5.1	.4	.9	6.7	.8
50–59	3.5	7.7	.0	.4	4.4	.6
60 and over	8.2	8.2	2.2	2.2	5.0	1.3

Note: Of the 2,841 families interviewed during the survey of families prior to removal, data on the number of acres cultivated were available for 2,783 families. Relocated families N = 618. All families prior to removal N = 2,783. Relocated owners N = 389. Relocated tenants N = 229. Owners before removal N = 1,830. Tenants before removal N = 953.

SOURCE: Tennessee Valley Authority, Department of Regional Planning Studies (Satterfield and Davlin), "A Description and Appraisal of the Relocation of Families," table 3.

stock.[25] Almost half of the owners (48.6 percent) and more than half (60.3 percent) of the tenants felt "that their present farms [were] not so good as the ones they had prior to removal." Among owners, 23.1 percent and among tenants 16.1 percent felt that they had secured a better location, with more families expressing satisfaction when relocated outside the reservoir area than inside.[26]

Figures from table 29 indicate some slight improvements in housing. But 17.3 percent of the owners and 63.7 percent of the tenants were still living in dwellings with three rooms or less.[27] As might be expected, the owner dwellings were on the average newer and of better construction than those available to tenants. There was not a great improvement in sanitary facilities or water supply, for two-thirds of the tenants and slightly over a third of the owners obtained water from springs (45.4 percent overall). Prior to removal, 41.0 percent of the tenants and 28.7 percent of owners were without toilet facilities of any kind. After, 52.4 percent of the tenants and 18.3 percent of the owners lacked toilets. Houses electrically lighted increased from 1.8 to 9.6 percent.[28]

The sample removed population felt more positively about their homes than their farms. Among the owners, 44.2 percent considered their house better than the one they had prior to relocation, 27.0 percent "about the same," and 28.8 percent not as good as the former. Only 29.3 percent of the tenants regarded their homes as

TABLE 29   *Relocated Owners and Tenants and Owners and Tenants of the Norris Flowage, by Number of Rooms per Dwelling (in Percent)*

Size of dwelling	Relocated families		All families prior to removal	
	Owners	Tenants	Owners	Tenants
All dwellings	100.0	100.0	100.0	100.0
1 room	0.8	8.3	1.3	7.9
2 rooms	3.4	24.0	8.3	28.2
3 rooms	13.1	31.4	26.9	35.1
4 rooms	21.9	22.7	22.9	15.3
5 rooms	24.2	6.6	17.0	7.3
6 rooms	16.0	5.7	12.4	3.2
7 rooms	7.7	.0	5.3	1.5
8 or more rooms	12.9	1.3	5.9	1.5

Note: Relocated families $N = 617$. All families prior to removal $N = 2,814$. Relocated owners $N = 389$. Relocated tenants $N = 229$. Owners before removal $N = 1,849$. Tenants before removal $N = 965$.
SOURCE: Tennessee Valley Authority, Department of Regional Planning Studies (Satterfield and Davlin), "A Description and Appraisal of the Relocation of Families," table 4.

better, while 41.9 percent felt that their homes were "not as good as" those lived in prior to relocation.[29]

In addition to economic pressures restraining movement of the displaced population, one must consider the tendency to remain within familiar environments and familiar personal relationships. High proportions of owners and tenants (78.4 percent and 69.4 percent respectively) relocated in the same locality as one or more friends from days before TVA. "All of these families," reported Satterfield and Davlin, "except three owners and one tenant reported frequent visits with these friends." Nor were the removed populations situated differently with respect to roads, schools, and trade centers. More than a quarter of the tenants and 15.4 percent of the owners lived on roads that were impassable during certain times of the year. Families were a median distance of 1.7 miles from their trade centers, with 7.2 percent relying upon itinerant peddlers for their necessities,[30] and over half of the owners and tenants reported no improvement in their trading centers after relocation. The median distance of the sample relocation population from elementary schools was 1.6 miles for owners and 1.8 miles for tenants.[31]

Given the fact that the spatial patterns remained much the same before and after removal and generally reflect the boundaries of communities in rural East Tennessee in the thirties, the chance of relocating in a familiar environment was excellent. Traditional spatial patterns and occasional neighboring can allay the shock of uprooting and relocation, but the Norris communities before TVA had been dependent upon church activities to fill out social contacts in a broader sense. The proximity of a former friend or neighbor could not completely fill the social gap created by removal, and here one finds evidence of adjustment difficulties. The follow-up study was made in 1937 before enough time had passed to assure full integration in new communities. Even so, it is surprising to find that 80.0 percent of the owners and 92.6 percent of the tenants were "not participating in . . . community sings, box suppers, and other gatherings of a similar nature." Church participation dropped radically: 23.1 percent of the sample said that they were not churchgoers, whereas only 4.1 percent belonged to that category prior to relocation.[32] This seems more striking in the face of oral evidence stressing the cohesiveness of both church participation and church-related activities in the year prior to the coming of TVA, as well as the local opposition to the federal burying ground proposed by TVA. Churches and their congregations formed the cement of sociability in many instances. While whole congregations, unlike families, could not be removed, the buildings in some cases could—and often became the sole reminders of what had once been a living organism rooted in the community's past.

The conclusion of the report by Satterfield and Davlin dealt with the amount of assistance received from "established relocation services" in finding a new home.[33] Only 35.7 percent reported such help (owners 40.4 percent, tenants 26.3 percent). Of these, only 35.6 percent of the owners and 57.1 percent of the tenants bought or rented a farm shown them by the relocation service. Not only was relocation aid extended more to owners than to tenants, but among landowners a larger number of those purchasing farms of $4,000 or more received assistance than did purchasers in poorer categories. Tenants complained that while they were promised help prior to removal, they were "compelled to move before such help became available." A larger group felt that the "relocation agencies had nothing to offer them; the farms listed were either too costly or were otherwise unsuited to their needs."[34]

Satterfield and Davlin reported that $213,953.39 had been expended by TVA through March 1937 for the removal and resettlement of 2,572 families from the Norris Reservoir area. The Agricultural Division of TVA in conjunction with the University of Tennessee Agricultural extension Division had spent $133,367.10, a cost which included the administration of the 1934 questionnaire to families who were potential candidates for removal. The authors noted in their report that "the cooperative activities of the Tennessee Valley Authority and the Agricultural Extension Division of the University of Tenessee did not include an agricultural training program for the readjustment of displaced families such as is being carried on in some of the other reservoir areas." Sixty-two percent of all the money expended in relocation and resettlement was basically for the cost of the 1934 questionnaire survey, of compiling available real estate lists, and for taking families to look at the properties. In contrast, the Removal Section of TVA expended

$64,242.25 in carrying out the most difficult and creative job of removal. According to Satterfield and Davlin, only 35.7 percent of the sample relocation families claimed to be aided in resettlement by TVA relocation agencies, a percentage which if applied to the total 2,572 families would show 1,025 families aided in relocation at a gross cost to TVA of $209 per family.[35]

In sum, the program for resettlement and removal could not be judged a success. Even the modest expectations of the removed population, as ascertained in 1934, were not met upon relocation. Few prospective buyers looked at available farms through TVA, and this was a service primarily for landowners and not tenants. The results of a lack of training and readjustment programs can only be guessed at, but speculatively speaking, it must have been highly negative, since the needs for such programs among a population that resumed upon relocation the same type of farming, often upon less productive land, would remain the same or would increase. It is ironic that TVA did more to ease the pressures of relocation upon many families through employment than through the rather ineffectual relocation services. Satterfield and Davlin pointed out that 22.9 percent of the owners and 17.9 percent of the tenants had family members working for TVA.

The final assessment of TVA's activities in the Norris Basin was the 1940 Regional Planning Council report, much of which was devoted to an apologia for county tax-base decrease through TVA purchases. But this report did make a general survey of what it termed "outstanding changes" and, euphemistically, "other modifications." The summary attached to this report itemized what TVA regarded as "the outstanding changes that have occurred which should operate to raise income, living standards, and the quality of public services in the area immediately surrounding Norris." Most of these had been caused "more or less directly" by TVA activities. If these points are examined one by one from the viewpoint of the removed population, they appear less outstanding. Along with the outstanding changes, TVA analysts presented some "other modifications," "effects which may be considered deterimental to the area." These were cited as follows, and for the most part their background and elaboration have provided one of the themes of this work.[36]

254

1. The previous isolation of rural peoples in parts of the area has made difficult the social and economic readjustments which the reservoir has required of them. More than six out of every ten of the reservoir's 2,900 families necessarily resettled in Norris counties which were already agriculturally overpopulated.

2. The already weak economic base of the Norris counties is currently weakened further by the TVA purchase and removal of more than 152,000 acres of land from private use; some difficulty will be encountered in supporting the present population, pending a broadening of the area's economic base.

3. The loss of property tax base resulting from TVA land purchase amounts to $2,000,000, or 8.3 per cent of the 1934 valuation. Rural land tax base reductions made voluntarily by the counties since TVA land acquisition account for an additional $440,000, or 2 percent of the 1934 valuation. An enforcement of tax assessment machinery would go far toward offsetting these losses. The valuation of property other than rural land increased $525,000.

4. The 800 new houses and the 42 per cent increase in farm values are evidences of increased farm population density and more intensive, agricultural operations. Representative farm families from the Norris reservoir now average only 17 acres of cropland whereas they formerly averaged 22 acres. An offsetting factor to this more intensive land use is the introduction of new farm practices to conserve soil and stabilize income.

5. The arms of the reservoir have blocked direct access to certain parts of the Norris area, causing shifts in natural trade areas, and in the case of Union County, making effective county administration most difficult. Such difficulties may be a blessing in disguise, if they bring about an early adjustment of county lines or county consolidation. [Pp. viii–ix]

These were the points against which the outstanding changes produced by TVA's impact were to be weighed. In the language of the reports, the "detrimental effects" were "being offset at least in part" by the following eight points, which will be considered from the removed population's point of view.

1. TVA activities appear to be chiefly responsible for an increase of $5,500,000 in farm values in the districts around the reservoir, as reported by the 1935 census. This increase, amounting to 42 per cent over 1930, occurred in the fact of falling values reported elsewhere in the state. [P. vi]

Among other things, these increases were due to the removal of large numbers of farms by TVA. Consequently those who relocated in the immediate vicinity were forced by buy in a rising market property which had become valuable because of the removal of so much land from the market. From the viewpoint of the removed population this could be regarded as detrimental.

2. TVA activities are chiefly responsible for the appearance of currently taxable properties in the Norris area since 1934, such as over 800 privately owned new houses, new stores, filling stations, and tourist camps. Furthermore, potential tax values have been created in the form of important real estate improvements on TVA property. [P. vi]

New properties to provide beneficial economic recovery would have had to come under an assessment schedule revised stringently upward to increase revenue. TVA thought that tax assessment procedures prevented the Norris Basin counties from realizing their economic potential. But increased property assessments would fall heavily upon the recently relocated. Stores, filling stations, and the like could have benefited the removed families if they had had enough capital and training to become owner/operators of new enterprises. Relocation attempts to do this through the Resettlement Administration failed. Whatever they were ultimately to become, most relocated families continued to be farmers, not owner/operators of new businesses. If these opportunities had directly offered so many disadvantages by 1940, why was there such continued strong out-migration from the region until recently?

3. By purchase of school properties TVA activities have been an important factor in the net reduction of 41 school units from the 316 operating in 1934; 22 of the net abandonments were one-teacher establishments. School plants have been constructed, improved and modernized by the expenditure of between $300,000 and $400,000 of TVA, WPA, and PWA [Public Works Administration] funds, in addition to county expenditures. [P. vii]

TVA cited the value in reduction of one-teacher establishments and the building of new school plants. Much of the expenditure was borne by counties out of tax bases diminished through TVA purchases. At any rate "improvements" in some respects can be taken simply as trade-offs. Relocation of families placed new burdens upon extant regional school systems, which had to absorb the influx of resettled families. This should be regarded as more of a "neutral" or compensatory aspect of the coming of TVA than a definite plus.

4. The TVA reservoir has caused the abandonment of 227 miles of county roads the TVA has built 88 miles of new county roads. For the replacement of affected state and county roads, the TVA has spent over $2,000,000, not including the cost of the Norris Freeway. In addition, the WPA has spent over $1,000,000 on the improvement of county roads. The state and federal governments have spent over $5,700,000 on the construction of state and federal highway systems since the systems were set up over 20 years ago. The Norris counties now contain 162 miles of federal-aid highways, 128 miles of other state highways, nearly all of those hard surfaced, and 2,200 miles of county highways; about half of the latter are graveled, over 50 miles are hard surfaced, and the remainder are earth. [P. vii]

The road improvements are significant in reducing isolation and should be taken positively. One would want to set this benefit against shifts in trade patterns caused by the intrusion of TVA. The lowering of aggregate bonded debt by $480,000 must be balanced against the $2,000,000 loss resulting from a reduced tax base. It is worth keeping in mind, however, that upon relocation 25 percent of the tenants and 15 percent of the owners lived on roads that were impassable for part of the year.

5. The TVA payment of over $118,500 for purchased schools to four of the five Norris counties, the $141,000 TVA final settlement to Union County, the increased back tax collections resulting from the TVA purchases of land and services, all were factors in lowering the aggregate bonded debt of the counties from $4,480,000 in 1934 to $4,000,000 in 1939. In spite of tax base losses, the ratio of bonded debt to assessed values increased only from 17.7 to 18.0 during the period. The decrease in bonded debt was accomplished at the same time that county capital assets were being increased by new school buildings and new roads.

6. The TVA has constructed within the area a model town costing $3,500,000, with housing accommodations for 350 families. The town has a $170,000 school which serves the residents of Norris and the surrounding area and is valuable for demonstration purposes. The TVA has constructed two recreation parks with cabins which operation 17,400 person-days during the 1938 season. In cooperation with other agencies it has planted nearly 20,000,000 trees on public and private lands in the area. The forest as established is of value for soil saving and demonstration purposes and as a source of

part-time employment. The TVA has distributed 4,450 tons of fertilizer to farmers for demonstration purposes or in lieu of AAA [Agricultural Adjustment Administration] payments, and has provided 950 farm homes with electricity. [P. vii]

Norris as a model town was never an answer to the region's rural overpopulation. If it became a model town, it did not do so by demonstrating what could be done through resettlement or through mixed rural/industrial community resettlement. Norris became a "technocratic" village of the TVA, looked upon as a pleasant rural retreat by many TVA employees. There was no immediate rural agricultural training program for the relocated population, and area test demonstration farmers were never the poor subsistence farmers, but rather those who were more successful and better off. The decreased size of the farms among the relocated population together with the reductions in cropland belies a situation that fertilizer cannot correct. The relocated population had expressed misgivings about rural electrification and participated in it only slightly upon relocation, and many areas were not electrified until the 1940s.

7. The Norris attractions have been partly responsible for 120 filling stations and 10 or 12 tourist cabin developments on the main highways surrounding the reservoir, and altogether responsible for 22 cottages on private lands, and a number of privately operated concessions along the shores of Norris Lake. Eighteen cottage sites have been leased on TVA lands. The permanent Norris community has created a demand for goods and services that has been translated into income and employment for nearby merchants and other local residents.

8. The TVA development has been the principal cause of a favorable differential between the Norris counties and otherwise comparable counties in such business indexes as retail sales, merchant's licenses, spendable income, and bank deposits. [P. viii]

One must refer to lack of capital for development among the aggregate removed population, and to the number of those who were, in that population, to continue the same type of farming. The otherwise comparable counties include Scott and Morgan counties in the Cumberlands and Cocke County on the edge of the Great Smokies; and to say that the Norris area showed growth improvement over those other poorer counties, considering the presence of

TVA in the Norris region for seven years, is not really to say very much. As the regional studies report noted with regard to spendable income: "Most of the differential between the Norris and sample counties is concentrated in Anderson, whose remarkable increase of 55 percent is traceable to the influence of the town of Norris." Positive impacts from the town of Norris and tourist traffic would doubtless benefit the region in the long run and increase aggregated business indices, but the fact remained that the region's most noticeable export continued to be its youth. Of course, an influx of tourism in the area would most likely have had the effect of raising regional trade prices.

Although it was not included in the specific points of the regional studies report summary, there was reference to the out-migration for economic advantage which had been part of the area's historical pattern before TVA came. Isolation of the Norris inhabitants had checked that population drain, but it was felt that "this natural tendency to migrate for economic advantage should be more evident in the future." The restraint on population reduction would now be removed: "TVA employment, new transportation facilities, the opening up of the area to the outside world of tourists and vacationists should all greatly increase population mobility." These factors should combine to "make people in the Norris area more sensitive than formerly to employment possibilities elsewhere which, particularly in Knoxville, have been enhanced by TVA activities."[37]

Unpublished provisional net migration figures for the Norris Basin counties do indeed indicate strong out-migration patterns between 1930 and 1940, the time of the regional studies report (see table 30). Out-migration was particularly strong in the productive age groups, and was stronger generally than one would be led to expect, given TVA's impact, since so much of the removed population settled in the same five-county area. The Satterfield/Davlin analyses were made in 1936, two years after removal, and one can only guess at the number of unsuccessful relocations that were turned into out-migrations by 1940. Out-migration patterns had been familiar to inhabitants of the Norris Basin as a safety valve against the effects of poor man/land ratios, and it is doubtful that they had been impeded by isolation, as the regional studies report

TABLE 30 Provisional Net Migration, Norris Basin Counties, 1930–40

Age in 1940	Anderson			Campbell			Claiborne			Grainger			Union		
	Total	Male	Female	Total	Male	Female	Total	Male	Female	Total	Male	Female	Total	Male	Female
0–4	210	107	103	495	243	252	102	35	67	−29	−17	−12	−43	−31	−12
5–9	535	252	283	564	158	406	132	65	67	120	76	44	−238	−95	−143
10–14	481	259	222	138	81	57	−410	−243	−167	79	38	41	−431	−249	−182
15–19	317	152	165	−186	−125	−61	−534	−248	−186	−66	−17	−49	−488	−217	−271
20–24	149	60	89	−363	−265	−98	−716	−343	−373	−222	−87	−135	−631	−297	−334
25–29	3	−46	49	−483	−276	−207	−697	−377	−320	−255	−143	−112	−627	−339	−288
30–34	273	121	152	−124	−22	−102	−357	−136	−221	−55	−26	−29	−312	−153	−159
35–39	411	248	163	80	79	1	−148	−73	−75	70	41	29	−168	−80	−88
40–44	281	137	144	51	44	7	−157	−64	−93	51	47	4	−124	−71	−53
45–49	181	102	79	53	62	−9	−119	−63	−56	−7	13	−20	−171	−88	−83
50–54	209	148	61	109	78	31	−65	7	−72	83	67	16	−74	−16	−58
55–59	29	57	−28	−21	8	−29	−58	−25	−33	38	19	19	−114	−53	−61
60–64	5	−6	11	−126	−91	−35	−117	−61	−56	−51	−12	−39	−115	−51	−64
65–69	102	69	33	19	9	10	35	12	23	72	62	10	−117	−65	−52
70–74	62	19	43	0	1	−1	−24	−3	−21	15	10	5	−70	−26	−44
75–79	11	15	−4	−22	−15	−7	−50	−14	−36	34	−10	−24	−81	−55	−26
80–84	3	4	−1	−4	−5	1	−10	−3	−7	−6	0	−6	−19	−15	−4
85+	22	14	8	15	10	5	6	7	−1	4	3	1	−10	−5	−5
All	3,284	1,712	1,572	195	−26	221	−3,187	−1,527	−1,660	−193	64	−257	−3,833	−1,906	−1,927

SOURCE: Richard A. Engels and Annie A. Moore, unpublished tabulations (center for Business and Economic Research, University of Tennessee, Knoxville, 1973).

indicated. The out-migratory pattern had been broken once before the coming of TVA by the depression-induced return-to-the-farm movement and then had apparently resumed, showing strong net losses through out-migration by 1940. The resumption of this familiar pattern of out-migration simply indicates, in the intermediate term, that TVA had not halted the population drain from the area, nor would it in the term, since net out-migration continued steadily into the seventies, only recently being reversed.

Out-migration has traditionally been seen as a means of seeking economic advantage through mobility, and indeed in factors of modernization, rural-to-urban migration has loomed very large in modern history. But was this the vision of modernization contained in TVA's broad socioeconomic improvement goals for the Tennessee Valley? Out-migration from rural areas like the Norris Basin also means the functional failure of regional economic opportunity, a classical one being a poor man/land ratio. The regional studies report was frank in its assessment of the situation: TVA's short-term and intermediate-term impact had exacerbated the problem it had found upon its arrival. Either the cited points which were to "offset" this situation and its side effects were basically too optimistic in terms of the seven years that had elapsed since TVA's coming, or they constitute a kind of overreach, counting items as beneficial impacts which are routine replacements made necessary by TVA's appearance on the scene. The material in the Satterfield/Davlin report in many respects complements that in the regional studies report. Defects of rural overpopulation and poor man/land ratios are acknowledged. The degree to which the beneficial impacts of the regional studies report offset the problems of relocation is dubious, and at any rate these "benefits" for the most part could not be directly participated in by the removed population. It is easy to see that negative short-term impacts would lead to a resumption of out-migratory patterns.[38] But should this be regarded as beneficial?

The burden of planning to improve the socioeconomic status of inhabitants of the Tennessee Valley was laid upon the Tennessee Valley Authority both implicitly and explicitly in its act. It can hardly be argued that an agency conceived by, among others, Roosevelt and Norris in the depth of the depression envisaged

261

socioeconomic improvement in terms of migratory mobility when millions of jobless youths and adults were on the road seeking work. A. E. Morgan, the planners, visionaries, and "super-idealists" within TVA correctly interpreted the planning intention of TVA as some form of socioeconomic improvement in place—for the inhabitants of the Tennessee Valley region rather than an alleged improvement through out-migration. TVA should have followed a vision seeking to attain "modernization" for the removed population neither through the channels of out-migration nor through the resumption of subsistence farming but through planned rural-industrial societies. Such societies should have been of some type which would have retained a greater organic sense of the meaning of what had vanished under the waters of Norris Reservoir, coupled with a restructured economic life built into a familiar and traditional environment.

When the Department of Regional Planning Studies finished its assessment of TVA's impact on Norris in 1940, prosperity was indeed "just around the corner" for a vast number of Americans who had suffered through the depression. Wartime-generated economic growth would create a situation where a reinvigorated economy could swell its labor force with out-migrants from poorer regions. But that situation was an accident of history and not the result of planning. Perhaps, in the last analysis, economic recovery and the promise of prosperity quenched the last fires of idealism within TVA. Still, that idealism had been engendered by a profound humanistic urge to lift up the dispossessed Americans whose plight, invisible in prosperity, was so visible when TVA was conceived in 1933. It is perhaps a tragedy of sorts that the best of TVA's planning efforts, conceived in crisis and economic depression, vanished with the onset of prosperity.

9 Conclusion

O N DECEMBER 11, 1934, President Franklin Roosevelt admonished members of the National Emergency Council against construing TVA as having been "initiated or organized for the purpose of selling electricity," which he proceeded to characterize as a "side function" of TVA. The president then proceeded eloquently to define TVA:

There is a much bigger situation behind the Tennessee Valley Authority. If you will read the message on which the legislation was based you will realize that we are conducting a social experiment that is the first of its kind in the world, as far as I know, covering a convenient geographical area—in other words, the watershed of a great river. The work proceeds along two lines, both of which are intimately connected—the physical land and water and soil end of it, and the human side of it. It proceeds on the assumption that we are going to the highest mountain peak of the Tennessee Watershed and we are going to take an acre of land up there and say, "What should this land be used for, and is it being badly used at the present time?" And a few feet farther down we are going to come to a shack on the side of the mountain where there is a white man of about as fine stock as we have in this country who, with his family of children, is completely uneducated—never had a chance, never sees twenty-five or fifty dollars in cash a year, but just keeps body and soul together—manages to do that—and is the progenitor of a large line of children for many generations to come. He certainly has been forgotten, not by the Administration, but by the American people. They are going to see that he and his children have a chance, and they are going to see that the farm he is using is classified, and if it is not proper for him to farm it, we are going to give him a chance on better land. If he should use it, we are going to try to bring him some of the things he needs, like schools, electric

263

lights, and so on. We are going to try to prevent soil erosion, and grow trees, and try to bring in industries. It is a tremendous effort with a very great objective. As an incident to that it is necessary to build some dams. And when you build a dam as an incident to this entire program, you get probably a certain amount of water power development out of it. We are going to try to use that water power to its best advantage.[1]

TVA was one of the notable agencies of the New Deal era deliberately constructed with a warrant to plan for the socioeconomic improvement of "forgotten Americans." This study has attempted to describe, analyze, and assess TVA's "social experiment" in modernization at the grass-roots level using population removal in the Norris Basin as a test case.

In the short term TVA's "social experiment" was a failure—a failure brought about by the lack of a coherent and unified grass-roots policy; by conflicting directorial roles and administrative structures; and by highly variant and persistent conceptual views held by people within TVA of the agency's aims and goals.

The major risk inherent in writing about TVA "from the ground up" and focusing upon a particular facet of TVA's work as a test case lies in the tendency to overlook mitigating circumstances and larger issues.

The first of these was that TVA in the early years was embroiled in a number of highly controversial and significant legal suits regarding its constitutionality. It was fighting for its very existence, a point which makes socioeconomic experimentation with local populations perhaps loom less large in the overall picture.

Second, there was considerable variation in the way the three early directors interpreted the broad goals and aims of TVA, variations which began to show signs of executive and administrative stress as early as 1933 and were aggravated by the reappointment of David Lilienthal over A. E. Morgan's objections in 1936. From then on, the situation worsened, culminating in Arthur Morgan's contumacious and erratic behavior and his subsequent removal by the president as TVA's chief executive, a process capped by a lengthy congressional investigation of Morgan's bitter charges against his co-directors. By the time the smoke of these internecine debates had cleared, TVA was already gearing up for its war role in the areas of power production, munitions, and transportation, and the problems of "modernization" had receded into the background—in many respects to be eclipsed by national recovery during World War II—a recovery that blurred the inherent socioeconomic problems of Appalachia and the Valley region alike.

Third, TVA was restricted in its role of modernization by real legal limitations. TVA planning powers were broadly construed and were never geared to an activist role in socioeconomic development. Rather than pushing for an active and interventionist role, however, the Authority chose to settle down within its legal limits, even to the point of taking refuge in them.

Fourth, there is the matter argued by Philip Selznick in *TVA at the Grass Roots* that much of TVA's program was coopted by elites within the Valley. In particular, what could be termed activist elements within TVA were tamed and subdued by the agricultural program under H. A. Morgan. Thus the planning role of TVA was adapted to the interests of the agricultural extension program, the county agents, and the Farm Bureau Federation. The argument is persuasive, and certainly in the limited field of population removal there is some evidence that the agriculturalists within TVA resented and resisted allegations about their administration in the family removal program, which came principally from planners and from the Family Removal Section of the Coordination Division. Agriculturalists ultimately brought the whole process under their control, stressing constantly the conservative and limited side of the population removal program.

A fifth and final argument which could be used against Norris Basin removal activities as a test case for TVA's modernizing activities would be that it is too confining. If we take this to mean that not enough can be learned of the experiences of population removal in one dam, there appears on the surface to be some valid objection. But the literature in TVA for all population removals in the period covered by this work bears out contentions similar to the ones made here for Norris. If one means that the impacts of population removal must be coupled with analysis of the broader range of TVA economic impacts, there are also some grounds for objection, but here invariably the argument takes on the insistence that all analyses be done on the long term.

Any of the above arguments could be used as reasons to deemphasize the Norris population removal as a test case for planning and socioeconomic development. None, however, really invalidates its use. Population removal impacts of TVA are admittedly immediate and short-term, but since information is available, they can be subjected to analysis. The same cannot be easily said for long-term economic impacts. To take an examination of measurable economic impact of TVA beyond the scope of this work is to move into an area which, for the historian, could be labeled terra incognita. An excellent article by Lance Davis using the problems of such an analysis of TVA concludes that it may well be a task beyond the reach even of the sophisticated tools of econometricians.[2] And Gilbert Banner has provided a fascinating example of the difficulties of such analysis in pointing out that TVA is fond of using aggregate figures, say on per capita income, to compare TVA states and counties with other states and counties. TVA figures, he argues, are based on assumed heterogeneous "land and economic areas." TVA counties of the Norris Basin, like Anderson, Campbell, and Union, do not reflect on the aggregate TVA-separable impacts from non-TVA impacts.[3]

The short-term analysis of the Norris Basin has the advantage of revealing impact in more than aggregate economic terms; it adds a real and human dimension which could never be expressed in an econometric model. It is perhaps an example of immediate, limited, short-term, and negative impact, but all those features keep us in touch with the fact that modernization is seldom, to the people it first touches, a long-term process.

Roosevelt had evoked an image of TVA which was mirrored, if generally and vaguely, in the planning sections of the TVA Act. But there was a considerable gap between planning for the modernization and well-being of the "forgotten Americans" and the realities of TVA at the grass roots. When TVA took land for the reservoir under eminent domain, socioeconomic planning for rural communities does not appear to have been its primary goal. When work on the dam was begun, there had been little or no thought given to translating the modernization process into realistic terms insofar as the removed populations were concerned. At the time when Roosevelt made his talk on the "forgotten Americans" to the

National Emergency Council, TVA's method of population removal had not advanced much beyond helping displaced farm owners find real estate for sale, despite the fact that the population removal of tenants and owners was well under way. Decisions concerning land purchase were made on the basis of the needs of the reservoir and watershed, and not on the basis of what would best suit the needs of the agricultural communities of the Basin.

Though many within TVA in the early years deplored their agency's lack of attention to the problem of marginal and submarginal farmers of either the tenant or owner class, little evidence of successful planning is related to them. Indeed, the first instance of inattention and lack of adequate planning consists in the maintenance of a legal position which disallowed tenantry any reimbursement for removal. While unquestionably TVA's position on this was within the law, it can be argued that the modernization goals implied a need to expand the law and to test it against the needs of the portion of the population to be modernized. The purchase of the land of the central peninsula, which added 500 families to the nearly 3,000 already marked for removal, was accomplished under the auspices of retirement of marginal land, but in reality the decision was made largely because the purchase of the land was cheaper than building access bridges to the peninsula. If it had been done entirely under the auspices of marginal land retirement, it would not have made the removal more palatable in light of the fact that there were not adequate plans for relocation of those who sold out.

The protective strip or "large purchase policy" which was followed for the TVA dams and reservoirs was itself structured largely on recreational planning and conservation arguments (along with those of reservoir protection) rather than being dictated by the needs of displaced or soon-to-be displaced families. And the number of those removed was considerably increased by such a decision.

The principal results of the relocation process have already been summarized and analyzed. This study has argued that the intrusion of TVA upon an indigenous population of some 3,500 rural families would have constituted the primary grounds for an experiment in regional planning; that the actual dispossession of a population which Roosevelt argued had been forgotten by Americans was the best opportunity to show that now forgetfulness was to be reversed. But insofar as these people of the Norris Basin were concerned, TVA appeared to place its planning goals in the long term with little attention to short-term and intermediate impacts. A population removal program which did not reimburse tenants in any form and which culminated in the resettlement of more than 60 percent of its removed population in the same five counties of the Norris Basin, already characterized as suffering from "rural overpopulation," can hardly be judged a success in providing modernization.

The end results of the resettlement program at Norris do not point to the existence of a viable planning structure, but rather to the lack of one. Marginal and submarginal subsistence farms and large numbers of poor tenants and smallholders are not turned around economically by a hoped-for long-term stimulation of industry and agriculture through cheap power generation or test-demonstration farms.

Gilbert Banner has suggested, in a provocative paper, that TVA's ideas of regional economic recovery left too much to chance, since they were based on the misconception that industrial growth would follow automatically upon the development of cheap power; that agricultural improvement would be stimulated through farm demonstration programs and the plentiful application of triple phosphate fertilizer; that riverine navigation improvement would stimulate commerce in conjunction with these developments; and that unproductive farm labor would be absorbed by the industries attracted by cheap power.[4]

In opposition to TVA's expectations, one can argue that the agriculture of the Norris Basin suffered from so many drawbacks (poor soil, small farm size, undercapitalization, rural overpopulation, and row-cropping, for instance) that it was, to paraphrase Banner, not sick but chronically ill. The Norris population needed something more than the promise of test-demonstration farms and aid in finding new real estate with which to replace that sold to TVA. What the population needed, in terms of planning and action, can be debated, but certainly it would have acquired greater planning powers and a more active intrusion into the population than either

Congress or the people of the region might have accepted, a point similarly borne out in Paul Conkin's excellent study of the Resettlement Administration's projects. But TVA withdrew from the risks of such an undertaking. It pursued a desultory cooperation with logically linked agencies like the Resettlement Administration and the Farm Security Administration, and rather than allowing planning program needs to dictate to its Legal Division what powers to ask for, it allowed its Legal Division to be the arbiter of existing limits. In some respects TVA's planning posture was thus determined by hastily conceived and inadequate planning powers, a situation made worse, since no new powers were asked for to supplement the weak ones possessed. And while it may be true that such powers would not have been forthcoming, to have formulated arguments for them and to have undertaken commitments to them may well have been the process by which a measure of idealism and a dedicated commitment to these dispossessed Americans could have been maintained.

Without the hoped-for industrial build-up and the reversal of an agricultural economy in a state of malaise, farmers had recourse only to let their feet speak for them as they out-migrated. TVA did not stop a flow of out-migration from the region that has only been reversed in this decade—and one could argue that nearly half a century has been enough to indicate results, even in the long run.

Clearly, this assessment is not intended to argue that TVA should never have been created or to place the blame of regional out-migration of the native labor pool on TVA any more than to say that TVA is to assume responsibiltiy for the fact that the Norris Basin counties today rank among the lowest in the state in per capita income. It is to suggest that a more active and viable planning program should have been attempted and that regional socioeconomic defects were not adequately dealt with by TVA.

It can be argued that no branch of the federal government or any institution should be judged in terms of its ideal goal formulations —that there are too many practical and empirical compromises along the way that must be made. Still, if some assessment is not made in ideal terms, what terms shall be used? TVA's problem, in many respects, was not that there was no ideal but that there were conflicting ideals. Roosevelt's ideal was one, and it was shared for

269

some time with A. E. Morgan. But Morgan's disputes within the board of directors, with H. A. Morgan and Lilienthal, were nearly continuous from 1933. And while the immediate and pressing differences between the directors occurred in disputes over organization, TVA's power program, the fertilizer program, the Berry marble claims, and the Fontana project, there was always constant a series of underlying radical differences, especially between A. E. Morgan and David Lilienthal over the meaning and intent of TVA.

Arthur Morgan's community-oriented dream of an industrial capitalism reduced to rural proportions and executed in rural communities which were only part-time industrial participants was intended to reinforce a wholly decentralized industrial component in the name of retaining the rural character of American life. Lilienthal, opposed to this, urged TVA's power program as the key to bringing a "backward" area into full modernity and assumed that industrial opportunity would follow power, a view encapsulated in his *Democracy on the March* and enshrined in much of TVA's public posture up to the present. Hence in a sense TVA at the topmost level was badly divided in defining itself as an instrument of modernization.

In the actual administration of its Norris programs—land acquisition, population relocation, and grave removal—TVA in the early years entertained a broad range of possibilities—all reflecting some variant opinions as to how modernization could be achieved. In the last analysis what actually was achieved either did not go far enough or went too far, depending on the point of view of the critics. What is certain is that the confusion and ambiguity of the directions in this hoped-for stimulation of modernity mirror certain ambiguities and contradictions in terms of American progressive reform vis-à-vis the definition of the good life for Americans. This study has not dealt extensively with the personalities of TVA's early directors, preferring to develop analysis at intermediate and lower-level administration, but a study of the relevant literature would reveal all three of the directors to have been imbued with considerable progressive idealism. Their enthusiasm took on conflicting and variant forms, but they had in common an inability to deal with the "masses" of people in other than abstract and idealized forms.

Perhaps this inability to translate idealistic reformist concepts into radical action programs that would transcend self-help notions and truly embrace regional planning at a grass-roots level is where the ultimate failure of TVA's population removal program lies. TVA as an instrument of modernization was complex and fragile, its modernization goals tangled and tension-ridden. With these limitations, TVA's early socioeconomic planning processes often brought about unintended consequences and the practical difficulty of translating ideals into action.

If, in the last analysis, many of the inhabitants of the Norris Basin continued their out-migratory trek to real opportunities, as opposed to the hoped-for opportunities at home which TVA would bring, it is equally certain that TVA has been formative as an educator in the Valley and as an exemplar for transition and change (what Banner has called the "rate and direction" of change).[5] But an educator's role can be too passive and abstract, and one can ask in less abstract, less aggregate, less long-term ways, how much TVA's guidance and educative role benefited those whom Roosevelt called "forgotten Americans" and whom Jack Weller has more recently called "yesterday's people."

TVA's 1979 annual report had on its front cover a recent picture of poverty—a young boy in a "small, drafty, wood frame house just a few miles from TVA offices in Knoxville." On the reverse side of this cover is another photograph of poverty forty-six years old. Though it is not identified in the report, the picture is of a Norris Basin removal tenant family. The caption in the report reads that the recent photograph could easily have been made "when TVA was founded during the depression. It serves as a reminder; in spite of TVA accomplishments, people and natural resources are still left to waste in some areas of the region." Indeed this is the case, although had planning at the grass roots proceeded in a coherent and unambiguous manner, it perhaps need not have been. Quoting from David Lilienthal's *Democracy on the March* "that all the people of the whole region are to do the job of transforming their valley—all the people . . . ," the report concludes: "David Lilienthal's message is simple. TVA must get back to its roots and to the people."[6] But from the perspective of the Norris Basin, TVA abdicated its planning role in the 1930s by leaving it to the dispossessed people to transform their valley through random migration and settlement. Concurring that TVA must get to the people, one must affirm that in so doing TVA will not so much be "getting back" as breaking new ground.

In a curiously Hegelian sense, TVA's development guidance, its success as the Valley's educator, and its water management program and recreational advantages have attracted newcomers who have swelled the Valley's population as "yesterday's people" have left. These technologically skilled outsiders have in many respects formed the nucleus of those who today would halt TVA's continued expansion in the name of environmental and ecological interests. It is ironic that TVA's development has encouraged the process of modernity to the degree that new people have entered the Valley who want to preserve the region as it was, while those who lived in it as it was have either left it or have been unable, in many respects, to secure the advantages which TVA was created to provide.

Notes

Notes for Chapter 1

1. Although formal usage would normally require TVA to be preceded by "the," it is common usage to refer to it without the article, a practice which shall be followed throughout this book.

2. For full citations of these authors' works consult the bibliography.

3. Selznick, *TVA and the Grass Roots.*

4. Pritchett, *Tennessee Valley Authority*, 126.

5. One of the best and most straightforward accounts of the evolution of the TVA Act, with specific references to the planning sections of the act, is: TVA, "Correspondence between Howard K. Menhenick and Tracy B. Augur." Menhenick was then director of regional planning studies, while Tracy B. Augur and L. L. Durisch, who compiled the brief history contained in the correspondence, had been, in the earliest days of TVA, with the Research Section, Social and Economic Division, later coopted into the Regional Planning Studies Department of TVA. The correspondence consists of the following: Tracy B. Augur to Howard K. Menhenick, "Origins of Sections 22 and 23 of the TVA Act," Dec. 31, 1942, 2–4; L. L. Durisch and Tracy B. Augur to Howard K. Menhenick, "Origin of the National Planning and Development Concept in TVA Legislation," Feb. 6, 1943, 1–6; Tracy B. Augur to Howard K. Menhenick, "History of Sections 22 and 23 of the TVA Act," March 1, 1943, 1–4. While Augur questioned the idea that in scope the New York State planning ideas of Roosevelt were fully developed regional planning concepts, he stated that the program Roosevelt inherited from Gifford Pinchot, Theodore Roosevelt, Al Smith, and Clarence Stein constituted "the most comprehensive and best thought-out planning activity developed up to that time" (Augur to Menhenick, "Origins of Sections 22 and 23 of the TVA Act," Dec. 31, 1942, 2).

6. L. L. Durisch and Tracy B. Augur to Howard K. Menhenick, "Origins of the Regional Planning and Development Concept in TVA Legislation," Feb. 6, 1943, 2–3.

7. Tracy B. Augur to Howard K. Menhenick, "Origins of Sections 22 and 23 of the TVA Act," Dec. 31, 1942, 3.

8. Ibid., 3–4.

9. Quoted by L. L. Durisch and Tracy B. Augur to Howard K. Menhenick in "Origin of the Regional Planning and Development Center in TVA Legislation," Feb. 6, 1943, .3.

10. Quoted by Durisch and Augur. As they comment:

A merging of the President's thinking with that of Senator Norris is illustrated by a number of phrases in the TVA Act which hark back to the New York State experience. His [Roosevelt's] interest in land utilization appears in the second phrase of the title, namely, an "Act to provide for reforestation and proper use of marginal lands in the Tennessee Valley." This thought appears again in Section 23 where the President is directed to recommend to Congress legislation "for the especial purpose of bringing about in said Tennessee drainage basin and adjoining territory . . . ; (4) the proper use of marginal land; (5) the proper method of reforestation of all lands in said drainage basin suitable for reforestation." In the Norris bill the above points (4) and (5) were followed by point (6), "the most practical method of improving agricultural conditions in the valleys of the said drainage basin." [L. L. Durisch and Tracy B. Augur to Howard K. Menhenick, "Origin of the Regional Planning and Development Center in TVA Legislation," Feb. 6, 1943]

11. Ibid., 6. Durisch and Augur conclude (p. 6): "There is no doubt that many leaders of thought in the subjects of land utilization and regional planning and development had a part in the evolution of the President's thinking, but it also seems clear from the record that the regional planning idea was basically the President's own, that it was he who introduced it to the Tennessee Valley legislation."

12. Tracy B. Augur to Howard K. Menhenick, "Origins of Sections 22 and 23 of the TVA Act," Dec. 31, 1942, 1.

13. The broad, open, and nonspecific role of TVA as envisaged in Roosevelt's congressional message was contrasted with the TVA Act itself, "where concern is centered on the execution of Norris for river development, fertilizer manufacture, and power distribution, and the broad planning for the economic welfare of the region is added as something to follow and grow out of the other programs" (Tracy B. Augur and Howard K. Menhenick, "Origins of Sections 22 and 23 of the TVA Act," Dec. 31, 1942, 1).

14. Pritchett, *Tennessee Valley Authority*, 30.

15. Selznick, *TVA and the Grass Roots*, 187. Selznick's comment follows a citation of part of Roosevelt's congressional message on April 10, 1933 and a portion of the preamble to the TVA Act: "to improve navigability and to provide for the flood control of the Tennessee River; to provide for reforestation and the proper use of marginal lands in the Tennessee Valley; to provide for the agricultural and industrial development of the said valley; to provide for the national defense . . ." Selznick emphasizes the point that while TVA had little "direct authority for large-scale planning" in a statutory sense, the act "permitted such discretion in the execution of primary purposes as would invite those in charge to recognize the social consequences of specific activities—such as the effect upon populations and urban communities of the creation of large reservoirs—and to assume responsibility for them" (Selznick, *TVA and the Grass Roots*, 6).

16. Morgan related that when President Roosevelt first spoke to him about TVA, "he did not speak at length concerning power development or fertilizer, but talked generally about the total improvement of the area" (see Morgan, *The Making of TVA*, 6–7; also pp. 54–55). Those within TVA who, like A. E. Morgan, opted for the broader planning goals of TVA over concrete programs like fertilizer and power were called the "superidealists" within TVA (Selznick, *TVA and the Grass Roots*, 190).

17. Morgan, *The Making of TVA*, 19. It is indicative that Morgan contrasts his "clear ideas" about TVA with the existence of a board of equals, an attitudinal position that may have had much to do with the disintegration of the board's relationships. This development is fully described in detail in the excellent work by Thomas K. McCraw, *Morgan versus Lilienthal*. Less adequate and with a strong bias against A. E. Morgan is the treatment in Marguerite Owen, *Tennessee Valley Authority*. Arthur Morgan's defense of his own position is set forth in his work: *The Making of TVA*. For excellent analysis of the administrative defects and problems in the early board structure see: Pritchett, *Tennessee Valley Authority*. Another good account based upon much research in the Morgan Papers at Antioch is Roy Talbert, "The Human Engineer."

18. Morgan, *The Making of TVA*, 19.

19. Ibid., 26.

20. Pritchett, *Tennessee Valley Authority*, 153.

21. Roy Talbert, "Beyond Pragmatism." See also Talbert, "Human Engineer," 58 and 11.

22. U.S. Congress, Joint Committee, *Investigation of the Tennessee Valley Authority, Hearings before the Joint Committee to Investigate the Tennessee Valley Authority*, 75th Cong., 3rd sess. (Washington, D.C.: U.S. Government Printing Office, 1939), pts. 1–4, p. 107 (hereafter referred to as *Hearings*).

23. Ibid.; Owen, *Tennessee Valley Authority*, 46.

24. H. A. Morgan, Testimony, *Hearings*, pts. 1–4, p. 103; C. H. Pritchett, *Tennessee Valley Authority*, 187–88.

25. Phillip Broughton (aide to A. E. Morgan) to A. E. Morgan Aug. 29, 1933, Morgan Papers. Morgan noted on the memorandum that Harcourt's statement preceded the August 3 board meeting and added marginally: "How New York City reports came in telling of conflict in the TVA Board. My assistant, Broughton, told me of these reports and then gave me this memo." A. Morgan also wrote marginally that since joining TVA, Harcourt Morgan "had wholly failed to realize a plan for TVA."

26. Arthur Morgan, *The Making of TVA*, 6–7.

27. Harcourt Morgan and David Lilienthal, "Memorandum on Organization," Aug. 3, 1933, Morgan Papers.

28. A. E. Morgan, "Memorandum on Progress toward Organization to August 5, 1933," Morgan Papers. The whole process of this administrative quarrel is described in some detail in A. J. Ackerman to E. H. Cassels, 18 June 1936, Morgan Papers, General Correspondence, E. H. Cassels, 1936–37. See also *Hearings*, pts. 1–4, 109.

29. Pritchett, *Tennessee Valley Authority*, 153–54. The division of functions allocated to A. E. Morgan the general engineering program, educational and training program (other than agriculture), land and regional planning, subsistence homesteads, social and economic organization and planning, forestry, soil erosion, and relationships with the Civilian Conservation Corps. He was also charged with "integration" of the parts into a unified whole. Harcourt Morgan was charged with all agricultural matters, rural life planning, and rural agricultural industries, chemical engineering (fertilizer, cement, dry ice) and public relations in East Tennessee and adjoining areas. Lilienthal received the power program, supervision of the legal department, the land acquisition program, and

"the economics of transportation." (Pritchett, *Tennessee Valley Authority,* 155–56; Ackerman to Cassels, June 18, 1936, Morgan Papers, General Correspondence.)

30. Pritchett, *Tennessee Valley Authority,* 157.

31. In H. A. Morgan's and Lilienthal's "Memorandum on Organization," which specifically broke down the allocation of administration, Arthur Morgan had written "no" in the margin next to the land acquisition function assigned to Lilienthal. Morgan Papers, General Correspondence.

32. *Hearings,* pts. 1–4, 314–15.

Notes for Chapter 2

1. The oral data presented in this chapter are edited from handwritten transcriptions from the oral tapes. No formal typescript of the data has yet been made. Because of the lack of a formal, deposited record of the interviews, references are made through brief biographical notes rather than to footnoted citations to access a file.

A good number of inhabitants of the reservoir area were sensitive to what they felt was a misrepresentation of the thirties in their way of life by TVA, the national news media, and others who depicted them as backward and ignorant hillbillies. There is some truth and not a little bias in this view, but in fact the bitterness still persists among many who lived in the region. Because of these feelings, the interview strategy was to build up lists of potential interviews through a few local contacts who knew the details of the research project so as to avoid an intrusive presence which could lead to resentment and fears of misrepresentation. Nearly everyone interviewed was recommended by a personal acquaintance, and in all of the cases save one, prior permission to interview was obtained. The result was generally a more relaxed and receptive interview.

2. Oral history more often than not appears as the core of a project rather than as supplementary data, and its inclusion in a book with other kinds of analysis is limited by some constraints of space. From the whole record, the authors have chosen material selectively to illuminate areas regarded as essential: farm self-sufficiency, local trading patterns, the sense of the rural community, religion, education, recreation, and some views of how TVA affected individuals. The fragmented views do not pretend to capture the totality of rural life in the Norris Basin.

3. Killibrew, *Resources,* 447.

4. Interview, Aug. 19, 1976, Big Valley, Union County, Tenn.

5. Interview, Aug. 23, 1976, Union County Courthouse, Maynardville, Tenn.

6. Interview, Aug. 23, 1976, Union County Courthouse, Maynardville, Tenn.

7. Interview, Aug. 19, 1976, H. Clay Stoner Store, Leadmine Bend, Union County, Tenn.

8. Interview, Aug. 18, 1976, Fountain City, Tenn.

9. Interview, Aug. 18, 1976, Knoxville, Tenn.

10. Interview, Aug. 18, 1976, Corryton, Tenn.

11. Interview, July 27, 1976, Knoxville, Tenn.

12. Interview, Aug. 17, 1976, Maynardville, Tenn.

13. Interview, July 17, 1976, Fountain City, Tenn.
14. Interview, July 17, 1976, Concord, Tenn.
15. Interview, July 8, 1976, Clinton, Tenn.
16. Interview, July 16, 1976, Andersonville, Tenn.
17. Interview, July 16, 1976, Knoxville, Tenn.
18. Interview, July 13, 1976, Andersonville, Tenn.

Notes for Chapter 3

1. For the reservoir 136,918 acres were purchased, with additional lands purchased for the townsite of Norris (3,679 acres), highway right of ways (723 acres), and marginal and inaccessible lands isolated by the reservoir (11,683 acres). Of all the land purchased for the reservoir, only 34,000 acres normally lie under water.

2. The Norris Reservoir purchase in the five counties was 214.0 square miles; the total county areas 1,811 square miles. Acquisition by county was as follows: Anderson, 8.5 square miles; Campbell, 67.0 square miles; Union, 91.0 square miles; Claiborne, 38.0 square miles; and Grainger, 9.5 square miles. Total county areas prior to acquisition were as follows (in square miles): Anderson, 342; Campbell, 459; Union, 235; Claiborne, 468; and Grainger, 307. Tabulations do not include 51 acres of flowage easements (TVA, "Real Property Appraisals," mimeograph ed, table 2, p. 43).

3. The best general physiographic description of the Norris Basin is in U.S. Soil Conservation Service, *Soil Survey: Norris.* J. B. Killibrew's *Resources* contains a detailed survey of the lands, soils, geography, and physiography of Tennessee counties made after the Civil War. see also: TVA, "Real Property Appraisals."

4. TVA, "Real Property Appraisals," 7. Atop the Cumberland escarpment above the reservoir, the elevation is 2,500 feet, dropping to 1,200 feet in the Powell Valley bench above the rivers and to about 850 feet in the river valleys. Between the Clinch and Powell rivers is a series of rough dolomitic hill crests at about 1,500 feet, rising, as the rivers are left behind, to an elevation of 2,000 feet on Lone Mountain, south of the Clinch River.

5. U.S. Soil Conservation Service, *Soil Survey: Norris,* 111–13. The land classification is based on the "productivity, workability, and conservability" of the soil and is not intended as a recommendation for use but the "relative suitability for the present agriculture of the area."

6. Ibid., 8–10. Some climatological reference points for the area include the following: average yearly rainfall, 47–50 inches; average winter temperature, 42 degrees; average summer temperature, 77 degrees; first killing frost, October 12–November 15; latest killing frost, about April 1; and average length of growing season, 168–222 days (TVA, "Real Property Appraisals," 25). There are seven distinct areas in the Norris Basin: Powell Valley; Powell and Lower Clinch River lands; Central Peninsula; Big Valley; Poorland Valley and Dark Hollow; upper Clinch River lands; and Sycamore Creek. Powell Valley, lying in Campbell and Claiborne counties at the foot of the Cumberland Mountains, is a fertile bluegrass section. The Powell and lower Clinch river lands in Campbell, Claiborne, and Union counties consist generally of broken hills and ridges. Central Peninsula, in Union and Claiborne Counties, lies between the Clinch

and Powell rivers in "a hilly tableland with no continuous ridges or valleys." Big Valley, southeast of Central Peninsula, is mainly in Union and Anderson counties and contains some moderately or gently rolling farm lands known for their fertility and good bluegrass pasture. Poorland Valley and Dark Hollow are mainly ridge sections. The upper Clinch River lands in Union, Claiborne, and Grainger Counties are moderately or steeply rolling, and Sycamore Creek contains wide and flat creek bottoms along its six-mile length.

7. TVA, "Real Property Appraisals," 17. Forty-eight percent of the poorer ridge and hill land was also in cultivation or open pasture.

8. TVA, "Real Property Appraisals," 18.

9. Ibid. The abandonment of the slopes was not always useless, since young timber growth and brush in the abandoned lands helped secure the soil against further erosion unless they burned off, which was periodically the case in some areas.

10. A description of these dossiers is in the bibliography at the end of the book.

11. U.S. Department of Agriculture, *Grainger County*.

12. Ibid., 8–9.

13. Ibid., 9–10. The average per acre productivity of corn in Grainger County was below 20 bushels. McLendon and Layman noted that in addition to showing a tendency always to grow the same crop without regard to soil type or productivity, farmers used fertilizer without qualification on soils deficient in humus, with the result that the soil was burned out.

14. Ibid., 14. The range of the less productive lands was in the ridge and hill land soils (Clarksville loam, DeKalb silt loam—43.9 percent) through the mountain land soils (Clinch shale loam, Grainger shale loam, DeKalb stony loam, and Newman stony loam—25.9 percent), and rough stony land (7.6 percent).

15. TVA, "Real Property Appraisals," 17. The ratio of other lands, topographically, was as follows: river bottom, second bottom, and terrace (8 percent of cleared land); creek and branch bottom (5 percent of cleared land); and Valley uplands (9 percent of cleared land).

16. The TVA Technical Library possesses a two-volume typescript report concerning the Tennessee Valley above Muscle Shoals, Alabama, which was compiled by USDA in 1933. These volumes have many sections, the most valuable of which were edited by H. H. Bennett of the Bureau of Chemistry and Soils and C. F. Marbut, chief, Division of Soil Survey. Tugwell was urged to compile this report by Arthur E. Morgan, the principal director of TVA, in 1933. Reference to this typescript report will hereafter be by volume and page as USDA, "Tugwell Report." H. H. Bennett's interesting career in the field of soil conservation is the topic of Wellington Brink's *Big Hugh, The Father of Soil Conservation* (New York: Macmillan, 1951).

17. USDA, "Tugwell Report," II, 9–10. Bennett claimed that even on Clarksville loam, the best of the area's ridge and hill land soils, slopes of no greater declivity than 10 to 12 percent would experience erosion of the entire surface if they were continuously row-cropped.

18. USDA, "Tugwell Report," II, 13. "Slopes are still being cleared," stated Bennett, "for a few years of cultivation with the intention of abandonment as soon as the soils have washed off, and then taking in new land to be put through

the same process of irreparable waste. This procedure can be seen all along the slopes of the Clinch Mountain and other high ridges running through the valley of East Tennessee."

19. Some of the 20 neighboring counties, such as Sevier, Monroe, and Polk, contain mountainous land and substantially large segments of the great valley. The 20 counties are: Sullivan, Carter, Cocke, Greene, Washington, Hamblen, Hawkins, and Sevier; Jefferson, Blount, Knox, Loudon, Monroe, McMinn, Polk, Bradley, Hamilton, Rhea, Roane, and Anderson. Of these only Anderson comprised a part, and a small part at that, of the Norris area acquisitions. In 1930 these 20 counties, which could reasonably be expected to have a higher density of population than the four most affected by the Norris Dam, had, excluding incorporated places of more than 2,500, a nonurban region of 8,336 square miles and a nonurban population of 407,618, with an average density of 48.9 persons per square mile. The four Norris counties (less Anderson) were as follows in average density: Campbell, 58.4; Claiborne, 52.0; Grainger, 41.5; and Union, 48.5. The crowding of rough country is not peculiar to Tennessee. Harlan County, Kentucky, containing some of the roughest land in the East, according to Fenneman, had 1930 nonurban density of 116.7 persons per square mile. See: Fenneman, *Physiography,* 334.

20. "Appalachia" is defined in U.S. Congress, House, *Economic Development Programs,* pt. 3, sect. 403, 87.

21. Rough computations based upon the 2,800 to 3,000 families living in the reservoir area with median family size of 4.8 persons. This is in the early stages of removal. Nearly 3,700 families were removed by 1937.

22. DeJong, *Appalachian Fertility Decline,* 40. See also: Beebe, *Conception and Fertility;* Vance, *All These People;* L. C. Gray, *Economic and Social Problems;* Goodrich, *Migration and Economic Opportunity;* and Smith, *The Sociology of Rural Life.*

23. Crude birth rate expresses the annual number of births per thousand in the population. The fertility ratio expresses the number of children 4 years of age and below per 1,000 women in the population ages 15 to 44. General fertility rate expresses the number of births per year to women in the population aged 15 to 44. DeJong points out, relative to the figure he uses:

> of particular concern is the timespan of the birth data upon which the measure is based. The five year period used to compute the fertility ratio can obscure relatively short-term features, but the one year period used as a basis for the crude birth rate is susceptible to yearly migrations, especially in many Appalachian counties where birth registration is not entirely complete. Because of these limitations a three year average of registered births was computed. [DeJong, *Appalachian Fertility Decline,* 33–37] Statistical measurements of fertility in this area were precarious because of underregistration. While U.S. rural white completion of registration was calculated at 90.2 percent in 1930, the five counties involved in this study were all well below this figure, some spectacularly so. The completeness figures (by county) are as follows: Anderson (68.9 percent), Campbell (63.8 percent), Claiborne (60.0 percent), Grainger (78.5 percent), and Union (40.0 percent). Rural white figures are used because of an exceptionally low black population for the Norris Basin. DeJong's computations use data adjusted for 1940 county registration completeness (p. 34 n 10).

24. DeJong, *Appalachian Fertility Decline,* appendix A, table 1, pp. 109–14.

Figures based on average annual births for the period 1929–31 and 1939–41.

25. Ibid. While Anderson County decreased in crude birth rate from 31.0 to 28.8, all the other counties gained substantially: Campbell (34.5 to 38.5), Claiborne (25.7 to 35.3), Grainger (25.7 to 28.2), and Union (50.2 to 55.9).

26. The Southern Appalachian general fertility rate in 1930 was 135.7, falling to 127.4 in 1940. The county rates for 1930 and 1940 were as follows: Anderson (139.9, falling to 121.6), Campbell (161.2, rising to 166.4), Union (246.0, rising to 253.0), Claiborne (120.7, rising to 156.5), and Grainger (121.1, rising to 130.5). Figures based on average annual births for the periods 1929–31 and 1939–41 (DeJong, *Appalachian Fertility Decline*, appendix A, table 3 pp. 121–26).

27. Fertility ratios for the United States dropped from 390.0 to 323.5 between 1930 and 1940, while the Southern Appalachian ratio dropped from 585.0 to 501.3; Campbell (625.9 to 552.2); Union (634.9 to 545.1); Claiborne (659.3 to 535.7); and Grainger (577.0 to 523.0).

28. See above, note 25.

29. Death rate is defined as the number of deaths per 1,000 population.

30. From 1930 to 1940 the death rate in Tennessee generally stayed slightly below or even with U.S. figures. Knox, *The People of Tennessee*, 113.

31. Tennessee State Planning Commission, "Preliminary Population Report," sect. IV–B, 1. Hereafter referred to as: TSPC, "Population Report."

32. Improved land was defined as "all crop land in use, idle or fallow; all meadows and pasture; and all improved woodlands used as pasture" (TSPC, "Population Report," sect. IV–C, 1).

33. Ibid., sect. IV–C, 3. Another factor to be considered in high improved land ratios is the declining fertility of the soil with expansion onto marginal lands.

34. Ibid., sect. IV–C, 1.

35. TVA (Satterfield and Davlin), "A Decription and Appraisal," 2; TVA (Lowry), "A Review of Social and Economic Conditions," viii, 9–10; USDA, *Economic and Social Problems*, 2–5. Apropos of the effects of out-migration, Lowry's report notes: "If age distribution for the Norris counties were the same as for the state, there would be 50,000 adults (20 to 54 years) to produce for the 48,500 children (19 years and under) reported for the area. Instead there were only 37,380 adults, indicating a 25 percent handicap in potential productivity" (p. 10).

36. TVA, "A Land Classification Approach." This report, noting the seriousness of agricultural overpopulation, stated that Grainger County was 43 percent overpopulated with regard to land resources and present farm practices.

37. The broader general implications of the return-to-the-farm movement are excellently depicted in Goodrich, *Migration and Planes of Living*.

38. TVA (Howard), "Some Social and Economic Characteristics," 1–2. T. Levron Howard did this study under the direction of T. J. Woofter of Chapel Hill. Howard later became an administrative assistant of the research section of the Social and Economic Division directed by Floyd Reeves.

39. Analysis of the aggregate data obtained from reservoir families through the questionnaire is found in: TVA (Durisch and Burchfield), "Tenant Families of the Norris Flowage;" TVA, "Families of the Norris Reservoir"; and TVA, "Urban-Rural Migration of Norris Reservoir Families."

40. TVA, "Urban-Rural Migration of Norris Reservoir Families," 1–17 passim. A small number of those who had left and returned had sought employment in the nearby coal fields of the Cumberlands.

41. The highest decade for total farm acreage in the five counties was attained in 1910, after which it began to decline to its lowest point in 1930 and thereafter began to increase in the thirties (*U.S. Census, 1930: Agriculture*, vol. II, pt. 2, county table 1, 870–85; *U.S. Census, 1940: Agriculture*, vol. I, first and second series, pt. 4, county table 2, 176–91.

42. Mean farm acreage between 1930 and 1935 in the Norris Basin counties dropped as follows: Anderson, 83.3 to 60.6 acres; Campbell, 62.8 to 51.6 acres; Claiborne, 56.4 to 48.7 acres; Grainger 76.1 to 62.2 acres; and Union 65.2 to 62.7 acres (*U.S. Census, 1930: Agriculture*, vol. II, pt. 2, county table 2, 870–85; *U.S. Census, 1940: Agriculture*, first and second series, pt. 4, county table 1, 170–79.

43. For the five Norris Basin counties between 1900 and 1940, tenant farms comprised (by decade) the following percentage of total farms: 1900, 31.79 percent; 1910, 29.21 percent; 1920, 23.46 percent; 1925, 20.38 percent; 1930, 24.47 percent; 1935, 29.20 percent; and 1940, 20.49 percent (*U.S. Census, 1930: Agriculture*, vol. II, pt. 2, county table 1, 870–85; *U.S. Census, 1940: Agriculture*, vol. I, first and second series, pt. 4, county table 1, 170-79).

44. Compiled from fifteenth and sixteenth censuses of the United States, TVA, "Classification of Families," 10–11 and table 1, Group 3. The most in need of help were regarded as "incapable of supporting themselves under existing conditions" (pp. 10–11).

45. TVA, "Classification of Families," 10–11. This group contained 2.2 percent owners and 3.7 percent tenants.

46. Ibid. Compare with Group 2, "needing advisory assistance only," which was made up of 70.8 percent of the owners and 42.3 percent of the tenants (pp. 5–6, tables 1 and 2).

47. Ibid.

48. The TVA board of directors appointed a special committee in the summer of 1934 to collect data from families of the Norris area who were to be removed. Various components of the study were allocated to TVA's Agricultural Division, the Research Section of the Social and Economic Division, and the University of Tennessee Agricultural Extension Division. All three units cooperated in preparing the questionnaire, and it was administered by the Agricultural Extension Division and TVA's Agricultural Division. Computations and tabulations were done by the Research Section of the Social and Economic Division. The data generated from the questionnaire were used in the three TVA studies mentioned above in footnote 39, chapter 3. The two major studies, "Families of the Norris Reservoir" and "Tenant Families of the Norris Flowage," used material from 2,841 families (1,864 owners and 977 tenants). The authors obtained access to the original questionnaires and placed the data in machine-readable form. The files were moved several times before their final deposit at the Regional Archives Branch, Federal Archives and Records Center, in Atlanta, and this probably accounts for differences in numbers of families used by the authors and those used in the 1935 TVA studies. The number of questionnaires used by us are broken down by county and land tenure as follows:

	Owners		Tenants		Total	
County	No.	%	No.	%	No.	%
Anderson	30	2	11	1	41	2
Campbell	616	33	307	37	923	34
Claiborne	507	27	255	31	762	28
Grainger	112	6	69	8	181	7
Union	592	32	193	23	785	29
N	1,857	100	835	100	2,692	100

49. TVA, "Families of the Norris Reservoir"; "Tenant Families of the Norris Flowage."

50. In analyzing and presenting the data from the TVA questionnaires, the authors decided to use land tenure as an independent variable, dividing the removed population into landowners and tenants. It may be argued that such a division creates groups which are too broad. But the authors' decision was based on the premise that owner/tenant divisions were more appropriate to the analysis of TVA's impact on the communities of the Norris basin and that that impact was felt more radically along the lines of land tenure than upon any other variable. Owners who had to move had the benefit of their money from land sales to TVA to aid in relocation, while tenants were uncompensated. The Norris Basin tenants, then, were placed at much greater risk upon removal than owners. It seemed more advisable to choose an independent variable more reflective of the future weight of relocation than to choose independent variables which, though delineating more sharply the nuances of community structure, might have obscured the greater impact of removal. An analysis committed solely to community life in the Norris Basin rather than to TVA's impact upon communities in the Norris Basin would likely demand a different strategy. Not only did tenants have to move without compensation, but they were, in most socioeconomic indicators, well below the population mean, while the owners were considerably above it. Measurements of central tendency obscure the diversity, especially in the owner group, of many socioeconomic characteristics but serve to depict a population generally of marginal wealth and circumstances that is faced with the formidable task of removing and relocating.

51. TVA (Howard), "Some Social and Economic Characteristics," 35.

52. Census figures for Norris Basin counties' annual mean labor, feed, and fertilizer expenditures (in dollars) for 1929 were $69.86 and for 1939 were $61.42. For the state, the corresponding expenditures for those years were $106.02 and $89.65, respectively (U.S. Census, 1920: Agriculture, vol. II, pt. 2, county table 12, pp. 960–68; U.S. Census, 1940: Agriculture, first and second series, vol. I, pt. 4, county table 10, pp. 240–47.

53. For 2,640 removed families annual mean farm expenditures on livestock, feed, labor, fertilizer, seed, and taxes was $73.97, with a standard deviation of $147.98 (TVA, "Family Removal Questionnaire," 1934).

54. TVA, "Some Social and Economic Characteristics," 21–22. Enumerations by TVA of the displaced families (N = 1,851 owners, 834 tenants) reported landowners as having 0.6 mules and 0.6 horses, tenants as having 0.3 mules and 0.2 horses. TVA enumerators, however, reported all zero values, while the census figures used by Howard do not. The fifteenth census of the United States, from which Howard's figures are derived, uses the number of farms reporting to

derive its averages. The term "farms reporting" means the farm reporting possession of the particular items indicated. The zero values, so common among poor subsistence farmers, would actually lower its averages, but because of the criteria of "farms reporting" usage, zero values are not included in the computations (*U.S. Census, 1930: Agriculture, Tennessee*, vol. II, pt. 2, "Explanation of Terms," p. 2).

55. Gross farm income is represented in the census, and in the authors' tabulations of TVA data, on the dollar value of all farm products sold, traded, or used by the farm household. For 1929 Goodrich found that almost all the lowest income counties were in the Southern Appalachians, which include the Norris Basin. See: Goodrich, *Migration and Economic Opportunity*, ch. 1, "Contrasts in Economic Levels," 14 and passim. Goodrich's data for the Southern Appalachian income levels concentrate upon the Cumberland coal counties, which include some of the Norris Basin counties, but it should be kept in mind that although some of the area's counties are coal counties, the removed population was essentially agricultural.

56. Significant unpublished sources on farm income indicators of interest for this period include: TVA (Cole), "Tennessee, A Study"; TVA (Lowry and Douglas), "Income Analysis"; TVA (Gant), "Consumption"; and Allred, "Report." The Allred study was a TERA-funded project completed in 1935, and his detailed economic data is compiled and ranked by counties. Most of the material in Allred is for individual years 1930–35 for selected data, with some short time series. Cole's study was a jointly sponsored TVA-CWA research project and contains some extremely useful comparative data and extensive time series compiled from census data. There is a good bit of textual analysis in Cole, whereas Allred is essentially a compilation.

57. For purposes of comparison, estimated per capita gross farm incomes in 1929 for the Norris Basin counties, with their rankings, are: Claiborne, $164.45 (53 of 95); Grainger, $156.75 (58 of 95); Union, $143.09 (70 of 95); Campbell, $137.97 (74 of 95); and Anderson, $140.29 (72 of 95). The state per capita gross farm figure was $191.84. (Allred, "Report," 163.)

58. The mean tenant income for labor off the farm, including tenants reporting zero, was $75.44, with a standard deviation of $204.88, a median of $2.25, and a mode of zero. The range of tenant income for labor off the farm was zero to $2,813. Owner mean was $67.26, with a standard deviation of $268.68, a median of $0.18, a mode of zero, and a range from zero to $6,500.00. (Tabulated from TVA, "Family Removal Questionnaire," 1934).

59. $N = 1,821$ owners, 829 tenants. Tabulated from TVA, "Family Removal Questionnaire," 1934. Oral interviews established that many who were classed as tenants rented small amounts of cropland and instead of raising food purchased it from their earnings as agricultural day laborers. An interesting comparative base on living and food consumption which can be run against the Norris area removed population is: TVA, Social and Economic Division, Research Section, "Consumption in Selected Population Groups in the Norris Area." The purpose of the report was to analyze the "economic possibilities of self-containment" in the Norris area. Much of the data used in the report had an interesting history. In the summer and fall of 1933, the Social Science Research Council and the Department of Home Economics of the University of Tennessee conducted the Tennessee Living Study, which examined 575 families in the state, including 146 families from the Norris Basin (Grainger County excluded).

Of the Norris families, 66 were farm families, 26 farm-industrial, 16 industrial, and 34 commercial. Mining families and regional upland families were excluded, all families had four, five, or six members, and families who were "apparently poverty-stricken" were omitted. The sample represents, then, a cross section rather different from the Norris area removed population, and a much more prosperous one. Gant, who wrote the TVA report utilizing the Tennessee Living Study data, commented (p. 11): "This family selection, although it does not describe statistically all living levels in the Norris area, lends particular significance to this study. The consumption habits and deficiencies of families included in the Tennessee Living Study reflect the greater deficiencies of their poorer neighbors." The Norris area sample families consumed $566 in food per year, producing $478 of it and purchasing $88 of it. The removed population at Norris consumed $275.68 in food per year which they produced on the farm, bearing out the "greater deficiencies" argument of Gant. Gant's study is useful in establishing the great degree of variance in quality of life in the area generally.

60. Material from the U.S. Census of 1940 shows the percentages of gross income made up of food raised and consumed by the farm operator and family to be as follows (percentages for 1929 and 1939, respectively): the state (25.0 percent, 31.4 percent); Anderson County (39.4 percent, 40.8 percent); Campbell County (40.6 percent, 61.9 percent); Claiborne County (43.5 percent, 41.5 percent); Grainger County (36.9 percent, 37.2 percent); and Union County (42.3 percent, 47.6 percent). U.S. Census, 1940: Agriculture, vol. III, series 3, county table 17, pp. 472–81.

61. Median family size for areas other than the Norris area is taken from TVA (Cole), "Tennessee," 109–13. Cole's definition of "family" as well as TVA's and ours (used interchangeably with "household") is the one employed in U.S. Census (1930): "A family may therefore be defined in general as a group of persons, related either by blood or by marriage or adoption, who live together as one household, usually sharing the same table. Single persons living alone are counted as families, however, as are a few small groups of unrelated persons sharing the same living accommodations as partners" (TVA, "Families of the Norris Resevoir," 2).

62. TVA's analysis of the Norris Basin removed families, which derived figures for relief and nonrelief tenants, showed that 19.6 percent of the relief tenant families had homes of four or more rooms, as opposed to 33.6 percent of the nonrelief group, despite a median family size of 5.0 persons for the relief tenants and 3.9 persons for the nonrelief tenants (TVA, "Families of the Norris Reservoir," 44).

63. Johnson and Jackson, City Behind a Fence, 43.

64. Of the families in the 84 counties of the Appalachian coal plateau in 1930 studies by Goodrich and his associates, 20.5 percent had autos, 3.6 percent trucks, 1.1 percent tractors, 0.8 percent electric motors for farm work, 1.4 percent stationary gas engines, 9.3 percent telephones, 5.0 percent piped water to house, 2.1 percent piped water to bathroom, and 4.0 percent house electricity; 34.4 percent were located on improved roads. For the United States, in comparison, the same percentages, in order, were: 58.0 percent, 13.4 percent, 13.5 percent, 4.1 percent, 15.0 percent, 34.0 percent, 15.8 percent, 8.4 percent, 13.4 percent, and 63.7 percent (Goodrich, Allin, and Thornthwaite, Migration and Economic Opportunity, 58, tables).

65. Levron Howard states: "In 1930, the percentage of farms located on unimproved dirt roads varied from 39.4% in Campbell to 67.2% in Grainger, 63.0% in Claiborne, 46.6% in Union County . . . ," and he concludes, "in rainy weather there was little difference between improved and unimproved roads" (TVA [Howard], "Some Selected Social Characteristics," 25).

66. TVA (Cole), "Tennessee," 199–205.

67. Percentages of schools without libraries were noted by Cole as follows for each county: Anderson, 26 percent; Campbell, 56 percent; Claiborne, 57 percent; Grainger, 51 percent; and Union, 85 percent. Males per 100 females in the populations of the counties were as follows: Anderson, 100; Campbell, 103; Claiborne, 103; Grainger, 101; and Union, 104. (TVA [Cole], "Tennessee," table 16, 71–72, table 28, 102–103, table 47, 200–201.

68. Ibid., 106.

69. Killibrew, *Resources*. See in particular, in addition to specific East Tennessee counties, pt. II, 483–614; ch. 19, pt. I, "Conditions of Agriculture," 350–69.

70. Ibid., 354–55.

71. Ibid.

72. Ibid., 356–57.

73. Ibid., 433.

74. Ibid., 451, 454, 467, 468.

75. Ibid., 454. Killibrew was well aware of the juxtaposition of the good and bad features of this type of life. Of the Claiborne Countians he wrote: "Neighbors help each other in harvest, in the clearing of land, and of times in the planting of crops, and what would be a dry, hard, irksome labor for one is made a pleasant pastime for the many." He concluded, however, by saying: "The lofty virtues of simplicity, frugality, and honesty are cultivated and appreciated, but there is a woeful lack of enterprise" (p. 482).

76. Ibid., 354.

Notes for Chapter 4

1. Nash, "Reservoir Land Management," 138–39.

2. TVA, "Real Property Appraisals," 43. The Norris Reservoir tracts, exclusive of lands purchased around the dam site for the town of Norris, marginal lands, and right of ways, amounted to 214 square miles.

3. TVA, "Real Property Appraisals," 43. While not classified "marginal lands" as such, much of the property included in the Norris Reservoir tracts was, from a utilitarian point of view, marginal, including much of the Central Peninsula.

4. TVA, "Real Property Appraisals," 43. Flowage easements, as will be seen, later became the rule in acquisition of reservoir property, rather than the exception of the early days.

5. Nash, "Reservoir Property Management," 138. During an interview, C. M. Stephenson, formerly with the economic division of TVA and a pioneer in the development of TVA's in-lieu-of-taxes payment policy, stated that at Norris the "most generous" taking line was pursued and that large purchase policy continued through the construction of Wheeler, Pickwick, and Guntersville dams, being modified in the course of the construction of the Chickamauga, Watts Bar, and Loudoun dams. Stephenson added that the agriculturalists opposition to heavy purchase was consistent and that one of the strongest

reasons for the eventual modification of the policy was the pressure exerted by Harcourt Morgan and his associate J. C. McAmis (C. M. Stephenson, interview held in TVA office, Knoxville, June 3, 1975.)

6. Pritchett, *Tennessee Valley Authority*, 177. The following documents, in the Morgan Papers, are interesting for the material they contain on the administrative reorganization of 5 August: A. J. Ackerman to E. H. Cassels, June 18, 1936 (General Correspondence, E. H. Cassels, 1936–37); Harcourt Morgan and David Lilienthal's "Memorandum on Organization," dated Aug. 3, 1933, and A. E. Morgan's response, "Memorandum on Progress toward Organization to August 5, 1933," dated Aug. 5, 1933 (General Correspondence).

7. Charles E. Hoffman to Michael McDonald, Feb. 27, 1975. Charles Hoffman was, in A. E. Morgan's chairmanship, assistant secretary to the board of directors. The authors submitted an extensive set of questions to Arthur Morgan in Antioch in 1975, which he answered orally. Morgan sent the questions to Charles Hoffman, who was gracious enough to give his responses in a thirteen-page typescript. In this instance Hoffman was responding to queries concerning land acquisition and afforestation.

8. A. E. Morgan, *The Making of TVA*, 7.

9. Nash, "Reservoir Property Management," 138. TVA engineers' siltation profiles for the Norris Basin are on file with the TVA materials in the Regional Archives Branch, Federal Archives and Records Center, Atlanta, Georgia: RG142, "Records of the Tennessee Valley Authority."

10. Arthur E. Morgan, interview at his home, Antioch, Yellow Springs, Ohio, Feb. 1975.

11. The Tugwell Report strongly urged maximum afforestation of a large portion of East Tennessee farm land and was highly critical of abuse of the soil in the East Tennesseee area generally and the Norris Basin specifically.

12. Charles E. Hoffman to Michael McDonald, Feb. 27, 1975.

13. A. E. Morgan, *The Making of TVA*, 61–65. This section of Morgan's book also contains his views on land misuse and abuse. For Morgan's fascination with forest genetics, see pp. 65–67.

14. Ibid., 61–65. See also the published testimony of Edward C. M. Richards in U.S. Congress, House, *Five Fundamental Issues*.

15. Quoted in Selznick, *TVA and the Grass Roots*, 190, 191. This view was essentially reflected in the Tugwell Report and, as Selznick points out, by the Soil Erosion Service, the Bureau of Agricultural Economics, and the National Resources Committee.

16. C. M. Stephenson, interview held in TVA offices, Knoxville, June 3, 1975.

17. Charles E. Hoffman to Michael McDonald, Feb. 27, 1975. Hoffman stated that H. A. Morgan "evidenced practically no interest in afforestation, reforestation, or in forest management." It should be reiterated that owing to the general configuration of the land and the type of soil, a great deal of land purchased by TVA for Norris tracts was uncleared woodland and that 77.6 percent of their purchase was in ridge or hill land.

18. Nash, "Reservoir Land Management," 138.

19. Charles E. Hoffman to Michael McDonald, Feb. 27, 1975. Hoffman added to the above comment: "This was not surprising because the man tilling small acreage was being neglected by everybody."

20. Ibid. Hoffman felt that Harcourt Morgan lacked a "lively, deep, and

abiding interest in the problems and needs of the small farmer. He appears to have placed greater importance on the independence of the small farmer—to use his land and farm it as he saw fit—than such freedom merited." In an interview with the authors, A. E. Morgan characterized Harcourt Morgan's attitudes toward the small farmer as "elitist" (A. E. Morgan, interview, Feb. 1975).

21. Testimony of Edward C. M. Richards, in U.S. Congress, Houwe, *Five Fundamental Issues*. Richards felt that the appointment of Neil Bass, a Harcourt Morgan protété, sounded the death knell for the forestry program which he had envisioned under Arthur Morgan's direction, and that Bass was a person who cared little for the forestry program or indeed knew very little about it.

22. Nash, "Reservoir Property Management," 141.

23. Ibid. See also: TVA, "Review of Norris Reservoir Properties," 1–46 passim.

24. Pritchett, *Tennessee Valley Authority*, 253–54. The best detailed description of TVA's land acquisition process is Charles J. McCarthy (former assistant general counsel of TVA), "Land Acquisition." See also: Nash, "Reservoir Land Management," and H. J. Hitching and P. P. Claxton, Jr., "Practice and Procedure."

25. McCarthy, "Land Acquisition," 53.

26. Ibid., 54.

27. For a specific analysis of the factors considered in land purchase in the Norris area, see: TVA (Wooten and Hind), "Real Property Appraisals."

28. McCarthy, "Land Acquisition," 56.

29. Ibid.

30. Under authorization of section 4(i) of the TVA Act. McCarthy points out in his analysis the close cooperation existing between TVA's Land Acquisition and Legal divisions in the work of identifying well in advance of condemnation those properties which would offer problems (McCarthy, "Land Acquisition," 57).

31. Quoted in full in McCarthy, "Land Acquisition," 57–58 and 22n, and discussed in Hitching and Claxton, "Practice and Procedure," 952. McCarthy gives a number of pages to the discussion of condemnation proceedings.

32. McCarthy, "Land Acquisition," 52–58 and 22n.

33. Ibid., 61.

34. Ibid., 63. And the prices paid "have been in the neighborhood of only 15 percent above the amount of TVA's appraisal."

35. *Hearings*, pts. 1–4, pp. 313–14.

36. Ibid., 314–15.

37. "There had been almost no recognition of the fact that tens of thousands of land sales to the government involved an important and often tragic human experience" (A. E. Morgan, *The Making of TVA*, 76).

38. A. E. Morgan, *The Making of TVA*, 77.

39. A. E. Morgan, *The Making of TVA*, 78. "From My Speech to the Summer Student Group," Norris, Tennessee, 3 Aug. 1934.

40. See: Foster and Roberts, *Tennessee Democrats: Knoxville Journal*, May 25, 1934.

41. J. W. Cooper to V. D. L. Robinson, Jan. 12, 1934, TVA administrative files (hereafter referred to as TVA AF). Cooper indignantly said, "It is the old story of

robbing the government, and when I get ready to do that, I will resign and get on the other side, get me a horse and a pair of six shooters and go to."

42. Copies of petitions sent to Sen. Kenneth McKellar, Feb. 27, 1934, TVA AF.

43. This petition was signed by 55 persons including the superintendent of the Union County school system, the principal of a local high school, the director of the Maynardville State Bank, the chairman of the Republican Executive Committee, four members of the Democratic Executive Committee, and several teachers. Petition to Senator McKellar, Feb. 24, 1934, TVA AF.

44. "To the Honorable Kenneth D. McKellar, United States Senator," petition, Feb. 26, 1934, TVA AF.

45. L. L. Campbell to Arthur E. Morgan, *Confidential*, March 2, 1934, TVA AF.

46. Neil Bass to Kenneth D. McKellar, March 10, 1934, TVA AF; see also H. A. Morgan to David Lilienthal, memorandum, Feb. 26, 1934, TVA AF. This is particularly curious, since Bass had in his own hands Cooper's answer to the petition and, it would seem, could investigate the charges on their own merits without consulting McKellar. Cooper's telegram to Bass read as follows: "Neil: McKellar sent the original of the Union County Petition I have answered it and am handing you herewith a copy of my answer" (telegram, undated, TVA AF).

47. *Hearings*, pts. 1–4, pp. 314–15.

48. A. E. Morgan, *The Making of TVA*, 76.

49. See letters exchanged between State Representative S. D. McReynolds and J. W. Cooper relative to the employment with TVA of S. D. McReynolds's nephew in TVA AF. See also letters exchanged between Floyd Reeves and Gordon Clapp, of TVA's personnel division, and David Lilienthal, in Roy Talbert, "The Human Engineer," appendix, 154–68.

50. Kenneth McKellar to Neil Bass, March 12, 1934, TVA AF.

51. Neil Bass to the board of directors, March 19, 1934, TVA AF. If Bass and McAmis made more extensive attempts than this to collect evidence pertaining to the allegations, there is no evidence to support it.

52. *Hearings*, pts. 8–10, pp. 3432–33. Snyder was also to state in testimony that there was no question of misfeasance on Cooper's part, only nonfeasance (p. 3469).

53. Ibid., 3432.

54. A. E. Morgan to President Roosevelt, 1936 (undated rough draft, not sent), box 19, miscellaneous notes of A. E. Morgan and others on board organization and administrative relationships, Morgan Papers. In order fully to evaluate this, it must be kept in mind that this draft began: "I respectfully request the removal of David E. Lilienthal from his present position as Director of the Tennessee Valley Authority." See also A. E. Morgan, *The Making of TVA*, 76. In congressional testimony Morgan stated that as a result of the investigation of Cooper's work Lilienthal gave up direct control of land acquisition and it was placed under the general coordinator's (later general manager's) office, and that "the principle of land purchase that I outlined to the board early in the program came into operation" (*Hearings*, pts. 1–4, pp. 316–17).

55. *Hearings*, pts. 8–10, p. 3431.

56. Ibid., pp. 3432–34. It is interesting that while both Snyder (a Lilienthal appointee) and A. E. Morgan (a Lilienthal foe) agree that a revision was neces-

sary, the credit for revision and the blame for Cooper's ineptitude are attributed according to divisions among the board of directors. This is typical of the labyrinthine manipulation which marred the early years of TVA after the board's reorganization.

57. "Revision of Land Acquisition Procedure as the Result of a Conference between Messrs. Blandford (coordinator), Cooper (land commissioner), Robinson (administrative assistant), and Sayford (Engineering Services Division)," memorandum, undated, TVA AF. A covering letter indicates that the memorandum was drawn up on March 21, 1934.

58. John I. Snyder, assistant general solicitor, to Messrs. J. B. Blandford, Ned H. Sayford, and V. D. L. Robinson, March 21, 1934, TVA AF. The only recommendations, basically in approval of the plan but suggesting modifications in the timetable, came from the Engineering Services Division (Ned Sayford, engineering services director, to John I. Snyder, March 23, 1934, TVA AF).

59. Cooper would claim at the time of his resignation that he had information "weeks in advance that Mr. Snyder was planning to take charge of Land Acquisition and put into effect plans which I deemed impracticable." (John D. Erwin, "Cooper Claims Act Not Hasty," *Knoxville Journal*, May 29, 1934.)

60. J. W. Cooper to David E. Lilienthal, "Plan of Acquisition Submitted by Mr. Snyder," April 6, 1934, TVA AF. It seems inexplicable that while Cooper knew he was responsible to David Lilienthal, he did not know that Lilienthal was at the same time head of the legal department and general counsel for TVA. In point of fact Cooper was not really the head of a division but simply held the title of land commissioner.

61. Ibid.

62. Ibid.

63. *Hearings*, pts. 8–10, p. 3470.

64. Ibid., 3434.

65. A. E. Morgan, *The Making of TVA*, 76; *Hearings*, pts. 1–4, pp. 315–16.

66. Cooper to Lilienthal, "Plan of Acquisition," 6 April 1934, TVA AF; James Cooper to John I. Snyder, April 4, 1934, TVA AF. Cooper, notwithstanding memoranda to the contrary, was absolutely right about permitting farmers to stay on the land. Charles E. Hoffman, legal aide to the board, pointed out that in September 1933 the board had resolved to allow occupancy for up to two years, providing certain conditions were met (Charles E. Hoffman, legal aide, to V. D. L. Robinson, administrative assistant, April 6, 1934, TVA AF).

67. James Cooper to David Lilienthal, memorandum, April 6, 1934, TVA AF. Cooper appended to his second and personal letter to Lilienthal of April 6 this brief note marked "IMPORTANT":

> David: I hand you herewith a statement which I hope you will take the time to read. I have been misrepresented to the Board, and I want to get the truth to them. There are many, many small incidents which have hindered me, and I know were lied about, and I would like to tell the Board about it. . . . I do hate to be accused of incompetency by somebody who does not know what he is talking about.

68. *Hearings*, pts. 1–4, pp. 343–44. Interestingly enough, it was not until Cooper's resignation, one year after the creation of TVA, that such a program was begun. By a joint contract of TVA and the Agricultural Extension Service, University of Tennessee, a relocation service was set up to find available real estate for families who had to move. Not until September 1935 was a highly

structured section known as "family removal" constituted within TVA.

69. James Cooper to the board of directors, May 23, 1934, TVA AF.

70. City Editor, "James W. Cooper Hits TVA As he Quits Post," *Knoxville Journal*, May 25, 1934. Cooper alleged that Snyder had actually sent over men to take over his office and that Snyder had earlier told him: "you know you are going to lose out. I always play square, and I want to tell you I am going to try to get your job."

71. John D. Erwin, "Cooper Airs Views on TVA," *Knoxville Journal*, May 27, 1934.

72. John D. Erwin, "Cooper Again Cites Support," *Knoxville Journal*, May 28, 1934.

73. Ibid.

74. Kenneth McKellar to H. A. Morgan, May 26, 1934, TVA AF. McKellar concluded: "I wish you would kindly advise me, I have already protested very strongly against this treatment of Mr. Cooper."

75. A. H. Roberts to Sen. Kenneth McKellar, telegram, May 25, 1934, TVA AF; see also Roy H. Beeler to Sen. McKellar, May 24, 1934, TVA AF; Kenneth McKellar to A. E. Morgan, May 25, 1934, TVA AF; McKellar to Morgan, May 26, 1934, TVA AF. Others who publicly endorsed Cooper were Judge J. M. Gardenshire, state RFC manager and former state counselor general, Roy Wallace, comptroller of Tennessee, Ernest N. Haston, secretary of the state of Tennessee, and J. J. Bean, state treasurer.

76. "Lilienthal Fears Fund Difficulties," *Chattanooga Times*, May 26, 1934. The article was based on a press release made in Knoxville, May 25, 1934 (unated copy, TVA AF).

77. Benton Stong, "Hasty Mr. Cooper," *Knoxville News-Sentinel*, May 26, 1934. In a *Journal* article of the twenty-ninth, Cooper repudiated the accusation that his resignation was hasty, saying it was "untrue and unwarranted" and that he would let the fully developed facts speak for themselves (*Knoxville Journal*, May 29, 1934).

78. Harvey H. Hannah, W. H. Turner, Porter Dunlap to Sen. McKellar, May 24, 1934, TVA AF; "Utilities Board Interested in Resignation of Cooper," *Knoxville News-Sentinel*, June 11, 1934.

79. Contemporary attachment to the idea of "swapping" and "bargaining" is illustrated in Fetterman, *Stinking Creek*, and Matthews, *Neighbor and Kin*.

80. Both Hoffman and A. E. Morgan indicate that little was done in the early phases of the agency to educate the removed population in the relevant phases of TVA's work. By contrast H. A. Morgan and Lilienthal made a plethora of speeches about TVA to civic groups and various societies all over the United States.

Notes for Chapter 5

1. Beginning with the May 1, 1934 project authorization request by J. C. McAmis, "Relocation and Re-establishment of Landowners and Tenants Who Are to Be Displaced by Projects Carried Out by the Tennessee Valley Authority" (TVA, central file, microfilm, hereafter referred to as TVA CFM).

2. A. E. Morgan, "The Subsistence Homestead Program," a memorandum

sent presumably to the co-directors Lilienthal and H. A. Morgan, 28 July 1933, TVA CFM. An undated rough draft to this is in Box AL, Morgan Papers.

3. "Rough Draft for Proposed Land Corporation Showing Need, Source of Finance, and Operation," Aug. 15, 1933, TVA, Division of Reservoir Properties file (hereafter referred to as TVA DRP).

4. Ibid. As an example of the difficulties involved, Morgan, who had made extensive inquiries about the National Park Service removals in the Great Smoky Mountains, commented that of the farmers bought out by the government, 63 percent were worse off after removal than before, despite the fact that many were moved to more productive land. Land values in some cases inflated to the extent of 46 percent (page 2 of draft).

5. The work of acquiring lands, however, was to be carried on "in cooperation with the Federal Land Bank so that the latter will service mortgages on individual parcels where purchasers have been able to finance at least half the purchase price thereof. In this way the duplication of machinery for the extension of long term credit may be avoided in cases where the purchaser is eligible for Farm Credit loans" (ibid.).

6. Ibid. An unsigned rough draft of an act of corporation conforming to the suggestions for the proposed corporation was found in TVA AF.

7. Ibid. Attached to this draft was "Itemized Statement of Cost of Relocating and Reestablishing a Farmer Who Has No Funds [tenants] on an Economic Farm Unit in the Tennessee Valley," Washington, D.C., Aug. 15, 1933. The source of funds and the amounts for land, dwellings, and other buildings were to be $1,350 from the proposed corporation, $1,275 from the Farm Credit Association, and $375 in labor from the removed tenant. The total anticipated investment (or cost of relocation) was $3,000 per relocation. An analysis by TVA would later state that the actual cost of relocation was approximately $209 per family. TVA, Social and Economic Research Division (Satterfield and Davlin), "A Description and Appraisal of the Relocation of Families from the Norris Reservoir," 37.

8. "Establishment of Replacement Bureau (General Cooper)," memorandum, Aug. 30, 1933, TVA CFM.

9. Arthur E. Morgan to the board of directors, "Proposal for a Service to Help Landowners," Sept. 14, 1933, TVA CFM.

10. Robert Sessions, "Proposed Solution for Readjustment of Farmers Removed from Condemned Areas," Feb. 19, 1934, TVA CFM.

11. Arthur E. Morgan, "Re: Possible Means of Financing the Relocation of Landowners of the Lands to Be Flooded by TVA Projects," TVA CFM. Undated, but location in files and content indicate early 1934 as the most likely period of its composition.

12. Ibid.

13. Ibid. The memorandum cited the Chancellorsville Homesteads as the project, and Morgan noted that it was for "stranded industrial families" and families living on submarginal land. The project, not a stranded industrial community but a farm community in Jasper County, Georgia, was called the "Chancellorsville Homestead Community"; it was established in 1933 by agreement between the Subsistence Homesteads Division and the University of Georgia Board of Regents. The latter withdrew its support in 1934 and the name

of the project, now much reduced in magnitude, was changed to Piedmont Homesteads. Under this name it eventually passed to the Resettlement Administration. See: Holmes, *The New Deal in Georgia*, 272–73; and Conkin, *Tomorrow a New World*, 123.

14. Arthur E. Morgan, "Re: Possible Means of Financing the Relocation of Landowners." The memo stated that such cooperation from the Subsistence Homesteads Division would not be likely "in view of its attitude on our Norris project." TVA had requested a loan from the Subsistence Homesteads Division for its planned town of Norris, which was initially intended as a subsistence homestead program. The loan was denied, and Norris remained TVA's own project. (Conkin, *Tomorrow a New World*, 113, 51n.)

15. Arthur E. Morgan, "Re: Possible Means of Financing the Relocation of Landowners," TVA CFM.

16. Ibid.

17. Ibid. It was argued that possibly TVA could not bear the expense of this additional burden.

18. Earle S. Draper to A. E. Morgan, "Coordination of Rehabilitation Activities in the Tennessee Valley," March 22, 1934, TVA CFM.

19. E. S. Draper to A. E. Morgan, April 26, 1934, TVA CFM.

20. H. A. Morgan to A. E. Morgan and David Lilienthal, "Proposal Statement of Policy in the Planning Activities of the Tennessee Valley Authority," Oct. 3, 1933, Morgan Papers.

21. The late Prof. William Cole, former head of the sociology department, University of Tennessee, was engaged in work for a WPA committee at the university in 1933 helping to organize projects with money funded to TVA by the WPA. Cole was especially knowledgeable about the planning functions of TVA and was acquainted with E. S. Draper and Tracy Augur. Cole stated that there was considerable difference of opinion among the agriculturalists and planners and that the latter regarded the former as "grown-up county agents" who had some rapport with local farmers but lacked perspective insofar as planning functions were concerned. Planners were "bitter" about the agriculturalists' attitudes. Cole felt that H. A. Morgan himself did not see TVA as an agency with a permanent future and that in the interim he was determined to use it to build up the agricultural forces in the Tennessee Valley (William Cole, interview at the Univ. of Tennessee, May 15, 1976).

22. The use of the Agricultural Extension Service seems to have originated with both Harcourt Morgan and J. C. McAmis. Harcourt Morgan to Neil Bass, 1933; Neil Bass to J. C. McAmis, Sept. 19, 1933, TVA CFM.

23. J. C. McAmis to Harcourt Morgan, "Financing the Relocation of Farmers," March 9, 1934, TVA CFM.

24. TVA, project authorization request, May 1, 1936, TVA CFM. The project title was: "Relocation and Re-establishment of Land Owners and Tenants Who Are to Be Displaced by Projects to Be Carried Out by the Tennessee Valley Authority."

25. E. S. Draper to A. E. Morgan, "Provision for Dispossessed Farmers from Norris Watershed Area," May 22, 1934. Draper did not refer to the project by name; it was called "Shenandoah Homesteads" by the Subsistence Homesteads Division and was made up of seven resettlement communities in five Virginia counties, a project which incurred the wrath of Sen. Harry F. Byrd of Virginia,

who railed against the "stench coming from gross inefficiency and Russian Communism" (cited in Paul Conkin, *Tomorrow a New World*, 163).

26. Tracy B. Augur to E. S. Draper, "Project of J. C. McAmis for Relocation and Re-establishment of Displaced Population," June 6, 1934, TVA CFM. These comments came after the plan had been approved by the board of directors of TVA, a process which Draper and Augur apparently did not participate in, the evidence indicating that the plan was forced through without broad discussion within concerned divisions of TVA. See A. A. Twitchell to Tracy B. Augur, "Project for Relocation of Norris Population," June 5, 1934, TVA CFM.

27. Augur to Draper, June 6, 1934, "Project of J. C. McAmis," TVA CFM.

28. Ibid.

29. Ibid. Augur did point out that there were probably three groups of families being displaced and that the McAmis plan would benefit the successful farmer as well as the one who, though unsuccessful, refused to change his life style "even though that might mean a continually losing fight for a decent existence." For those who desired "wider opportunities" and new patterns of existence, however, the plan represented a "backward and ineffective step." Augur also favored the building of "cottage colonies or group houses" for displaced elderly persons at the town of Norris. (Tracy B. Augur to E. S. Draper, "Resettlement of Aged Persons in the Norris Reservoir Area," June 7, 1934, TVA CFM.

30. Carroll A. Towne, Land Planning and Housing Division, to Tracy B. Augur, chief, Land Planning and Housing Division, "Notes on Resettlement," Oct. 31, 1934, TVA CFM. While subsistence homesteads could serve as a model, the concept was not wholly embraced by the planners. In response to a memorandum from a TVA employee urging an attempt to copy the Cumberland Plateau experiment at Crossville, Tennessee, which its author described as a "compromise between individualism and communism much like the *MIR*," Draper, head of the Land Planning and Housing Division, urged a wait-and-see attitude with regard to the actual results of the Crossville Subsistence Homestead before undertaking such a project for TVA. (E. S. Draper to C. C. Haun, Nov. 5, 1935, TVA CFM.)

31. John I. Snyder, Land Acquisition Division, to Neil Bass, administrative assistant to Harcourt Morgan, Dec. 21, 1934, TVA CFM. Snyder and Augur, of the land planning department, were in serious disagreement about leasing as opposed to renting land in and around Norris. Augur thought that TVA should purchase land and lease it back to the owner. In what was to become the township of Norris, land was purchased, the owner or tenant evacuated, and the land then rented to "strangers," a process which Augur thought contrary to TVA's relationship with the people they removed (Tracy Augur to E. S. Draper, Dec. 5, 1934, TVA CFM).

32. Floyd Reeves was director of the Personnel and Social Development Division of TVA, a counterpart to Earle Draper's Land Planning and Housing Division.

33. Tracy B. Augur to Floyd W. Reeves, "Colonization of Norris Families," Jan. 19, 1935, TVA CFM. Some of Augur's conclusions about the efficacy of this plan were revealing. He suggested that for "problem families" in general, such a colonization scheme might have possibilities, "treating camp life as an interview period before permanent assignment." Typical of both the inherent paternalism

and the caution often behind such plans was the statement, "In order that the arrangement not be too attractive it is proposed to require certain work of persons helped."

34. TVA, "Classification of Families."

35. Carroll Towne to Paul Ryan, "Minimum Standard for Resettlement," Feb. 4, 1935, TVA CFM.

36. Earle Draper to Tracy Augur, Feb. 9, 1935, TVA CFM.

37. The following decisions were cited as establishing precedent in federal condemnation proceedings that payment should not exceed the value of the land: "United States vs. Myers, 190 Fed. 688; Mitchell vs. United States, 237 U.S. 241; Petrovsky vs. United States (C.A.D.C. 1933) 26 Fed. 24 (215) and cases therein cited." B.C. Dunklin and Conrad M. Kennedy to William G. Davis, Esq., Feb. 9, 1935, TVA CFM.

38. B.C. Dunklin and Conrad M. Kennedy to William G. Davis, Esq., Feb. 9, 1935, TVA CFM.

39. James Lawrence Fly, general solicitor, to T. Levron Howard, administrative assistant, Social and Economic Division, "Relocation of Indigent Families in the Area to be Flooded by Norris Dam," Feb. 11, 1935, TVA CFM. After examination of the provisions of the act, Fly stated: "The families in question are tenants of lands to be condemned and any disbursements in moving and temporarily housing and feeding such families would seem to be expenses incidental to the condemnation proceedings . . . for federal purposes, the inconvenience and expense of removal from the condemned premises are not proper elements of damages and no item therefore can be allowed or awarded in such condemnation proceedings."

40. James L. Fly to A.E. Morgan, "Relocation of Indigent Families in the Norris Reservoir Area," March 4, 1934, TVA CFM. Fly stated:

Any obvious move on the part of the Authority to prepare to care for these people is likely to lead to reliance thereupon: one, by increased numbers of people; two, for indefinite periods of time; three, by the regularly organized charities and government relief organizations that are charged with the duty. I should feel that the Authority would be making a mistake in opening itself to such probabilities. . . . I would suggest that we not take any open steps which will indicate the expectancy of the Authority that it will have the task thrust upon it.

41. C.W. Farrier was assistant to John B. Blandford, Jr., the coordinator of TVA and head of the Coordination Division.

42. "Synopsis of Events to April 8, 1935," TVA CFM; C.W. Farrier to James L. Fly, April 16, 1935, TVA CFM.

43. C.W. Farrier to James L. Fly, April 16, 1935, TVA CFM. Farrier estimated that at least 1,600 Norris Basin families needed "varying degrees of assistance in obtaining farm locations outside the basin" and that the TERA had cited a shortage of at least 1,500 housing units in East Tennessee: "By requiring the evacuation of 4,000 families approximately from the Norris Reservoir area, this existing shortage has been greatly increased. The point has been reached where it is necessary to provide means for the subdivision of large farms into smaller farms for the relocation of the evacuated families."

44. Ibid.

45. John Blandford, Jr., to Arthur E. Morgan, May 15, 1935, TVA CFM. Blandford asked Morgan to suggest a liaison officer, and Morgan recommended

that Farrier continue in the position he had already informally occupied. Presidential Executive Order 7027 created the Resettlement Administration, and Executive Order 7028 (April 30, 1935) transferred the FERA's Rural Rehabilitation Division to the RA. Executive Order 7041 transferred the function and funds of the Division of Subsistence Homesteads, Department of the Interior, to the RA. Later the Land Policy Section of the AAA was transferred to the RA. From May 1935, TVA's population removal program concerning resettlement was under the RA.

46. Entry from C. W. Farrier, notes, Coordination Division, undated, TVA CFM.

47. TVA (Marshall A. Wilson), "Activities of the Reservoir Family Removal Section, Coordination Division, Norris Reservoir Area," typescript, Jan. 1937. Fear of flooding discussed in C. W. Farrier to W. L. Sturdevant, Information Division, Sept. 20, 1935, TVA CFM.

48. Entries from C. W. Farrier's notes, Aug. 5–31, Sept. 9–15, 1935, TVA CFM.

49. TVA, "Activities of the Reservoir Family Removal Section," 4.

50. Ibid., 5–6.

51. Ibid., 9–14.

52. Marshall Wilson, chief social caseworker, Norris, memorandum, Dec. 20, 1935, TVA DRP.

53. W. G. Carnahan, Reservoir Family Removal Section, TVA, to Bruce Poundstone, chief, Rural Resettlement Division, Resettlement Administration, telegram, Jan. 11, 1936, TVA DRP. By the first of January, with removal progressing at a rapid rate, only 21 families had actually been accepted by the Rural Rehabilitation Corporation of the Resettlement Administration (Reservoir Family Removal Section, Coordination Division, "Progress Report," Jan. 4, 1936, TVA DRP).

54. Bruce Poundstone, chief, Rural Resettlement Division, Resettlement Administration, to W. G. Carnahan, chief, Family Removal Section, Jan. 15, 1936, TVA DRP.

55. C. W. Farrier to R. W. Swatts, representative to Tennessee, Resettlement Administration, Feb. 28, 1936, TVA DRP. The project called for the purchase of lands adjacent to the Norris Reservoir by the RA and the provision of RA supervision, as well as the purchase of grazing and croplands leased by TVA to Resettlement Administration clients. TVA was to make these lands available on a rental basis and provide work projects for RA clients on the Norris Lake forest land managed by TVA. This labor in lieu of cash would "recompense TVA for crop and grazing lands" and give the RA clients "favorable consideration for other employment over and above this labor in lieu of cash for rental." TVA also agreed to supply the RA with 500,000 board feet of salvaged lumber.

56. W. G. Carnahan to L. C. Sowell, March 3, 1936, TVA DRP.

57. W. G. Carnahan to John B. Holt, coordinator, Division of Farm Population and Rural Life, Bureau of Agricultural Economics, USDA, April 16, 1936, TVA DRP.

58. Julian Brown, state director, Resettlement Administration, to W. G. Carnahan, March 14, 1936, TVA DRP.

59. C. W. Farrier to R. W. Swatts, March 30, 1936, TVA DRP.

60. John B. Holt to W. G. Carnahan, April 13, 1936, TVA DRP. Ironically, Holt

was conducting a survey of the techniques of selection of families for persons displaced by the Resettlement Administration and was asking TVA for its experiences in the matter.

61. W. G. Carnahan to John B. Holt, April 16, 1936, TVA DRP.

62. Ibid.

63. Ibid.

64. Ibid. By "workers" of the Tennessee Valley Authority, Carnahan clearly meant those caseworkers of the Resevoir Family Removal Section.

65. W. H. Carmichael to W. G. Carnahan, Aug. 20, 1936, TVA CFM.

66. Ibid. Families undergoing the stress of being uprooted, felt Carmichael, needed a central system to deal with: "One section that could and would arrange their contracts with the proper Tennessee Valley Authority unit . . . would rectify this situation and result in less antagonism and misunderstanding."

67. W. H. Carmichael to W. G. Carnahan, Aug. 20, 1936, TVA CFM.

68. Ibid. Carmichael felt the failure of outside agencies was that they had their own problems to deal with, and that in the case of the RA "it was not flexible enough to handle the peculiar problems of the Tennessee Valley Authority Population Readjustment."

69. W. H. Carmichael to W. G. Carnahan, Aug. 20, 1936, TVA CFM.

70. W. G. Carnahan, population readjustment adviser, to L. N. Allen, director, Reservoir Property Management Department, "Recommendations for Future Plans for Population Readjustment," Oct. 12, 1936, TVA DRP. Carnahan's main concern was that by placing reservoir family removal under reservoir property management, the work was being fragmented.

71. W. G. Carnahan to L. N. Allen, "Recommendations," Oct. 12, 1936, TVA CFM.

72. Taylor, "The Resettlement Problem," Jan. 12, 1937, TVA DRP.

73. Ibid. Those most needing immediate assistance were 39 families who had received rehabilitation loans and 8 more who were living in temporary tents pending some resolution of their difficulties.

74. W. G. Carnahan to Resettlement Administration, Attn.: E. R. Henson, Rural Resettlement Division, Dec. 24, 1936, TVA DRP. See also: Paul Taylor, "The Resettlement Problem," Jan. 12, 1937, TVA DRP.

75. W. G. Carnahan to Resettlement Administration, Attn.: E. R. Henson, Rural Resettlement Division, Dec. 24, 1936, TVA DRP; TVA to Secretary of Agriculture, Attn.: Administrator of Resettlement Administration, "Resolution Passed by the Board of the Tennessee Valley Authority at This Meeting," undated, TVA DRP.

76. W. G. Carnahan to Bernard Frank, assistant director, Forestry Division, Jan. 8, 1937, TVA DRP; J. J. Goulden, Forest Development Section, Knoxville, to George S. Perry, Forest Development Section, Norris, "TVA Forestry Division Tentative Statement on a Rural Resettlement Division Cooperative Project of Highway 33 Bridge [on the Clinch River]," Jan. 15, 1937, TVA DRP.

77. Taylor, "The Resettlement Problem," 13.

78. Ibid., 18–20. Taylor figured readjustment costs, with the aid of TVA, to be roughly $4,000 per family "on a security basis" if the funds "are expended to the best advantage of everyone concerned." For the Norris area families only, he figured $1,200,000 minimum and $2,000,000 maximum for 300 families. TVA

was to contribute aid in transportation, acquisition of land, and temporary housing.

79. Ibid., 20.

80. Ibid. 22.

81. W. G. Carnahan to Resettlement Administration, Attn.: E. R. Henson, Rural Resettlement Division, Dec. 24, 1936, TVA DRP. Carnahan hoped eventually to establish Resettlement Administration liaison in developing not only the Highway 33 Clinch River cooperative, but also Norris and Big Ridge parks, in whose development the National Park Service had already aided TVA. The advantage of such projects, to his mind, was that they naturally sought "to readjust the population living adjacent to the developments, in contrast to present developments which have given less consideration to population readjustment needs."

82. W. G. Carnahan, chief, Reservoir Family Removal Section, to John B. Blandford, Jr., general manager, "Request for Board Approval of Tentative Plans for Clinch-Norris Recreational Cooperative," Feb. 8, 1937, TVA DRP. In the fall of 1936, local residents requested a TVA planner, H. E. Hudson (recreation and trailways projects) to inspect the site and compute costs and income derivable from its use in recreational development (W. G. Carnahan to Walter Packard, Resettlement Administration, Feb. 9, 1937, TVA DRP).

83. W. G. Carnahan to John B. Blandford, Jr., "Request for Board Approval," Feb. 8, 1937, TVA DRP.

84. TVA representatives from various divisions and departments were represented: forestry, planning, engineering, reservoir property management, Removal Section, Extension relocation service, and the administrtion of TVA (Walter Kahoe, administrative assistant). TVA, "Conference Minutes," Jan. 18, 1937, TVA DRP.

85. TVA, "Conference Minutes," Jan. 18, 1937, TVA DRP. Walter Kahoe also suggested that it would be better for TVA to keep title to the lands and use restrictions and long-term leases than to transfer title to the Resettlement Administration. He "suggested a public amendment to the Act in order to do in the open what we are desiring to do under cover. . . . He suggested this because not only do we have this particular problem [at Norris] but others up and down the River like it . . . ."

86. TVA, "Conference Minutes," Jan. 18, 1937, TVA DRP.

87. W. G. Carnahan, chief, Reservoir Family Removal Section, to John B. Blandford, Jr., General Manager, TVA, "Transmittal of Attached Data from the Resettlement Administration," Feb. 11, 1937, TVA DRP. Carnahan pointed out to Blandford that although the Reservoir Family Removal Section and the Agricultural Extension Relocation Service had supplied data to the Resettlement Administration, "it is the opinion of workers in the Reservoir Family Removal Section that the remedies suggested cannot be applied to all families and that some plan should be developed to initiate a less ambitious program for the marginal and submarginal families who are adversely affected by the construction program of the Tennessee Valley Authority."

88. Walter E. Packard, director, Rural Resettlement Division, Resettlement Administration, U.S. Department of Agriculture, to W. G. Carnahan, chief, Reservoir Family Removal Section, Jan. 29, 1937, TVA DRP. Enclosed with the

letter was a "Proposed Program for Resettlement, Prior to June 30, 1938, of Families Affected by the TVA Program." Packard said his proposals were being sent to RA regional directors George S. Mitchell in Raleigh, N.C., and Robert W. Hudgens in Montgomery, Ala. Packard stated that he would like a meeting in Knoxville on February 5 or 6 between E. R. Henson and Paul Taylor of the Resettlement Administration (with others from regional offices) and some TVA representatives.

89. W. G. Carnahan to John Blandford, Jr., "Request for Board Approval of Tentative Plans for Clinch-Norris Recreational Cooperative," Feb. 8, 1937, TVA DRP; Charles E. Hoffman, assistant secretary to the board, to W. G. Carnahan, "Board Action Concerning a Proposal to Cooperate with the Rural Resettlement Division in Organizing a Community Cooperative," Feb. 25, 1937, TVA DRP; Walter Packard to W. G. Carnahan, telegram, Feb. 16, 1937, TVA DRP.

90. L. N. Allen to John B. Blandford, Jr., "Summary of Conference Concerning Proposed Relationship with Resettlement Administration," Feb. 24, 1937, TVA DRP.

91. L. N. Allen to Dr. H. A. Morgan, March 10, 1937, TVA DRP.

92. See: Walter Packard to W. G. Carnahan, March 4, 1937, TVA DRP; Carnahan to Packard, March 5, 1937, TVA DRP; Frank Cooper, Resettlement Administration, regional chief appraiser, Region 4, to W. G. Carnahan, March 11, 1937, TVA DRP; and J. O. Walker, director, Rural Resettlement Division, Resettlement Administration, to W. G. Carnahan, April 5, 1937, TVA DRP.

93. L. N. Allen to Paul Taylor, informational coordinator, Farm Security Administration, May 19, 1938, TVA DRP.

94. Tracy B. Augur to E. S. Draper, "Relocation of Displaced Families in New Communities," April 17, 1935, TVA DRP.

Notes for Chapter 6

1. Primary responsibility for the grave removal program in the Norris Reservoir area rested in TVA's Engineering Services Division. The chief of that division was Ned H. Sayford, who assigned the direct supervisory work of grave removal to his assistant, Harry Wiersema. Jervey Kelly was also active in this work for the Engineering Services Division. The TVA's field engineer at LaFollette, Tennessee, John F. Barksdale, supervised the surveying, mapping, removal agreements, and the preparation and filing of grave removal records. The Authority also created a cemetery committee composed of representatives of the Authority's board of directors: Ned Sayford, Carl Bock (director of engineering and geology), and W. R. Woolrich (mechanical engineer) of the Agricultural Industry Division. This committee delegated much of the actual work to a subcommittee, chaired by the assistant director of the Engineering Services Division, Harry Wiersema, and representing many branches of TVA: land planning, land purchases, population removal, agriculture, industry, and engineering. Counselor Thaddeus Adams of the Authority's Legal Division was instrumental in the work of the grave removal program and affected the decisions made in committee, subcommittee, and divisions concerned with the reinterment and disinterment phase of the Authority's work at Norris.

2. W. R. Woolrich to H. A. Morgan, Aug. 17, 1933, TVA, Division of Water Management: Mapping Services Branch, Archaeological, Cemetery, and Utility

Relocation Section, Cemetery and Relocation Unit (hereafter referred to as TVA MSB).

3. John D. Freeman to W. R. Woolrich, Aug. 19, 1933, TVA MSB.

4. *Knoxville News-Sentinel,* Aug. 20, 1933.

5. "Minutes of the TVA Board of Directors Meeting," Aug. 21, 1933; C. A. Bock to N. Sayford and W. R. Woolrich, memorandum, Sept. 5, 1933; "Memorandum for the Establishment of a National Cemetery," undated, TVA MSB.

6. TVA, press release, Washington, D.C., Aug. 22, 1933, TVA MSB.

7. *Knoxville News-Sentinel,* Aug. 25, 1933; W. B. Morgan to W. R. Woolrich, Aug. 25, 1933, TVA MSB.

8. Mrs. E. Barksdale, "Immortal Pioneers," *Chattanooga Sunday Times,* Sept. 13, 1936. For this article Mrs. Barksdale won the Libble Luttrell Morrow prize for best feature, awarded by the Tennessee Woman's Press and Author's Club.

9. Copy of the original report of the meeting of the Campbell County Missionary Baptist Association, Aug. 25, 1933, TVA MSB. The requests made of the Authority by this body, contained in this document, were marginally annotated by someone in the Authority but were neither dated nor initialed.

10. Ibid. Four days following this meeting, the executive secretary of the Tennessee Baptist Convention wrote to TVA authorities that he had made a visitation in the region, and "was delighted with the plans already being worked by the trustees of the Campbell County Association, of which the Rev. George Ridenour is a member. Being a native son and knowing the heart of these people, he is better able to serve them and the Authority than any one person" (Freeman to Woolrich, Sept. 5, 1933, from the file of H. A. Morgan, director, TVA MSB).

11. TVA, press release, Washington, D.C., Oct. 11, 1933, TVA MSB.

12. Rev. T. C. Wyatt, Tennessee Valley Church Advisory Committee, to Woolrich, Sept. 12, 1933, TVA MSB.

13. Earle S. Draper, Land Planning Division, to Ned H. Sayford, memorandum, Nov. 3, 1933, TVA MSB.

14. G. L. Ridenour to W. R. Woolrich, Nov. 13, 1933, TVA MSB.

15. Freeman to Woolrich, Nov. 28, 1933, TVA MSB.

16. Copy of the resolutions adopted by the Tennessee Baptist Convention, Murfreesboro, Tenn., Nov. 16, 1933; Freeman to Woolrich, Nov. 28, 1933, TVA MSB.

17. Draper to Woolrich, Nov. 28, 1933, TVA MSB.

18. Transcript, cemetery conference, Knoxville, Tenn., Dec. 15, 1933, TVA MSB. Participants were the Rev. G. Ridenour; Mr. J. C. Carden, an undertaker of LaFollette; and Messrs. Bock, Sayford, and Woolrich.

19. T. C. Shannon, undertaker, to J. W. Cooper, chief, Land Acquisition Division, TVA, Nov. 25, 1933; copy to Woolrich, Nov. 6, 1933, TVA MSB.

20. Transcript, cemetery conference, Knoxville, Tenn., Jan. 26, 1934. Participants: Gen. J. W. Cooper, W. R. Woolrich, George Ridenour, and J. C. Carden (TVA MSB). As an indication of the hostile opinion allegedly raised against the scheme of a national memorial cemetery, Woolrich received a memorandum from a TVA employee who allegedly heard a local Baptist minister address his Sunday school with the statement, "It was high time that the Baptists organize to

combat the horde of atheists invading the community" (P. Horton to Woolrich, Feb. 5, 1934, TVA MSB).

21. "Proposed Procedure for Grave Removals in the Norris Reservoir Area" and "Cost Estimate B" (grave removal costs with national cemetery calculated), undated, unsigned, handwritten estimate and proposal, TVA MSB.

22. Woolrich to Sen. Kenneth McKellar, undated, TVA MSB.

23. "Recommended Procedure for Cooperation with Those Desiring to Move Graves from the Submerged Areas of Norris Dam." Entered in the board of directors meeting, Feb. 15, 1934, as Exhibit L–15–34a and approved. Notice of approval sent to Ned H. Sayford, Feb. 19, 1934, TVA MSB.

24. Sayford to John I. Snyder, assistant solicitor, Legal Division, May 11, 1934, TVA MSB.

25. John F. Barksdale to Luther C. Harris, memorandum, May 17, 1934, TVA MSB.

26. "Cemeteries in the Norris Dam Area," unsigned memorandum, undated, TVA MSB. Marginal annotations on this document suggest that its date is roughly mid-June 1934. It was contained in a folder of materials forwarded by N. Sayford and H. Wiersema to C. C. Haun of TVA, who was active in the public relations work of the grave removal operation.

27. Harris to Barksdale, "Public Sentiment as a Basis for the Grave Removal Program," memorandum, June 18, 1934, TVA MSB.

28. Ibid.

29. Edward Kane, Legal Division, to John I. Snyder, director of land acquisition, memorandum, July 13, 1934, TVA MSB. The Legal Division stated that not only were the resolutions "so vague as to now show a clear intent to give the Association representatives any power to act in the sale of properties or to receive purchase monies," but that proof by affidavit could be obtained showing that local churches intended that the association be so empowered.

30. "Normal," routine purchase of church lands and cemeteries was somewhat complicated by the fact that some churches possessed deeds with reverter clauses to the effect that when land ceased to be used for religious purposes, it would revert to the original grantor. Where, in such a case, TVA bought the land from trustees, it would become land not used for religious purposes and hence would revert to the original grantors, thus causing a second purchase theoretically to be made by TVA from the deed reversion to the grantors. The Authority looked upon this as a problem that could only be resolved by negotiation, and it no doubt furthered their antipathy toward dealing with an enlarged board of trustees for each church which would so deeply have involved the Authority with the Campbell County Baptist Association.

31. Edward Kane to John I. Snyder, memorandum, July 13, 1934, TVA MSB.

32. Woolrich to A. E. Morgan, chairman, board of directors, July 13, 19234, TVA MSB.

33. Thaddeus Adams to David S. Porter, Legal Division, March 9, 1936, TVA MSB. Adams, who in 1934–35 had been legal counsel to the TVA cemetery committee, here reviewed concisely the legal background of the problem of grave removal in the Norris area.

34. Tennessee Code of 1932, sec. 1825: "*Dead Bodies of Persons Dying of Yellow Fever.* It shall not be lawful to disinter or remove the body of any person dying with Yellow Fever within fifteen months after the death of such person, or

when the thermometer indicates a temperature of more than thirty-two degrees Fahrenheit (1879, Ch. 43)." The right of *removal* was by implication contained in this statute. Cited in Adams to Porter, March 9, 1936, TVA MSB.

35. Ned H. Sayford to John I. Snyder, "Special Rules Governing the Disinterment, the Removal, and the Reinterment of Deceased Persons . . . in Order to Comply with the Tennessee Valley Authority Requirement," memorandum, May 11, 1934, TVA MSB. The power to make rules in this case was vested in the Tennessee Department of Public Health under authority granted in the Tennessee Code of 1932, sects. 325 and 5756.

36. Adams to Porter, March 9, 1936, TVA MSB. The precedents establishing the fundamentals were cited as: Kincaid's Appeal, 66 Pa. 411, 5 AM.R. 377 (1870); Little v. Presbyterian Church, 68 S.C. 489, 47 S.E. 974 (1904); and Grinnan v. Fredericksburg Lodge No. 4, 118 Va. 588, 88 S.E. 79 (1916). Adams concluded his letter to Porter by praising the efficiency of the grave removal program and the residents: "and the people in the basin among whom we worked, and whose buried dead we were removing were usually always reasonable, kind and cooperative."

37. Adams to Snyder, Aug. 11, 1934, TVA MSB.

38. Adams to James Lawrence Fly, general solicitor, TVA, Aug. 21, 1934, TVA MSB.

39. Harry Wiersema to the Committee on Cemeteries, TVA, Aug. 17, 1934, TVA MSB. There were three types of contracts: TVA–297, TVA–298, and TVA–299. One designated that the individual arrange for the removal and receive monetary compensation from TVA. In the second, the individual designated TVA to remove the body; and in the third contract the individual designated that the grave was to be left untouched. TVA, "Regulations for the Removal of Graves," undated, TVA MSB.

40. Adams to Fly, Sept. 29, 1934, TVA MSB.

41. "Minutes of Grave Removal Conference, LaFollette, Tenn.," Oct. 13, 20, and 27, 1934, TVA MSB.

42. Adams to Barksdale, Nov. 5, 1934, TVA MSB.

43. Ibid.

44. Adams to Porter, March 9, 1936, TVA MSB.

Notes for Chapter 7

1. Rosenman, *Public Papers and Addresses*, II, 127–29. See also Gray, "The Maturing of a Planned New Town," 1–25, for an excellent summary history of Norris from 1933 to 1973.

2. Typical of these articles were Chase, "TVA, the New Deal's Best Asset," 705; Milton, "Dawn for the Tennessee Valley," 32–34; and Davenport, "The Promised Land," 38.

3. See A. E. Morgan, "Benchmarks"; see also David E. Lilienthal to A. E. Morgan, "Inquiry on Norris Dam Town Project," memorandum, Oct. 13, 1933, and A. E. Morgan to David E. Lilienthal, "Your Inquiry on the Norris Townsite Project," memorandum, Nov. 11, 1933, A. E. Morgan Papers; Morgan, "Benchmarks," XXIII, 551–52.

4. Morgan, "Benchmarks," XXIII, 552.

5. Ibid., 552, 577.

6. Arthur E. Morgan, speech, Aug. 31, 1933, in *Speeches and Remarks by Arthur E. Morgan,* I, 1933—35, TVA Technical Library, 8.

7. For a concise discussion of Roosevelt's concept of regional planning, see TVA, "Correspondence," 1–6.

8. TVA Board of Directors, "Minutes," June 16, 1933. (Hereafter "Minutes" will refer to meetings of the board of directors.)

9. "Minutes," July 29, 1933.

10. "Minutes," July 30, 1933.

11. Earl S. Draper to Arthur E. Morgan, "Report on Progress with Reference to Cove Creek Town Site and Regional Planning," memorandum, Aug. 22, 1933, TVA AF.

12. "Minutes," Aug. 5, 1933.

13. "Minutes," Sept. 18, 1933.

14. TVA, *Norris Project,* 174.

15. Tracy B. Augur, "Norris," 21.

16. TVA, *Norris Project,* 86.

17. Augur, "Norris," 21–23.

18. TVA, *Norris Project,* 186.

19. Ibid., 186–91.

20. Ibid., 201–2; see TVA (Grandgent), "Houses at Norris." Excluding the cost of the Norris school, which amounted to $161,000, the total sum expended on housing construction at Norris came to $1,445,304. See also *Hearings,* pts. 1–4, p. 1198; pts. 11–14, pp. 4654–55.

21. By June 30, 1935, TVA had expended the sum of $3,051,499 for the total construction of Norris (TVA, *Norris Project,* 218).

22. Despite interest in Norris as a model town, there is comparatively little material on the history of the town. In addition to the previously cited article by Augur, there are Moutoux, "The TVA Builds a Town"; Cushing, "An American Phenomenon"; and Dunn, "Model Worker's Town." A not-so-flattering portrait can be found in Stevenson, "A Contrast in Perfect Towns." None of the above discussions deals with the history of the town, however. Thus one of the principal sources upon which the authors have relied is an unpublished essay by J. W. Bradner, Jr., Norris town manager, located in the regional studies files on Norris. Entitled "The Evolution of a Community," it has been an invaluable source.

23. TVA (Bradner), "Evolution of a Community," 4–5.

24. Ibid., 7.

25. Ibid., 8.

26. Ibid., 8–9.

27. "Minutes," Aug. 7, 1935.

28. Kenneth Rouse, chairman of the board of directors, Norris Cooperative Society, to TVA board of directors, Aug. 22, 1935, regional studies files, Norris town.

29. Frank J. Carr, comptroller, to H. A. Morgan, "Memo on Norris Cooperative Society Incorporated," July 6, 1936, p. 2, TVA AF. See also *Hearings,* pt. 11, pp. 4658–61; t. 14, pp. 6095–97.

30. Frank J. Carr, comptroller, to H. A. Morgan, "Memo on Norris Cooperative Society Incorporated," July 6, 1936, p. 2, TVA AF.

31. Ibid., 1. See also TVA (Cunningham and Tallman), "Summary"; and "TVA Installs a Model Drug Store."
32. Norris Cooperative Society, "Annual Report," 1937.
33. TVA (Bradner), "Evolution of a Community," 10.
34. TVA (Durisch), "Proposed Local Government Organization," 1–19. See also *Hearings*, pts. 1–4, pp. 1197–1202.
35. Ibid. TVA (Durisch), "Proposed Local Government Organization," 6.
36. Ibid., 8–9.
37. TVA (Bradner), "Evolution of a Community," 13; see also *Hearings*, pts. 1–4, pp. 1210–11.
38. Davenport, "There'll Be Shouting in the Valley," 10–11; 36–40.
39. Davenport, "There'll Be Shouting in the Valley," 39.
40. Houston and Davis, "TVA: Lily-White Reconstruction," 291. For more information on Negroes and Norris Dam, see *Hearings*, pts. 5–7, pp. 2381–90; pts. 8–10, pp. 3239–40.
41. Houston and Davis, "TVA: Lily-White Reconstruction," 291.
42. John P. Davis, "The Plight of the Negro in the Tennessee Valley," *The Crisis* 42 (Oct. 1935), 315.
43. Ibid., 291.
44. TVA CFM, Norris.
45. "Churchless Norris," *Christian Century*, Nov. 14, 1934, pp. 1448–49; see also "Minutes," April 25, 1935.
46. "Churchless Norris," 1449; see also *Hearings*, pts. 1–4, pp. 1208–09, 1218–20, 1587–91; pts. 8–10, pp. 3690–91.
47. TVA (Bradner), "Evolution of a Community," 6–7.
48. Ibid., 7.
49. Ibid., 12–13.
50. TVA (Lowry and Cadra), "Local Social and Economic Effects," 133–34; see also *Hearings*, pts. 1–4, pp. 1202–3; pts. 8–10, pp. 3177–81, 3183–85, 3188–89.
51. TVA (Lowry and Cadra), "Local Social and Economic Effects," 134; see also "School at Norris, Tennessee," 55; McLeod, "TVA Sets Up a New Type of School," 47.
52. TVA (Lowry and Cadra), "Local Social and Economic Effects," 134; TVA (Bradner), "Evolution of a Community," 12.
53. TVA (Lowry and Cadra), "Local Social and Economic Effects, 135; TVA (Bradner), "Evolution of a Community," 15–16.
54. TVA (Lowry and Cadra), "Local Social and Economic Effects," 135.
55. TVA (Bradner), "Evolution of a Community," 14.
56. Ibid., 14–15.
57. Gray, "Maturing of a Planned New Town," 11.

Notes for Chapter 8

1. TVA (Lowry), "A Review of Social and Economic Conditions," 2–3. The use of the term "development program" in this context is somewhat misleading, since a broader reading of the TVA Act of 1933 would classify regional planning and land use and water use planning as "developmental," not just flood control, navigation, and power.

2. TVA (Satterfield and Davlin), "A Description and Appraisal."

3. The two questionnaires differ essentially in the amount of data generated. The 1936 schedule was quite brief in comparison with that of 1934.

4. Nielsen's thesis is a comprehensive résumé of the work undertaken by Pat Kerr of the Agricultural Extension Service, but it is difficult to use as a proxy for first-hand evaluation of relocation for a number of reasons: through either Kerr's or Nielsen's ommssions, one is not told how the sample was derived. As nearly as can be determined from material in the Nielsen thesis, three sets of stratified samples, with variant n's (roughly 10 percent of all those "affected" by the reservoir's construction, whether they had to move or not) were obtained on the basis of county of residence before relocation by farm tenure; of tenure by new worth upon relocation; and of how affected by tenure (tenants displaced or not displaced; owners who had to sell all, part, or none of their property). In the voluminous tables and figures cited, one is never informed at precisely what strata the conclusions are operating, and some of the most valuable data are computed for only a part of the sample without any notations as to how the n's are derived. The three strata of the sample do vary somewhat (n values from 355 to 273), and the n for the significant socioeconomic data is not 355 but 152. These numbers are very small for the affected population, and it is not known on what basis they either provide an accurate sample or are based on reliable sampling techniques. In much of the data analysis of the subgroups of farm families (removed tenants by income grouping, for example) the n's are so small, even with regard to the sample population, that findings are more misleading than not (n is 4, 5, 16, and 25). In addition to sampling defects, Kerr's (and Nielsen's) data suffer from cognitive balancing. Respondents were asked to reconstruct from memory both discrete and attitudinal data for their condition in the years 1933–34 (before relocation) and compare these data with their present situation (after relocation). Since the intervening experience of relocation would normally color the mnemonic responses, the value of the data is questionable. See Nielsen, "Socio-Economic Readjustment of Farm Families." A second master's thesis on the general topic of relocation within TVA is not for the most part much more than a broad restatement of the family removal program as envisaged by TVA and has little analytic content (Brown, "Family Removal in the Tennessee Valley").

5. TVA (Satterfield and Davlin), "A Description and Appraisal," 14. As of Dec. 1, 1936, the Extension Relocation Service stated that 3,418 families had been relocated. There were at that date 86 families still to be removed, most from the Central Peninsula. Allowance must be made, however, for the fact that the service did not consider 831 families "removal cases" because although they were influenced by the impact of TVA, they were not compelled to seek new locations: "In some cases either none or only part of the land on which the families were living was purchased by the Tennessee Valley Authority; in some instances the land purchased belonged to non-resident owners; some families reported as living in the reservoir area were really transient whose regular residence was outside the area. By March 31, 1937, the total of removal cases stood at 2,872."

6. TVA (Satterfield and Davlin), "A Description and Appraisal," 15–16. Of the total of 2,587 families only 6.8 percent (176) located outside Tennessee; 56.8

percent of these resettled in Kentucky, the majority of whom (73.0 percent) were found in Bell and Whitley counties.

7. Satterfield and Davlin used as their comparative data base TVA's analysis and compilation of the data from the 1934 questionnaire, administered to 2,841 families and analyzed in TVA (Durisch and Burchfield), "Families of the Norris Reservoir."

8. In chronological order the reports are: TVA (Durisch), "The Effect on County Government"; TVA (Macon and Morrison), "The Effects upon Local Finance"; and TVA (Lowry), "A Review of Social and Economic Conditions." Owing to the fact that purchases of land were incomplete in 1934, the first report made only a tentative assessment of Campbell and Union counties, where purchases were nearly complete.

9. The conclusions and summary were presented separately: TVA, "Summary and Recommendations." The complete report consisted of 134 pages, including appendices and tables, and was submitted by Earle Draper to Gorden Clapp, then general manager, on March 6, 1940. The regional planning council was made up of representatives from various departments within TVA. Participating were representatives from agricultural relations, commerce, forestry relations, health and safety, regional planning studies, and reservoir property management.

10. USDA, *Economic and Social Problems;* TVA, "A Land Classification Approach." Cited in: TVA (Satterfield and Davlin), "A Description and Appraisal," 2–5; 2, n.2.

11. TVA, "A Review of Social and Economic Conditions," 79. While the report argues that "this remarkable acceleration between 1930 and 1935 cannot be explained directly by the pressure of reservoir family removals" because large-scale removals had not begun before January 1935, it is doubtful whether intensive farming and overpopulation alone could have caused it, since the same conditions without TVA apply to many other counties in East Tennessee which registered falling farm values. Value change would not need to wait upon actual large-scale removals, and the region's inhabitants were aware of the necessity of such removals by September 1934 at least.

12. TVA (Satterfield and Davlin), "A Description and Appraisal," 14.

13. Ibid., 8, nn. 2 and 3. It was estimated that to provide "an average opportunity" for a farm family, a farm should be at least 64 acres, including 38.6 acres of cultivatable land. The median size farm in the Norris area prior to removal was less than this figure (62.2 acres). Of course, "average opportunity" and the standardized acreage needed to produce it should be defined with some caution, as there are too many invisible variables attached to both the term and the figure.

14. TVA (Satterfield and Davlin), "A Description and Appraisal," 19.

15. Ibid., 20. Six others in this group were clients of the Resettlement Administration who, after the time of the survey, were forced to remove, since their rental arrangements were for one year only (20, 1n). Of the four more families in this group, two believed that they had achieved permanent settlement, and two more said that they had rented the only places they could find and that they would not permanently settle there (20).

16. Ibid., 20.

17. Ibid., 22. The median appraisal value of farms sold to TVA was $3,040; the median price paid for a new farm, $2,285. Such figures must be used with caution because different prices may indicate the presence or absence of improvements on both old and new land. Owners received a mean $50 per acre for land sold to TVA (25).

18. TVA (Lowry), "A Review of Social and Economic Conditions," 82. It was noted that "in response to their [the removed families] demand for land, many of the farms in the remaining parts of the counties were split up" and that south of LaFollette in the Powell Valley "small subsistence and truck plots have replaced the former large farms of 150 or more acres."

19. In the under-$1,000 category, owners increased in number from 43 to 89 (11.4 percent to 24.2 percent); in the $4,000-and-over category, 140 owners decreased to 100 (37.3 percent to 27.2 percent). Prices paid are for agricultural lands and do not reflect town lots or nonagricultural property. TVA (Satterfield and Davlin), "A Description and Appraisal," text and table, p. 22.

20. TVA (Satterfield and Davlin), "A Description and Appraisal," 23–24. Of those families who purchased farms worth $1,000 to $3,999, upon relocation, 59.7 percent located in the reservoir counteis, 27.6 percent in adjoining counties, and 12.7 percent in the second tier of counties around the reservoir. Among the families purchasing farms worth $4,000 or more, 33.7 percent purchased in the five-county reservoir area, 41.6 percent in adjoining counties, and 24.7 percent in other counties. The average price per farm in reservoir counties was $2,026; in nonreservoir counties, $4,525. Indebtedness against farms was a factor among only 10 percent of relocated owners and typically, farm mortgages, generally a sign of farm affluence and willingness and ability to improve farms and farming techniques, appear to be substantial only in the case of wealthier owners. Among those indebted on their farms, 24.4 percent were in the group that paid under $1,000 for their farms, as compared to 48.8 percent in the $1,000-to-$3,999 group, and 28.6 percent for the $4,000-plus group. The average indebtedness of the latter was $2,048; the middle group, $777; and the under-$1,000 group, $160.

21. TVA (Satterfield and Davlin), "A Description and Appraisal," 23. Thirty percent of those investing invested less than $500.

22. Ibid., 24–25. "Twenty-seven percent of the sample relocated owners and 85.2 percent of the tenants now have farms of less than 20 acres as contrasted with 20.9 percent and 73.4 percent respectively, for the same families prior to removal." (25) Of the owners, 18.5 percent now hold land of 100 acres or more, as contrasted with 23.6 percent prior to removal (25).

23. Ibid., 25; table 3, 26.

24. Median acres in cultivation by owners in reservoir counties was 12.2 acres; in adjoining counties, 27.5 acres; in nonreservoir counties, 33.8 acres. Among tenants, 64.6 percent of those relocated in the reservoir counties cultivated less than 10 acres, compared with 52.3 percent in adjoining counties and 26.7 percent in nonreservoir counties. (TVA [Satterfield and Davlin], "A Description and Appraisal," 26.)

25. Ibid., 27. Among owners, 15.4 percent owned more farm machinery after than before relocation; 9.0 percent owned less. Only 9.3 percent of the tenants owned more; 4.4 owned less. Of the owners, 19.3 percent, and of the tenants, 14.8 percent, purchased livestock after relocation; 15.2 percent of owners and

15.3 percent of tenants had sold all or part of their stock before removal.

26. Ibid., 28. Despite expressed dissatisfaction, the greatest number of owners (92.0 percent) regarded their relocation as permanent. Less than half of the tenants (44.5 percent) felt their relocation permanent. In light of the fact that tenants had no permanent investment in the land, this is not surprising.

27. Ibid., 29. Tenant's average dwelling size increased from 3.1 to 3.2 rooms; owner's average dwelling size went from 4.4 to 5.2 rooms.

28. Ibid., 30–31. Frame dwellings were more prominent among owners (75.1 percent) than among tenants (32.7 percent). More than half the tenants lived in box dwellings upon relocation. Of all the relocated dwellings in the sample, 7.1 percent were of log construction, 31.1 percent of box construction, and the remainder of frame construction. The median age of the owners' houses was 10.2 years; of tenants' houses, 13.5 years. Classifications of housing made by field men of the total sample were 38.0 percent, good; 41.6 percent, fair; and 20.4 percent, poor. Only 10.0 percent of the owner dwellings were classed as poor, as compared with 38.0 percent of the tenant dwellings.

29. Certain discrepancies in percentages of population prior to removal on items cited in the TVA report, "A Description and Appraisal," and in the authors' data in chapter 3 occur because the data used by the authors contain fewer cases than the original set used in TVA compilations. On the follow-up questionnaire, data for house size, sanitary facilities, and water supply prior to removal were not requested, hence the sample data have to be compared to data from the whole removed population.

30. TVA (Satterfield and Davlin), "A Description and Appraisal," 33.

31. Ibid. Compared with 1.5 miles and 1.6 miles, respectively, prior to removal. Five and a half percent of all families lived more than 5 miles from an elementary school upon relocation.

32. Ibid., 36.

33. The term "established relocation agencies" is ambiguous, since it does not indicate which of TVA's relocation services are being referred to.

34. TVA (Satterfield and Davlin), "A Description and Appraisal," 37. In the sample population 22.9 percent of the owners and 17.9 percent of the tenants were aided in relocation with money earned from working for TVA.

35. TVA (Satterfield and Davlin) "A Description and Appraisal," 38.

36. Page numbers following the cited modifications refer to TVA (Lowry), "A Review of Social and Economic Conditions," viii–ix.

37. Ibid., 74, v.

38. Ibid., 5–6. See: TVA and Institute for Research in Social Science, Univ. of North Carolina, Chapel Hill (Folger), "Migration"; and TVA (Draper), "Interstate Migration Problem." The Folger typescript deals mainly with subregional migratory patterns in the Tennessee Valley area. Draper, although sanguine about reversing net losses to the Valley through interstate migration, nonetheless regarded the out-migration as a serious problem rather than a benefit.

Notes for Conclusion

1. Seligman and Cornwell, *New Deal Mosaic*, meeting no. 19, Proceedings of the National Emergency Council, Dec. 11, 1934, 368–69.

2. Davis, "'And It Will Never Be Literature,'" 69–74.
3. Banner, "Toward More Realistic Assumptions," 123–34.
4. Ibid., 127–28.
5. Ibid., 123.
6. TVA, *Annual report, 1979,* 85 (epilogue).

Bibliography

ARCHIVAL SOURCES

TVA's archival concerns are essentially oriented toward the preservation and utilization of materials necessary to create working reference files for the agency's ongoing projects rather than toward the creation of an historical archive as such. Moreover, changes in TVA's organizational table on the one hand, and in forms of record classification on the other, have created some complex problems in the location and identification of documents. A bibliographical essay, therefore, may be of more use to students of TVA's development than many standard bibliographical citations would be. This essay deals in large measure with materials of TVA's population removal program at Norris in the early years of TVA, but similar materials for other dams and reservoirs can be found in the same location, and all should prove useful to historians interested in TVA's early developments.

In 1961 the Chattanooga Records Center of TVA transferred forty file drawers of population removal material to the Regional Archives Branch, Federal Archives and Record Center (FRC), East Point, Georgia. These population removal materials form part of Record Group 142, which consists of 114 cubic feet of materials classed as "Record of the Tennessee Valley Authority: Records from the following divisions of TVA: Division of Health and Safety, 1938–1973; Land Planning and Housing Division, Cartographic Records, 1934–1936; Division of Forestry, Fisheries and Wildlife, Project History File, 1933–1955; Engineering Design Division, records relating to Lend Lease program to Soviet Union, 1942–

1945." The section of RG 142 pertaining to family removal from reservoirs is the group (FRC accession number 61A1597) headed (on the shelf index) "Family Removal and Population Readjustment Case Records."

The family removal records are made up of "case histories, code cards, removal sheets, social studies, and other related forms and correspondence for the period of January 1934–1954, filed alphabetically, geographically, numerically by code numbers, and subjectively." In reality some of the material, notably social studies, antedates 1934, having been compiled in 1933, the year of TVA's creation.

The most significant materials in Record Group 142 are the interview sheets of families removed from reservoir areas by TVA. Since the Authority brought to completion seven major dams and reservoirs between 1933 and 1942 alone, the interview sheets provide superb quantifiable data for the construction of views of rural life in the Tennessee Valley in the thirties. The removed populations themselves were cross sections of rural life, from Appalachian subsistence farms to plantation economies of the cotton belt, and are of inestimable value in reconstructing, in socioeconomic detail, the lives of smallholders, tenant farmers, and sharecroppers throughout the valley. The removal sheets vary in form and content from reservoir to reservoir as some changes were made in the taking of schedules, but they are uniformly rich in detail. RG 142 also contains code cards which reference the use TVA made in the relocation of each family to various state and local agencies.

In addition to the above-mentioned records, RG 142 contains social studies: a group of typed and mimeographed analyses and studies of cities, counties, and states in the Tennessee Valley. These studies were completed under the auspices of joint TVA-CWA grants beginning as early as 1933 and were compiled by scholars from various academic institutions in the Tennessee Valley states. The social studies comprise Project 10,000, which was made up of 200 numbered individual studies ranging from analyses of school systems and county fiscal procedures to compilations of basic socioeconomic data for the various states. Of particular interest are studies of urban housing in Knoxville, Tennessee, by the late William Cole, a sociologist at the University of Tennessee, and "Social and Economic Status of Blacks in Tennessee," by Charles S. Johnson of Fisk University. T. J. Woofter of the University of North Carolina directed numerous socioeconomic studies of rural life in North Carolina in the depression (including excellent material on tenantry) , and there are some intriguing studies of black communities in Alabama.

GRAVE REMOVAL FILES

A vast amount of information is available concerning the operation of disinterment and reinterment procedures undertaken by TVA in reservoir areas. These materials are located in Chattanooga, Tennessee, at TVA's Division of Water Management: Mapping Services Branch, Archeological, Cemetery, and Utility Relocation Section, Cemetery and Relocation unit. Some duplications of the removal records of this unit (but not its correspondence files) are available in Special Collections, Hoskins Library, the University of Tennessee, Knoxville. The file in Chattanooga gives reference to correspondence relating to particular grave removals as well as containing all memoranda on the formulation of grave removal policy and all field reports and surveys.

LAND ACQUISITION FILES

In Chattanooga, TVA's Division of Properties and Services, Land Branch, possesses a large amount of quantifiable and nonquantifiable material of utility to the historian. This material is in the land book and the land tract files. The land book is a series of ledgers containing record of each parcel of land acquired by TVA. The ledger indicates the disposition of each tract according to ownership, and this item alone gives interlocking familial relationships pertaining to land ownership through a citation of the heirs and assigns for each parcel. The land book also references the acreage of each parcel and how much was paid for the land itself and for improvements, as well as the taxes and liens upon each parcel at the time of purchase. For Norris much of these data are aggregated in: Tennessee Valley Authority (H. H. Wooten and Jack Hind), "Real Property Appraisals of the Norris Reservoir Purchase Area," mimeographed confidential report (Knoxville, 1937).

The Division of Properties and Services also houses the land tract files. These are legal dossiers pertaining to each land transfer filed by the reservoir parcel number. Most of the information in these files is not likely to be easily quantified but is significant, including the following: transcription of each original deed pertaining to the tract in question, with a full transcription of the process required to remove clouds from the title, as well as all correspondence which took place between the owner and TVA. These files literally follow each piece of property, step by step, through the process from first contact to individual sale. The quantifiable segment of these files is made up of the appraisal reports for each property. The attached correspondence and deed transfers of property provide not only insights into the process of purchase but fascinating histories of the properties themselves and the changing patterns of land ownership. Interested readers may refer to the following published items on land acquisition. See: Kris Kristjonson, "TVA Land Acquisition Experience Applied to Dams in the Missouri Basin," *Bulletin* 432 (Aug. 1953) of the Agricultural Experiment Station, South Dakota State College, Brookings, S.D.; C. J. McCarthy, "Land Acquisition Policies and Proceedings in TVA—A Study of the Role of Land Acquisition in a Regional Agency," *Ohio State Law Journal* 10 (Winter 1949), 46–63; Claude W. Nash, "Reservoir Land Management," in Roscoe C. Martin (ed.), *TVA: The First Twenty Years—A Staff Report* (Knoxville: Univ. of Tennessee Press, 1956); and W. O. Whittle, "Movement of Population from the Smoky Mountain Area," typescript (Knoxville: Univ. of Tennessee Agricultural Experiment Station, 1934). See also the working bibliography on land acquisition compiled by Charles Stephenson of TVA's research section of the Social and Economic Division (Central Service Office Files 601.002).

RECORD STAGING AREA FILES, TVA, KNOXVILLE

TVA's Record Staging Area, in Knoxville, is the repository of some of the most valuable historical records TVA possesses. These materials can be roughly divided into three groups: the old central file material, administrative files, and division files.

TVA initially operated upon a central file system with a decimal classification between 1933 and 1936. The decimal classification utilized was adopted from the War Department classification manual. A copy of the early file classification manual is available at the office in Knoxville of TVA's Eastern Area Records Office. The old central file system was microfilmed in the 1940s, but since much of the copy was of onionskin and colored duplicates and was badly stored, the copy is extremely difficult to read. Storage box numbers in this microfilm file give access to decimal classification, thus necessitating the use of the file classification manual. In 1936 an administrative file was created as a branch of the old central files, the purpose being to serve the office of the general manager. The administrative file (sometimes referred to as the general manager's file) contains material generally consisting of the chairman's file, the director's file, volume files, information office, budget and government relations and economic staff. The file systems are confusing because the decimal classification was not discontinued until 1940, whereupon an alphanumeric/departmental system was adopted, to be replaced later by a subject/numeric classification. There are 520 drawers of materials in the administrative file, made up of correspondence, reports, and cross-index sheets. At least 40 percent or more of the file is comprised by cross-index sheets. These files may be reached through the Eastern Area Records Office, TVA, and are located in the TVA Record Staging Area, TVA, Knoxville: Division of Office and Property, section 2A–1–42, Knoxville, Tennessee.

When TVA's old central file system was retired and an administrative file developed, a division file was also created. This division record file was created to serve each division. But owing to the changing organizational table, some of these files are centralized and some decentralized. To the historian of TVA the most significant of these files are the old Commerce Department files and Regional Studies Department files, many of these being volume files. To those interested in population removal programs in the reservoirs, the most valuable of these files is the Division of Reservoir Properties file (sometimes referred to as the reservoir property management file).

The Division of Reservoir Properties is now part of the current Division of Office and Property, and the files constitute part of the 364 file drawers which supplement the administrative files. There were formerly about 200 transfer cases of these records, but they have recently been cleared to about 40 file boxes. Much of the material in the DRP files is microfilmed in the old central files collection, but the DRP files are preferable, being more easily accessible and easier to read and duplicate.

DRP files contain material from all the reservoirs concerning population removal. Most Norris area material is in boxes 1, 2, and 33 but is duplicated for other reservoir areas. The most important general and specific (Norris area) material is as follows:

1. TVA correspondence with the Resettlement Administration and the Farm Security Administration through 1939, extremely valuable material including much information on the proposed joint RA-TVA project of the Clinch River Recreational Cooperative;

2. DRP excerpts from testimony before the 1938 congressional committee, and DRP-related minutes of early TVA board meetings;

3. The day-to-day working files of population removal activities, some specifically referenced to the Norris area, some related to other removals in other reservoirs. These include correspondence, and caseworker progress reports;

4. Volume files, DRP. These are duplications of reports made by TVA officials concerning population removal and related matters. Copies of virtually all of these reports are filed with the Technical Library, Information Office, Office of the General Manager, TVA, and are referenced in the library's card catalogue;

5. Family case record summary sheets and files (TVA970B). Each family to be aided in relocating by TVA's Reservoir Family Removal Section, Coordination Division, possessed a file and a case record summary sheet. The sheet contains quantifiable socioeconomic data for these families as well as a detailed record of caseworker visits to families and all correspondence relating to the family's removal. While much of these data are not quantifiable, the qualitative sectors of the file provide a close look at both the problems and the mechanics of population removal by TVA. They are the most complete records of the "problem cases" of family removal activities. Some photographs are appended to these case files.

All DRP files and other division files in the TVA Record Staging Area, Knoxville, are, like the administrative files, accessed through the Eastern Area Records Office, TVA, Knoxville.

PHOTOGRAPHIC FILES

TVA possesses several excellent collections of photographs taken in the early years. The Information Office, office of the general manager, TVA, possesses in the Technical Library of TVA the photographs taken by the renowned Lewis Hine. The Hine Collection, which may be reached through the director of TVA's Technical Library, consists of roughly 200 eight-by-ten-inch photographs with descriptions. These photographs are on a variety of subjects: construction of Norris Dam; activities in the town of Norris; portraits of Norris area residents; many pictures of schools, churches, and homes in the Norris reservoir area; and some superb compositions illustrating the effects of soil erosion in the area of the Norris reservoir. While these photographs cannot be faulted for their professionalism, they must only cautiously be interpreted as representing an accurate cross section of life in the Tennessee Valley in the thirties. Many were taken with an eye for drama rather than faithful representation.

The Technical Library also holds the scrapbook of Marshall Wilson, the chief resident caseworker for the Removal Section of TVA at Norris. Wilson's photos are far from professional, but they are fully representative of the range of building types and family life in the reservoir area. The snapshots in this collection are accompanied by extensive cutlines. Both the photographs and cutlines in this and the Hine Collection may be reproduced with the courtesy of TVA.

A significant photographic source is the Technical Information Office's negative file located in Knoxville, Tennessee. This is a very large file of negative and positive prints, classed by envelope and individual exposure number. Each print is identified, most with descriptions, but some possess only reservoir property tract numbers to indicate the particular property photographed. There are literally thousands of envelopes containing both negative and positive prints (the authors searched over 10,000 envelopes themselves). These TVA negative file prints are the most representative photographic records available. They show the various house types, stores, and churches and the topography of the whole Tennessee Valley area and are extremely useful to the social historian. Another available photographic record is contained in TVA's Technical Information Office in Knoxville in the public relations photograph file. Here are some excellent eight-by-ten-inch publicity prints and the most extensive file of pictures of distinguished visitors to TVA, as well as some interesting early pictures of Norris, Tennessee, and construction of the dam.

A. E. MORGAN PAPERS

The Arthur Morgan Papers are located in the Olive Kettering Library, Antioch College, Yellow Springs, Ohio. Morgan's secretary, Margot Ensign, has been classifying this material for easier access. Much of the collection is very helpful insofar as Morgan's early life is concerned, but the later material is essentially devoted to Morgan's defense of himself against his dismissal and the criticisms of his co-directors. Access to the Morgan Papers can be obtained through Nina Wyatt, associate curator, Olive Kettering Library, Antioch College, Yellow Springs, Ohio. Two interesting accounts of Arthur Morgan's development are based upon the A. E. Morgan papers, both by Roy Talbert: "The Human Engineer: A. E. Morgan and the Launching of the Tennessee Valley Authority" (M.A. thesis, Vanderbilt Univ., 1967); "Beyond Pragmatism: A Biography of Arthur Morgan" (Ph.D. diss. Vanderbilt Univ., 1971). Much of the TVA material in the Morgan Papers was reproduced by A. E. Morgan himself for use in his *The Making of TVA*.

FRANKLIN D. ROOSEVELT LIBRARY

TVA materials in the Franklin D. Roosevelt Library at Hyde Park, New York, are not as extensive as one might have hoped for TVA material. The presidential papers contain letters, various memos or memoranda, press releases, and other routine items many of which may also be found in various TVA files in Knoxville. There is, however, a verbatim transcript of Arthur Morgan's hearing before FDR at the White House, a valuable source. The material is well indexed and easily retrieved.

TVA ARCHIVES, TECHNICAL LIBRARY

Contained here are all published TVA materials and some unpublished TVA material (withheld from publication or not judged publishable). Many historically significant TVA reports are contained in the library, but not all, since the library usually gets them when division and branch files are cleared. The Technical Library also possesses outside published and unpublished material about TVA.

One of the most useful features of the Technical Library from the historian's standpoint is the extensive newsprint clippings file from 1933 to the present. There is automated retrieval for these clippings from 1965 to the present. Clippings before 1965 are arranged chronologically by subject. The archives also contain background material on TVA, pertinent laws, hearings, reports, and government documents, as well as some legislative histories. Of particular interest in the clipping files is the public record of disputed property transfers in the Norris Basin, from the *Knoxville News-Sentinel* and the *Knoxville Journal*. Two Norris area newspapers, *The Claiborne Progress* and the *Anderson County News*, are useful for the period studied. Of special interest in both papers are editorials concerning the impact of TVA, with much information in *The Claiborne Progress* devoted to local CCC camps and their impact. The history of TVA can also be traced, in certain ways, through other sources which could be classed, in their interest for the historian, with the newsprint collections housed in TVA's Technical Library. The following may be cited: TVA press releases, 1933–38; David Lilienthal, "Speeches and Remarks" (four bound volumes in the Technical Library, TVA); A. E. Morgan, "Speeches and Remarks" (two bound volumes in the Technical Library, TVA); A. E. Morgan, "Speeches and Writings" (two volumes of excerpted material), compiled by R. H. Denton of the Technical Library, TVA. A. E. Morgan and Lilienthal were prodigious public speakers and projected their views of TVA quite forcibly in public addresses. The speeches and remarks of both would provide some stimulating data for a content analysis study of both directors' personalities.

For a list of Tennessee newspapers for the period which may be of some use, see: "Tennessee Newspapers: A Cumulative List of Microfilmed Tennessee Newspapers in the Tennessee State Library" (August 1969 Progress Report), mimeograph (Nashville: Tennessee State Library and Archives, 1969).

Finally, mention should be made of the records of Harcourt Morgan and David Lilienthal. For Harcourt Morgan two sets of personal papers exist, one collection, housed in Special Collections, Hoskins Library, University of Tennessee, Knoxville, contains material pertaining to his presidency of the University and some miscellaneous materials contributed by his family. The papers for his years as a TVA director are also at the Hoskins Library as well as in the administrative files of TVA.

David Lilienthal's records pertaining to his TVA years are on microfilm in the TVA Technical Library as well as in the administrative files. Both were consulted in the course of reviewing materials in the TVA archives and Technical Library. As part of the project to microfilm Lilienthal's papers, TVA also microfilmed all of Arthur Morgan's records while he was a member of the board of directors.

SELECTED PUBLISHED AND UNPUBLISHED DOCUMENTS

Allred, C.E., James H. Marshall, and W. Eugene Collins. "Report of the Economic and Fiscal Capacity of Tennessee Counties." Knoxville: Univ. of Tennessee School of Agriculture, 1934. Typescript.

Augur, Tracy B. "The Planning of the Town of Norris." *American Architect* (April 1936), 1–8.

Banner, Gilbert. "Toward More Realistic Assumptions in Regional Economic Development." In *The Economic Impact of TVA*, ed. John R. Moore. Knoxville: Univ. of Tennessee Press, 1967.

Beebe, Gilbert W. *Conception and Fertility in the Southern Appalachians*. Baltimore: Williams and Wilkins, 1942.

Brown, Ralph Geron. "Family Renewal in the Tennessee Valley." Master's thesis, Univ. of Tennessee, 1940.

Case, Harry L. *Personnel Policy in a Public Agency: The TVA Experience*. New York: Harper, 1955.

Chase, Stuart. "TVA, The New Deal's Best Asset." *The Nation* (June 3, 10, 17, and 24, 1936), 702–5, 738–41, 775–77, 804–5.

Chattanooga Sunday Times.

Chattanooga Times.

Christian Century, editorial, Nov. 14, 1934.

Clapp, Gordon R. *The TVA: An Approach to the Development of a Region*. Chicago: Univ. of Chicago Press, 1955.

Conkin, Paul K. *Tomorrow a New World: The New Deal Community Program*. Ithaca: Cornell Univ. Press, 1959.

Cushing, Edith S. "An American Phenomenon." *Radcliffe Quarterly* (Jan. 1935), 38–40.

Davenport, Walter. "There'll Be Shouting in the Valley." *Collier's* (June 30, 1934), 10–11, 36–40.

Davis, John P. "The Plight of the Negro in the Tennessee Valley." *The Crisis* 42 (Oct. 1935), 294–95, 314–15.

Davis, Lance E. "'And It Will Never Be Literature': The New

Bibliography

Economic History, A Critique." In *The New Economic History: Recent Papers on Methodology*, ed. Ralph Andreano. New York: Wiley, 1970.

DeJong, Gordon F. *Appalachian Fertility Decline: A Demographic and Sociological Analysis*. Lexington: Univ. of Kentucky Press, 1968.

Droze, Wilmon Henry. *High Dams and Slack Waters: TVA Rebuilds a River*. Baton Rouge: Louisiana State Univ. Press, 1965.

Duffus, R.L. *The Valley and Its People*. New York: Knopf, 1946.

Dunn, Annette H. "Model Workers' Town is New Deal Product." *The Jeffersonian* (Aug. 1935), 18–19.

Fenneman, N.M. *Physiography of the Eastern United States*. New York: McGraw-Hill, 1938.

Fetterman, John. *Stinking Creek*. New York: Dutton, 1967.

Finer, Herman. *The TVA: Lessons for International Application*. Montreal: International Labour Office, 1944.

Foster, Austin, and Albert Roberts. *Tennessee Democrats: A History of the Party and Its Representative Members—Past and Present*. Nashville: Democratic Historical Association, 1940.

Goodrich, Carter, Bushrod W. Allin, and Marion Hayes. *Migration and Planes of Living: 1920–1934*. Philadelphia: Univ. of Pennsylvania Press, 1934.

Goodrich, Carter, Bushrod W. Allin, and C. Warren Thornthwaite. *Migration and Economic Opportunity: Report of the Study of Population Redistribution*. Philadelphia: Univ. of Pennsylvania Press, 1934.

Gray, Aelred J. "The Maturing of a Planned New Town, Norris, Tennessee." *The Tennessee Planner* 32 (1974), 1–25.

Gray, L.C. *Economic and Social Problems of the Southern Appalachians*. U.S. Department of Agriculture Miscellaneous Publication 205. Washington, D.C.: U.S. Government Printing Office, 1935.

Hitching, H.J., and P.P. Claxton, Jr. "Practice and Procedure in Eminent Domain Cases under the TVA Act." *Tennessee Law Review*, 16 (1941), 952–59.

Hobday, Victor C. *Sparks at the Grass Roots: Municipal Distribution of TVA Electricity in Tennessee*. Knoxville: Univ. of Tennessee Press, 1967.

Hodge, Clarence L. *The Tennessee Valley Authority: A National Experiment in Regionalism*. Washington, D.C.: American Univ. Press, 1938.

Holmes, Michael S. *The New Deal in Georgia: An Adminsitrative History*. Contributions in American History 36. Westpoint, Conn.: Greenwood Press, 1975.

Houston, Charles H., and John P. Davis. "TVA: Lily-White Reconstruction." *The Crisis*, 41 (Oct. 1934), 290–91, 311.

Hubbard, Preston J. *Origins of the TVA: The Muscle Shoals Controversy, 1920–1932*. Nashville: Vanderbilt Univ. Press, 1961.

Johnson, Charles W., and Charles O. Jackson. *City Behind a Fence: Oak Ridge, Tennessee, 1942–1946*. Knoxville: Univ. of Tennessee Press, 1981.

Killibrew, J.B. *Introduction to the Resources of Tennessee*. Rpt. Spartanburg, S.C.: Reprint Co., 1974.

Knox, John. *The People of Tennessee: A Study of Population Trends*. Knoxville: Univ. of Tennessee Press, 1949.

Knoxville Journal.

Knoxville News-Sentinel.

Kyle, J.H. *The Building of TVA: An Illustrated History*. Baton Rouge: Louisiana State Univ. Press, 1958.

Lilienthal, David E. *Journals*. Vol. I, *The TVA Years: 1939–1945*. New York: Harper, 1965.

———. *TVA: Democracy on the March*. New York: Harper, 1953.

Lowitt, Richard. *George W. Norris: The Persistence of a Progressive, 1913–1933*. Urbana: Univ. of Illinois Press, 1971.

McCraw, Thomas K. *Morgan versus Lilienthal: A Feud within the TVA*. Chicago: Loyola Univ. Press, 1970.

———. *TVA and the Power Fight, 1933–1939*. Philadelphia: Lippincott, 1971.

McCarthy, Charles J. "Land Acquisition Policies and Proceedings in TVA—A Study of the Role of Land Acquisition in a Regional Agency." *Ohio State Law Journal* 10 (Winter 1949), 46–63.

McDonald, Michael J., and John Muldowny. "Reburying the Dead: Disinterment and Reinterment at TVA's Norris Dam." *Publications of the East Tennessee Historical Society* 47 (1975), 118–38.

McLeod, Ruth. "TVA Sets Up A New Type of School." *Progressive Farmer* (Nov. 1935), 47.

Matthews, Elmora Messer. *Neighbor and Kin: Life in a Tennessee Ridge Community*. Nashville: Vanderbilt Univ. Press, 1965.

Milton, George Fort. "Dawn for the Tennessee Valley." *Review of Reviews* 77 (June 1933), 32–34.

Moore, John R., ed. *The Economic Impact of TVA*. Knoxville: Univ. of Tennessee Press, 1967.

Morgan, Arthur E. "Benchmarks in the Tennessee Valley." *Survey Graphic* 23 (Jan. March, May, and Nov. 1934), 5–9, 42–44, 46; 105–110, 138–39; 233–37, 251; 548–52, 575–76; 23 (March and Nov. 1935), 113–16, 140; 529–32, 575.

———. *The Making of the TVA*. Buffalo: Prometheus Books, 1974.

Moutoux, John T. "The TVA Builds a Town." *The New Republic* (Jan. 1934), 330–31.

Nash, Claude W. "Reservoir Land Management." In *TVA: The First Twenty Years*, ed. Roscoe C. Martin. Knoxville: Univ. of Tennessee Press, 1956.

Bibliography

Nielsen, Ralph Leighton. "Socio-Economic Readjustment of Farm Families Displaced by the TVA Land Purchase in the Norris Area." Master's thesis, Univ. of Tennessee, 1940.

Owen, Marguerite. *The Tennessee Valley Authority*. New York: Praeger, 1973.

Pritchett, Charles Herman. *The Tennessee Valley Authority: A Study in Public Administration*. Chapel Hill: Univ. of North Carolina Press, 1943.

Ransmeier, J.S. *The Tennessee Valley Authority: A Case Study in the Economics of Multiple Purpose Stream Planning*. Nashville: Vanderbilt Univ. Press, 1942.

Robock, Stefan H. "An Unfinished Task: A Socio-Economic Evaluation." In *The Economic Impact of TVA*, ed. John R. Moore. Knoxville: Univ. of Tennessee Press, 1967.

Rosenman, Samuel I., ed. *The Public Papers and Addresses of Franklin D. Roosevelt*. Vol. II, *The Year of Crisis, 1933*. New York: Random, 1938.

Satterfield, M.H. "Removal of Families from Tennessee Valley Authority Reservoir Areas." *Social Forces* 16 (Dec. 1937), 258–61.

"School at Norris, Tennessee." *School Executive* (Oct. 1935), 55.

Seligman, Lester G., and Elmer E. Cornwell, Jr., eds. *The New Mosaic: President Roosevelt Confers with His National Emergency Council, 1933–1936*. Eugene: Univ. of Oregon Press, 1965.

Selznick, Phillip. *TVA and the Grass Roots: A Study in the Sociology of Formal Organization*. New York: Harper, 1966.

Smith, Lynn T. *The Sociology of Rural Life*. New York: Harper, 1940.

Stevenson, Charles. "A Contrast in Perfect Towns." *Nation's Business* (Dec. 1937), 114–15.

Talbert, Roy, Jr., ed. "Arthur E. Morgan's Ethical Code for the Tennessee Valley Authority." *Publications of the East Tennessee Historical Society* 40 (1968), 119–27.

——. "Arthur E. Morgan's Social Philosophy and the Tennessee Valley Authority." *Publications of the East Tennessee Historical Society* 41 (1969), 86–99.

——. "Beyond Pragmatism: A Biography of Arthur Morgan." Ph.D. diss., Vanderbilt Univ., 1972.

——. "The Human Engineer: A.E. Morgan and the Launching of the Tennessee Valley Authority." Master's thesis, Vanderbilt Univ., 1967.

Tennessee State Planning Commission. "Preliminary Population Report—General Population Statistics and Trends." Nashville, 1935. Bound typescript.

Tennessee Valley Authority. *Annual Report, 1979*. Knoxville: TVA, 1980.

————. William E. Cole. "Tennessee, A Study in Basic Social Data." Knoxville, 1934. Typescript.

————. "Correspondence between Howard K. Menhenick and Tracy B. Augur Regarding Origins and History of Sections 22 and 23 of the TVA Act." Knoxville, 1934, Mimeographed.

————. Ross M. Cunningham and Gerald Tallman. "Summary of and Supplement to Studies of Research Sections in the Social and Economic Division Relating to Norris Commercial Facilities." Knoxville, 1935. Typescript.

————. Earle S. Draper. "Relationship of Tennessee Valley Authority Program to the Interstate Migration Problem." Knoxville, 1940. Mimeographed.

————. L.L. Durisch. "The Effect on County Government of Tennessee Valley Authority Land Purchases in Campbell and Union Counties." Knoxville, 1934. Mimeographed.

————. L.L. Durisch. "Proposed Local Government Organization for Norris, Tennessee." Knoxville, 1935. Mimeographed.

————. L.L. Durisch and Laverne Burchfield. "Families of the Norris Reservoir: A Presentation of Basic Data." Knoxville, 1935. Mimeographed.

————. George F. Gant. "Consumption in Selected Population Groups in the Norris Area." Knoxville, 1935. Typescript.

————. Louis Grandgent. "Houses at Norris, Tennessee: A Review of Costs." Knoxville, 1936. Mimeographed.

————. T. Levron Howard. "Some Social and Economic Characteristics of Selected Counties within the Norris Dam Area." Knoxville, 1933. Typescript.

————. Robert Lowry. "A Review of Social and Economic Conditions in the Five-County Norris Area." Knoxville, 1940. Mimeographed.

————. Robert Lowry and Paul Cadra. "Local Social and Economic Effects of the Norris Dam Project." Knoxville, 1938. Mimeographed.

————. Robert Lowry and Lorrie Douglas. "Income Analysis of Thirty-two Counties." Knoxville, 1939. Mimeographed.

————. Hershal L. Macon and Vernon G. Morrison. "The Effects upon Local Finance of Real Property Purchases by the Tennessee Valley Authority: Survey No. 1—Norris Reservoir Counties." Knoxville, 1936. Mimeographed.

————. *The Norris Project: A Comprehensive Report on the Planning, Design, Construction and Initial Operation of the Tennessee Valley Authority's First Water Control Project.* Technical Report No. 1. Washington, D.C.: U.S. Government Printing Office, 1940.

————. "Population Readjustment Handbook." Knoxville, 1940. Mimeographed.

————. "A Review of Social and Economic Conditions in the Five-

County Norris Area: Summary and Recommendations." Knoxville, 1939. Mimeographed.

————. Charles M. Stephenson. "Problems of the Stranded Fragment of Union County, Tennessee, on the Peninsula between the Clinch River and Buffalo Creek Area of Norris Reservoir." Knoxville, 1936. Typescript.

————. Charles M. Stephenson. "Relocation of 1,834 Families from the Norris Purchase Area." Knoxville, 1935. Mimeographed.

————. "Tenant Families of the Norris Flowage." Knoxville, 1935. Mimeographed.

————. "Urban Rural Migration of Norris Reservoir Families." Knoxville, 1935. Typescript.

————. Marshall A. Wilson. "Activities of the Reservoir Family Removal Section, Coordination Division, Norris Reservoir Area." Knoxville, 1937. Typescript.

————. Marshall Wilson. "Families of the Norris Reservoir Area." Knoxville, 1949. Unofficial Typescript.

————. Marshall Wilson. "Norris Area." Knoxville, 1937. Typescript.

Tennessee Valley Authority. Board of Directors. "Minutes." June, July, July, Aug. 5, Sept. 18, 1933; Aug. 7, 1935.

————. Department of Regional Planning Studies. M. Harry Satterfield and William Davlin. "A Description and Appraisal of the Relocation of Families from the Norris Reservoir Area." Knoxville, 1937. Typescript.

————. Land Acquisition Division. Appraisal Section. H.H. Wooten and Jack Hind. "Real Property Appraisals of the Norris Reservoir Purchase Area." Knoxville, Feb. 1937. Mimeographed.

————. Land Acquisition Division. Department of Property and Supply. "Review of Norris Reservoir Properties to Determine Surplus Land." Knoxville, 1945–46. Mimeographed.

————. Land Planning and Housing Division." A Land Classification Approach to Land Use Problems." Knoxville, 1936. Typescript.

————. Norris Cooperative Society. "Annual Report," 1937. Regional Studies Report, Town of Norris. Knoxville, 1937.

————. Regional Studies Department. J.W. Bradner. "The Evolution of a Community." Knoxville, 1940. Typescript.

————. Social and Economic Division. Research Section. "Classification of Families of the Norris Flowage According to Assistance Necessary for Relocation." Knoxville, 1935. Mimeographed.

Tennessee Valley Authority and the Institute for Research in Social Science, Univ. of North Carolina. John Kenneth Folger. "Migration in the Tennessee Valley Area, 1935 to 1940." Chapel Hill, 1951. Typescript.

"TVA Installs a Model Drug Store," *North Western Druggist* (Oct. 1935), 46.

U.S. Congress. House. *Economic Development Programs under the Jurisdiction of the Committee on Public Works.* pt. 3, "Appalachian Regional Development Act of 1965 as Amended; Definition of the Appalachian Region," sec. 403. Washington, D.C.: U.S. Government Printing Office, 1971.

―――. Joint Committee. *Investigation of the Tennessee Valley Authority. Hearings before the Joint Committee to Investigate the Tennessee Valley Authority.* 75th Cong., 3rd sess. Washington, D.C.: U.S. Government Printing Office, 1939, pts. 1–4.

―――. *Five Fundamental Issues Affecting the TVA and Its Forest Conservation Program.* Testimony of Edward C.M. Richard, Former Chief Forester of the TVA. 75th Cong., 3rd sess. Washington, D.C.: U.S. Government Printing Office, 1938.

U.S. Department of Agriculture. Bureau of Chemistry and Soils. W.E. McLendon and W.S. Layman. *Survey of Grainger County, Tennessee.* Washington, D.C.: U.S. Government Printing Office, 1907.

―――. *Economic and Social Problems of the Southern Appalachians.* Miscellaneous Publication 205. Washington, D.C.: U.S. Government Printing Office, 1935.

―――. Rexford G. Tugwell. "Report on That Part of the Tennessee River Basin above Muscle Shoals." 2 vols. Washington, 1933.

U.S. Department of Commerce. Bureau of the Census. *Fifteenth Census of the United States, 1930: Agriculture,* vol. II, pt. 2, *Tennessee.*

―――. *Fourteenth Census of the United States, 1920: Agriculture,* vol. II, pt. 2, *Tennessee.*

―――. *Sixteenth Census of the United States, 1940: Agriculture,* vol. I, first and second series, pt. 4, *Tennessee.*

―――. *Sixteenth Census of the United States, 1940: Agriculture,* vol. III, series 3, *Tennessee.*

U.S. Resettlement Administration. Rural Resettlement Division. (Paul Taylor.) "The Resettlement Problem Resulting from Families Displaced through the Land Purchase Program of the Tennessee Valley Authority." Washington, 1937. Typescript.

U.S. Soil Conservation Service. *Soil Survey: Norris, Tennessee.* Series 1939, No. 19. Washington, D.C.: U.S. Government Printing Office, 1953.

University of Tennessee. Agricultural Experiment Station. (W.O. Whittle) "Movement of Population from the Smoky Mountains Area." Knoxville, 1934. Typescript.

Vance, Robert W. *All These People.* Chapel Hill: Univ. of North Carolina Press, 1945.

Wengert, Norman I. *Valley of Tomorrow: The TVA and Agriculture.* Knoxville: Bureau of Public Administration, Univ. of Tennessee, 1952.

Whitman, Willson. *God's Valley: People and Power along the Tennessee River.* New York: Viking, 1939.

Index

Index

Cumberland Mountains: and the Norris Basin, 70

Cumberland Plateau: and the Norris Basin, 4, 70; its physiography relative to the Norris Basin, 70; and the poverty level analyses of Carter Goodrich, 100, 112

Davis, Lance, 5

Davlin, William (Social and Economic Research Division, Dept. of Regional Planning Studies, TVA): and the analysis of impact of relocation, 241, 243, 244–45; farm ownership, tenancy, and type after relocation analysis, 247–52; conclusion of analysis of TVA relocation, 252–54

Draper, Earle (TVA division head, Land Planning and Housing): concern with federal agency coordination of resettlement activities and TVA, 163; and early criticism of the relocation service, 165; advocates resettlement communities at Norris to A. E. Morgan, 165; uses Shenandoah National Park acquisitions as good example compared to Smoky Mountains policy, 165–66; and colonization of tenants, 170; asked to prepare Norris town plan, 219; and recommendation for town site, 220

Droze, Wilmon, 5

Duffus, R. L., 6

Durish, L. L. (Social and Economic Section of TVA's Land Planning and Housing: and tenant resettlement scheme, 170

Electric Home and Farm Administration, 161

Engineering Services Division, TVA: and grave removal, 206–207

Extension Relocation Service, Norris: formerly TVA's Family Removal Section, 159; created (1934) by contract between TVA and UT Agricultural Extension Division, 167; reaches its limits of operation, 174; and analysis of TVA impact of relocation, 24

Family Removal Section, TVA: and UT Agricultural Extension Division, 159; officially established as Extension Relocation Service, 159

Farm Credit Administration: and A. E. Morgan's concepts of resettlement, 157–59; and loan qualifications for resettlement, 165

Farrier, C. W. (TVA Coordination Division): talks with FERA about resettlement, 173; and Judge Barton Brown of TERA, 173; and tenant resettlement, 173–74; notes on Rexford Tugwell, 174; and liaison with Paul Taylor of RA, 184

Federal Emergency Relief Administration: and A. E. Morgan's plans of resettlement, 157–59, 161; and Surplus Relief Corporation, 162; and funding for TVA and TVAC, 162; and tenant resettlement, 173; and A. E. Morgan, 173

Federal land purchase policy, 136–37

Fetterman, John, *Stinking Creek*, 108

Finer, Herman, 5

Fly, James Lawrence (General Solicitor of TVA): and disapproval of tenant resettlement plans, 172–73

Frankfurter, Felix, 17

French Broad River, 4

Freeman, John D. (executive board, Tennessee Baptist Convention): and Union County meeting on grave removal, 196

Goodrich, Carter: and poverty level analyses on the Cumberland Plateau, 100, 112

Grainger County, Tenn.: and site of Norris Dam and Reservoir, 69; and USDA soil report of 1907, 74, 246; and 1870 population density, 75; and its 1930 Crude Birthrate, 76; and 1936 TVA report on relocation impact, 246

Great Depression: and the Norris Basin, 7; and dam construction, 127

Green, William (AFL), 18

Gutheim, Frederick: and the planning sections (22 and 23) of the TVA Act, 10

Henegar, Andy: and Life in the Norris Basin, 31–32; and the Norris Basin Community, 44, 48, 53

Henson, E. R. (Rural Resettlement Division of RA): and W. G. Carnahan: 184–85

Hill, Myers: and life in the Norris Basin, 34–35; and the Norris Basin community 38–39, 41, 42, 34–44, 45, 47, 49, 53; and the coming of TVA and population removal, 58, 60

Hine, Lewis, 5

Hobday, Victor, 5

Hodge, Clarence, 5

Hoffman, Charles (former Secretary of TVA Board of Directors): and comments on heavy purchase policy, 130; and A. E.

327

Index

THE UNIVERSITY OF TENNESSEE PRESS
KNOXVILLE

CPSIA information can be obtained at www.ICGtesting.com
Printed in the USA
LVOW07s2325290115

424942LV00001B/154/P